KENT STATE AND MAY 4TH

A SOCIAL SCIENCE PERSPECTIVE

SECOND EDITION

Thomas R. Hensley
DEPARTMENT OF POLITICAL SCIENCE
KENT STATE UNIVERSITY

Jerry M. Lewis
DEPARTMENT OF SOCIOLOGY
KENT STATE UNIVERSITY

KENDALL/HUNT PUBLISHING COMPANY
4050 Westmark Drive   Dubuque, Iowa 52002

Map–inside front cover: Courtesy of Kent State University Archives

Photos–cover and interior: Courtesy of Kent State University Archives

CONTENTS

PREFACE

On May 4, 1970, members of the Ohio National Guard fired into a crowd of protestors at Kent State University, killing four undergraduate students and wounding nine others. This tragic act and its aftermath generated national and international social, legal, and political controversy. In this volume, we present social science research which provides various perspectives for analyzing the controversy.

All of the authors whose research is presented in this book were members of either the departments of political science or sociology at Kent State University when they undertook their research. They observed or took part in many of the activities reported in this book. Even so, the authors have tried to present factual reports and analyses in as objective a manner as possible.

The second edition of this volume is divided into four sections. The first is an overview of the events of May 1-4, 1970. This section presents a detailed description and analysis of May 1970 at Kent State University. In addition, three essays are presented which review the vast literature that has arisen from these events. The second section looks at the legal aftermath of the shootings. The third section provides a social science perspective on the impact of the shootings. The fourth section examines from several perspectives the gymnasium controversy that erupted on Kent State's campus in 1977. Eight of the articles in this edition also appeared in the first edition, and five articles are new to the second edition.

We wish to thank the Office of Faculty Development at Kent State for support in the development of a preliminary version of his book. We also wish to thank Nancy Birk of the Kent State Libraries and Media Services and Gary Harwood of University Relations and Marketing for assistance in obtaining the pictures used in the book. These pictures were taken by Doug Moore of Kent State. Donna Redden and Elaine Huskins provided excellent secretarial assistance. We also wish to thank all of the authors who contributed to this volume. All royalties will be donated to the May 4 Memorial Fund, a project which created markers at the sites in the Prentice Hall parking lot where Jeffrey Miller, Allison Krause, William Schroeder, and Sandra Scheuer died on May 4, 1970.

Thomas R. Hensley

Jerry M. Lewis

Students taking cover as the Ohio National Guard fires into the Prentice Hall parking lot on May 4th, 1970. Photo by Doug Moore.

INTRODUCTION

The four essays in this section provide an overview of the events associated with May 4, 1970 when four students -- Allison Krause, Jeffrey Miller, Sandra Scheuer, and William Schroeder -- were killed and nine others -- Alan Canfora, John Cleary, Thomas Grace, Dean Kahler, Joseph Lewis, Donald MacKenzie, James Russell, Robert Stamps, and Douglas Wrentmore -- were wounded by the Ohio National Guard.

James Best, a member of Kent State University's political science department, describes the events through a secondary analysis of a large number of resources. Written in the late seventies, his essay provides the reader with a factual background for looking at the events on the days prior to the shootings as well as the events of May 4.

Jerry M. Lewis, an emeritus member of Kent State's sociology department, reviews in two essays, one written (Update) for this volume, the books that have been published about May 4 and related events including legal controversies, memorials, and novels about May 4.

Lewis and Thomas R. Hensley, a member of Kent State's political science department, conclude this section with an essay using many of the sources discussed in the Best and Lewis essays, attempting to locate and correct the historical inaccuracies associated with May 4. Their approach is to raise and provide answers to twelve of the most frequently asked questions about May 4 and its aftermath.

THE TRAGIC WEEKEND OF MAY 1 TO 4, 1970

James J. Best
Kent State University

In this chapter we present an historical narrative of the events of May 1 - 4, 1970 and an analysis of the context within which those events took place, a narrative which serves a number of purposes. For those unfamiliar with what happened in Kent, Ohio, during the period of May 1 to 4 the narrative provides a time-ordered description of the major actors and activities, making use of all the major published as well as many unpublished descriptions and analyses of the events, as well as testimony given by the participants during the 1975 civil suit trial. From these sources we reconstruct in sufficient detail the fateful events of those four days.

Since no action occurs in a vacuum it is important for us to present and analyze the social, historical, and political context within which the shootings took place. We concentrate our efforts on several factors which we consider important: the social context provided by the city of Kent, the historical context of demonstrations on the campus of Kent State University, and the political context provided by the statements and actions of President Nixon and Vice-President Agnew, as well as the Republican primary campaign of Governor James Rhodes.

THE KENT STATE INCIDENT

We have asked a number of questions during this narrative: What factors led to the fatal confrontation between National Guardsmen and demonstrators on Monday, May 4? Why did Kent Mayor Leroy Satrom call for the Ohio National Guard after only one night's disturbances? Why did city and university officials think that the National Guard had complete control of the campus on May 4? Why did Governor James Rhodes make a speech on Sunday morning, May 3, which served to inflame the emotions of many who heard or read about it? Were radicals involved in the events of May 1-4? How did townspeople and students react to the shootings? What impact did the shootings have on the larger society in which they occurred?

In reconstructing these events we have had to choose which sources to use and, when sources conflicted, which sources to believe. Extensive use has been made of two major works—Michener's *Kent State: What Happened and Why*[1] and *The Report of the President's Commission on Campus Unrest*[2] (the Scranton Commission Report)— although each work has its defects. Michener's book suffers from his research methods and his political and educational biases; he selectively interviewed participants in the weekend's events and uncritically accepted what he was told. Politically, Michener believes in the democratic process and, while he understood the frustrations students felt when they learned of the U.S. invasion of Cambodia, he could not condone the damage to downtown businesses on May 1 or the burning of the ROTC building on May 2. Educationally, he has an obvious affection for Kent State University and its administration, particularly President Robert White, which colored his evaluation of White's role in the weekend's events. These criticisms notwithstanding, Michener has the uncanny ability to recreate the ambience of a situation, particularly Blanket Hill on the morning of May 4: you can almost smell the tear gas and see the tear gas-masked Guardsmen striding up the hill.

The Scranton Commission Report is concerned with establishing for the public record what "really" happened. The quest to describe what happened is both the strength and weakness of this book; it stands as the most authoritative statement of what happened but it rarely explores inconsistencies between various participant's testimony, leaves unanswered a number of questions regarding the motivation of many participants, and is relatively unconcerned with the impact of the shootings on subsequent events.

A number of other reports were useful as well. The Knight newspaper report[3], published less than three weeks after the shootings, is important because the reporters interviewed many of the participants, particularly Guardsmen, shortly after the shootings. The decision to focus on the events of May 4, however, leaves unanswered a number of questions regarding events earlier in the weekend. Nonetheless, "The fact that the Journal got this report out so rapidly and with relatively few serious errors set the tone for facts that govern the remainder of the studies."[4] The report subsequently won a Pulitzer Prize.

The Joe Eszterhas and Michael Roberts' book on Kent State[5] is a journalistic quickie, published after the Knight newspaper report but before the Scranton Commission report and the Michener book. It is replete with inaccuracies, and the authors rarely cite the sources of their information.

Peter Davies' *The Truth About Kent State*[6] argues, primarily through an analysis of photographs of the shootings and testimony before the Scranton Commission, that the shootings were the result of a conspiracy on the part of certain Guardsmen. Readers of this work should remember that it was written in an attempt to convince the Justice Department to convene a federal grand jury to investigate the shootings.

Another conspiracy theory is advanced by Charles Thomas in "The Kent State Massacre: Blood on Whose Hands?"[7] For Thomas the Guardsmen and students were merely pawns in a larger game being played by the Nixon administration; Kent State was a demonstration of President Nixon's get-tough policy toward student dissent, and after the shootings President Nixon and John Mitchell consciously attempted to cover-up the administration's role in the fateful events. Thomas's allegations are at variance with other research on the subject and many are unsubstantiated: he reconstructs conspiratorial conversations by Guardsmen on May 4 which have never been verified by anyone else. His research is based, however, on materials to which he had access as an archivist working in the National Archives, material generally not available to other researchers. As a result his analysis and conclusions may be correct but are impossible to corroborate independently.

The Phillip Tompkins and Elaine Anderson[8], and Stuart Taylor *et al.*[9] books are based on research conducted by Kent State faculty and students shortly after the shootings. The former focuses on communication failures within the administration and between administrators and students as they contributed to the events of May 1 to 4. Taylor and his colleagues focus on KSU student perceptions of the events, and their survey research data represent our best knowledge of the phenomenon.

Only two works have been written which present the perspective of the Guardsmen. Ed Grant and Mike Hill's book,[10] although factually incorrect on occasion and leaving time gaps, does provide some insight as to what Guardsmen were thinking on Saturday and Sunday night. William Furlong's piece in the *New York Times Magazine*[11] also provides some insight as to why Guardsmen turned and fired on the demonstrators.

Three unpublished sources have been useful as well. The Justice Department Summary of the FBI Report was entered by Congressman John Seiberling in the Congressional Record.[12] Volume IV of the *Report of the Commission on KSU Violence*[13] (the Minority Report) represents an attempt by a group of KSU faculty and students to write a history of the events; division within the committee is reflected in the fact that the volume is called the "Minority Report," although a "majority" report has never been published. The Minority Report's principal weakness stems from its attempt to prove that radicals and outside agitators were responsible for the shootings. The report is valuable because it includes a great deal of information from people who did not testify before the Scranton Commission or talk to Michener and his researchers.

The third source has been the transcript of the 1975 civil suit trial,[14] in which the major participants testified. Unfortunately, the plaintiffs case was poorly handled and potentially illuminating questions were rarely asked.

These materials constitute the primary data sources for our description of the events of the period. They have been supplemented by a body of research by social scientists at Kent State who have focused on one or more aspects of the events, some of which appear in the current book.

Our primary job in this chapter will be to compare and contrast these sources so that we might construct as accurately as possible an historical narrative of events. From this narrative we have asked and sought answers to a number of questions which we feel are of primary importance. We have not asked all the questions possible nor have we answered all the questions we have asked.

THE SOCIAL, POLITICAL, AND HISTORICAL CONTEXT

Kent, Ohio is a small city located approximately thirty miles South of Cleveland and ten miles east of Akron, an intrinsic part of the industrial heartland of northeastern Ohio which is so heavily dependent on the steel of Youngstown, the rubber of Akron, and the manufacturing and commerce of Cleveland. Kent was first settled in 1805 and the water power of the Cuyahoga River made industrial development attractive and inevitable. Later, the construction of the railroad through Kent insured that local manufacturers would have access to markets and that freight trains would daily tie up traffic in the center of the town. In 1910, after substantial lobbying, the state legislature agreed to create a state normal school in Kent on fifty-four acres of land donated by W. S. Kent; the purpose of the school was to train elementary school teachers but its early leaders had greater ambitions. The first students were admitted in 1913, and the school achieved the status of a four year college in 1929 and university status in 1938.[15]

As the university grew so did the town. In 1913 the normal school enrolled forty-seven students, while the town had a population of approximately 5,000; by 1970 the university had grown in enrollment to over 21,000 while the town (now a city) had a population of 28,000. Much of the growth for both the city and university had occurred

in the twenty-five years between the end of World War II and 1970. By 1970 the city had developed into the largest population center in Portage County and the university had become the second largest in the state and one of the twenty-five largest in the United States. The size of the university insured that it would be the dominant industry in the city as well as the county. In the early 1970s KSU employed over 2,500 people and had an annual payroll in excess of $20 million and a budget of over $50 million.

There are three Kents—the downtown area, the residential areas, and the university. Downtown Kent, centered around the intersection of state routes 43 and 59, is unlike the center of most college towns. Aside from the two banks, two drug stores, two movie theaters, the post office, and a grocery store that you expect in a college town, there are no art galleries, boutiques, men's specialty shops, or good restaurants. Michener describes downtown Kent in these terms:

"Route 59, which runs east and west, is a tacky, grubby thoroughfare onto which all the ugliest enterprises of Kent have been piled.... But the apex of this ugliness comes on North Water Street in the center of town, for here are collected all the sleazy bars frequented by the university students."[16]

The downtown area is a continual point of friction between university students and merchants. Students dislike shopping in an area where they have little choice and where they feel prices are inflated, while the merchants feel that students don't provide enough business to compensate for the trouble involved—checks that bounce and beer bottles littering the streets after a long weekend. After 9:00 p.m. the only lights in downtown Kent are those in the movie theater marquee and the bars on North Water.

A block or two from routes 43 and 59, you find another more attractive Kent. The residential areas are spacious, tree-lined, and generally middle-class. Neighborhoods are mixed. Clusters of modem, tract-built houses, as well as older, restored or restorable frame homes share maple and oak-shaded streets, highlighting Kent's reputation as "the Tree City." The residential areas provide homes for many of the university faculty and staff, people who work in nearby cities and towns but prefer the amenities of a university locale, and those who provide services for the university. Students who live in Kent tend to live in apartments on the edge of the city or in subdivided older homes close to the campus. The people who live in Kent are predominately white (96.7 percent) and native-born (88.8 percent), well-educated (30.4 percent have at least a college education), and most work in Kent. The median family income for 1970 was $10,886, with only 5.7 percent of the families having incomes below the poverty level[17]. Behind the tacky facade of the downtown area live middle and upper-middle class people, proud of themselves and their homes.

Kent State University is the third Kent—a city within a city, located in, but not part of, the city which surrounds it. The yellow stone buildings which initially composed the normal school, college, and then the fledgling university, are clustered on Hilltop Drive, where they formed the heart of the early campus. More recently, the university built new dormitories and classrooms to house, feed, and teach the thousands of new students who swelled the university during the late 1950s and 1960s. From its original fifty-four acre grant the university had grown by 1970 to more than 600 acres. President White, KSU's president during the 1960s, viewed the period in these terms; "With the tremendous growth after World War II and the results of this baby boom hitting us in the 1960's, we had to find buildings to put the students in and professors to teach them. Our primary obligation was to keep the place running."[18]

Because of its rapid growth Kent State in the late 1960s was described by students and faculty as "the largest unknown university in the United States."[19] Students tended to be first generation college students, the sons and daughters of working class parents who saw college as a way for their children to advance themselves. But on weekends and during vacations those same parents began to realize that their children were changing, were different, were no longer the same. Robert O'Neill, John Morris, and Raymond Mack suggest that, as a result, parents began to see Kent State "as the institution that takes their children away, changes their values, expands their horizons, and thus drastically realigns family and social relationships. Kent graduates will probably never join their fathers and uncles making tires in Akron, steel in Cleveland, or heavy machinery in Elyria."[20]

Although Kent State may have broadened the lives and minds of its students, it did not make many of them radicals, or even very liberal.[21] According to Michener the first Vietnam war protest on campus

took place in 1965 and drew thirteen people[22]. In the late 1960s, however, student activism began to increase at Kent State as it did at other universities. On November 13, 1968 the Black United Students (BUS) and the Kent Students for a Democratic Society (SDS) staged a protest against the appearance on campus of recruiters from the Oakland, California police department. When the university announced that it planned disciplinary action under the student code against the protestors, the black community threatened to withdraw from school unless all protestors were given amnesty. Two days later, President White, citing a procedural technicality, decided not to press charges and the black students returned to campus.

In the spring of 1969 the SDS chapter at Kent State began to press the university to meet four demands: abolition of the ROTC program on campus, removal of the Liquid Crystals Institute (whose research was funded in part by the U.S. Department of Defense), removal of a state criminal investigation laboratory from campus, and abolition of the university's program in law enforcement. On April 8, 1969 a group of students, including SDS leaders, marched to the Administration Building to post a list of demands. They were met at the doors to the building by campus police. Fights broke out between campus police and demonstrators, and six demonstrators (four of them students) were arrested for assault and battery. The four students (subsequently known as the "Kent State Four") were summarily suspended from school and were later tried in county court, found guilty of assault, and sentenced to six months in the county jail. In addition the SDS chapter lost its campus charter, thereby depriving it of a share of student fees and access to university facilities.[23]

Eight days after the demonstration a disciplinary hearing was held in the Music and Speech Building for two of the suspended students. Campus police chained and locked the doors of the building, preventing a large crowd from entering the building and attending the hearing. Fights broke out between supporters and opponents of the suspended students. Somehow—no one is quite clear how[24]—supporters of the suspended students found their way into the building and gained access to the third floor where the hearing was being held. The clamor in the hallway was loud enough to disrupt the hearing and the noise rose even louder when the demonstrators discovered that the campus police had locked all doors leading down from the third floor. A stalemate resulted: the demonstrators could not get through the locked doors (although some did get out of the building by using an unwatched elevator) and the campus police lacked the personnel to deal effectively with them. The Ohio State Highway Patrol was called, and they arrested fifty-eight people for inciting to riot or criminal trespass.

The arrested demonstrators felt they had been entrapped by the campus police—allowed into the building by the campus police and then locked in so they could be arrested for trespassing. The day after the Music and Speech arrests a new organization was formed, the Concerned Citizens of the Kent Community (CCC or 3-C or Tri-C); it was a coalition of moderates, liberals, and radicals united in their concern for procedural due process and student rights. Tri-C demanded:

1. all charges and suspensions be dropped since they were not in accordance with the Student Conduct Code.
2. the university follow the November, 1968 Student Conduct Code.
3. the SDS charter be reinstated since the revocation did not follow the regulations in the Student Conduct Code.

The CCC demands struck a responsive chord in the student body. Those concerned with procedural due process joined in the protest with those supporting SDS. The focus of their activities was a campus-wide referendum on the CCC demands to be held in late April. A counter-group, quickly formed by student leaders and with the tacit support of the university administration, attacked the CCC and tried to link it with SDS and other radical organizations. Leaflets appeared warning students that 400 radicals from other schools had descended on KSU. An "extra" edition of the *Daily Kent Stater* featured a front page editorial showing an alleged link between CCC and SDS.[25] These tactics made many CCC supporters resentful and forced CCC to shift its strategy to one of arguing it was not dominated by radicals nor linked to radical organizations. Many liberal faculty members became alienated from the university administration because of its role in the campaign.[26]

The election results were ambiguous. The Tri-C position lost but the referendum, which drew the largest campus vote in university history,

demonstrated substantial support for their position. Shortly after the referendum CCC folded as an organization and their final statement reflects the frustration and bitterness which many moderates and liberals on campus must have felt:

> In 3-C's short, three week existence, many sincere and dedicated members of the steering committee have learned that moderate tactics are meaningless here.
>
> To conclude: we played the administration's game in good faith. We hoped to win a larger measure of justice at KSU, and we hoped to move the university in a democratic direction. But we find ourselves ineffective and powerless. Needless to say, an impotent organization, one which has lost credibility with its student supporters, cannot long survive. Consequently, 3-C, a coalition of moderate students, hereby disbands.[27]

A subsequent investigation and report by the Kent chapter of the American Association of University Professors is generally critical of the administration's handling of the Music and Speech demonstration, arguing that academic due process had been infringed upon and the university had not operated within the letter and spirit of the student code.[28] By the time the report was issued it was too late. Tompkins and Anderson argue that

> although the administration received applause from elements outside the university for its handling of the April (1969) incidents, it also succeeded in alienating a large part of the faculty and students—overwhelmingly unsympathetic to the SDS—for acting in a way perceived to be inconsistent with the Student Conduct Code, for overreacting, for discrediting the CCC and for failing to listen.[29]

Much of the criticism of the administration was aimed at President White and the difficulty of people in gaining access to and communicating with him. Decision making in the university was centralized in his office and he rarely delegated that authority to others; vice-presidents and deans were rarely involved in university-wide policy making and occasionally found the president making policy in their areas of competence. Ordinarily this administrative style worked well enough, but in crises it placed the burden of decision making on White and left other administrators without direction. This unwillingness to delegate authority was to cause difficulties on May 1 and 2 when White was out of town.

The Music and Speech incident seemed to establish a pattern for the university's handling of demonstrations. Campus police would serve as the first line of defense, with the Ohio State Highway Patrol serving as back-up, making arrests after criminal acts had been committed. What would happen if the campus police could not effectively cope with a demonstration and the Highway Patrol were not available were questions left unasked.

While the fall quarter 1969 began quietly at KSU, the situation was tense and potentially explosive at a number of other universities. The war in Vietnam was unpopular with many university students, and in October the New Mobilization Committee to End the War in Vietnam organized nationwide antiwar demonstrations. In November 250,000 people gathered in Washington, D.C. to protest the war. The Nixon administration's response to these demonstrations was indifference—Nixon and his staff watched the Purdue-Ohio State football game during the November demonstration—or hostility: Vice-President Agnew told a New Orleans meeting that the October demonstrations were "encouraged by an effete corps of impudent snobs who characterize themselves as intellectuals."[30]

In Ohio, a group of black university students at Akron University took over the administration building for four hours on December 10, before they were evicted by the National Guard, called by Governor James Rhodes. Early in February, 1970 demonstrations at Ohio University resulted in a bomb explosion outside the campus police building. Protests over the war in Vietnam and ROTC on campus took place at Denison University in March and at Ohio University, Dayton University, Miami University and Ohio State in April. At Ohio State several hundred Guardsmen were called out on April 30 to break up a demonstration and in the process several hundred people were injured. The situation at Ohio State remained unstable, and it was almost four weeks before the National Guard began to withdraw from the campus.

Thus, by the first week in May, 1970, violence on Ohio's state-supported campuses was an old story. Few institutions had been spared. Governor Rhodes had already acquired a reputation for prompt and firm response; he had called out the National Guard forty times during the preceding two years. In fact, Ohio's expenditure for National Guard duty is said to have exceeded the total for all other forty-nine states during 1968-70.[31]

Antagonism on campus toward the Nixon administration escalated when, on April 30, President Nixon ordered U.S. and South Vietnamese troops to invade Cambodia, further widening the scope of the conflict. On Friday, May 1, President Nixon added to student dissatisfaction by contrasting the "bums" on campus with the "kids" fighting in Vietnam:

> You see these bums, you know, blowing up the campuses. Listen, the boys that are on the college campuses today are the luckiest people in the world, going to the greatest universities, and here they are burning up the books, storming around about this issue. You name it. Get rid of the war there will be another one. Then out there (in Vietnam) we have kids who are just doing their duty. They stand tall and they are proud.... They are going to do fine and we have to stand in back of them.[32]

President Nixon's decision to invade Cambodia must have been a mixed blessing to Ohio Governor Rhodes, coming during the last week of his long and intense Republican primary campaign against Robert A. Taft, Jr. for the U.S. Senate nomination. The family name had given Robert Taft an enormous advantage initially, but Rhodes seemed to be closing the gap between the two men during the last few weeks of the campaign. As a result the race was a close one, and the last weekend of the campaign, May 1-4, promised to be crucial for Rhodes's political future (he was prohibited from serving more than two consecutive terms as governor).

Another group of actors important in the events of May 1 to 4 were also busy during the last week in April. The 107th Armored Cavalry and the 145th Infantry (National Guard units based in northeastern Ohio) had been called to active duty in Akron on April 29 as a result of a truckers' strike which had been periodically violent. These were the Guardsmen ordered to Kent on May 2, after four days of hard, grueling, and potentially dangerous duty in Akron.

The factors which we have discussed in this section did not cause the events of May 1 - 4, but they did serve as the context within which those events took place and within which those events must be understood. As we shall see in the following pages, it is important to know how President White's administrative style shaped the way he responded to the demonstrations and the presence of the National Guard on his campus. It is also important to understand why students reacted as they did to President Nixon's announcement of the Cambodian invasion and why city and university officials reacted as they did to the resultant demonstrations.

Although the announcement of the Cambodian invasion had sparked a large and violent demonstration at Ohio State on Thursday, April 30, the scene in Kent had been relatively calm. The Cambodian invasion was a source of conversation and many students were upset and frustrated over the turn of events in southeast Asia. But the first demonstration did not occur until Friday, May 1.

FRIDAY, MAY FIRST

In response to the invasion of Cambodia, a group of history graduate students—World Historians Opposed to Racism and Exploitation (WHORE)—quickly organized a protest demonstration for noon at the Victory Bell on the Commons. The Commons provided a natural amphitheater setting and was a convenient meeting ground for students moving between dormitories and classes; the Victory Bell, located near one corner of the Commons, had traditionally served as a center for student speeches and rallies.

Approximately five hundred people attended the rally, listening with quiet attention to a variety of student speakers. "The general theme of the speeches was that the President had disregarded the limits of his office imposed by the Constitution of the United States and that, as a consequence, the Constitution had become a lifeless document, murdered by the President."[33] To symbolize its "murder" a copy of the Constitution was buried; several students volunteered their draft cards and discharge papers to be burned as well. The speeches ended with a call for another rally to be held in the same spot at 12:00 noon on May 4, to protest further the war in Vietnam, the U.S. invasion of Cambodia, and other students demands, including the abolition of the ROTC program on campus.[34] Overall, it was a quiet, peaceful rally, certainly not the start of what would be a long and violent weekend. The most important event during the rally was the call for another meeting at noon on Monday, a rally which would precede the killing of four students.

Later that afternoon the Black United Students (BUS) held a rally to hear blacks speak about disturbances that were taking place at Ohio State. This rally, which also took place on the Commons and attracted 200-400 people, ended peacefully at 3:45 p.m. The BUS rally was to be the last black political activity on campus that quarter. Michener suggests that black student leaders anticipated trouble on campus and had warned blacks to stay out of it,[35] "which they did."[36] The desire of black students to "cool it" contradicts one report of the BUS rally which states that one of the speakers had invited his listeners to come down to the street affair in Kent tonight at 9:00 p.m.[37]

President White waited until he had received reports on both rallies before leaving for a weekend in Iowa with his sister-in-law and a Sunday meeting of the American College Testing Program, of which he was chairman of the Board of Trustees. The reports convinced him there was little cause for concern; at the BUS rally "only 47 blacks appeared," he said, "no more than 20 radicals."[38] His decision to leave campus was a fateful one. By the time he returned to Kent on Sunday at noon the town and campus had experienced two nights of confrontation and conflict, the ROTC building had been burned to the ground, and the Ohio National Guard had effectively taken command of White's university.

Friday night started like many other spring nights. The first warm weather of the spring made those on campus anxious to avoid the drudgery of studying for mid-term exams. A Lab Band concert was scheduled for Friday night as were films from the recent Ann Arbor film festival. The All-University Spring Ball, scheduled for Saturday night, had been cancelled due to lack of interest—only seven tickets were sold. At the local movies students could see *Midnight Cowboy*, *Alice's Restaurant*, or *Zabriskie Point*. For those with autos the Route 59 Drive-In offered *Destroy All Monsters* and *Scream and Scream Again*.

For many students Friday night meant beer drinking on North Water Street, whose bars and rock music were well known to college and high school students throughout northeastern Ohio. This Friday with warm weather and impending exams, the bars were even more crowded than usual. Two topics dominated conversation in the bars—the pro-basketball playoff series between the New York Knicks and the Los Angeles Lakers and the invasion of Cambodia. Many students that night were angry and frustrated over President Nixon's decision to invade Cambodia, which seemed to stifle any hope that the war in Vietnam would be winding down soon.

Throughout the early evening people spilled from the bars onto the sidewalks and into the streets. Between 10:00 and 11:00 p.m. petty vandalism occurred when firecrackers were lit, beer bottles were thrown at passing cars, and the rare city police car driving down Water Street was booed. Soon the excitement was on the streets rather than in the bars. Shortly after 11:00 people formed a human chain in the middle of Water Street, doing a snake dance and forcing cars and trucks to back up toward the center of the city. The atmosphere was lighthearted, if frenetic.

From 11:20 p.m. on the mood of the crowd on North Water changed. City police cars patrolling North Water were bombarded with bottles. A trash fire was started in the center of the street. "Soon the crowd blocked the street and began to stop motorists to ask their opinion about Cambodia."[39] Shortly before midnight the crowd turned its attention toward the center of the city; a group moved en masse down Water Street, breaking windows in local business establishments and causing an estimated $10,000 damage.[40] Kent City Police Chief Roy Thompson, initially hopeful that the crowd would "simmer down,"[41] finally decided that the situation was getting out of hand and all twenty-one members of the Kent police force were summoned to duty.[42] In addition, a request for assistance was sent to the Portage County Sheriff and law enforcement agencies in surrounding communities. The first clash between "rioters" and police occurred near the intersection of Main and Water Streets, where fifteen policemen in riot gear dispersed the crowd which had been breaking windows on North Water Street.[43]

Mayor Leroy Satrom, who had been in Aurora, Ohio at a Law Day celebration and a subsequent poker game, returned to Kent at 12:20 a.m. to find a chaotic scene.[44] The remains of the trash fire burned on North Water, broken glass littered the streets and sidewalks on Water and Main streets, and the police were moving in full riot gear through the center of the city. After conferring with Chief Thompson, the mayor made a strategic mistake—he declared a state of emergency, ordered all bars in the city closed, and established an 11:00 p.m. curfew for the city and a 1:00 a.m. curfew for the campus. Police informants had warned that SDS Weathermen were on campus

and when the disturbances began downtown, Chief Thompson and Mayor Satrom assumed that it was part of a radical plot.[45] A few minutes later Mayor Satrom telephoned Governor Rhodes' office in Columbus and reported to the governor's administrative assistant "that SDS students had taken over a portion of Kent."[46] Within minutes of Satrom's call the governor's office telephoned the commander of the Ohio National Guard, Major General Sylvester T. Del Corso, who immediately dispatched a National Guard liaison officer, Lt. Charles J. Barnette, to Kent to keep him informed about the situation.

The declaration of a state of emergency was a mistake not only because it was based on incomplete evidence (there was no evidence that Weathermen were in Kent or on campus that night) but in closing all the bars the police forced hundreds of people who were primarily interested in drinking beer, listening to rock music, or watching the end of the Knicks-Laker basketball game, into the streets. "This arbitrary action threw a new mass of young people into the streets and infuriated many who up to now had done nothing wrong."[47] On the streets they found themselves being herded by city police and sheriffs deputies using tear gas away from the center of the city and toward the campus. Those who refused to disperse were arrested.

By 2:00 a.m. the downtown area had been cleared of people, although people were still visible through clouds of tear gas on East Main Street. The warm weather, the uphill walk toward campus, the tear gas, and constant prodding from riot-geared police frayed tempers. Finally, at the intersection of East Main and Lincoln Streets—next to the university entrance at Prentice Gate—the crowd stopped and faced the pursuing police. Standing on one side of the street and on campus property, the crowd seemed to challenge the local police to violate the campus sanctuary. Local police stopped and waited for assistance from the university police, but the assistance never came. Michener reports that this annoyed city police who were unaware that University Police Chief Donald L. Schwartzmiller had felt it necessary to utilize his men to protect buildings on campus.[48]

A potentially violent confrontation was avoided when a car collided with a Tree City Electric truck repairing the traffic light in the center of the intersection, leaving one of the electricians hanging from the light. Police and "rioters" cooperated to form a rescue team, and the dangling repairman was the center of attraction until he was rescued. By that time the tension had dissipated, and the crowd quickly and quietly melted away.[49]

By 2:27 a.m. both the campus and town were reported quiet once more, and shortly thereafter Lt. Barnette of the National Guard reported to Mayor Satrom at City Hall to get a status report. The first National Guard presence had arrived in Kent.

Looking back on Friday night one must ask, "Why did it happen?" Michener, in his interviews with participants and bystanders, finds a lack of agreement on motivation—the invasion of Cambodia, the weather, a need to let off steam, or the premeditated plans of radicals were all given as reasons. Michener leans toward a theory of radical involvement, based on the presence of one of the Kent State Four on Water Street early in the evening and a number of demonstrators wearing red armbands.[50] Chief Thompson felt that the disturbance was "instigated by a bunch of agitators and subversive groups."[51] Based on responses from over 7,000 students to a survey conducted soon after May 4, Stuart Taylor concluded:

> According to these results and the many letters written by the students who witnessed the events, one might conjecture that the "style" and actions of the Nixon Administration "primed" or increased the "readiness" of students for action. The disturbance, however, appears to have been instigated or "triggered" by a few persons, possibly "radical KSU students."[52]

The Minority Report of the Commission on KSU violence perhaps best summarizes the feeling of many. "The participation of outsiders in the events of May 1-4 ought not to be summarily dismissed as fantasy. The kind of participation is what cannot be established."[53] Although many people feel that the Friday night disturbances were part of a radical plot, there is little concrete evidence to support that conclusion. The Justice Department Summary of the FBI Report makes no mention of radicals in the Friday night activity, noting that fifteen people were arrested, all of them Ohio residents. The Scranton Commission, which had access to the full FBI Report, notes, "The FBI uncovered no evidence that the Kent State Four were involved in planning or directing any of the events of the May 1-4 weekend."[54] In addition, the activities engaged in—a trash fire, throwing bottles, and breaking windows—are not normally ones which revolutionaries choose. The FBI findings and the Scranton Commission report did not stop Michener from concluding that Friday night's activities were led by "a hard core of radical activists—abetted by a few real revolutionaries, not necessarily from the university—who grasped at the disturbance as a means of advancing their own well-defined aims."[55]

Without the invasion of Cambodia, the violence at Ohio State the preceding night, President Nixon's speech earlier in the day about "bums" on campus, and city officials' fears of SDS activities, it is possible that Friday night's action might have been treated merely as students celebrating the first good weather of spring. Traffic had been disrupted and windows broken on North Water Street in the past, a price which businessmen seemed willing to pay. But May 1, 1970 was unlike any spring day in the past. Frustration over the Cambodian invasion, anger because they were turned out of bars, and the sting of tear gas turned what might have otherwise been a relatively harmless release of emotion into an ugly incident. The local officials were inept in their handling of the event:

> The pattern established on Friday night was to recur throughout the weekend. There were disorderly incidents; authorities could not or did not respond in time to apprehend those responsible or to stop the incidents in their early stages; the disorder grew; the police action, when it came, involved bystanders as well as participants; and, finally, the students drew together in the conviction that they were being arbitrarily harassed.[56]

While resentment against the authorities grew among those involved, directly or indirectly, in the Friday disturbances, many other people— townspeople, students, university officials, and city officials—were disturbed at the magnitude of the damage done on Friday night. For many the glass shards on Main and Water streets were concrete evidence that "student radicals" or "outside agitators" were out to destroy their city and they became convinced that the community was under siege.

SATURDAY, MAY SECOND

Saturday morning witnessed one of those cruel ironies that were to permeate the weekend; while rumors spread through the city that radicals were planning to burn down the city, a number of students were downtown helping to clean up the debris from the preceding night. Store owners, fearful of being burned out or having their windows smashed, posted antiwar signs in the windows of their businesses.

City and university officials also began to prepare for what they feared would happen Saturday night. At the first of many meetings that day, university officials decided to seek an injunction against 500 "John Does," barring them from doing further property damage on campus. According to the Justice Department Summary, "it is not known ... if the injunction was served upon any person or disseminated in any way."[57] As we shall soon see, notice of the injunction was contained in leaflets distributed to students on campus that afternoon.

When Mayor Satrom returned to his office on Saturday morning, he formalized the proclamation of civil emergency which he had promulgated eight hours earlier. He banned the sale of liquor, beer, firearms, and gasoline (except for that pumped directly into an automobile), and established an 8:00 p.m. to 6:00 a.m. curfew for the entire city (including the campus).

At 11:00 a.m. Mayor Satrom held the first of four meetings with university officials and Lt. Barnette, the National Guard liaison officer.

> Although the university officials regarded the action as unnecessary, in that they felt that local law enforcement personnel could cope with any situation that might arise, the Mayor, other city officials and the National Guard representative decided at that time to put a company of 110 National Guardsmen on standby.[58]

Apparently in response to pressure from university officials Satrom exempted the campus from the 8:00 p.m. curfew and established a 1:00 a.m. curfew instead.[59] The change in curfew was recognition that if students could not go beer drinking downtown after 8:00 p.m. and were confined to their rooms on campus after that time, the situation would become even more tense. University officials, particularly Vice-President for Student Affairs Robert Matson, began arrangements for social activities on campus for the period after 8:00 p.m.

At a 1:00 p.m. meeting Lt. Barnette and Vice-President Matson discussed how to handle disturbances that might occur on campus. Matson explained that the campus police would be used first; if they failed, the Sheriff's Department would be called in, and then, as a last resort, reliance would be placed on the Ohio State Highway Patrol which, in riot situations where state laws had been violated, could make arrests. Lt. Barnette replied that if the National Guard were called, they would make no distinction between city and campus and would take jurisdictional control of the entire area.[60] Barnette's description of the National Guard mission is very different from that of General Del Corso, Barnette's immediate superior officer in the National Guard, whose concept of the guard's mission was that it would be used to *assist* rather than *replace* local law enforcement agencies.[61] Barnette's concept of the National Guard mission, however, was the only authoritative source that city and university officials had, and it shaped their perceptions all weekend of what would happen if the Guard were called to Kent—they would assume total control of the city and the university.

Sometime during the morning or early afternoon Lt. Barnette told Mayor Satrom that he would have until 5: 00 p.m. to ask for National Guard help, since it would take some time to move them from their strike duty in Akron to take up positions in Kent. This deadline meant that Satrom would have to make a decision on using the National Guard before knowing whether there would be any disturbances in the city or on campus Saturday night.

He was not without information, however incorrect or distorted it may have been. Businessmen told of receiving threatening phone calls. Throughout the day Police Chief Thompson heard rumors of guns, Weathermen, burning down the city, and putting LSD in the city water supply.[62] "False fire alarms, bomb threats and violent rumors kept the day ugly, and always at the mayor's elbow stood Lieutenant Barnette of the National Guard, warning him, 'If you're going to call the Guard, you have to do it before 5:00 this afternoon.'"[63]

While Satrom was trying to decide whether to call for the National Guard, Vice-President Matson and student leaders were making plans on campus. Recognizing that university students would not be allowed in the city after 8:00 p.m., the dormitory cafeterias were ordered to stay open late, and live entertainment and dancing were arranged for several dormitory complexes. In addition, a leaflet was printed and distributed to dormitory residents informing them of the injunction and the 8:00 p.m.

curfew in the city. However, the leaflet failed to mention the 1:00 a.m. curfew on campus. The leaflet also stated that peaceful campus assemblies were not banned (such a prohibition would have made much of the evening's planned entertainment illegal).[64]

Anticipating that there might be some disturbances on campus that night—there were rumors that a rally would take place—university officials established a rumor control center and activated an emergency operations center in the Administration Building. This window-less room would be the administration's command post for the remainder of the weekend. Vice-President Matson also asked Glenn Frank, Harold Kitner, and Jerry Lewis to organize a faculty group to serve as faculty marshals for the time being, wearing armbands to identify themselves. Many faculty marshals were unsure of their role in case of a disturbance. "Ultimately, most marshals decided that they would not physically intervene in case of disturbances but would confine their activities to discussion and persuasion, fact-finding, and reporting events to the university emergency operations center."[65]

Mayor Satrom's final meeting of the day took place in City Hall at 5:00 p.m., the deadline for telling Lt. Barnette whether or not the Guard would be needed. There were a number of factors that influenced Satrom's decision. Rumors had been circulating that plans were afoot to destroy the ROTC building on campus and the local Army recruiting office and post office downtown.[66] In addition, Mayor Satrom had received two disturbing reports of "Weathermen observed on campus and positively identified, and evidence of weapons on campus."[67] Neither of these reports was substantiated, but they did fit Satrom's sharpening perceptions of Kent as a city under siege by radicals. Threats to downtown businesses, if they didn't show overt signs of opposition to the Cambodian invasion, and memories of the destruction of the preceding night undoubtedly played a role in his decision.[68]

In view of these rumors and threats, Mayor Satrom felt he needed help. He hoped for assistance from the county sheriff while university officials hoped for assistance from the highway patrol; Satrom learned that the sheriff's deputies would not be available and that the Highway Patrol would be available only to make arrests for law violations. There also would be a time lag while they were mobilized. The unavailability of law enforcement

back-up assistance highlighted a problem of coordination between the city police and the campus police which had surfaced the night before—neither wanted to coordinate operations. Campus police would make no commitment to help city police control disturbances off-campus, just as city police were unwilling to move on-campus.

As the meeting broke up, Mayor Satrom felt he had no option except to call on the National Guard for help. Unfortunately, when the university representatives left the meeting, "they were under the impression that the National Guard was being requested for duty only in Kent, not on the Kent State campus."[69] University officials assumed that their strategy of relying on campus police, backed up by the highway patrol, would be sufficient to handle problems on campus. Earlier in the day, however, Lt. Barnette had told university officials that if called, the National Guard would not differentiate between the city and the campus.

Mayor Satrom then called the governor's administrative assistant (the governor was campaigning in Cleveland) to order up the National Guard, and the assistant called both Governor Rhodes to authorize the commitment of the Guard to duty in Kent and General Del Corso to mobilize the Guard for duty in Kent. Del Corso, in turn, ordered Guardsmen bivouacked in Akron on strike duty to be ready to move in one hour.[70] Shortly after 6:00 p.m., the National Guard was on alert and ready to move into Kent, although there had been no disturbances on campus or in the city yet that day.

Around 7:00 p.m. a crowd began to gather at the Victory Bell for the rumored rally, a crowd which by 7:30 had grown to around 600.[71] According to the Scranton Commission, the group was "an idle collection of students whom the curfew had prevented from going downtown."[72] According to Michener, however, "there was also a substantial cadre of hard-core radical leaders and perhaps one or two revolutionaries who had their eyes on much more than the rickety old ROTC building; among them, too, were many who had no connection with the university."[73]

The crowd soon moved off the Commons toward the dormitories where students were attending dances. A number of students were "liberated" from the dorms so that by the time the crowd returned to the Commons it had grown substantially—to approximately 1,000 to 2,000.[74] Once back on the Commons the crowd, some chanting antiwar slogans, moved purposely toward the ROTC building on one edge of the Commons.

As the crowd surrounded the old, wooden two-story structure, some shouted, "Get it" and "Burn it." Initially rocks were thrown at the building; then a trash can was thrown through a first floor window. Railroad flares were lit, and people threw them at the building or through the broken windows, hoping to start a fire. Their only success was a curtain which flamed briefly but soon sputtered out. Most of the crowd took little part in the efforts to destroy the ROTC building; some watched quietly while others cheered and chanted antiwar slogans. The lack of success in starting a fire was not a deterrent. A rag dipped in gasoline from the tank of a nearby motorcycle was lit and at 8:45 p.m. the ROTC building was aflame at last.[75]

The mood and intent of the people who participated in the fire Saturday night has been the subject of some debate. The Minority Report describes them as a "mob" with leaders,[76] which seems to fit Michener's view of the crowd as being led by radical leaders and revolutionaries, who sought to burn down the ROTC building and then to extend the rioting to the rest of the campus and the city.[77] For a leadership cadre who supposedly knew what they were doing and how to do it, they were remarkably inept. It took approximately thirty minutes of diligent effort to set the ROTC building afire, and then the fire went out. In addition, the bulk of the participants at the fire were hardly "riotous." The Scranton Commission differentiates between three groups of people involved on Saturday night: those who actively tried to set the building on fire and whose mood was one of anger, another group who cheered and shouted as if the fire were part of a carnival, and a third group who merely watched.[78] These three groups, called the "active core," "cheerleaders," and "spectators," respectively, by Lewis,[79] were not equal in numbers. Most of the crowd were "cheerleaders" or "spectators," although the "active core" did the physical damage to the building. Taylor's student survey data show that people's perceptions of the mood of the crowd depended on one's role. There was disagreement as to whether the mood of the crowd was "angry," "unconcerned," "lighthearted," or "fearful," depending on whether one participated or merely observed the events on Saturday night.[80] There is also a discrepancy between observers and participants and their perceptions of the role of "outside agitators." Of the observers, 54 percent as opposed to 16 percent of the participants, thought that outside agitators were "very" or "moderately" responsible for the Saturday night disturbance.[81] But one student noted:

> Those who claim to have recognized "outside agitators" must be praised for the remarkable feat of memorizing the faces of 20,000 KSU students to know that there were in fact outsiders in the crowd. Only an FBI agent who is looking for someone in particular could know for certain who caused the mob action.[82]

At 8:35 p.m., Mayor Satrom, informed of the trouble on campus and without consulting university officials, called for the National Guard, and they were ordered to Kent immediately, arriving between 9:30 and 10:30 p.m.

Shortly after the ROTC building began to blaze in earnest, the fire was reported to the Kent Fire Department and within fifteen minutes a city fire truck arrived at the scene. The firemen soon found themselves battling the crowd as well as the fire; hoses were wrestled away from the firemen, and others were punctured and chopped with ice picks and machetes. Rocks were also thrown at the firemen and, since they had no police protection, they withdrew from the campus. Shortly thereafter (approximately 9:15), the fire went out by itself. It began again a short time later, this time detonating live ammunition stored inside the building.

With the renewed fire at the ROTC building and the explosion of live ammunition, the campus police finally arrived at the scene. As Michener notes caustically, "They were two hours and twelve minutes late"[83] Where had the campus police been while the crowd was trying to burn down the ROTC building? According to the Minority Report, Chief Schwartzmiller's logic was that until the destruction started he didn't want to start a riot by having his men appear on the scene, but after the destruction had begun he felt it was too dangerous for his men to intervene.[84] When the ROTC building was initially threatened, the campus police had called the city police for help, but the Kent police said they were busy protecting the downtown area. "Schwartzmiller said later he received the impression that the Kent police department was 'getting even' with him for his failure to dispatch his men to Prentice Gate to disperse the crowd there on Friday night."[85]

While the campus police were trying to decide when and how to intervene, twenty state highway patrolmen entered campus and took positions near the residence of President White, with the intent of protecting his home from destruction.[86] Whether the campus police knew that the highway patrol was on campus is not known, but the highway patrol, law enforcement officials of the state of Ohio, did nothing to prevent the destruction of the nearby ROTC building.

Ten county sheriff's deputies arrived on the Commons at about the same time as the campus police, and together, using tear gas, they cleared the demonstrators from the Commons with some demonstrators heading back toward the dorms. While the campus police and sheriff's deputies were clearing the Commons, the National Guard was entering Kent, and the ROTC building was burning more brightly than ever. As one Guardsmen described the scene, "The sky was all lit up. It was something out of 'Gone With the Wind' with Atlanta burning."[87] In response to the renewed fire in the ROTC building, another Kent fire truck was dispatched to campus.

General Del Corso, who had accompanied Brigadier General Robert H. Canterbury and his men to Kent, after conferring with Mayor Satrom, ordered one detachment downtown to prevent destruction of businesses and another detachment to campus to protect the firemen who were answering the second alarm. Neither Del Corso nor Canterbury requested permission of any university official before sending troops onto campus. General Canterbury said later that because the building was located on state property, the Guard needed no specific invitation to enter the campus.[88] While Del Corso was ordering the Guard to protect the firemen on campus, an unidentified Guardsman called Vice-President Matson at the emergency operation center, and, after conferring with university officials and campus police, Matson agreed that the National Guard was needed.[89]

By 10:10 p.m., when the firemen arrived back on campus with National Guard protection and were met by the contingent of campus police and sheriff's deputies, the fire had completely gutted the ROTC building. The detachment of Guardsmen ordered downtown intercepted a group of demonstrators who had moved from the campus, and the Guardsmen, using tear gas, drove them back toward the campus. For approximately two hours (from 10:00 p.m. to

midnight) the Guard cleared the campus, using tear gas to force people into the dorms, some of whom were not KSU students and had no rooms in the dorms, and others who were KSU students but were forced to spend the night in other dorms on campus. By midnight the situation on campus and in the city was "secure."

A number of questions remain regarding Saturday night. Who burned the ROTC building? Michener and others see the fire as part of a radical conspiracy, led by radicals and revolutionaries.[90] The Scranton Commission regards the presence of machetes, ice-picks, and flares as evidence of preplanning, perhaps by radicals.[91] Charles Thomas believes Saturday night's events were orchestrated by agents of the federal government, thereby creating an opportunity and rationale for Governor Rhodes and President Nixon to "get tough" with radical protestors.[92] Although a number of authors see the burning of the ROTC building as a radical plot, there is little direct evidence that radicals were directly involved in Saturday night's events. Certainly the bulk of the crowd at the fire were neither radical nor revolutionary.

The presence of the National Guard in Kent on Saturday night was a mixed blessing at best. Michener argues that "if the Guard had not been present, it seems clear that several more university buildings, and perhaps some downtown, would have been burned."[93] If the Guard was instrumental in preventing further destruction on Saturday night, its role in clearing the campus with the use of tear gas created resentment on the part of many students. "Students who had nothing to do with burning the building—who were not even in the area at the time of the fire —resented being gassed and ordered about by armed men."[94] After reviewing the Guard's activities on Saturday night the Minority Report suggests, "The Guard ... was perceived by a large number of the student body as 'outsiders.' . . . They possessed 'power' rather than 'authority.'"[95]

The delay in deploying the campus police raises an interesting question: if the bulk of the crowd by the ROTC building consisted of "cheerleaders" and "spectators," would Schwartzmiller's men have faced any major danger in trying to stop the burning of the ROTC building? Schwartzmiller assumes that they would have been in danger, but was that a valid assumption? Rapid deployment of the campus police might have prevented the complete destruction of the ROTC building and negated the need for the National Guard to appear on campus, thereby altering the events of the next two days.

Although students may have seen the Guardsmen as "outsiders" who possessed "power" rather than "authority," townspeople reacted differently. Grant and Hill describe the reactions of some townspeople as the National Guard entered the city:

> People from some of the neighborhoods on our route ran out to our jeep. They said things like, 'Kill those S.O.B.'s if they cause any more trouble.' 'Get tough with them.' Maybe we agreed with some of these statements when we were entering a riot situation in a city, but now we were facing white young people like us and we thought that these remarks were stupid.[96]

Kent residents were clearly unhappy with what was happening to their city and its university. They saw the damage of Friday night and listened to rumors of what was happening on campus Saturday night, and the town-gown split, hidden below the surface under normal circumstances, emerged. Lewis argues:

> In Kent, middle-American townspeople and their officials tended to equate anti-war sentiment with unpatriotic, subversive activity. Moreover, equally important, they regarded the violent outbursts, from the breaking of store windows to the burning of the ROTC, as illegitimate ways of resolving domestic conflict.[97]

Not only were the demonstrators illegitimate and unpatriotic, but the National Guard represented "authority" which could and would reimpose "order" on the campus. For many Kent residents, taking sides with the students was an act of disloyalty, an endorsement of lawlessness, and a threat to the established social and political order.

SUNDAY, MAY THIRD

Governor Rhodes helicoptered into the KSU airport at 9:00 a.m. from Cleveland where he had been campaigning. He was met at the airport by Mayor Satrom and National Guard officials who showed him the damage on campus and in the city. After his tour Rhodes met with representatives of the highway patrol, the county sheriff, the county

prosecutor, General Del Corso, and three university vice- presidents to determine what should be done. Rhodes was described as "angry"[98] but not intemperate.[99] The discussion, which took place in the City Fire Station, centered on whether to keep the university open, which Rhodes favored, and on how to do so. The university officials who were present played virtually no role in the discussion, even though it was their institution whose future was being discussed. This curious lack of effort to keep control of the campus in their own hands, which surfaced again on Monday morning in the same fire station, may have been the result of a reluctance to question or challenge the governor of the state, or it may have reflected a recognition that with the Guard now on campus, control had passed from their hands. Governor Rhodes did not ask their opinions.

The meeting had not been in session long when it was decided to admit the press; what had been a policy-making session quickly degenerated into a press conference. According to one of the participants, "At that moment Jim Rhodes changed completely. He became a candidate for United States Senate."[100] After the press entered the room and pictures were taken, Rhodes launched into a fifteen-minute statement whose impact has been the subject of substantial debate.

Rhodes began by describing disturbances at Ohio State and Miami universities and argued that Kent State was merely one more in a coordinated series of attacks on authority, the National Guard, and the Ohio State Highway Patrol, using the state universities as sanctuaries. He called the disturbances at KSU "probably the most vicious form of campus-oriented violence yet perpetrated by dissident groups and their allies in the state of Ohio," and he vowed to use "every force of the law" to control them.[101] The troublemakers, who moved from campus to campus fomenting trouble, were described as

> worse than the brown shirts and the communist element, and also the night riders and the vigilantes. They are the worst type of people that we harbor in America. And I want to say this-they are not going to take over the campus and the campus now is going to be part of the county and the state of Ohio. It is no sanctuary for these people to burn buildings down of private citizens, of businesses (sic), in the community, then run into a sanctuary. It is over with in the state of Ohio.[102]

Rhodes went on to state that the vast majority of students at Kent State weren't interested in violence and destruction but were on campus for an education.[103]

What was Governor Rhodes trying to do by making this statement? As the Knight newspaper investigating team discovered, "It was impossible to learn what was going on in Governor Rhodes' mind at this time."[104] After analyzing Rhodes's statements, the Minority Report concluded that they were consistent with his statements in the past; they were not inflamatory and were not incendiary.[105] In essence, Governor Rhodes was merely repeating what he had said so often in the past. Michener argues that the statements were inflammatory because they were reported out of context and that if there was any difficulty it stemmed from the fact that "they were uttered in the hortatory style of a politician seeking votes rather than the persuasive style of a leader trying to defuse a perilous situation."[106] Unfortunately, the situation called for leadership rather than horation, and during those fifteen minutes when James Rhodes was a candidate for the Republican nomination to the Senate, rather than Governor of the state of Ohio, his words served to inflame rather than heal the wounds of the community.

Five years later Governor Rhodes offered his evaluation of his remarks.:

Q Sir, by those pronouncements about Brown Shirts, Communist elements, Night Riders and vigilantes, did you consider that you were, perhaps, inflaming a volatile potentially explosive situation?

A It was not inflamatory, no, sir.[107]

Peter Davies offers an alternative explanation for Rhodes' statements: they were to be a symbolic warning to the National Guard. Governor Rhodes warned:

You men are up against the scum of America, but be careful. They are vicious, organized, and dangerous. Your job is to protect the citizens of Kent and Portage County, where no one will be safe if we fail, and remember, your commanding officer has said, we can stop them with gunfire if necessary.[108]

One important result of Rhodes' statements was that they changed the mission of the Guard from one of protecting lives and property to one of breaking up any assembly on campus, peaceful or otherwise.[109] This change in mission lends some credence to Davis' interpretation of Rhodes' statement and is reflected in the Governor's promise at the end of his press conference to have the courts declare a "state of emergency" in Kent. This promise was repeated shortly after noon when Governor Rhodes met briefly with President White, who had just returned from Iowa. (He had tried to return Saturday night but had been unable to arrange air transportation). Rhodes reaffirmed his pledge to keep the university open and told White that he was going to the courts to seek a state of emergency. After Rhodes's pledge on Sunday morning, many people thought Kent was operating under a state of emergency, which would have prohibited any public gathering, but Governor Rhodes never sought such relief from the courts. "After the governor departed, widespread uncertainty regarding rules, prohibitions, and proclamations remained. Many people were unsure about what was to be legal and what not, particularly with regard to rallies."[110]

University officials, who were part of, but never participants in, the meeting with Governor Rhodes, were unsure of what was permitted under a state of emergency. Were rallies legal? If so, under what circumstances? Equally important, did a state of emergency relieve university officials of control of the campus? Did the National Guard now officially control the campus? There were more questions than answers.

Conversations between university administrators and Guard officers convinced university officials that Governor Rhodes's proposed state of emergency order gave the Guard complete legal authority on campus. Based on this information Vice-President Matson and student body president Frank Frisina printed and distributed on campus 12,000 leaflets, which stated that the National Guard had assumed control of the campus, that all rallies were banned, that a curfew was in effect (and curfew hours were listed), and that the Guard had the authority to make arrests. With the publication and dissemination of this leaflet, the mission of the Guard changed from assisting local law enforcement officials to replacing them. The leaflet was based on the assumption that the state of emergency was in effect (which was not true) and, as a result, "the only accurate information in this document are the curfew hours."[111]

Sunday afternoon a group of twenty-three faculty members drafted and published a statement deploring the appearance of the National Guard on campus, the burning of the ROTC building, violence, the war in Vietnam, the police vendetta against the Black Panthers, President Nixon's policies and Governor Rhodes' statements at the morning press conference. It read, in part:

> We call upon our public authorities to use their high offices to bring about greater understanding of the issues involved in and contributing to the burning of the ROTC building at Kent State University on Saturday, rather than to exploit this incident in a manner that can only inflame the public and increase the confusion among the members of the university community.[112]

Sunday newspaper headlines in Akron and Cleveland announced to northeastern Ohio the details of the Saturday night fire. *Akron Beacon Journal* readers discovered that "rioters" had burned down the ROTC building,[113] while *Cleveland Plain Dealer* readers learned that those "rioters" were "student radicals."[114] The *Beacon Journal* readers were aware that the National Guard was on campus,[115] while *Plain Dealer* readers were not.[116] Intrigued by the headlines and spurred by clear and mild spring weather, crowds of sightseers descended on Kent. Traffic became so thick that by 1: 00 p.m. no more traffic was permitted on campus, and traffic in the city and on approach roads put a severe strain on local law enforcement agencies already tired from two nights of disturbances. Tourists found the campus deceptively calm under the watchful eye of the National Guard. Guardsmen and sightseers talked quietly with one another, and an air of stability pervaded the campus. The charred remains of the ROTC building were a "must" attraction, as was the Guard helicopter parked on the university high school football field.

As darkness returned so did the tensions of the previous two nights. Shortly after 7:00 p.m. the Victory Bell began to toll and by 8:00 a crowd had begun to gather around the burned-out ROTC building. The crowd "was certainly less unified in temper and less dominated by a purpose that (sic) the crowd on Saturday night," [117] although Taylor found that the majority of students who participated in Sunday's events did so to protest the presence of the National Guard on campus.[118] By 8:45 the crowd had grown so large that the campus curfew was

moved from 1:00 a.m. to 9:00 p.m. At 9:00 the Ohio Riot Act was read to the crowd; they were given five minutes to disperse, being liable to arrest if they did not. When the crowd failed to disperse, tear gas was fired at them and the crowd broke in two—one group heading for President White's home and another for Prentice Gate at the corner of Main and Lincoln Streets. Those who headed for White's house were tear-gassed by National Guardsmen, and this crowd retreated to the Commons. The group heading toward Prentice Gate sat down in the intersection of Main and Lincoln, effectively blocking traffic on both streets. Remnants of the group from President White's house, as well as a group of demonstrators from downtown, joined them. According to the FBI, "Law enforcement officers from the city and county faced the students while National Guardsmen took a position behind them. State police helicopters were overhead with searchlights being played on the crowd."[119]

An uneasy truce lasted until 10:10 p.m. when the demonstrators demanded to talk to Mayor Satrom and President White about six demands: abolition of ROTC on campus, removal of the Guard from campus by Monday night, lifting of the curfew, full amnesty for those arrested Saturday night, the granting of all demands made by BUS (Black United Students), and the reduction of student tuition. A young man was given access to a police car public address system, and he announced that Mayor Satrom would soon be there to talk with them and that efforts were being made to contact White.[120] Vice-Presidents Matson and Roskens decided that White should not go, since the Guard was in charge of the campus and "there was no point negotiating in the streets," a decision in which they say White concurred. White does not recall that he was personally contacted by Matson regarding the matter.[121] Mayor Satrom tried to get to the scene but by the time he arrived the crowd was being dispersed.

At 11:00 p.m., the Riot Act was read once again, and the demonstrators were ordered to clear the intersection. The demonstrators, who up to this point had behaved peacefully, became hostile and angry at what they felt was a betrayal by the authorities who had promised to talk with them. Rocks were thrown, obscenities shouted, while tear gas and a bayonet charge by the National Guard were used to clear people from the intersection and drive them back across campus. One group was driven into the

Rockwell Library, where they were imprisoned by police and Guardsmen until given a forty-five minute grace period to clear the building. Another group was chased across campus toward the Tri-Tower dormitories by Guardsmen firing tear gas and wielding bayonets. A number of people were injured Sunday night—several Guardsmen from rocks, and two or more people bayoneted by Guardsmen.[122]

Sunday night witnessed an escalation in violence between demonstrators and authorities, indicating that both groups were losing patience with the other. Demonstrators were resentful of what they viewed as broken promises made by the police and the excessive force used to clear the intersection. Policemen and Guardsmen seemed to be increasingly impatient with demonstrators who cursed them, threw stones, and refused to obey them. The National Guard seems to have become particularly resentful. During Sunday it became apparent to many Guardsmen that demonstrators did not view them as citizen/soldiers—the view that many Guardsmen had—"but as something like Nazi Storm Troopers who would delight in having an excuse to attack them."[123] The verbal abuse, the bombardment of rocks, their long duty, and fear were beginning to take a toll. The Sunday night confrontation resulted in ". . . the first rumblings of resentment toward the students. Even the Guardsmen who were students at Kent were mumbling about how insane they were."[124]

By early Monday morning the situation on campus had deteriorated badly. Thinking the city and university were operating under a state of emergency, university officials had forfeited control of the university to the National Guard. The campus police would never again be a factor in the events that followed. Demonstrators were also becoming increasingly antagonistic toward the Guard; the National Guard represented the military, governmental authority, tear gas, and bayonets. The National Guard, in turn, began to see demonstrators as foul-mouthed, rock-throwing radicals, threatening the safety of the Guardsmen as well as the security of the nation.

MONDAY, MAY FOURTH

Classes resumed on Monday morning and students who had been away over the weekend stared at the charred remains of the ROTC building and talked with classmates who had been part of the action. Many students were upset by the appearance of the National Guard on campus. The noon rally, originally scheduled to protest the Cambodian invasion, now took on a new focus: to protest the presence of the National Guard on campus.[125] Although a substantial proportion of the student body knew that the noon rally was prohibited, many felt strongly enough about the presence of the Guard to go to the rally, nonetheless.

At 10:00 a.m. the last meeting of the weekend, called by General Canterbury, was held at the Fire Station. President White, Vice-President Matson, Mayor Satrom, Police Chief Thompson, the Kent safety director, a representative from the highway patrol, and the Guard legal officer were also present.[126] There were several items which had to be settled. Confusion over curfew hours had to be cleared up; it was decided that the city curfew hours of 8:00 p.m. to 6:00 a.m. would apply to the campus as well.[127] General Canterbury also made known his desire to withdraw his troops from campus as soon as possible, even as early as Monday evening. Late in the meeting the noon rally scheduled for the Commons was discussed. Who said what has been the subject of some dispute—a dispute of some importance since the Guard's interpretation of what was decided governed their actions on campus at noon. The Justice Department concluded that the National Guard determined that the rally would not be held.[128] Canterbury stated to the Scranton Commission that he deferred to President White, who said, "No, it would be highly dangerous (to hold the rally)."[129] White testified that he played no role at all in banning the noon rally.[130] The contrast in perceptions between General Canterbury and President White is clearly seen in testimony given at the 1975 civil suit trial.

First, General Canterbury's description of the Monday morning meeting:

Q What discussion was there concerning what, if anything, to do about the noon rally?

A There was a discussion entered into by just about everyone there about that rally and all rallies and the decision was made by the Mayor, by the Sheriff, by the Chief of Police, by everyone including the University people, that the rallies should not be permitted.

Q Tell us what the conversation was between you and Dr. White on the subject of dispersals (of rallies)?

A I asked Dr. White if the assembly was to be permitted, and his response was, that it would be highly dangerous.

Q Did he say he wanted you or the Guard to disperse any and all assemblies?

A I have given you the total of that conversation.[131]

From his conversation with White, Canterbury assumed that White agreed with everyone else at the meeting that all rallies would not be permitted. If rallies were not permitted, then the Guard's mission on Monday was clear—to disperse any assembly on the Commons.

White's description of the Monday morning meeting is at variance with that of General Canterbury.

Q Was there anything discussed with respect to permitting assemblies on the Commons?

A There was no general discussion that I recall concerning the status of assemblies in general.

Q Did you say anything at the meeting with respect to whether it would be dangerous to permit a rally on Monday, May 4th?

A No, sir.

Q Did General Canterbury ask you whether or not you wanted to have the assembly dispersed?

A I don't recall such a question.

Q Now, did General Canterbury suggest to you or say anything to you that there was going to be a rally?

A No, I don't believe he said that.

Q You knew there was going to be a rally, didn't you?

A No, I didn't know that.[132]

Obviously, President White and General Canterbury had different perceptions of what happened and what was said at the Monday meeting. Testimony of other participants at the meeting tends to support Canterbury's view that a "consensus" of the meeting emerged, with none of the university officials voicing strong opposition to the proposal that rallies not be allowed on campus.

Why White and Matson didn't speak in favor of holding a rally is not clear. With the deteriorating climate of opinion on campus, it was sure to be dangerous for the National Guard to ban a rally. In his testimony before the Scranton Commission

President White stated, "From past history, all know that my response would have been affirmative to a rally."[133] It is doubtful, however, that public officials and Guard officers were aware of White's "past history" on holding rallies, and his support for the noon rally was not apparent to those attending the meeting. The acquiescence of university officials to the rally ban fits into a pattern of behavior which emerged after the National Guard's appearance on campus and Governor Rhodes' statement that he would seek a state of emergency; the acquiescent behavior was based on the assumption that the National Guard had taken over effective control of the campus and, under the state of emergency, could determine whether rallies were prohibited. The assumption that a state of emergency existed, an assumption shared by all of the participants in the Monday morning meeting, was erroneous. Because everyone assumed a state of emergency existed, there was little need to debate whether to ban rallies; under the state of emergency they were naturally banned. The meeting concluded with the agreement that the noon rally should not be allowed.

At the conclusion of the meeting (11:15 a.m.) White and Matson returned to campus for a brief meeting with other university officials and then went to the Brown Derby restaurant for a luncheon meeting to discuss a Faculty Senate meeting scheduled for later that afternoon; they were eating when they heard news of the shooting.

After the meeting General Canterbury returned to Guard headquarters in the Administration Building on campus, informing those present that the noon rally had been banned.[134] Canterbury had at his command Companies A and C of the First Battalion, 145th Infantry Regiment and Troop G of the Second Squadron, 107th Armored Cavalry Regiment, all of whom had been on duty for much of Sunday night, getting three hours sleep at most before being summoned back to duty on Monday morning.

People began to gather on the Commons as early as 11:00 a.m. Some were aware of the proposed noon rally and wanted to take part. Many went out of curiosity, because they "wanted to see what was going on."[135] Both Michener and the Scranton Commission conclude that the rally was an anti-Guard rally rather than an antiwar rally (as originally planned) and that many people gathered on the campus to find out what could be done to get the Guard off campus.[136] Lewis also notes that some students "felt they had a right to be on the Commons and that the Guard was saying symbolically that they did not have this right."[137] If Lewis is correct, participation in the noon rally was viewed by some as a symbolic protest of and challenge to the authority of the Guard on campus. Taylor's student data indirectly support Lewis' argument—students felt the mood of the crowd was one of concern and anger rather than fear, and few of them felt they were risking injury in appearing at the rally.[138]

By 11:45 a.m. ninety-nine Guardsmen faced a crowd across the Commons estimated at 1,200 to 4,500.[139] Seventy percent of the students in Taylor's survey thought there were less than 2,000 people on the Commons at the time.[140] There is agreement that there was an active core of people around the Victory Bell, numbering 200 to 1,500,[141] shouting slogans at the Guard; on the surrounding hill there were 1,000 to 3,000 "cheerleaders" and "spectators."[142] The total number of demonstrators was probably between 2,000 and 3,000.[143]

Enforcing the morning decision that no rally be allowed, a Kent State police officer, Harold Rice, standing near the ROTC ruins and using a bullhorn, ordered the crowd to disperse. When they didn't the National Guard commander put Rice in a jeep with a driver and two riflemen, and the group drove across the Commons toward the crowd, who responded by chanting "Pigs off campus" and "One, two, three, four, we don't want your fucking war," as well as hurling rocks at the jeep. Officer Rice told the crowd through the bullhorn that their rally was prohibited and they would have to disperse. Those who heard him didn't move, and the jeep returned to the main body of the Guard.

Although Taylor found that many students knew the rally was prohibited,[144] there were still many, particularly those who commuted and did not hear the announcements on the local radio stations or read the Matson-Frisina flyer, who first learned the rally was prohibited when the campus police and the National Guard ordered them to disperse. Interestingly, there were no university officials involved in the attempt to stop the rally, and few writers fault university officials. Tompkins and Anderson, however, place much of the responsibility for what happened subsequently on the shoulders of President White. "That the President had failed to prepare them for this announcement, that he failed to appear at the rally, that he failed to 'legitimize' the Guard's orders, in our judgment, contributed to the

metamorphosis of what had been a peaceful, almost playful rally into a fatal confrontation."[145] This criticism of White overlooks the point made earlier —White apparently assumed that the Guard was now in control of the campus and there was no need for him to be involved personally. In addition, appearing before the crowd to explain the Guard's presence on campus was not White's style.

When Officer Rice returned to the main body of troops, General Canterbury ordered his troops to load and lock their rifles, ready to fire if necessary. Use of weapons by the National Guard in civil disorder duty is governed by Section F of Annex F to OPLAN 2, which states:

> f. Weapons. When all other means have failed or chemicals are not readily available, you are armed with the rifle and have been issued live ammunition. The following rules apply in the use of firearms:
>
> (1) Rifles will be carried with a round in the chamber in the safe position. Exercise care and be safety-minded at all times.
>
> (2) Indiscriminate firing of weapons is forbidden. Only single aimed shots at confirmed targets will be employed. Potential targets are:
>
> > (a) Sniper-(Determined by his firing upon, or in the direction of friendly forces or civilians) will be fired upon when clearly observed and it is determined that an attempt to apprehend would be hazardous or other means of neutralization are impractical....
> > (b) Other. In any instance where human life is endangered by the forcible, violent actions of a rioter, or when rioters to whom the Riot Act has been read cannot be dispersed by any other reasonable means, then shooting is justified.[146]

Unfortunately, as Taylor's data clearly show, students were unaware that the Guard had live ammunition in their weapons and did not think they would fire.[147]

As he stood by the ROTC building looking at the crowd across the Commons, General Canterbury saw his mission quite clearly; if the crowd would not disperse voluntarily he would be forced to use whatever means he had at his disposal. As he testified before the Scranton Commission: "The assemblies were not to be permitted because of the previous two days of rioting and to permit an assembly at this point would have been dangerous."[148] Many Guardsmen must have agreed with Grant and Hill:

> We were now, I believe, in an untenable situation from which there could be no turning back. For the first time in the many riots in which I participated, I believed there was a possibility that the demonstrators could attack us and be successful in overrunning our position, with little or no effort. This could have been accomplished in just a few seconds. I felt that we could have been killed with our own rifles if they got hold of them. This feeling was not mine alone. Most of the Guardsmen shared it.[149]

On orders from General Canterbury eight to ten Guard grenadiers used their grenade launchers to fire tear gas cannisters at the crowd. Two volleys of the pungent gas soon began to scatter some of the crowd, but a stiff cross-wind and poor aim by the grenadiers made the barrage largely ineffective. In addition, "the indiscriminate gassing of spectators had the effect of arousing anger among the crowd"[150] and led some spectators to become actively involved in harassing the Guard. Errant tear gas canisters were lobbed back at the grenadiers who fired them.

Seeing that the tear gas had no effect in dispersing the crowd, the men of Companies A and C and Troop G were ordered to advance against the crowd. Their rifles were loaded, safeties on, bayonets in place. Each Guardsman wore a gas mask. Most carried M-1 rifles, a combat weapon, some carried .45 caliber pistols as sidearms, and there were several shotguns loaded with birdshot and buckshot, non-lethal except at very close range. According to the Justice Department Summary, but cited nowhere else, no firing instructions were issued except that Company C was told that the order to fire would come from one man, presumably the commanding officer, firing in the air.[151]

As the troops moved out from the ROTC building and across the Commons, Company A was on the right flank, Company C was on the left flank, and Troop G was in the center. General Canterbury, in a business suit, marched behind his men. The advance of the Guard and the tear gas forced the crowd to retreat, some of them going back up and over the hill behind the Victory Bell (Blanket Hill) and around Taylor Hall.

Canterbury's original plan was to march to the crest of Blanket Hill, a knoll beyond the bell, between the northern end of Johnson Hall and the southern end of Taylor Hall. When some of the students ran to the north end of Taylor Hall he sent a contingent of men around there to disperse them. He had hoped, after clearing the Commons, to withdraw his troops to the ROTC building.[152]

Tactically this plan made good sense. The crest of Blanket Hill gave Canterbury control of the immediate high ground and insured that the Commons had been cleared and the noon rally dispersed—his mission for the day. Company C, detached to the other side of Taylor Hall, provided protection for his flank and prevented people from end-running his position and returning to the Commons.

When Canterbury reached the crest of the hill, however, he decided that it would be necessary to push the demonstrators even further away from the Commons and toward the nearby dormitories. His immediate target was a nearby athletic practice field. When the Guard contingent reached the practice field, they formed a skirmish line and patiently awaited further orders. Once on the practice field Canterbury discovered that he had not been very effective in dispersing the crowd; when his troops marched down the back side of Blanket Hill toward the practice field, the crowd separated and let them through, closing ranks again after the Guard's passage. The practice field was also a poor site for his men to form a skirmish line; it was fenced on three sides, effectively preventing movement except back in the direction they had come, and it enabled the crowd, which had now split into two groups, to harass the Guardsmen from the Prentice Hall parking lot and the walk at the bottom of Blanket Hill. As they stood on the practice field the Guard were under a heavy barrage of rocks and verbal abuse, and the tear gas volleys merely produced a "tennis match," with the demonstrators hurling the tear gas cannisters back at the Guardsmen.[153]

While the National Guard was being barraged with rocks, their own tear gas cannisters, and verbal abuse, the mood of the students changed.

> By this time, the crowd seemed more united in mood. The feeling had spread among students that they were being harassed as a group, that

state and civic officials had united against them, and that the university had either cooperated or acquiesced in their suppression. They shouted "Pigs off campus" and called the Guardsmen "green pigs" and "fascist bastards."[154]

The Scranton Commission also suggests that many students felt that the Guard was violating the students' "turf," their traditional sanctuary, and interfering with their freedom of expression.[155] Taylor, for example, found that many students were aware that the rally had been banned but didn't think the ban was right.[156] The Guard charged across the Commons with rifles at the ready, and using tear gas merely reenforced their perceptions of the Guard as an alien entity on the campus.

The Guard contingent spent ten fruitless minutes on the practice field, with only stone bruises, frayed nerves, and growing discomfort to show for their time. The weather was warm, the situation was tense, and the gas masks which the Guardsmen had been forced to wear as they crossed the Commons fogged up in the heat, making sight and breathing difficult.[157] With each passing minute in the practice field, the Guardsmen became increasingly uncomfortable.

At one point during their stay on the field some Guardsmen kneeled and pointed their rifles at the crowd facing them, but did nothing further. According to the Scranton Commission a .45 caliber pistol was fired into the air by an officer on the practice field, but the only officer with such a weapon denies firing it.[158] The act of kneeling and pointing their weapons at the crowd without firing may have seemed to the crowd to be evidence that the Guardsmen had no ammunition or they wouldn't use it.

Finally, General Canterbury decided that the Guardsmen should retrace their steps to the top of Blanket Hill and back down into the Commons and across to the ROTC building. He defended his move in these words: "My purpose was to make it clear beyond any doubt to the mob that our posture was now defensive and that we were clearly returning to the Commons, thus reducing the possibility of injury to either soldiers or students."[159] To the watching crowd the Guard maneuver looked like a retreat, as though the demonstrators had "won," and this emboldened some of them, who marched in mock lock-step with the departing Guardsmen and heaped a great deal of verbal abuse on them.[160] The crowd did not act en masse; some stayed at the foot of

Blanket Hill watching the Guardsmen march away; others ran around the end of the Taylor Hall toward the Commons. Individuals and small groups followed the Guardsmen as they trudged up the hill, their backs to the people below.

At the crest of the hill, near a small pagoda, a group of Guardsmen turned and fired. According to the Scranton Commission:

> Twenty-eight Guardsmen have acknowledged firing from Blanket Hill. Of these, 25 fired 55 shots from rifles, two fired five shots from .45 caliber pistols, and one fired a single blast from a shotgun. Sound tracks indicate that the firing of these 61 shots lasted approximately 13 seconds. The time of the shooting was approximately 12:25 p.m.[161]

Four students—Jeffrey Miller, Allison Krause, William Schroeder and Sandra Lee Scheuer—were killed and nine others wounded. The closest casualty was twenty yards from the Guardsmen, the farthest 245 to 250 yards away; Jeffrey Miller was 85-90 yards away, Allison Krause, 110 yards away, and William Schroeder and Sandra Lee Scheuer were both 130 yards away. The Scranton Commission found that Allison Krause, Jeffrey Miller, and William Schroeder had been on or near the Commons during the noon rally, although Miller is the only one of the three known to have been directly involved in harassing the Guard. Sandra Lee Scheuer was on her way to class when she was shot and killed.[162]

Why did the Guardsmen fire? A number of explanations have been advanced. At the 1975 civil suit trial several Guardsmen argued that the crowd was within twenty feet of them and posed a serious threat to their lives.[163] Guardsman Barry Morris described his perceptions as he marched back up Blanket Hill:

> **Q** And what were the students doing as you were walking toward the Pagoda?
>
> **A** At first they were just walking kind of fast behind us, because we were walking at a quick pace. As we quickened our pace, they started running, and at that point, it just, it seemed obvious that they were set on overtaking us. The noise, you know, the noise level increased just to point that it, you know, that I was scared to death.[164]

Several other Guardsmen testified that they felt their lives were in danger.

After interviewing a number of Guardsmen, Eszterhas and Roberts concluded that while the Guardsmen felt they were being threatened, and some were afraid, most realized that they were in no danger of being killed.[165] There was noise and some stones were thrown, but there was no evidence that the demonstrators had weapons. Michener suggests that the Guardsmen shot because they feared for their lives and were tired of being harassed by people with whom they no longer had patience or sympathy.[166] In essence, the Guardsmen had been pushed to the limit of their physical and psychological endurance—and they broke. The Scranton Commission, recognizing that some of the Guardsmen were frightened and many were tired of being harassed, nonetheless, concluded: "The indiscriminate firing of rifles into a crowd of students and the deaths that followed were unnecessary, unwarranted, and inexcusable"[167]

Peter Davies raises an interesting point:

If the Guardsmen's claim that a crowd was charging them to within ten, fifteen, twenty, and thirty feet was true, then obviously most of the casualties would have been less than two hundred feet away. Why were they shooting at students two hundred, three hundred, and four hundred feet away from them, distances that remove any danger whatever to the soldiers?[168]

The Scranton Commission found that relatively few of the Guardsmen were firing at people who were immediately threatening them—at least forty-one shots were fired into the air or the ground.[169] Those Guardsmen who admit firing at specific people seem to have fired at people closest to them, although the closest casualty was sixty feet away, not the twenty or thirty feet claimed by some Guardsmen.[170]

The answer to Davies' question may lie in the topography of the area of the shooting. The pagoda on Blanket Hill is the high point of the area and shots fired over the heads of people twenty or thirty yards away would carry in a downward trajectory and inflict mortal wounds hundreds of feet away to people at whom the Guardsmen weren't aiming. Thus, the Guardsmen who thought they were safely aiming over the heads of people near them may have inflicted wounds on others quite some distance away.

Several other explanations have been suggested. The Minority Report examines two alternatives—the "they followed orders" thesis and the "sniper" theory.[171] The "they followed orders" thesis stems from the statement of one Guardsman that he heard the order to fire; the authors of the Minority Report wonder about the officer with a .45 caliber pistol aimed at the crowd before the shooting began and the single shot which preceded the barrage of rifle fire.[172] At the 1975 civil suit trial Harry Montgomery, a student standing by Taylor Hall, testified that he saw a Guardsman with a .45 tap several Guardsmen on the back as they walked up Blanket Hill, before he turned and fired his pistol.[173] The Guardsman identified by Montgomery, First Sergeant Myron Pryor, testified that he did not tap his men on the back and did not turn and fire the first shot, since his .45 was empty at the time.[174] Since no check of ammunition was made by the Guard immediately after the shooting, it is difficult to know whether Pryor is telling the truth. However, Pryor did admit that he turned and aimed his empty pistol at the demonstrators but that he turned when his troops turned, which he assumed was because they had been ordered to take a stand.[175] Guardsman Richard K. Love also testified that he heard an order to halt and turn as the Guard neared the pagoda[176], but there is no supporting testimony, and the Scranton Commission concluded, "The weight of the evidence indicates, however, that no command to fire was given, either by word or by gesture."[177]

The "sniper" theory—that the first shot was fired by a sniper and the Guardsmen fired in retaliation—was initially proposed by Generals Canterbury and Del Corso, but there has been little supporting evidence. The Scranton Commission, noting that neither the FBI nor the Ohio State Highway Patrol—after extensive investigations—found evidence of a sniper, suggests that what appears to be a sniper's gun in the photographs is nothing more than the telephoto lens of a camera on a tripod atop a nearby building.[178] Perhaps the most telling criticism of the "sniper" theory is found in the Minority Report, which concludes, "What chiefly weakens the hypothesis that the Guardsmen shot thinking themselves endangered by student snipers is that they did not fire in any direction where snipers might be presumed to have been."[179]

Peter Davies suggests still another explanation for the shooting: while the Guardsmen stood on the practice field, an agreement was reached to take action against those harassing them.[180] This theory, of course, assumes premeditation on the part of the Guardsmen and/or their commanders. Based on the evidence available to him at the time Davies is forced to accept that

> We still do not know whether or not a few Guardsmen had conspired during those few minutes when they were immobile on the football practice field, compelled, by the folly of their commanders, to endure harassment by a handful of students in the parking lot and the particularly vocal abuse from many among the large crowd spread out in front of Taylor Hall.[181]

Davies' theory was one of the factors which subsequently led the Justice Department to open a grand jury investigation of the shooting in 1973, an investigation which resulted in the indictment of eight Guardsmen for violating the civil rights of the wounded and dead students. In the subsequent criminal trial the case was dismissed for lack of evidence.

Charles Thomas argues that "Major Jones had informed his men that if the students encroached on the Guard from behind on the return march, the soldiers were to wheel around and fire a volley over their heads, to brush them back."[182] Thomas presents no direct evidence to substantiate these allegations nor is there any in the public record. Following his logic Thomas argues that Major Jones, at the top of the hill, shouted "Turn around and fire three rounds!"[183] leading to the fatal fusillade. Nowhere in the public record, in films of the events, or in the tape recordings made at the time, is Major Jones' voice to be heard issuing that command.

The central question remains unanswered. Was the shooting a conspiracy between officers and enlisted men to punish those who had been harassing them? Or were the Guardsmen pushed, by the heat, the rocks, and the verbal abuse, beyond the breaking point? These questions have not been completely answered, even after nine years of litigation.

Upon hearing the gunfire, Majors Fassinger and Jones ran up and down the line of Guardsmen yelling, "Cease Fire!" Major Jones had to hit several men on the helmet to stop their firing. Immediately after the Guardsmen at the top of Blanket Hill stopped firing, Captain Snyder of Company C (stationed at the other end of Taylor Hall and out of the action) took seven men to examine those students in the Prentice Hall parking lot who had been shot. They found Miller and Schroeder dead. The presence of a Guard contingent nearby inflamed those who slowly began to realize what had happened, and Captain Snyder's contingent beat a retreat back to Taylor Hall and later back across the Commons. General Canterbury, after the firing had halted, ordered the men of Troop G and Company A back down Blanket Hill and across the Commons.

The reaction of the crowd to the gunfire is well described by the Scranton Commission:

> As shooting began, students scattered and ran. In the parking lot behind Prentice Hall, where two were killed and two wounded, students dove behind parked cars and attempted to flatten themselves on the pavement. On the slope east of Taylor Hall, where four were wounded, students scrambled behind a metal sculpture, rolled down the incline, or sought cover behind trees. The scene was one of pell-mell disorder and fright.
>
> Many thought the Guardsmen were firing blanks. When the shooting stopped and they rose and saw students bleeding, the first reaction of most was shock. Jeffrey Miller lay on the pavement of an access road, blood streaming from his mouth.
>
> Then the crowd grew angry. They screamed and some called the Guardsmen "murderers." Some tried to give first aid. One vainly tried mouth-to-mouth resuscitation on Sandra Lee Scheuer, one of the fatalities. Knots of students gathered around the fallen.[184]

In shocked and stunned silence people viewed the desolation created by the gunfire. Some stayed to try and help the living or weep for the dead, while others moved toward the Commons after the Guard. Those who gathered on the Commons to face the National Guard once more had a strident, defiant, fatalistic mood. Michener describes the scene: "From the crowd rose many voices demanding that a frontal assault be made on the Guard. 'Let them spatter us if they want to,' was the defiant cry."[185] Guardsmen, some of whom had earlier feared that the crowd would take their weapons away and use them, now faced people who felt they had nothing to lose by doing just that. As the National Guard stood nervously in a circle on the Commons, rifles in position, surrounded by an ever-growing and increasingly hostile crowd, the bloodshed of a few minutes earlier looked as though it was merely a prelude.

Further bloodshed was averted by the intervention of faculty marshals, who worked to cool down the emotions of the crowd and prevent hostile and provocative actions by the Guard. Major Jones and General Canterbury seemed intent on dispersing the crowd through the use of force, but they were convinced to give the marshals a chance to plead with the crowd to disperse before further violence occurred. A tense twenty minutes ensued, while the marshals—visible in their white armbands—talked with the crowd and the National Guard officers. By 1:30 p.m. the marshals were successful, leaving the Commons and Blanket Hill clear of demonstrators and the Guard standing at "parade rest" in a circle around the burned-out ROTC building.

Word of the shooting reached President White at the Brown Derby where he was eating lunch. He immediately returned to his office, and after conferring with his staff, decided to close the university for the rest of the week. Once again, however, effective control of the campus was taken from White's hands. Portage County Prosecutor Ronald Kane heard of the shooting over the radio, and after failing in his attempt to talk with Governor Rhodes he obtained an injunction from Common Pleas Court Judge Albert Caris closing the university indefinitely.

The injunction gave the National Guard complete control over the campus (the first specifically legal authorization granted them) and gave students until noon on May 5 to vacate the campus. Students packed what they could and left the rest in their dorms, using university buses and cars to get home as best they could. Worried parents also tried to call their children in Kent, putting such an overload on the city phone system that it had to close down, leading some students to think that the FBI was trying to isolate them and convincing many parents that a "revolution" was taking place in Kent.[186] Despite the enormous difficulties involved, the campus was virtually empty by evening, except for the police and National Guard, who patrolled its 660 barren and war-scarred acres.

During the afternoon and evening of May 4 city police and National Guardsmen closed down the city to outsiders. All traffic in and out of the city was halted, and military vehicles patrolled the streets. A dusk-to-dawn curfew was in effect and everyone was off the streets; many spent the evening listening to the radio for news—much as they had when John F. Kennedy had been killed. "Rumors flew more

swiftly than the military helicopters which circled the town incessantly, shining giant spotlights over houses and yards in an eerie treetop dance. Kent knew real fear."[187]

In retrospect, the events of Monday are more understandable if we realize that most of the participants in the drama believed that Governor Rhodes had ordered a state of emergency in Kent, which would have effectively placed legal control of the city and university in the hands of the National Guard. The Monday morning meeting in the fire station thus yields a different interpretation: General Canterbury and the officials at the meeting were not debating whether the Guard had the authority to disperse the noon rally (that was assumed) but whether the rally was or should be prohibited. President White's oblique response that the rally "would be dangerous" provided Canterbury with the necessary rationale for his subsequent actions. The lack of overt opposition by university officials at the meeting can also be understood as tacit acceptance of the Guard's status on campus. White's decision to go to lunch with his staff at the Brown Derby at the time of the rally is still another indication that he regarded dispersal of the noon rally as the Guard's responsibility.

Although city, university, and National Guard officials were under the impression that Kent was under a state of emergency and that rallies were banned, many of the demonstrators were not. They were unaware of what Rhodes had planned to do, and those who knew that the rally was banned disagreed with the ban. Thus, the Guard's newly defined mission of dispersing the noon rally was regarded by many demonstrators as one more example of an illegitimate exercise of arbitrary military power.

Guardsmen and demonstrators thus viewed the legitimacy of the Guard's mission as it moved across the Commons and up Blanket Hill in quite different terms. Because the demonstrators felt the Guard's presence on campus was illegitimate, they felt no qualms about harassing them, physically and verbally. The Guardsmen, who viewed their mission as a legitimate one, grew increasingly resentful of the physical and verbal abuse to which they were subjected. The consequence of these differing perceptions was the thirteen second fusillade which killed four people.

AFTERWARDS

Tuesday morning the mass media descended on Kent, insuring that KSU would no longer be the largest unknown university in the country. Some newsmen from the New York Times and CBS had been covering the story since the burning of the ROTC building on Saturday night. Along with the media came the FBI and the Ohio State Highway Patrol—each making a separate investigation of the shootings and neither making their complete report public.

The faculty, finding themselves barred from campus and wanting to take some form of collective action, held a mass meeting in the Akron Unitarian Church, attended by approximately half the faculty as well as many teaching fellows and graduate assistants. The resolution adopted by this assembly read, in part,

> We hold the Guardsmen, acting under the orders and under severe psychological pressures, less responsible than are Governor Rhodes and Adjutant General Del Corso, whose inflammatory indoctrination produced those pressures. We deplore the prolonged and unduly provocative military presence on the campus not only because we regard the use of massive military force against unarmed students as inappropriate in itself, but because it symbolizes the rule of force in our society and international life.
>
> We regard student protest against this rule of force as their moral prerogative. We profoundly regret the failure of the Governor and other civil officers to understand the complexity and variety of issues motivating our students, to comprehend the diversity of the students involved, and to adjust flexibly and humanely to their morally based unrest.[188]

Michener concludes that while the faculty manifesto contained some basic truths it showed "civic irresponsibility" because of the lack of appreciation for the difficult political situation in which the university was embroiled.[189] In essence, the charges—even though true—should not have been made public, or made public at that time. Michener, of course, fails to understand the sense of moral outrage which many faculty felt at the shootings, an outrage which demanded public expression.

Townspeople quickly took sides as well. The Knight news team investigating the shootings found:

> By Wednesday, two days after the shooting, public opinion on the Kent State incident was clearly divided. There were those who felt that the student demonstrators had received exactly what they deserved and those who were quite ready to charge the national Guardsmen involved with murder.[190]

Although there are no public opinion data from Kent for this period, letters to President White and the Kent-Ravenna Record Courier reflect this division of opinion, with the majority of letters sympathetic to the Guardsmen.[191] The Republican primary, which took place the day after the shootings, resulted in Governor Rhodes' loss of the Senate nomination; Rhodes won 47.5 percent of the primary vote statewide and won 41.4 percent of the vote in Portage County. His vote in Portage County declined precipitously from 1966, when he had carried 86.4 percent of the Republican vote for governor against a weak opponent.

Student opinion was also divided. Taylor found that at least 45 percent of the students surveyed felt that Guard officers, Governor Rhodes, and radical KSU students were "very" responsible for the shootings.[192] There was a reluctance to place responsibility on the Guardsmen who fired, many students feeling that the commanding officers had primary responsibility. Many students felt Governor Rhodes was more responsible than the Guard officers or the enlisted men. Many accused him of using the occasion to win votes in the primary. "Governor Rhodes had to show his power for the political scene and the up-coming primary by bringing in the troops. I put the entire blame on him...."[193] Those who viewed student radicals as being very responsible seemed to focus on two dimensions of the Monday demonstration: students who defied the ban on rallies deserved whatever happened to them, and what happened at KSU was part of a broader conspiracy. "I believe that outside agitators were totally responsible because through a plan they accomplished their purpose of closing KSU.... KSU was a mission for the group and they accomplished their 'mission impossible.'"[194] Perceptions of responsibility were colored by the extent to which students were involved in Monday's events. Participants were far more likely than observers and nonparticipants to say that Governor

Rhodes, National Guard officers, President Nixon, and Vice-President Agnew were "very" responsible for the shootings, and they were far less likely to perceive radicals, student and nonstudent, as being "very" responsible.[195] It is interesting to note that the participants hold the most visible symbols of civil and military authority, National Guard officers, governor, president, and vice-president responsible, rather than the enlisted men who fired the shots. For these people the context of events within which the shootings took place was an important determinant of responsibility.

The split between those who held radicals responsible and those who perceived the symbols of civil and military authority responsible is mirrored in a Q-sort by Steven Brown,[196] which found two major groupings—radicalized students, who were alienated from the established order, and intolerant townspeople, who were totally committed to the established order and intolerant of those who threatened it. A third group, the "reasonables," felt that the way to resolve conflict was by discussion and negotiation. The Brown data indicate that very shortly after the shootings student and townspeople's perceptions had differentiated.

A nationwide Gallup telephone poll, taken on May 13 and 14, found that 11 percent of the people thought that the National Guard was primarily responsible for the deaths, 58 percent that the demonstrating students were responsible, and 31 percent had no opinion.[197] The Gallup organization noted:

> The question on the Kent State killing produced an unusually high number of "no opinion," suggesting that the no opinion column might harbor some people with qualms about the guard's behavior who were reluctant to say so outright. It also seems likely that some of those polled were suspending judgment about who was most to blame until the conflicting accounts of the shooting could be cleared up.[198]

The willingness to suspend judgment, which the Gallup pollsters found in the national sample, was not evident in Kent. In characterizing the mood of the city after the shootings the Knight newspaper team found, "Often it seemed to reporters that there was a plenitude of spite in Kent and a sad shortage of sympathy.[199]

The shock waves from the shootings at Kent State, and the subsequent shootings at Jackson State in Mississippi, were felt on college campuses across the nation. A study by Peterson and Bilowsky found that 57 percent, or almost 1350 colleges and universities, experienced some "significant" impact on campus operations as a result of the Cambodian invasion, the Kent State and Jackson State shootings.[200] The campus response varied by type of school; public and private universities were more likely to experience strikes or demonstrations than colleges which, in turn, were more likely to experience disruptions than sectarian institutions. The authors suggest that the number of students attending the school was a critical factor in a school's response to the events of early May; they reasoned that the larger schools contained a "critical mass" of protest-prone students who could and would take advantage of events such as Kent State to mobilize students at their institutions.[201]

The presidents of colleges and universities were concerned with their students' reactions to the shootings at Kent State and Jackson State, since many of the presidents, particularly those heading public institutions, were concerned about the possible loss of public confidence in higher education and the reaction of state officials to demonstrations on their campuses. These fears were reflected in the presidents' perceptions of which constituents would be critical of happenings on campus; local area residents were viewed as being most critical, followed in turn by state legislators, and alumni—three very important clientele support for higher education in America.[202]

The fears of these presidents proved largely unrealistic. The campus demonstrations following Kent State, while large and frequently militant, were also peaceful. In analyzing the largely peaceful nature of the protest demonstrations the Scranton Commission concluded:

> The main reason for the general nonviolence is again to be found in the paradox of tactics: the massive number of moderates who had joined the protest, partly because of violent acts against students, then guaranteed by their involvement that the protests would be largely nonviolent. In part, moderates were able to do this because they outnumbered extremists. But more important were their decisions: on campus after campus, students, faculty, and administrators set up programs of action designed to provide politically viable alternatives to violent action.[203]

On campus after campus moderates took over control of the protest movement from campus radicals. There were speeches, there was rhetoric, there were marches, and there were demonstrations—frequently larger than during the Student Mobilization days—but they were more somber and thoughtful than before, and they attracted a broader cross-section of the campus community, some of whom supported U.S. foreign policy in southeast Asia but could not tolerate American students, like themselves, being shot and killed on college campuses.

Although post-Kent State demonstrations proved attractive to substantial numbers of moderates, activating and involving many who had not been involved previously, research by Adamek and Lewis suggests that involvement in protest demonstrations, particularly where violence results, served to radicalize participants.[204] Interviews with Kent State students suggested that the violence of May 4 served to radicalize the students, "that is, they became more accepting of the use of violence, moved to the left in their political attitudes, and became more politically and protest active."[205] The Adamek and Lewis data show that the violence of May 4, rather than making students more quiescent, angered and made them more radical.

Two days after the shootings six Kent State students, visiting Congressman William Stanton (R-Ohio) in Washington, were able to spend more than an hour talking with President Nixon. The students explained to Nixon that they felt that campus unrest was caused by student opposition to the Vietnam War and by a lack of communication between students, campus administrators, and the federal government. The President expressed appreciation for their candor and promised them a full report on the killings. In the following days President Nixon also met with the heads of eight major universities and with state and territorial governors to hear their evaluations of his policies.

In the week following May 4, President White and the Faculty Senate sought ways to complete the spring quarter instruction, which still had five weeks remaining. At a faculty meeting on May 8, President White and the faculty decided to continue classes through whatever means possible. Classes met at nearby universities and colleges (Oberlin designated itself as "Kent State in Exile"), church halls, faculty homes, business and commercial facilities, and many courses were completed by mail and telephone.

May 8 marked the withdrawal of the National Guard from campus and the departure of the Ohio State Highway Patrol and, due to a modification of the court injunction, the first day that faculty, staff, and administration were allowed back on campus (from 8:00 a.m. to 5:00 p.m., Monday through Friday).

When the faculty and staff returned to campus, they discovered the FBI and the Ohio State Highway Patrol busily gathering evidence in their investigations of the shootings. Neither report has ever been made public in its entirety, although the Portage County Grand Jury had access to the Highway Patrol report, and the Scranton Commission had access to the FBI report. On May 15, Portage County Prosecutor Ronald Kane revealed to the public "weapons" and "materials" confiscated in a search of empty dormitory rooms after the closing of the campus on May 4. The collection included a rifle, shotgun, several revolvers, baseball bats, knives, bows and arrows, and hypodermic syringes and needles. As Michener notes, however, these were the types of things one might expect to find in a college dormitory or in the homes of families with college-age students.[206]

In addition to these investigations by off-campus agencies, President White, on May 11, created the Commission on Kent State University Violence, chaired by Professor Harold K. Mayer. The Mayer Commission met with a large number of people and took documentary and tape-recorded evidence regarding the events of May 1-4. At the conclusion of their investigation the commission could not agree on a final report and a year after its establishment, published four volumes—three volumes represent subcommittee reports focusing on specific problems within the university and between the university and community, while the fourth volume, the Minority Report (so called because it was written by a minority of members of the commission), concluded that outside agitators played a predominant role in the events of the weekend.[207]

President White also created a forty-five member Commission to Implement a Commitment to Non-Violence, under the chairmanship of Professor Charles E. Kegley. The Kegley Commission had a twofold task:

(1) to consider and recommend various control procedures including, but not restricted to, a marshalling program, group discussions and the development of an administrative policy in response to violence or threats of violence and (2) to attempt to prevent violence by identifying those conditions which might produce it and to suggest means by which to eliminate it.[208]

Unlike the Mayer Commission, the Kegley Commission was established to explore administrative problems within the university and to suggest solutions. As a result it issued no report. Instead it decided upon a series of administrative changes, which it submitted to the appropriate administrative officers for adoption or rejection. Naturally, not all of the recommendations were accepted but much of the administrative reorganization which occurred in the year following the shootings stemmed from the Kegley Commission recommendations.

Forty days after the shootings, on June 13, over twelve hundred graduate and undergraduate students returned to the campus—to receive their diplomas. They were the first students to be on campus since May. During his commencement address President White announced that President Nixon, responding to pleas from White and area congressmen, had named a special commission headed by former governor William Scranton, to investigate campus unrest, particularly the cases of Kent State and Jackson State.

On June 15 Judge Caris lifted the injunction under which the university had been operating and returned control to the trustees. A week later classes began for the first summer session of 1970. Security was tight: faculty, staff, and students had to carry valid and up-to-date ID cards and there were more law enforcement officers on campus than usual. The only visible reminders of the weekend were the fire-blackened plot of ground where the ROTC building once stood and bullet holes in the metal sculpture downhill from the pagoda where the Guardsmen stood when they shot.

Although classes resumed their academic year schedule in September, 1970, the campus and community would never be the same. For people who live in Kent, who teach at or attend Kent State, or who were on or around the campus during this period, the events of May 1 - 4 will not be forgotten. Each year on May 3 and 4 there is an all-night vigil at the site of the killings, followed by a day of commemorative activities. Students attending KSU frequently must explain to their parents and friends what "really" happened on Blanket Hill that day and convince them that radicals no longer pose a threat on the campus. Finally, Kent State University is no longer "the largest unknown university" in the country—quite the reverse. KSU will not be known for the quality of its faculty (regardless of how talented they may be), nor the beauty of its now-quiet campus, but for what happened during thirteen fateful seconds on May 4.

CONCLUSIONS

Although the shootings brought notoriety to Kent State, they left a series of unresolved questions in their wake, the most important of which was: who was responsible for the shootings? Although it is easy to blame the demonstrators, "radicals," or Guardsmen for the shootings, it is my considered opinion that a large number of people must share responsibility for contributing to the events which led up to the shooting and whose activities led to the fateful Monday morning clash. In addition to the Guardsmen and the demonstrators, I would say the following people share at least some of the responsibility:

Mayor Satrom and Police Chief Thompson—whose actions on Friday night escalated a bad situation into an incendiary one and then spent much of Saturday listening to and believing rumors that the city and university were under seige by radicals. This left them with no alternative but to call in the National Guard.

Generals Del Corso and Canterbury—who redefined the National Guard's mission from assisting local law enforcement officials to one of assuming responsibility for the maintenance of order. In addition, they were remarkably inept field commanders—several times placing their men in unnecessary jeopardy and failing at a critical moment to maintain order and discipline among their men.

Governor Rhodes—whose statement on Sunday morning that he was going to seek a declaration of a "state of emergency"—which he never did—misled those involved in making decisions on Monday as to what was permissible.

President Whirte and his administrative staff—who relinquished control of the campus too willingly and then washed their hands of any subsequent participation in events, when such participation might have changed the course of events. One wonders what might have happened had White spoken out strongly at the Monday morning meeting in the fire station, or if university officials had been present on the Commons prior to the Monday morning rally.

The demonstrators—student and non-student, radical and non-radical—whose activities on Friday and Saturday nights brought the National Guard on campus and ultimately led to the fatal Monday confrontation.

The campus police—whose experience and empathy with students should have made them most qualified to deal with demonstrators but who did very little during the weekend except watch.

Why did the shootings take place at Kent State? Kent State was not a center of radical activity prior to the shootings—which is one reason why the shootings took place there. University administrators and city officials failed to understand the causes of the weekend demonstrations and had no effective strategy for dealing with them, short of calling in the National Guard. City and university officials in Madison, Wisconsin; Berkeley, California; and Seattle, Washington dealt with demonstrations of greater magnitude and more potential violence without loss of life.

The prolonged use of the National Guard, first for strike duty in Akron and then for police duty in Kent, insured that men whose tempers were growing short, who felt increasingly threatened by people whose actions they could no longer understand or agree with, would be on campus with weapons and live ammunition.

Perhaps most sadly, the shootings on Monday morning were the result of different perceptions regarding what was at stake. Demonstrators met on the Commons that day to rally in protest of the National Guard's occupation of the campus, while the National Guard was there to disperse a prohibited rally. Both groups felt they had a legitimate right to be there and to act as they did, and people who had no desire for a direct and fatal confrontation moved inexorably toward one.

ENDNOTES

1. James Michener, *Kent State: What Happened and Why* (New York: Random House, 1971).
2. *The Report of the President's Commission on Campus Unrest.* William Scranton, Chairman (Washington, D.C.: U. S. Government Printing Office, 1970), hereafter referred to as Report of the President's Commission....
3. Akron (Ohio) Beacon Journal, "Kent State: The Search for Understanding," 24 May 1970.
4. Jerry M, Lewis, "Review Essay: The Telling of Kent State," *Social Problems* 19 (Fall 1971): 276.
5. Joe Eszterhas and Michael D. Roberts, *Thirteen Seconds* (New York: Dodd Mead, 1970).
6. Peter Davies, *The Truth About Kent State* (New York: Farrar, Straus & Giroux, 1973).
7. Charles Thomas, "The Kent State Massacre: Blood on Whose Hands?" *Gallery* 7,5 (April 1977): 39ff.
8. Phillip K. Tompkins and Elaine Vanden Bout Anderson, *Communication Crisis at Kent State* (New York: Gordon and Breach, 1971).
9. Stuart Taylor, Richard Shuntich, Patrick McGovern, and Robert Genther, *Violence at Kent State: May 1 -4, 1970*: *The Student's Perspective* (New York: College Notes and Texts, 1971).
10. Ed Grant and Mike Hill, *I Was There: What Really Went On at Kent State* (Lima, Oh.: C. S. S. Publishing Co., 1974).
11. William Furlong, "The Guardsmen's View of the Tragedy at Kent State," *New York Times Magazine*, 21 June 1970, pp. 12-13, 64, 68-69, 71.
12. U.S. Congress, House, Representative John Sieberling's insertion of the Justice Department's Summary of the FBI Report, *Congressional Record*, 15 January 1973, pp. E207-E213, hereafter referred to as "Justice Department Summary."
13. Commission on Kent State University Violence, "Volume IV: Minority Report," Kent, Ohio, 1972 (mimeographed).
14. Trial Transcript, *Krause v. Rhodes*, 390 F. Supp. 1072 (N. D. Ohio, 1975).
15. For an excellent history of Kent State University see Phillip R. Shriver, *The Years of Youth* (Kent, Oh.: Kent State University Press, 1960).
16. Michener, *Kent State*, pp. 42-43.
17. U.S. Department of Commerce, *County and City Data Book: 1972* (Washington: U.S. Government Printing Office, 1973), pp. 750-61.
18. Quoted in Michener, *Kent State*, pp. 104- 5.
19. Jerry M. Lewis, "The Moods of May 4, 1970: The Student's View," *Political Science Discussion Papers*, Kent State University, Spring, 1971 (mimeographed).
20. Robert M. O'Neill, John P. Morris, and Raymond Mack, *No Heroes, No Villains* (Washington: Jossey-Bass, 1972), p. 6.
21. *Report of the President's Commission. . .* , p. 234.
22. Michener, *Kent State*, p. 470.
23. A good description of the confrontation can be found in Michener, *Kent State*, pp. 96-98 and the *Report of the President's Commission...* , pp. 235-36.
24. Michener, *Kent State*, pp. 99 - 100 and Kent Chapter of the American Association of University Professors, "Report of

the Special Committee of Inquiry," Kent, Ohio, 1969 (mimeographed).

25. Kent Chapter of the American Association of University Professors, "Report. . .," p. 43.
26. *Report of the President's Commission...* , p. 237.
27. Kent Chapter of the American Association of University Professors, "Report. . . ," p. 43.
28. *Ibid.*, pp. 14-15.
29. Tompkins and Anderson, *Communication Crisis at Kent State*, p. 8.
30. Quoted in Lester A. Sobel, ed., *News Dictionary:* 1969 (New York: Facts on File, 1970), p. 138,
31. O'Neill, Morris, and Mack, *No Heroes, No Villains*, pp. 24-25.
32. Sobel, *News Dictionary:* 1970 (New York: Facts on File, 1971), p. 300.
33. Justice Department Summary, p. E207.
34. *Report of the President's Commission*, p. 240.
35. Michener, *Kent State*, pp. 27-34.
36. *Report of the President's Commission. . . ,* p. 240.
37. Commission on Kent State University Violence, "Volume IV," p. 25.
38. *Akron Beacon Journal*, 24 May 1970, p. A18.
39. *Report of the President's Commission...* , p. 241.
40. *Ibid.*
41. Eszterhas and Roberts, *Thirteen Seconds*, p. 39.
42. Justice Department Summary, p. E207.
43. Michener, *Kent State*, p. 51.
44. *Ibid.*, p. 113.
45. Eszterhas and Roberts, *Thirteen Seconds*, p. 45 and Trial Transcript, *Krause v. Rhodes*, vol. 10, p. 801.
46. *Report of the President's Commission...* , p. 242.
47. Michener, *Kent State*, pp. 51-52.
48. Michener, *Kent State*, pp. 119-22.
49. *Report of the President's Commission*, p. 242.
50. Michener, *Kent State*, pp. 56-63.
51. *Kent-Ravenna (Ohio) Record-Courier*, May 2, 1970, p. 3.
52. Taylor, Shuntich, McGovern, and Genther, *Violence at Kent State*, p. 13.
53. Commission on Kent State University Violence, "Volume IV," p. 17.
54. *Report of the President's Commission*, p. 243.
55. Michener, *Kent State*, p. 123.
56. *Report of the President's Commission. . . ,* p. 243.
57. Justice Department Summary, p. E208.
58. *Ibid.*, E208.
59. *Report of the President's Commission*, p. 245.
60. *Ibid.*, p. 245 and Davies, *The Truth About Kent State*, p. 15.
61. Trial Transcript, *Krause v. Rhodes*, vol. 32, p. 8038. Grant and Hill, *I Was There*, p. 15, use much the same language to describe the traditional role of the National Guard.
62. Eszterhas and Roberts, *Thirteen Seconds*, pp. 74-75.
63. Michener, *Kent State*, p. 170.
64. *Report of the President's Commission. . . ,* p. 245.
65. *Ibid.*, p. 246.
66. *Ibid.*
67. *Akron Beacon Journal*, 24 May 1970, p. A18 and Trial Transcript, *Krause v. Rhodes*, vol. 43, p. 801.
68. *Akron Beacon Journal*, 24 May 1970, p. A18.
69. *Report of the President's Commission...* , pp. 246-47.

70. Grant and Hill, *I Was There*, pp. 40-41 and *Report of the President's Commission...* , p. 247.
71. Davies, *The Truth About Kent State*, p. 16.
72. *Report of the President's Commission...* , p. 247.
73. Michener, *Kent State*, p. 174.
74. Estimates range from "more than 500" (Taylor, Shuntich, McGovern, and Genther, *Violence at Kent State*, p. 29) to "2000" (Michener, *Kent State*, p. 176). The higher estimates are probably more accurate according to people who were there.
75. *The Report of the President's Commission...* , p. 248 and the Justice Department Summary, E208 agree on this point. *Michener, Kent State*, pp. 178-79 argues that the fire was started by flares and the gasoline soaked rags weren't used until after the firemen responded to the first alarm.
76. Commission on Kent State University Violence, "Volume IV," p. 51.
77, Michener, *Kent State*, p. 174.
78. *Report of the President's Commission...* , pp. 248-49.
79. Lewis, "The Moods of May 4, 1970," pp. 2-3.
80. Taylor, Shuntich, McGovern, and Genther, *Violence at Kent State*, p. 31.
81. *Ibid.*, Table 24, p. 43.
82. *Ibid.*, pp. 33-34.
83. Michener, *Kent State*, p. 179.
84. Commission on Kent State University Violence, "Volume IV," p. 61.
85. *Report of the President's Commission. . . ,* p. 249.
86. Michener, *Kent State*, p. 178 and Justice Department Summary, p. E208.
87. Furlong, "The Guardsmen's View...," p. 250.
88. *Report of the President's Commission...*, p. 251.
89. *Ibid.*, pp. 250-51.
90. Michener, *Kent State*, pp. 128 - 52 and Commission on Kent State University Violence, "Volume IV," p. 17.
91. *Report of the President's Commission. . . ,* p. 251.
92. Charles Thomas, "The Kent State Massacre."
93. Michener, *Kent State*, p. 204.
94. *Report of the President's Commission. . . ,* p. 253.
95. Commission on Kent State University Violence, "Volume IV," p. 80.
96. Grant and Hill, *I Was There*, p. 53.
97. Jerry M. Lewis, "A Study of the Kent State Incident Using Smelser's Theory of Collective Behavior," *Sociological Inquiry*, 42 (1971): 86.
98. *Akron Beacon Journal*, 24 May 1970, A18.
99. *Report of the President's Commission...*, p. 253.
100. Quoted in Michener, *Kent State*, p. 229.
101. *Report of the President's Commission...*, p. 253.
102. *Ibid.*, p. 254.
103. Michener, *Kent State*, p. 104.
104. *Akron Beacon Journal*, 24 May 1970, p. A18.
105. Commission on Kent State University Violence, "Volume IV," pp. 84-92.
106. Michener, *Kent State*, p. 232.
107. Trial Transcript, *Krause v. Rhodes*, vol. 35, p. 8891.
108. Davies, *The Truth About Kent State*, p. 22.
109. *Akron Beacon Journal*, 24 May 1970, p. A18.
110. *Report of the President's Commission...* , p. 255.
111. Davies, *The Truth About Kent State*, p. 24.

112. Quoted in John Hubbell, "A Point of Clarification," *Left Review*, 4,2 (Spring 1980): 32.

113. *Akron Beacon Journal*, 3 May 1970, p. 1.

114. *Cleveland Plain Dealer*, 3 May 1970, p. 6.

115. *Akron Beacon Journal*, 3 May 1970, p. 1.

116. *Cleveland Plain Dealer*, 3 May 1970, p. 6.

117. Commission on Kent State University Violence, "Volume IV," p. 94.

118. Taylor, Shuntich, McGovern, and Genther, *Violence at Kent State*, p. 48.

119. Justice Department Summary, p. E208.

120. *Report of the President's Commission...* , p. 257.

121. *Ibid.* and Michener, *Kent State*, p. 246.

122. *The Report of the President's Commission. . .* , p. 257 states that two people were bayonetted while Grant and Hill, *I Was There*, p. 57, state that there were ten.

123. Grant and Hill, *I Was There*, p. 52.

124. *Ibid.*, p. 57.

125. Taylor, Shuntich, McGovern, and Genther, *Violence at Kent State*, pp. 55-56.

126. Michener's account in *Kent State*, pp. 520-24, does not place Presiden White at this meeting, but all other accounts indicate that he was there.

127. *Report of the President's Commission...* , p. 260.

128. Justice Department Summary, p. E209.

129. *Report of the President's Commission...* , p. 260.

130. *Ibid,,* p. 261.

131. Trial Transcript, *Krause v. Rhodes*, vol. 33, pp. 8317, 8324.

132. *Ibid.*, vol. 34, p. 8748.

133. *Report of the President's Commission...* , p. 261.

134. *Ibid.*

135. Commission on Kent State University Violence, "Volume IV," p. 183.

136. *Report of the President's Commission. . .* , p. 267 and Michener, *Kent State*, p. 327.

137. Lewis, "A Study of the Kent State Incident. . . ," p. 91.

138. Taylor, Shuntich, McGovern, and Genther, *Violence at Kent State*, p. 76.

139. The FBI Report estimates 1200 - 1300 while Esterhas and Roberts estimate 4500. The Scranton Commission estimate of 2000 is probably the most accurate, p. 265.

140. Taylor, Shunfich, McGovern, and Genther, *Violence at Kent State*, Table 42, p. 202.

141. The Justice Department Summary, p. E209 estimates the crowd at 200 while Eszterhas and Roberts, *Thirteen Seconds*, p. 150, estimate 1500. The latter estimate is too high.

142. The Justice Department Summary, p. E209, estimates 1000 while Eszterhas and Roberts, *Thirteen Seconds*, p. 150, suggests a crowd three times as large. The latter estimate is too high.

143. This figure agrees rather closely with the estimates of Grant and Hill, p. 66, The Scranton Commission Report, p. 2, and Lewis, "Review Essay . . . ," p. 270.

144. Taylor, Shunfich, McGovern, and Genther, *Violence at Kent State*, p. 76.

145. Tompkins and Anderson, *Communicution Crisis at Kent State*, p. 41.

146. Quoted in the *Report of the President's Commission. . .* , p. 264.

147. Taylor, Shuntich, McGovern, and Genther, *Violence at Kent State*, p. 109.

148. *Report of the President's Commission...* , p. 264.

149. Grant and Hill, *I Was There*, p. 67.

150. Commission on Kent State University Violence, "Volume IV," p. 207.

151. Justice Department Summary, p. F909.

152. *Report of the President's Commission...* , p. 266.

153. *Ibid.*, p. 267.

154. *Ibid.*, p. 266.

155. *Ibid.*, p. 267.

156. Taylor, Shuntich, McGovern, and Genther, *Violence at Kent State*, p. 56.

157. Grant and Hill, *I Was There*, p. 77, suggest this was a major reason for the shootings.

158. *Report of the President's Commission. . .* , p. 268.

159. *Ibid.*, p. 268.

160. Michener's description of these events in *Kent State*, p. 304, is excellent.

161. *Report of the President's Commission...* , p. 273.

162. *Ibid.*, p. 275.

163. Trial Transcript, *Krause v. Rhodes*, vol. 7, p. 1415; vol. 11, p. 2549; and vol, 14, p. 3308.

164. *Ibid.*, vol. 11, p. 2605.

165. Eszterhas and Roberts, *Thirteen Seconds*, pp. 161-64.

166. Michener, *Kent State*, pp. 341, 371.

167. *Report of the President's Commission...* , p. 289.

168, Davies, *The Truth About Kent State*, p. 55.

169. *Report of the President's Commission*, p. 274.

170. Trial Transcript, *Krause v. Rhodes*, vol. 7, p. 1415 and *Report of the President's Commission. . .*, p. 270.

171. Commission on Kent State University Violence, "Volume IV," pp. 242-49,

172. *Ibid.*, p. 244.

173. Trial Transcript, *Krause v. Rhodes*, vol. 5, pp. 969-70.

174. *Ibid.*, vol. 14, pp. 3281, 3292.

175. *Ibid.*, vol. 14, pp. 3318-19.

176. *Ibid.*, Vol. 12, p. 2857.

177. *Report of the President's Commission.* p. 275.

178. *Ibid.*, pp 279-80,

179. Commission on Kent State University Violence, "Volume IV," p. 248.

180. Davies, *The Truth About Kent State*, p. 42.

181. *Ibid.*

182. Charles Thomas, "The Kent State Massacre," p. 101.

183. *Ibid.*, p. 102.

184. *Report of the President's Commission.. .* , p. 275.

185. Michener, *Kent State*, p. 358.

186. *Ibid.*, p. 376.

187. *Kent State University Alumni Magazine*, published by Kent State University, June, 1970, p, 3.

188. Ottavio Casale and Louis Paskoff (eds.), *The Kent Affair*. (Boston: Houghton Mifflin, 1971), p. 26.

189. Michener, *Kent State*, p. 380.

190. American Newspaper Publishers Association, *Reporting the Kent State Incident* (New York: ANPA Foundation, 1971), p. 12.

191. See Casale and Paskoff, *The Kent Affair*, pp. 91 - 115 and Michener, *Kent State*, pp. 389-401.

192. Taylor, Shuntich, McGovern, and Genther, *Violence at Kent State*, p. 98.

193. *Ibid.*, p. 94.

194. *Ibid.*, p. 96.

195. *Ibid.*, pp. 99-100.

196. Steven R. Brown, "The Resistance to Reason: Kent State University," *Political Science Discussion Papers*, Kent State University, 1971 (mimeographed).

197. *Newsweek*, 25 May 1970, p. 30.

198. *Ibid.*, p. 25.

199. American Newspaper Publishers Association, *Reporting the Kent State Incident*, p. 17.

200. Richard E. Peterson and John A. Bilowsky, *May, 1970: The Campus Aftermath of Cambodia and Kent State* (Berkeley, Cal.: Carnegie Commission on Higher Education, 1971), p. 15.

201. *Ibid.*, p. 50.

202. *Ibid.*, pp. 36-37.

203. *Report of the President's Commission...* , p. 45.

204. Raymond J. Adamek, and Jerry M. Lewis, "Social Control Violence and Radicalization: The Kent State Case," *Social Forces* 51 (March 1973): 342-47.

205. Raymond J. Adamek and Jerry M. Lewis, "Social Control Violence and Radicalization: Behavioral Data," *Social Problems* 22 (June 1975): 670.

206. Michener, *Kent State*, p. 383.

207. Commission on Kent State University Violence, "Volume IV."

208. *Kent State University Alumni Magazine*, June, 1970, p. 5.

REVIEW ESSAY: THE TELLING OF KENT STATE

Jerry M. Lewis
Kent State University

I stood on the Commons. I was watching the Guards and thinking they are telling us to leave, but this is our campus, we belong here and they don't. That is why I stayed mostly.

Barbara Knapp, a Kent State undergraduate at the Scranton Commission hearings.

On May 4, 1970, four days of student protest ended at Kent State University when 28 Ohio National Guardsmen fired their weapons at, over, and around a crowd made up largely of undergraduates who were protesting the presence of the Guard on campus. The immediate tragic result of this act was death for four students and wounding for nine others. All were undergraduates. The ramifications of this violence rapidly went beyond Kent State stimulating the first national student strike in the history of American higher education.

In the months that followed a major effort was made to understand what had happened at Kent. Five hundred media news personnel were accredited to cover the Kent story. In addition to stories written for the media, ten books were written about the tragedy.

In contrast to most reviews in *Social Problems*, this one focuses on works that have been written by people who are not, with one exception, behavioral scientists. Therefore, it seems appropriate to begin with an overview of each book and to look at the manner in which the authors studied the Kent story.

STUDIES OF KENT

1. Shortly after the shootings, the Knight Newspaper chain (locally the Akron *Beacon Journal*) made a decision to cover the Kent story in detail and quickly organized a team of eight reporters plus supporting personnel to do it. The result was a 30,000 word story (*Kent State: The Search for Understanding*) published on May 24, 1971, in all the Knight papers.[1]
2. *The Middle of the Country* (Warren, 1970) is one of three books with student authors. It is a series of rapidly written essays, printed double spaced and with typographical errors. The strength of this little book is that it reflects, through brutal comments in two of the essays, the impact of the killings on students who were eyewitnesses to the shootings. However, there are many factual

Reprinted from Social Problems, 19:2 (Fall 1971) pp. 267-279 by permission of The Society for the Study of Social Problems.

This study was supported by a National Institute of Mental Health Grant RO1 MNI7421-02SP. I am indebted to A. Paul Hare of Haverford College who encouraged me to write this essay. In addition, my colleagues Raymond J. Adamek and Diane L. Lewis made many helpful comments.

errors in the book; this volume should not be used as a factual source.

3. *The Report of the President's Commission on Campus Unrest* was published in October, 1970. The Scranton Report (after its Chairman, William Scranton, former governor of Pennsylvania) was based on FBI investigations, Commission staff work, and hearings held at Kent State, Jackson State, and in Washington. The FBI report on Kent State ran to 8,000 pages and was based primarily on the work of agents who began to arrive on campus within 24 hours of the shootings, reaching an estimated total of 100 agents at one point.[2] The hearings lasted three days; and the Commission took testimony from administrators, faculty, students, Guardsmen, and townspeople. Earlier there had been similar hearings at Jackson State College. The Kent report was published as a separate report to the main body of the Scranton Commission report.

4. Joe Eszterhas and Michael D. Roberts (1970), two Cleveland *Plain Dealer* reporters, published *13 Seconds: Confrontation at Kent State*, based primarily on their own interviews, university documents, and the well known newspaper technique of rewriting other reporter's news stories as their own material. Its major strength is its treatment, through the use of quotes, of student attitudes about the events of May 1-4, 1970. Unfortunately, it was hurriedly written and consequently has many errors[3] and reads like a 300 page newspaper story.

5. I. F. Stone (1970) wrote *The Killings at Kent State: How Murder Went Unpunished*, the first half of which was a reprint of pieces in his October, November, and December, 1970, newsletters. The November and December columns were based in part on two days of interviewing at Kent in the Fall of 1970. The second half of the book is a reprint of several Kent related documents, including the full text of the summary of the FBI report, which had not been published prior to Stone's book.

6. *The Kent Affair* (Casale & Paskoff, 1971) is a compendium of documents organized by two Kent State University English professors. It is particularly useful in that it gathers in one place many of the important political cartoons, news stories, and official documents dealing with Kent State. Further, it contains many of the let-

ters reflecting the polarization that took place after the shootings.

7. James Michener's *Kent State: What Happened and Why* (1971) was first published in abridged form in the March and April, 1971, issues of *Reader's Digest* and released about two weeks before May 4, 1971, in a completed version. Michener lived in Kent from August to November, 1970, and interviewed most of the participants in the events. His research efforts were supported by a full-time staff from the *Digest* as well as some part- time consultants from local newspapers (Michener, 1971:556-559).

8. *Communications Crisis at Kent State* (Tompkins and Anderson, 1971) and *Violence at Kent State: The Student's Perspective* (Taylor, et al., 1971) were both written by faculty- graduate student teams. In addition, they are also alike in that they are the only studies presented in this review that have a social survey empirical base. Tompkins and Anderson's study, begun in late May, is based on personal interviews with a university sample of 225 students, 120 faculty members, 29 departmental chairmen, and 11 top administration officials, including the President of the University. In addition, they had a small sample of interviews with some city and county officials. Much of the interviewing was done by the authors themselves.

9. The second book by Stuart Taylor, a professor of psychology at Kent State, and three of his doctoral students (Richard Shuntich, Patrick McGovern, and Robert Genthner), is based on a sample of 7,000 Kent students. The data were collected through a mail questionnaire sent to all graduate and undergraduate students on May 28. By June 24, 7,000 questionnaires had been returned. The strength of Taylor's work is that it is based on data taken when there was very little interaction among the students. Secondly, it is based on survey data collected before any of the major studies, except the Knight special report, had been published.

10. The final book, *Kent State: An Appeal for Justice* (Davies, 1971), has not been published as yet, although it has received wide media coverage; and the written part was entered into the Congressional Record. Peter Davies, a New York City insurance broker, develops a theory, using photographic evidence, that certain members of the Guard conspired about ten minutes

before the shooting to fire at students who had been harassing them from the parking lot where most of the slain and wounded were located. He wrote the report in order to demonstrate that there was enough evidence to justify calling a Federal Grand Jury.[4]

DRAMATIS PERSONAE

Future sociological studies of Kent may focus on many issues, the areas of collective behavior, student unrest, and organizational change probably among the more prominent. As one reads the various books on Kent State, four dimensions are consistently dealt with as these authors probe the drama. Without carrying the metaphor too far, the players in this tragedy are the students, the Guard, the administration and faculty, and the general public.

THE STUDENTS

How many students were on or near the Commons? As would be expected this question was answered with a wide variety of responses, ranging from the Scranton Report's (1970:265) 2,000 to Eszterhas and Roberts (1970:50) 4,500. My feeling is that the Scranton Commission was closer to the truth, because Taylor, *et al.* (1971:102) indicate that 90 percent of all students in the sample reported that the crowd in the immediate vicinity of the Commons was less than 3,000.[5]

There was considerably more agreement as to the size of the active core of students gathered around the Victory Bell on the Commons chanting such slogans at the Guard as "Pigs Off Campus," "Strike, Strike, Strike," and "One, two, three, four, we don't want your fucking war." The Scranton Commission (170:264) says the core was about 800 while Eszterhas and Roberts (1970:150) say it was about 1,500. All the studies agreed that the majority of the crowd on surrounding hills and buildings was made up of student spectators whose sympathy lay clearly with their fellow students gathered around the Victory Bell. Again, I believe the Scranton Commission estimate about the core was essentially correct.[6]

Why were the students on the Commons? Did they have a right to be there? These questions generated much controversy and debate. On Monday the first view of troops most students had as they arrived at the Commons was of the Guard formed into a skirmish line with the major concentration in front of the burned ROTC building. Several students indicated that students felt they had a right to be on the Commons and that the Guard was saying symbolically that they did not have this right.

The Scranton Report (1970:267) notes:

> Many students felt that the campus was their "turf." Unclear about the authority vested in the Guard by the governor, or indifferent to it, some also felt that their constitutional right to free assembly was being infringed upon. As they saw it, they had been ordered to disperse at a time when no rocks had been thrown and no other violence had been committed. Many told interviewers later, "We weren't doing anything."

Michener (1971:327) writes:

> At 11:00 in the morning of a bright, sunny day, students began collecting on the Commons as their 9:55-10:45 classes ended. They came casually at first, then in larger numbers when some of their 11:00-11:50 classes dismissed early because the confusion on campus made it too difficult to teach. Many students wandered by, as they always did to check on what might be happening. Another set of classes, 12:05-12:55, would soon convene, and it was traditional for students who were involved either in leaving one class or heading for another to use the Commons as their walkway. Without question, they had a right to be on the Commons. But were they entitled to be there on this day? A state of emergency had been declared by Mayor Satrom, presumably outlawing any unusual gatherings. Classes would meet, and that was about all. Yet testimony from students is overwhelming that they believed their campus to be operating as usual. On Friday a rally had been openly announced for Monday noon, and invitations to attend it had been circulated on succeeding days; in fact, announcements for this rally had been scrawled on certain blackboards and were seen by students when they reported for classes on Monday.

Thus, both major studies of Kent came to the same conclusion that Monday's rally was an anti-Guard rally and not an anti-war protest and more specifically a protest against the Guard's takeover of the campus. Further support for this conclusion is found in Taylor, *et al.* (1971:101) in that 57 percent of all students in the sample said the rally's major purpose was to protest the Guard's presence on campus. It should be noted that anti-war feeling had not disappeared, since all studies agreed that this seemed to be the cause of the action on Friday and Saturday, May 1, 2. Rather, in the words of a student (Taylor, *et al.* 1971:56) discussing the rally, "Cambodia was a reason, but its importance had died somewhat in that getting the troops off campus had become a big major issue."

One of the explanations for the large gathering of students was that most did not know the rally had been prohibited. However, both Tompkins and Anderson (1971:43) and Taylor, *et al.* (1971:101) report that over half of the students said they knew that the rally had been prohibited; but knowledge of the prohibition of the rally probably did not do much good in preventing attendance, for 69 percent of students Taylor, *et al.* (1971:1010) answered no to the question "Do you think peaceful assembly should have been prohibited on campus?"

One of the major failures of all the studies except Taylor, *et al.* (1971) was the fact that they did not explore why so many students did not go to the rally. If knowledge of a rally is a good base for predicting the size of the audience, then as many as 78 percent of Kent's 19,000 students (Taylor, *et al.* 1971:100) were in a position to decide to go or not to go. The Scranton Commission completely ignored this issue, and Michener looks only at the black students and their decisions not to attend the rally. Taylor, *et al.*, consistently and to their credit distinguished between those students who attended the rally and those who did not. They found important differences, for example, in the political persuasion of attenders and non-attenders. They (1971:68) write:

> While only two percent of the observers and one percent of the nonattenders considered themselves radical, 28% of the participants indicated that they were radical. This "self-description" appears to be quite accurate when one examines the participants' reactions to positions advocated by the "new left" movement. When asked, for example, if "the power of the President should be severely restricted and the power given to the people," 88% of the participants responded in an affirmative manner. Only 53% of the observers

and 38% of the non-attenders expressed agreement with this position.

What was the influence of radical students? Several of the studies dealt extensively with this issue. Michener described in considerable detail the activities of the radical community at Kent in years prior to May 1-4. When he discovered they had little influence on the events of the four days, he concluded that while the radical leaders had no direct influence on the events, they had laid (Michener, 1971:409) ". . . the groundwork for the May disturbances and were long absent from the scene." The Scranton Commission, although it also looked at the history of protest and radicalism at Kent particularly at the hearings, do not show any evidence that specific radical leaders influenced the events of the four days. They note that the radical activists who had been released from jail two days prior to the May 1 anti-war demonstration in downtown Kent were in no way ". . . involved in planning or directing any of the events of the May 1-4 weekend" (Scranton, 1970:243).

Taylor, *et al.* (1971:119), offer one account for confusion on this issue in their finding that 50 percent of their sample believed that radical students were very responsible for the Monday, May 4, incidents. In fact Kent's students believed that the radical students were more responsible than the National Guard enlisted men. I think this feeling expressed by students that radicals were responsible led Michener to the conclusion that radical students had laid "the groundwork" for disturbances. The Scranton Commission, with much better resources for investigating, reached a more balanced view of the radical influence. Unfortunately, the Scranton Commission report will, no doubt, not be as widely read as the *Reader's Digest* version of Michener's book, which stresses even more than the larger work the influence of the radical leaders.

The picture which emerges from these studies shows considerable agreement about the dynamics of the student protest at Kent State. Those students who did protest first directed their attention to the War and Cambodian invasion. However, as the National Guard took over, a growing hostility toward the Guard by students is depicted. There is considerable controversy as to the place of radical student leadership in fostering this hostility; but there is no doubt in any of the minds of the authors that this hostility developed because the Guard had taken over what the students believed to be their "turf" both in terms of real estate and symbolic territory.[7]

THE NATIONAL GUARD

Did the Guard use proper crowd control procedures? In general all the studies are critical of the crowd control procedures of the Guard on that Monday. The procedures the Guard used on that day, except for the firing, were those used from the time they arrived on Saturday until the shooting. The techniques included use of teargas and bayonets, patrolling in small groups with loaded weapons, and making no arrests.

The issue of whether the students and faculty knew that the Guard had loaded weapons when they were on duty has been widely debated. One position argues that all guns should be considered loaded, while another says that the Guard only loads in the possible presence of snipers and further directs only aimed at known snipers through the use of special sniper teams.

The Scranton Commission (1970:263) states that every time the Guardsmen came on duty, ". . . their weapons (mostly M-1s) were locked and loaded." The majority of students and faculty did not know this (Michener, 1971:372; Tompkins and Anderson, 1971:43; Warren, 1970:48). Taylor, *et al.* (1971:109) make the point dramatically when they note that only 27 percent of the total sample stated they knew the Guard had loaded weapons. Further (Taylor, *et al.*, 1971:109), less than one percent of the active participants in the rally felt the Guard would fire on them.

The Scranton Commission as well as Michener (1971:337) are critical of the Guard decision to march a small number of men a great distance through the crowd on Monday. The result of this action, the Commission concluded (1970:288), was:

> Guardsmen had been subjected to harassment and assault, were hot and tired, and felt dangerously vulnerable by the time they returned to the top of Blanket Hill. When they confronted the students, it was only too easy for a single shot to trigger a general fusillade.

Were the Guardsmen in danger when they fired? The Scranton Commission (1970:289) concluded that while some Guardsmen were frightened, the shootings ". . . were unnecessary, unwarranted, and inexcusable." Michener (1971:341) goes even further and suggests that a few Guardsmen who fired directly into the crowd did so because they were ". . . fed up with the riotous behavior of the students and in fear of their lives. . . ." In discussing the context of the shootings, Michener (1971:371) writes:

> After much negotiation, we were finally able to see the secret film. To have claimed, as some did, that the group of students hurrying up from the right constituted "a mortal danger" or "a howling mob bent on killing the Guard" required either extra-sensory perception or a new definition of words.
>
> But that is not what is really relevant, for it answers only the question, "What would a rational person viewing this film in a quiet library, long after the event, conclude?" The larger question must be, "What would a hot, tired Guardsmen think if he caught a glimpse of moving students coming at him on his blind right flank?" He could very reasonably think that he was about to be attacked by "a howling, vicious mob prepared to tear him apart."

Eszterhas and Roberts (1970:161-164) are very clear on this issue. Primarily through quotes, they show that with one exception the Guardsmen felt that they were being threatened but were not in danger of being killed. The one exception was the Commander of the National Guard who said, "I felt I could have been killed" (Eszterhas and Roberts, 1970:161).

Davies (1971) takes the most extreme position among all the books as he argues, primarily through the use of photographs, that not only did the Guard act to punish the students, but a few of the Guard conspired to do so about ten minutes before the shootings. Michener (1971:409) believes essentially the same thing, although he does not name specific Guardsmen as does Davies (1971:214-215).

What was the effect of the continuing interaction between the Guard and the students? The National Guard was ordered into Kent by the Governor of Ohio (the only person legally allowed to do so) at the request of City of Kent's Mayor. They came on campus on Saturday evening without specific invitation from University officials, although a request was in the process of being prepared at the time. The justification for coming on campus without the official permission of the University was made by the Commanding General of the Guard who felt that since the burned ROTC building was on state property the Guard (Scranton Report, 1970:250) needed ". . . no specific invitation to enter the campus." Michener (1971:198) and Tompkins and Anderson (1971:25) accept this conclusion.

The Scranton Commission (1970:253) felt that the continuing interaction between the Guard and students operated as a stimulant for developing student resentment because their orders and many of their control activities (particularly gassing) interfered with legitimate student activities. The Commission (1970:259) notes that resentment on the part of Guardsmen was building as well, and by Sunday evening May 3 they ". . . seemed to be growing more impatient with student curses, stones and refusals to obey."

The picture of the Guard is one of ineptness beyond belief. The Guardsmen, as a result of their orders, continually subjected themselves to harassment from groups of angry and hostile students, who dished it out with relish. However, in general, the various studies reflect very little about the feelings and attitudes of the Guardsmen. We know how they behaved, but we know very little of the why. In fact, until the Davies report (1971:214-215) was published, the names of all the Guardsmen who fired were not even available to the general public.

The reason for this paucity of data is because the Guard was very secretive in contrast to the other actors in this drama. In discussing the Beacon Journal special, the ANPF Foundation Report (1971:18) comments:

> . . . the National Guardsmen were the most difficult portion of the story to cover. Many of the Guardsmen feared possible prosecution and they did not want to talk. In general, Guard officers declined to supply names of enlisted men who were on Blanket Hill when the shooting occurred.

THE ADMINISTRATION AND THE FACULTY

Did President White and his staff adequately respond to the crisis? In general, most of the studies treated the University administration rather well. I think the reason for this is that the Guard so completely controlled the campus that there was

very little White and his administration could have done to change the situation.

There was one issue that generated much controversy: whether White had ordered the noon rally on May 4 to be called off or whether the decision had been made by the National Guard commanding officers. At the Scranton Commission hearings General Canterbury said that White had indicated that the rally should not be held. Later, noted the Commission (1970:261), White responded to this testimony saying, "From past history, all know that my response would have been affirmative to a rally." Eszterhas and Roberts (1970:147-148) note the issue but, like the Scranton Commission, came to no conclusion. Michener, who, according to faculty gossip, developed a strong friendship with White, does not even place him at the meeting, although he knew about the controversy since he followed the events of the hearings rather carefully (Michener, 1971:520-524).

Tompkins and Anderson (1971:36) conclude that the university requested that the rally be broken up.

> Our sources, however, seem to have cleared the confusion. The university advised against permitting the rally because to do so would be inconsistent with the leaflet which had been distributed the day before. It was argued that consistency from day to day on such matters was a "must." It was also argued that if such a reversal of the prohibitions were made, it would have to be announced "ahead of time by at least two hours." It was at least 11:00 a.m. when the matter was being discussed. Students were already assembling on the Commons.

However, they are quite irresponsible here, for they do not in any way identify their sources. Taylor, *et al.* (1971:121) conclude that most students felt White was not responsible for the incident on May 4.

How did the faculty involve itself in the events? Letters to the editor in newspapers suggested that radical faculty played an important part in stimulating students to dissent.

The Scranton Commission, as I noted, looked for agitators (both inside and outside) but could find no evidence that faculty played an agitator part. The Scranton Report (1971:278) and Michener (1971:399-408) go into the activities of the faculty marshals in considerable detail. In particular, they examined how marshals persuaded students to abandon the sit-in to protest the killings which began on the Commons about 15 minutes after the killings.

Both Michener and the Scranton Commission discussed the activities of 23 faculty members who wrote a letter of protest on May 3. Michener (1971:295-296) writes:

> The statement of the twenty-three concerned professors at the meeting held on Sunday afternoon would later come in for vigorous abuse by those who felt that the sentiments expressed therein were provocative and conducive to riot. Far from it. They were sentiments which had been expressed at various times on the floor of the United States Senate, in the editorial columns of great newspapers across the country, and in university senates everywhere; they were in the great tradition of free education, and if no one at Kent State had voiced them, the university would have been further derelict. There is, however, a question of timing, and it is possible to make a case against the publishing of these impeccable opinions at this particular and heated moment, except that we could find no one who had bothered to read them that day.

Taylor, *et al.* (1971) suggests that students felt faculty were not "very responsible" for the events of Monday, May 4. As was noted, 50 percent of Kent's students felt that the radical students were "very responsible" for the incidents. In contrast, Taylor, *et al.* (1971:121) state that two percent of the students felt the faculty was "very responsible" for the incident.

Another dimension of faculty involvement is painted by Tompkins and Anderson (1971:45), who see the faculty as a rather uninformed group:

> If anything, the faculty and chairmen were less well informed than the students. Only fifty-eight percent knew a rally was scheduled for noon (seventy-five percent for students). Only forty-four percent were aware that the rally had been prohibited (fifty-six percent for students). Thirty-seven percent (thirty-four percent for students) were aware that the Guard had live ammunition in their weapons.
> Perhaps most significant is the fact that fifty-three percent of the faculty and chairmen said they would have behaved differently had they known the facts. Seventy-three of the seventy-nine who so responded said they would have

used all of their influence — in the classroom and out — either to dissuade the students from confronting the Guard or to attempt to "cool" the situation.

In reference to the last sentence, it should be noted that several faculty members released their students from class to go to the rally (Michener, 1971:327).

THE PUBLIC RESPONSE

How did the general public react to the shootings? The issue explored here is that aspect of the response to the killings that reflected the general polarization in the society in regard to the Kent incident. Casale and Paskoff (1971:91-115) provide many pages of public reactions to the events, including letters sent to President White and letters sent to editors of newspapers (both local and national). They (Casale & Paskoff, 1971:91) report that the letters to President White totaled 5,000 by the end of 1970.

Michener (1971:436-446) devotes considerable time to looking at letters from one paper, the local Kent Record-Courier. He (1971:445-446) concludes:

> The most deplorable aspect of these letters was not the explosive outpouring of hatred (which could be forgiven as an autonomic response to phenomena not understood) nor the obvious obsession with property values as opposed to human life (which is often observed in American life) but rather the willingness to condemn all students, perceiving them as a mass to be castigated. Nothing can excuse this error. We must constantly remember that only a small percentage of the Kent student body was involved.

The hostility of the general public, which began to surface very soon after the killings, probably influenced the student's attitudes toward the future. Taylor, *et al.* (1971:139) report that 50 percent of all students felt that relations between the University and the State Legislature would be "greatly harmed"; even more (69 percent) felt that relations between the University and Community of Kent would be "greatly harmed" by the shootings.

The Scranton Commission, for some unknown reason, failed to deal with this outpouring of hostility. In fact, in the Special Report, the Commission only focused on the events through May 5 and failed to explore issues that took place after the shootings. I personally felt that it should have looked into the police search of rooms and the FBI's investigation of a professor's political beliefs.

A CONVERSATION AMONG THE BOOKS

In the concluding section of the essay, a somewhat different approach is taken. In previous sections, I tried to highlight aspects of the books which dealt with topics which might stimulate future sociological research, e.g., interaction patterns between students and social control agents. Here, I look at the books in an attempt to assess the motivations of authors and to show how they evaluated each other's work.

The Akron *Beacon Journal's* special report (1970) set the tone for most of the studies in its quest for hard facts. The staff wrote (1970:A-17):

> This society is built on the assumption that properly informed citizens can themselves decide to shape their future. It is our responsibility as a newspaper to provide information that allows public judgment to function.

The fact that the *Journal* got this report out so rapidly and with relatively few serious errors set the tone for facts that govern the remainder of the studies.

In the weeks that followed the report, the *Beacon Journal* received considerable criticism. Heisey (1971:8) found that 68 percent of the letters the *Beacon Journal* published were critical of the *Journal's* special report.

Warren (1970:17-18) saw his book of essays as ". . . an effort to provide America with as representative a guide as possible to what actually happened during the period leading up to and culminating in the action of May 4;" and it was widely distributed throughout the nation (one still sees it in airports). However, it received little attention from the other authors, primarily because the *Beacon Journal's* study provided a much better fact base.

Eszterhas and Roberts (1970) never state their objectives, but it is clear that their effort was an attempt to get the facts in the journalistic sense of that statement. However, this book is a travesty on good journalism for two reasons. First, it had so many factual errors and was so poorly written that it was difficult to take the book seriously. Second, it went to the publishers before the Scranton hearings; consequently Eszterhas and Roberts ignored an important body of data which would have vastly improved their study."[8]

Casale and Paskoff's (1971) book is a useful compendium of documents. Its major weakness is that they take a questionable point-of-view about the analysis of the events represented by the documents, simply noting (1971:xii) the difficulty of establishing facts and conclusions and leaving these tasks to the readers. This is not acceptable for any of us who lived through the events of May 4 and following. If Kent professors are unwilling to provide guidelines and perspectives for analyses of the events, then we have abdicated our first responsibility as scholars to write about what we believe to be true.

The Scranton Commission's charge was to determine the cause of campus violence and to suggest steps for resolving grievances through peaceful means (Scranton Report, 1970:533-534). President Nixon in his statement to the press (Scranton Report, 1970:535) indicated that the role of the Commission was, in part, to:

> help us to avoid future incidents of the sort that occurred this past spring, the most appalling of which were the tragedies at Kent State University in Ohio and Jackson State in Mississippi.

Two writers were critical of the Commission report. Stone (1970:16) felt that the central charge of the Commission was to find out what happened at Kent State and Jackson State. The fact that the Commission issued the reports on these two schools separately, and after the main report, suggested to Stone that killing and wounding of students were not of central importance to the Commission.

Stone (1970:15) also makes an important point about the quality of the Scranton Report. He writes:

> The danger in the Jackson and Kent State reports by the President's Commission on Campus Unrest lies in their very quality. If the Commission had white-washed the killings, the findings would be angrily dismissed by blacks

and students as more-of-the-same, but the hope would remain that a better investigation by better men might have produced better results. The destructive potential of the report comes from the fact that they have honestly and thoroughly shown that the killings were unjustified and unnecessary. The established order mustered its best and they fulfilled their moral and political obligation. And yet there is not the slightest chance that anything will be done about it.

Michener felt that the general report of the Commission was an excellent essay. However, he (1971:524) felt the special report on Kent State was not so impressive because:

> It was conceived in haste, inadequately researched, written under heavy duress so far as time and lack of staff were concerned, and barely finished before the expiring date of the Commission.

In regard to haste, there is a certain irony in that Michener wrote his own book (599 pages) in about six months.

While the Scranton Commission concluded that the shootings were "unnecessary, unwarranted and inexcusable," they did not communicate the deep sense of indignation found in other Presidential Reports. Nowhere in the evaluation of the Guard's actions do we find the passion of the Kerner Report's (1968:1) "Our nation is moving toward two societies, one black, one white — separate and unequal" or the bluntness of the Walker Report's (1968) "police riot."

Michener's (1971) book received considerable interest in the Kent community because many felt his efforts would help ease the polarized town-gown conflict. Unfortunately, the opposite occurred when the *Reader's Digest* version appeared with its emphasis on the role of radical leaders in the protest. The full version of the book was more favorably received, but the damage had already been done.

After the *Reader's Digest* came out, people began to say they had been misquoted or their point of view distorted. Two professors of speech at Kent undertook a study of Michener's methodology to explore the question of distortion. They (Moore and Heisey, 1971) found that his research procedures were somewhat careless. Further, his quoting was from memory, since he did not rely on any mechanical devices for recording interviews and only took a few notes during any given interview (Michener, 1971:558).

My own feeling is that his book is extremely well written and portrays the events of May 4, 1970, with such detail and accuracy that one can almost smell the teargas coming across the Commons. However, the book reflects the values of the *Reader's Digest*. As Wicker (1971:31) so pungently noted, Michener "is unable . . . to believe that there is anything wrong with the 'old life style' or that direct challenges to the authority behind it can never be necessary or worthwhile." (That Michener was concerned about American higher education and Kent State University is without doubt.)

Tompkins and Anderson (1971) and Taylor, *et al.*(1971) were concerned, as Kent State professors and students, with developing a sound data base for analysis of the Kent incident. Both studies succeeded in this task, although any interpretation must be evaluated from the standpoint of surveys conducted after the shootings had taken place, hence, the possibilities of *ex post facto* justifications.

Both studies interpret their finds. Tompkins and Anderson perhaps even overinterpret. Taylor, *et al.* generally present a balanced interpretation of findings often letting the data (presented in percentages) stand alone.

Each of the studies reviewed here attempted to grapple with and understand an event that had enormous social and political implications for the society. That none succeeded should not be seen as a criticism of authors but rather as a challenge to sociology. The Kent States, Jackson States, and Orangeburg's and other domestic and foreign misuses of force by American society must be seen as crucial social problems which our discipline must come to understand and to solve.

REFERENCES

Akron *Beacon Journal*. 1970. *Kent State: The Search for Understanding*. Akron: Knight Newspapers Inc.

Casale, Ottavio M. and Louis Paskoff. 1971. *The Kent Affair*. Boston: Houghton Mifflin.

Davies, P. 1971. *Kent State: An Appeal for Justice*. New York. (Mimeographed), reprinted in Congressional Record (July 22, 1971) pp. E8143-58.

Eszterhas, Joe and Michael D. Roberts. 1970. *13 Seconds: Confrontation at Kent State*. New York: Dodd, Mead and Company.

Heisey, D. R. 1971. *University and Community Reaction to the News Coverage of the Kent State Tragedy.* Kent State University. (Mimeographed).

Knight Newspapers, Inc. 1971. *Reporting the Kent State Incident.* New York: American Newspaper Publishers Association (ANPA) Foundation.

Michener, J. 1971. *Kent State: What Happened and Why.* New York: Random House and Reader's Digest Press Book.

Moore, Carl and D. Ray Heisey. 1971. "Not a Great Deal of Error. . .?" Kent State University. (Mimeographed).

Report of the National Advisory Commission on Civil Disorders. 1968. Washington, D.C.: U. S. Government Printing Office.

The Report of the President's Commission on Campus Unrest. 1970. Washington, D.C.: U. S. Government Printing Office.

Rights in Conflict. 1968. New York: Bantam Books.

Stone, I. F. 1970. *The Killings at Kent State: How Murder Went Unpunished.* New York: A New York Review Book.

Taylor, Stuart, Richard Shuntich, Patrick McGovern, and Robert Genthner. 1971. *Violence at Kent State: May 1-4, 1970: The Students' Perspective.* New York: College Notes and Texts.

Tompkins, Phillip K. and Elaine Vanden Bout Anderson. 1971. *Communications Crisis at Kent State.* New York: Gorden and Breach.

Warren, B. 1970. *The Middle of the Country.* New York: Avon.

Wicker, T. 1971. *The New York Times Book Review* (June, 6th) New York: New York Times Publishing Co.

ENDNOTES

1. For a more detailed account of the way the Knight organization went about developing the special report, see *Reporting the Kent State Incidents* (1971).

2. This figure is based on Senator Stephen Young's statement in Stone (1970:9). From personal experience and observations, I believe the figure is high. Nonetheless, there were many agents on the Kent campus.

3. For example, in the discussion of the sit-in that took place in November of 1968, Eszterhas and Roberts (1970:14) have 80 black students and 75 whites in the protest. However, the numbers became 200 and 150 respectively on page 56. The first figure was more accurate.

4. On August 13, 1971, Attorney General John N. Mitchell announced that a Federal Grand Jury would not be convened.

5. In my capacity as a faculty peace marshal, I was present on the Commons and nearby areas from a little before noon until a half-hour after the shootings. I believe the crowd was less than 3,000.

6. Taylor, *et al.*, does not speak to the size of the active core.

7. Professor Adamek notes one exception to this statement. There is considerable disagreement, even among eyewitnesses, as to the question of whether the burning of the R.O.T.C. building was a planned attack or a spontaneous outpouring of hostility.

8. The Scranton Commission was appointed after the Akron *Beacon Journal* (1970) Special Report and Warren (1970) had been published.

THE TELLING OF KENT STATE: AN UPDATE

Jerry M. Lewis
Kent State University

This essay is an update of the one printed in the previous pages and was written for this volume. In the earlier essay I organized the review around questions that I thought were appropriate at the time. Some of these questions included: How many students were on the Commons on May 4 at the time of shooting? What was the influence of radical students? Did the Ohio National Guard use proper crowd control methods? Did President White and his staff act appropriately? How did the public react to the shootings? Most of the books concerning Kent State dealt with the events of May 4, 1970. The ones reviewed in this essay are much broader that those reviewed in the earlier essay.

In this analysis I evaluate the books using two basic questions: (1) How well do the books help professors teach about May 4 and its aftermath? (2) How can the books assist us in conducting research on May 4 and its aftermath? For both questions I draw primarily on my own experiences as a teacher and researcher addressing various May 4 topics, although I have been greatly helped by the discussions I have with Tom Hensley in regard to teaching about May 4.

The books are reviewed in chronological order beginning with the earlier ones. The books are:

1. *I Was There*, 1974 (Grant and Hill)
2. *Kent State and May 4: A Social Science Perspective*, 1978 (Hensley and Lewis)
3. *The Kent State Coverup*, 1980 (Kelner and Munves)
4. *The Kent State Incident: Impact of Judicial Process on Public Attitudes*, 1981 (Hensley)
5. *Mayday: Kent State*, 1981 (Payne)
6. *Kent State/May 4: Echoes Through a Decade*, 1988 (Bills)
7. *To Heal Kent State*, 1990 (Sorvig)
8. *A Gathering of Poets*, 1992 (Anderson et al.)
9. *Four Dead in Ohio: Was There a Conspiracy at Kent State?*, 1995 (Gordon)
10. *Silent Bell*, 1998 (Drake)
11. *Hippies*, 1998 (Jedick)

REVIEW OF THE BOOKS

I Was There

Ed Grant and Mike Hill were Guardsmen at Kent State in 1970. Their book *I Was There* is very poorly written and confusing. It is never clear whose voice is speaking, Grant or Hill. Further, the implication of the title is that they were on the hill when the shootings took place, but neither of them were. One of the men, it is not clear who, was with Company C between Prentice Hall and Taylor Hall when the firing began. They would have not seen the firing but rather its consequences. Hill and Grant (p. 84) write, "Suddenly we [Company C] heard one shot, immediately followed by a volley of shots. The people in the parking lot were falling, diving and running for cover as the bullets shattered windows in the parked cars." Davies (1971) does not list Grant or Hill as being with Companies A or G when the firing began. There is material for scholars in the book, however. There are original interviews conducted by someone—it is not clear who—for this book. These interviews are with Kent City firemen at the time of the shootings and Professor Glenn Frank, the head of the faculty marshals on May 2,3, and 4, 1970. In addition to the interview there is a listing (Appendix B) of the employment of Ohio National Guard members prior to and after May 4, 1970.

Kent State and May 4th: A Social Science Perspective

Thomas R. Hensley, a professor of political science, and Jerry M. Lewis, an emeritus professor of sociology, teach at Kent State University. They have collected into one volume, *Kent State and May 4th: A Social Science Perspective*, many social science articles dealing with the shootings and its aftermath. It contains articles providing overviews of May 4, the Kent State trials, the radicalization hypothesis of those dealing with social control violence, and the Gym dispute. This volume is the second edition of the earlier work. There have been several changes and additions in the second edition of the book.

Professor Hensley and I have used the volume in both political science and sociology courses. For teachers, the overview of the weekend by James Best entitled "Kent State: Answers and Questions" (reprinted elsewhere in this volume as "The Tragic Weekend of May 1 to 4, 1970") remains the strongest resource for providing an efficient picture of the events leading to the shootings on May 4. Hensley's overview of the trials has been well received by both students and general readers.

The analytical articles about May 4, notably Lewis' treatment of the actual confrontation using Smelser's value-added model of collective behavior and the Adamek/Lewis research on radicalization, are less well received by students. When using these materials, professors should set clear theoretical contexts for the Smelser theory and methodological ones for the Adamek/Lewis studies of social control violence and radicalization. The material on radicalization developed in three articles, two of which are reprinted in this volume will likely be found useful by researchers (See Adamek and

Lewis, pp. 117-134) because very little social science research has been done on the direct impact of social control violence on those who experienced it. The volume also contains two detailed analyses related to the gym protest at Kent State in 1977-78. These articles are reprinted in this volume (Hensley, pp. 147-178 ; Lewis, pp. 179-190)

The Kent State Coverup

In *The Kent State Coverup*, Joseph Kelner, a well-known trial lawyer from New York, and James Munves, a professional writer, describe the 1975 civil trial which was won by the defendants—President Robert White, Governor James Rhodes, and the officers and enlisted men of the Ohio National Guard (See Hensley, "The May 4 Trials"). The book is a case history of the trial. Teachers will be able to use it as a way to describe how the legal system works in a civil trial (circa 1975). It is likely that it will be more helpful to researchers because of the documents contained in the appendix, including a chronology of the calling out of the National Guard from 1963 to 1973; aspects of the crowd control organizational plan of the National Guard showing its rules of engagement; and finally listings of the state and federal criminal and civil litigation in the Kent State case.

The Kent State Incident: Impact of Judicial Process on Public Attitudes

Thomas R. Hensley has written widely on the legal aspects of May 4. This volume, *The Kent State Incident: Impact of Judicial Process on Public Attitudes*, is primarily concerned with analyzing the impact of judicial decisions on public attitudes. Three judicial activities involving the May 4 shootings were studied:

1. The decision of the 1974 federal grand jury to indict eight members of the Ohio National Guard;
2. The decision in the 1975 federal civil trial finding none of the Guard defendants liable for the shootings; and
3. The 1979 federal civil trial reaching an out-of-court settlement involving the payment of $675,000 to the parents of the slain students and the wounded students as well as a statement of regret from the defendants. (See Hensley, "The Kent State Trials" in this volume.)

With each of these three judicial activities, surveys were sent to random samples of Kent State students both before and after the judicial decisions. The research was organized around cognitive dissonance theory; the primary concern was to use the questionnaires to assess whether students changed their attitudes to conform to judicial decisions.

The results of each of the data collection phases supported the hypothesized relationships. Hensley (1981:209) concludes that:

> Kent State students' attitudes about responsibility for the shootings did not change to conform with the decisions of authoritative judicial structures. Attitude change was observed frequently for those students who were placed in a [cognitive] dissonant situation by a decision and who disagreed with the decision; the pattern was significant lowering of support for the judicial structure issuing the decision.

Hensley's book is useful for both teachers and researchers. Hensley's essay "The May Fourth Trials" reprinted in this volume in updated format as "The Kent State Trials" is an excellent way to introduce students to the legal complexities associated with criminal and civil trials. Researchers can draw on Hensley's complex methodology using quasi-experimental designs to study the impact of judicial decisions.

Mayday: Kent State

Kent State was a docudrama made for a national television audience where it was first shown on NBC in February of 1981. Today it is known as actress Ellen Barkin's first film. She played Carol, a political activist. It tells the story of May 4 in chronological order from Nixon's Cambodian speech on April 30 to the killings on May 4. All of the major events of the five days are included in the film.

Gregory Payne, a professor of speech at Emerson College in Boston, develops in *Mayday: Kent State* an account of the making of a television movie, Kent State. Payne served as a consultant for the film made in Gadsden, Alabama. In addition to Payne's account of the making of the film, the book contains some excellent primary source materials about the slain students and their families as well as a copy of President Nixon's "Cambodian Address"

given on April 30, 1970. The material about Bill Schroeder (pp. 75-83) is worthwhile for both teacher and researcher.

Both teachers and researchers will find the latter part of Payne's book fascinating as he discusses his experiences in trying to maintain the intellectual integrity of a docudrama in the face of the Hollywood film mentality. He (Payne, 1981:158) writes, "The project was punctuated with healthy disagreements as to how much dramatic license had to be employed, and at what points to keep the audience interested." Payne (1981:158) continues, " The real test of the film is the types of reaction *Kent State* generates from its audience." While the film was billed as docudrama, Lewis (1981) has suggested that there were many errors in the film particularly in the presentation of composite figures such as faculty and activist students.

Kent State/May 4: Echoes through a Decade

Scott Bills is a professor of history at Stephen F. Austin University. His edited book *Kent State/May 4: Echoes through the Decade* was published in two editions in 1982 and 1988 by the Kent State University Press. It contains an overview narrative, town and gown reactions to the shootings, and a detailed annotated bibliography. It is basically in three parts. The first is a 60 page narrative by Bills providing an overview of the events leading to May 4 as well as the aftermath of May 4. The second part of the book, by the far the largest, is a series of interviews (by Bills) and written accounts of detailing various perspectives about May 4 and its aftermath. These accounts are drawn from a variety of categories of people including students, faculty, townspeople, researchers, and politicians. Of the 23 accounts and interviews, ten come from current or former Kent State faculty members. The third part of the book is an extensive annotated bibliography.

Both editions are very useful for teaching and research. My comments are based on the second edition. For teaching, I have used the volume in several ways. First, using the overview essay combined with the one by James Best, previously noted, is a good way to introduce the topics of May 4 and its aftermath to students.

The interviews with the various categories of people responding to May 4 can be used effectively as a teaching tool. In a collective behavior class dealing with crowds and the response to crowds, I had my students draw names of people in Bills' book who were interviewed or wrote accounts of their May 4 perceptions. Next, I had students discuss the May 4 events drawing on the persons whose account or interview they had read. To begin the discussion I asked such questions as "Were the Guard justified in shooting?" " Did students have the right to be on the Commons on May 4?" I also asked my students to respond to aftermath questions such as whether they thought there should be a May 4 memorial.

For researchers, scholars will find the annotated bibliography particularly helpful. It is one of the most through exercises of this type I have ever seen. Students also find the annotated bibliography helpful when writing terms papers on May 4 topics. The only draw back of the bibliography is that there is no material listed after 1987.

To Heal Kent State

Kim Sorvig, an architect, writes in *To Heal Kent State* an account of his experience as someone who submitted an entry into the May 4 Memorial competition. His submission was based on the Mary Vecchio picture (See Lewis, "The Anti-Vietnam War Pieta" in this volume, pp. __). Students will find his account of the impact of the Mary Vecchio picture very moving while researchers can understand why someone would put so much time and effort in preparing a submission for the competition. Sorvig (1990:169) writes, summarizing his experiences with the pictures and the memorial competition:

> Those of us who remember Kent State, and the hopes and disasters that surrounded it, have many dreams to mourn, and many more dreams still to build. We cannot remember our dreams unless we are willing to recall our nightmares. Perhaps the steps I have described from my own journey of remembrance can guide the hearts of others a little ways towards their own memorials to Kent State....

A Gathering of Poets

Poetry is greatly removed from social science. Yet, the insights of the poet can help both teachers and researchers. *A Gathering of Poets* was edited by

Maggie Anderson, Alex Gildzen, and Raymond Craig, all current or past members of the Kent State faculty. The book is based on poetry readings held as part of the 20th anniversary of the May 4 shootings from May 3 to 6. Over 300 poets participated in the reading (gathering). This volume contains 147 poems from 131 poets. The volume is organized into eight sections containing poems with the following themes:

> Background to the 60s
> The 60s
> Poems written in May of 1970 or about May 4
> Related tragedies
> Poems written for the gathering
> Children
> Poems about anger, pain and grief
> Gatherings of poets as political ritual

It is likely that those interested in May 4 will find sections II, III, and V of most interest.

Both teachers and researchers will find the poetry of value for their scholarship. The first insight is the great diversity of poets showing the breath of the real impact of May 4. The poets range from academics including the editors, to award winning authors such as Rita Dove and Alice Walker, to a member of the Kent 25—Bill Athrell.

This breath, depth and complexity of May 4 can be felt in the words of the poets. Alex Gildzen writing about "Allison" (Anderson, *et al.*,1992: 55):

> lured from corngreen commons
> to gather lilacs & poppies
> to stuff into gun barrels
>
> but May had a darker meaning
> & Allison of the flowers
> fell on parking lot asphalt
> her heart ripped apart
>
> & what of spring

Kathe Davis, a member of Kent State's English department, in "The Hardest Thing" (Anderson *et al.*, 1992:160) pens these lines:

> is that there's no undoing it.
> Probably every kid who fired
> would call his bullet back.
> The principled kids facing the guns
> would have negotiated, moderated,
> they would have talked.

Excerpts of poems by Alex Gildzen and Kathe Davis with permission of the Kent State University Press and the authors.

They weren't out to die
But it can't be undone

Four Dead in Ohio: Was There a Conspiracy at Kent State University?

William Gordon runs a small publishing company in California and is a Kent State University graduate of its journalism school. The first version of Gordon's book was published by Prometheus Books in 1990 under the title, *The Fourth of May Killings and Coverup at Kent State. Four Dead in Ohio: Was There a Conspiracy at Kent State?* is a paperback reprinted version of the hard back edition (Gordon, 1995: 273) by his own house. This review is based on the 1995 reprinting which does have an updated annotated bibliography which can serve as an update to Bills' bibliography. His discussion of the conspiracy theory of the shootings is based in part on the ideas of Peter Davies (pp. 61-71). Gordon concludes (pp. 70-71), "The evidence we have now is that a Guardsman with some authority—sergeant, perhaps—simply passed a threshold of tolerance for the demonstration"(pp.70-71). Most readers, including this author, do not believe that Gordon has made a compelling case for a conspiracy in the shootings.

Gordon's book can be used by both teachers and researchers as a reference book. Three parts of the book particularly provide interesting primary resource material for conducting social science inquiries into the events of May 4: his discussion of the Kent 25 trials (pp. 120-123), charges and results of the trials; an interview with John Ehrlichman, President Richard Nixon's domestic affairs advisor (Appendix I); and an interview with Colonel Charles Fassinger, the highest ranking uniformed National Guard officer on the field on May 4 (Appendix II).

Silent Bell/Hippies

The last two books are works of fiction. Gary Drake in *Silent Bell* writes of a love affair based in the academic year 1969-1970 at Kent State University. In a series of flashbacks the protagonist, Stuart Stern, a journalism major at Kent State, recalls his love affair with Melina Progonos (Mel), a music major, in the context of the turbulent events of that academic year. While the book is well written, it has a tourist guide book feel of the campus. All the buildings and streets are in the correct place, but there is no clear sense of the 60s culture or the anti-war movement as the book is really about an undergraduate love affair. Indeed, the couple has just finished making love when the shootings began.

Peter Jedick, a Cleveland, Ohio fireman, has written in *Hippies* a semi-autobiographical fictional account of the author's experiences of living in the city of Kent as a student during the academic year 1969-1970. The novel tells the story of four male undergraduates living in a house in Kent, Ohio. It traces the life of these four men through the academic year beginning with the fall quarter of 1969 and ends with the sound of gunfire on May 4, 1970.

Readers will find Jedick's treatment of the four days leading to the shooting of interest. He begins with Richard Nixon's speech on April 30, 1970 announcing the Cambodian invasion. The reaction of Matt, the main character of the novel, and his house mates are valid. They begin to discuss the lack of trust in Nixon, the joy of high lottery numbers for the draft, and worries about China and Russian reactions to the Cambodian invasion.

Later on Friday, May 1, Matt and others are downtown during the street actions that led to the National Guard coming on campus. Jedick captures what happened on Friday as well as the burning of the ROTC building on Saturday, May 2.

The morning of May 4 is treated well. The confusion that students felt about the Guard being on campus with such force is well described. The novel ends with gun shots and three well known pictures: the National Guard firing, students diving for cover, and Mary Vecchio screaming over the body of Jeffery Miller. Today's students will find in *Hippies* a much better recreation of the 1960s campus culture than in *Silent Bell*.

CONCLUSIONS

In rereading the original "Telling of Kent State," three things strike me as important to note about the differences between the first set of books reviewed and this present set of work. First, in the first review essay I noted that the volumes had as a primary focus the events of the May 4 and its immediate aftermath and/or their legal ramifications. In contrast the collection of books reviewed here deal with a much wider range of issues.

Second, the authors of the first review were social scientists, journalists, and lawyers. In addition to these categories of writers, the second set of books have authors from more varied walks of life including guardsmen, humanities professors, an architect, and a fireman.

Third, the medium of communication is more varied. Most of the first set of books are descriptive, with straight forward "academic style" prose. However, the books in the second set range from case histories to poetry to novels.

I come away from the reading of this second set of books with the conclusion that the killings at Kent State have truly had an impact on a considerable part of American culture. The responsibility of us all is to inquire, learn, and reflect on what happened at Kent State not as a local issue but one that is related to the national tragedy of the Viet Nam War experience.

REFERENCES

Anderson, Maggie and Alex Gildzen, with Raymond A .Craig (eds.). *A Gathering of Poets*. Kent, Ohio: Kent State University Press, 1992.

Bills, Scott L. (ed..) *Kent State/May 4: Echoes Through a Decade*. 2d Edition, Kent, Ohio: Kent State University Press., 1988.

Davies, Peter. *The Truth About Kent State: A Challenge to the American Conscience*. New York: Farrar, Straus & Giroux, 1973.

Drake, Gary. *Silent Bell*. Pittsburgh, PA.: Dorrence Publishing Co., 1998.

Gordon, William A. *Four Dead in Ohio: Was There a Conspiracy at Kent State?* Laguna Hills, CA: North Ridge Books, 1995.

Grant, Ed and Mike Hill. *I Was There: What Really Went on at Kent State*. Lima, Ohio: The C.S.S. Publishing Company, Inc., 1974.

Hensley, Thomas R. *The Kent State Incident: Impact of Judicial Process on Public Attitudes*. Westport, CT.: Greenwood Press, 1981.

Hensley, Thomas R. and Jerry M. Lewis. *Kent State and May 4th: A Social Science Perspective*. Dubuque, IA.: Kendall/Hunt Publishing Co., 1978.

Jedlick, Peter. *Hippies*. Cleveland, Ohio: (Self-published), 1998.

Kelner, Joseph and James Munives. *The Kent State Coverup*. New York: Harper and Row, 1980.

Lewis, Jerry M. "Kent State-The Movie". *The Journal of Popular Film and Televison*. Vol.9 (1981):1, pp.13-18.

Payne, J. Gregory. *Mayday: Kent State*. Dubuque, Iowa: Kendall/Hunt, 1981.

Sorvig, Kim. *To Heal Kent State*. Philadelphia, Pa: Worldview Press, 1990.

THE MAY 4 SHOOTINGS AT KENT STATE UNIVERSITY: THE SEARCH FOR HISTORICAL ACCURACY

Jerry M. Lewis
Thomas R. Hensley
Kent State University

INTRODUCTION

On May 4, 1970 members of the Ohio National Guard fired into a crowd of Kent State University demonstrators, killing four and wounding nine Kent State students. The impact of the shootings was dramatic. The event triggered a nationwide student strike that forced hundreds of colleges and universities to close. H. R. Haldeman, a top aide to President Richard Nixon, suggests the shootings had a direct impact on national politics. In *The Ends of Power*, Haldeman (1978) states that the shootings at Kent State began the slide into Watergate, eventually destroying the Nixon administration. Beyond their direct effects, the May 4 shootings have certainly come to symbolize the deep political and social divisions that so sharply divided the country during the Vietnam War era.

In the nearly three decades since May 4, 1970, a voluminous literature has developed analyzing the events of May 4 and their aftermath. Some books were published quickly, providing a fresh but frequently superficial or inaccurate analysis of the shootings (e.g., Eszterhas and Roberts, 1970; Warren, 1970; Casale and Paskoff, 1971; Michener, 1971; Stone, 1971; Taylor *et al.*, 1971; and Tompkins and Anderson, 1971). Numerous additional books have been published in subsequent years (e.g., Davies, 1973; Hare, 1973; Hensley and Lewis, 1978; Kelner and Munves, 1980; Hensley, 1981; Payne, 1981; Bills, 1988; and Gordon, 1997). These books have the advantage of a broader historical perspective than the earlier books, but no single book can be considered the definitive account of the events and aftermath of May 4, 1970 at Kent State University.[1]

Despite the substantial literature which exists on the Kent State shootings, misinformation and misunderstanding continue to surround the events of May 4. For example, a prominent college-level United States history book by Mary Beth Norton *et al.* (1994), which is also used in high school advanced placement courses,[2] contains a picture of the shootings of May 4 accompanied by the following summary of events: "In May 1970, at Kent State University in Ohio, National Guardsmen confronted student antiwar protestors with a tear gas barrage. Soon afterward, with no provocation, soldiers opened fire into a group of fleeing students. Four young people were killed, shot in the back, including two women who had been walking to class." (Norton *et al.*, 1994, p. 732) Unfortunately,

Reprinted from *Ohio Council for the Social Studies Review*, 34:1 (Summer 1998) pp. 9-21 by permission of the Ohio Council for the Social Studies.

this short description contains four factual errors: (1) some degree of provocation did exist; (2) the students were not fleeing when the Guard initially opened fire; (3) only one of the four students who died, William Schroeder, was shot in the back; and (4) one female student, Sandy Scheuer, had been walking to class, but the other female, Allison Krause, had been part of the demonstration.

This article is an attempt to deal with the historical inaccuracies that surround the May 4 shootings at Kent State University by providing high school social studies teachers with a resource to which they can turn if they wish to teach about the subject or to involve students in research on the issue. Our approach is to raise and provide answers to twelve of the most frequently asked questions as people search for the truth and meaning of the events of May 4 at Kent State. We will also offer a list of the most important questions involving the shootings which have not yet been answered satisfactorily. Finally, we will conclude with a brief annotated bibliography for those wishing to explore the subject further.

WHY WAS THE OHIO NATIONAL GUARD CALLED TO KENT?

The decision to bring the Ohio National Guard onto the Kent State University campus was directly related to decisions regarding American involvement in the Vietnam War. Richard Nixon was elected president of the United States in 1968 based in part on his promise to bring an end to the war in Vietnam. During the first year of Nixon's presidency, America's involvement in the war appeared to be winding down. In late April of 1970, however, the United States invaded Cambodia and widened the Vietnam War. This decision was announced on national television and radio on April 30, 1970 by President Nixon, who stated that the invasion of Cambodia was designed to attack the headquarters of the Viet Cong, which had been using Cambodian territory as a sanctuary.

Protests occurred the next day, Friday, May 1, across United States college campuses where anti-war sentiment ran high. At Kent State University, an anti-war rally was held at noon on the Commons, a large, grassy area in the middle of campus which had traditionally been the site for various types of rallies and demonstrations. Fiery speeches against the war and the Nixon administration were given, a copy of the Constitution was buried to symbolize the murder of the Constitution because Congress had never declared war, and another rally was called for noon on Monday, May 4.

Friday evening in downtown Kent began peacefully with the usual socializing in the bars, but events quickly escalated into a violent confrontation between protestors and local police. The exact causes of the disturbance are still the subject of debate, but bonfires were built in the streets of downtown Kent, cars were stopped, police cars were hit with bottles, and some store windows were broken. The entire Kent police force was called to duty as well as officers from the county and surrounding communities. Kent Mayor Leroy Satrom declared a state of emergency, called Governor James Rhodes' office to seek assistance, and ordered all of the bars closed. The decision to close the bars early increased the size of the angry crowd. Police eventually succeeded in using tear gas to disperse the crowd from downtown, forcing them to move several blocks back to the campus.

The next day, Saturday, May 2, Mayor Satrom met with other city officials and a representative of the Ohio National Guard who had been dispatched to Kent. Mayor Satrom then made the decision to ask Governor Rhodes to send the Ohio National Guard to Kent. The mayor feared further disturbances in Kent based upon the events of the previous evening, but more disturbing to the mayor were threats that had been made to downtown businesses and city officials as well as rumors that radical revolutionaries were in Kent to destroy the city and the university. Satrom was fearful that local forces would be inadequate to meet the potential disturbances, and thus about 5 p.m. he called the Governor's office to make an official request for assistance from the Ohio National Guard.

WHAT HAPPENED ON THE KENT STATE UNIVERSITY CAMPUS ON SATURDAY MAY 2 AND SUNDAY MAY 3 AFTER THE GUARD ARRIVED ON CAMPUS?

Members of the Ohio National Guard were already on duty in Northeast Ohio, and thus they were able to be mobilized quickly to move to Kent. As the Guard arrived in Kent at about 10 p.m., they encountered a tumultuous scene. The wooden ROTC building adjacent to the Commons was ablaze and would eventually burn to the ground that evening, with well over 1000 demonstrators surrounding the building. Controversy continues to exist regarding who was responsible for setting fire to the ROTC building, but radical protestors were assumed to be responsible because of their actions in interfering with the efforts of firemen to extinguish the fire as well as cheering the burning of the building. Confrontations between Guardsmen and demonstrators continued into the night, with tear gas filling the campus and numerous arrests being made.

Sunday, May 3rd was a day filled with contrasts. Nearly 1000 Ohio National Guardsmen occupied the campus, making it appear like a military war zone. The day was warm and sunny, however, and students frequently talked amicably with Guardsmen. Ohio Governor James Rhodes flew to Kent on Sunday morning, and his mood was anything but calm. At a press conference, he issued a provocative statement calling campus protestors the worst type of people in America and stating that every force of law would be used to deal with them. Rhodes also indicated that he would seek a court order declaring a state of emergency. This was never done, but the widespread assumption among both Guard and University officials was that a state of martial law was being declared in which control of the campus resided with the Guard rather than University leaders and all rallies were banned. Further confrontations between protestors and guardsmen occurred Sunday evening, and once again rocks, tear gas, and arrests characterized a tense campus.

WHAT TYPE OF RALLY WAS HELD AT NOON ON MAY 4?

At the conclusion of the anti-war rally on Friday, May 1, student protest leaders had called for another rally to be held on the Commons at noon on Monday, May 4. Although University officials had attempted on the morning of May 4 to inform the campus that the rally was prohibited, a crowd began to gather beginning as early as 11 a.m. By noon, the entire Commons area contained approximately 3000 people. Although estimates are inexact, probably about 500 core demonstrators were gathered around the Victory Bell at one end of the Commons, another 1000 people were "cheerleaders" supporting the active demonstrators, and an additional 1500 people were spectators standing around the perimeter of the Commons. Across the Commons at the burned-out ROTC building stood about 100 Ohio National Guardsmen carrying lethal M-1 military rifles.

Substantial consensus exists that the active participants in the rally were primarily protesting the presence of the Guard on campus, although a strong anti-war sentiment was also present. Little evidence exists as to who were the leaders of the rally and what activities were planned, but initially the rally was peaceful.

WHO MADE THE DECISION TO BAN THE RALLY OF MAY 4?

Conflicting evidence exists regarding who was responsible for the decision to ban the noon rally of May 4. At the 1975 federal civil trial, General Robert Canterbury, the highest official of the Guard, testified that widespread consensus existed that the rally should be prohibited because of the tensions that existed and the possibility that violence would again occur. Canterbury further testified that Kent State President Robert White had explicitly told Canterbury that any demonstration would be highly dangerous. In contrast, White testified that he could recall no conversation with Canterbury regarding banning the rally.

The decision to ban the rally can most accurately be traced to Governor Rhodes' statements on Sunday, May 3 when he stated that he would be seeking a state of emergency declaration from the courts. Although he never did this, all officials— Guard, University, Kent—assumed that the Guard was now in charge of the campus and that all rallies were illegal. Thus, University leaders printed and distributed on Monday morning 12,000 leaflets indicating that all rallies, including the May 4 rally scheduled for noon, were prohibited as long as the Guard was in control of the campus.

WHAT EVENTS LED DIRECTLY TO THE SHOOTINGS?

Shortly before noon, General Canterbury made the decision to order the demonstrators to disperse. A Kent State police officer standing by the Guard made an announcement using a bullhorn. When this had no effect, the officer was placed in a jeep along with several Guardsmen and driven across the Commons to tell the protestors that the rally was banned and that they must disperse. This was met with angry shouting and rocks, and the jeep retreated. Canterbury then ordered his men to load and lock their weapons, tear gas canisters were fired into the crowd around the Victory Bell, and the Guard began to march across the Commons to disperse the rally. The protestors moved up a steep hill, known as Blanket Hill, and then down the other side of the hill onto the Prentice Hall parking lot as well as an adjoining practice football field. Most of the Guardsmen followed the students directly and soon found themselves somewhat trapped on the practice football field because it was surrounded by a fence. Yelling and rock throwing reached a peak as the Guard remained on the field for about ten minutes. Several Guardsmen could be seen huddling together, and some Guardsmen knelt and pointed their guns, but no weapons were shot at this time. The Guard then began retracing their steps from the practice football field back up Blanket Hill. As they arrived at the top of the hill, twenty-eight of the more than seventy Guardsmen turned suddenly and fired their rifles and pistols. Many Guardsmen fired into the air or the ground. However, a small portion fired directly into the crowd. Altogether between 61 and 67 shots were fired in a 13 second period.

HOW MANY DEATHS AND INJURIES OCCURRED?

Four Kent State students died as a result of the firing by the Guard. The closest student was Jeffrey Miller, who was shot in the mouth while standing in an access road leading into the Prentice Hall parking lot, a distance of approximately 270 feet from the Guard. Allison Krause was in the Prentice Hall parking lot; she was 330 feet from the Guardsmen and was shot in the left side of her body. William Schroeder was 390 feet from the Guard in the Prentice Hall parking lot when he was shot in the left side of his back. Sandra Scheuer was also about 390 feet from the Guard in the Prentice Hall parking lot when a bullet pierced the left front side of her neck.

Nine Kent State students were wounded in the 13 second fuselage. Most of the students were in the Prentice Hall parking lot, but a few were on the Blanket Hill area. Joseph Lewis was the student closest to the Guard at a distance of about sixty feet; he was standing still with his middle finger extended when bullets struck him in the right abdomen and left lower leg. Thomas Grace was also approximately 60 feet from the Guardsmen and was wounded in the left ankle. John Cleary was over 100 feet from the Guardsmen when he was hit in the upper left chest. Alan Canfora was 225 feet from the Guard and was struck in the right wrist. Dean Kahler was the most seriously wounded of the nine students. He was struck in the small of his back from approximately 300 feet and was permanently paralyzed from the waist down. Douglas Wrentmore was wounded in the right knee from a distance of 330 feet. James Russell was struck in the right thigh and right forehead at a distance of 375 feet. Robert Stamps was almost 500 feet from the line of fire when he was wounded in the right buttock. Donald Mackenzie was the student the farthest from the Guardsmen at a distance of almost 750 feet when he was hit in the neck.

WHY DID THE GUARDSMEN FIRE?

The most important question associated with the events of May 4 is why did members of the Guard fire into a crowd of unarmed students? Two quite different answers have been advanced to this question: (1) the Guardsmen fired in self-defense, and the shootings were therefore justified and (2) the Guardsmen were not in immediate danger, and therefore the shootings were unjustified.

The answer offered by the Guardsmen is that they fired because they were in fear of their lives. Guardsmen testified before numerous investigating commissions as well as in federal court that they felt the demonstrators were advancing on them in such a way as to pose a serious and immediate threat to the safety of the Guardsmen, and they therefore had to fire in self-defense. Some authors (e.g., Michener, 1971 and Grant and Hill, 1974) agree with this assessment. Much more importantly, federal criminal and civil trials have accepted the position of the Guardsmen. In a 1974 federal criminal trial, District Judge Frank Battisti dismissed the case against eight Guardsmen indicted by a federal grand jury, ruling at mid-trial that the government's case against the Guardsmen was so weak that the defense did not have to present its case. In the much longer and more complex federal civil trial of 1975, a jury voted 9-3 that none of the Guardsmen were legally responsible for the shootings. This decision was appealed, however, and the Sixth Circuit Court of Appeals ruled that a new trial had to be held because of the improper handling of a threat to a jury member.

The legal aftermath of the May 4 shootings ended in January of 1980 with an out-of-court settlement involving a statement signed by 28 defendants[3] as well as a monetary settlement, and the Guardsmen and their supporters view this as a final vindication of their position. The financial settlement provided $675,000 to the wounded students and the parents of the students who had been killed. This money was paid by the State of Ohio rather than by any Guardsmen, and the amount equaled what the State estimated it would cost to go to trial again. Perhaps most importantly, the statement signed by members of the Ohio National Guard was viewed by them to be a declaration of regret, not an apology or an admission of wrongdoing:

> In retrospect, the tragedy of May 4, 1979 should not have occurred. The students may have believed that they were right in continuing their mass protest in response to the Cambodian invasion, even though this protest followed the posting and reading by the university of an order to ban rallies and an order to disperse. These orders have since been determined by the Sixth Circuit Court of Appeals to have been lawful.
>
> Some of the Guardsmen on Blanket Hill, fearful and anxious from prior events, may have believed in their own minds that their lives were in danger. Hindsight suggests that another method would have resolved the confrontation.

> Better ways must be found to deal with such a confrontation.
>
> We devoutly wish that a means had been found to avoid the May 4th events culminating in the Guard shootings and the irreversible deaths and injuries. We deeply regret those events and are profoundly saddened by the deaths of four students and the wounding of nine others which resulted. We hope that the agreement to end the litigation will help to assuage the tragic memories regarding that sad day.

A starkly different interpretation to that of the Guards' has been offered in numerous other studies of the shootings, with all of these analyses sharing the common viewpoint that primary responsibility for the shootings lies with the Guardsmen. Some authors (e.g., Stone, 1971; Davies, 1973; and Kelner and Munves, 1980) argue that the Guardsmen's lives were not in danger. Instead, these authors argue that the evidence shows that certain members of the Guard conspired on the practice football field to fire when they reached the top of Blanket Hill. Other authors (e.g., Best, 1981 and Payne, 1981) do not find sufficient evidence to accept the conspiracy theory, but they also do not find the Guard self-defense theory to be plausible. Experts who find the Guard primarily responsible find themselves in agreement with the conclusion of the Scranton Commission (*Report*, 1970, p. 87): "The indiscriminate firing of rifles into a crowd of students and the deaths that followed were unnecessary, unwarranted, and inexcusable."

WHAT HAPPENED IMMEDIATELY AFTER THE SHOOTINGS?

While debate still remains about the extent to which the Guardsmen's lives were in danger at the moment they opened fire, little doubt can exist that their lives were indeed at stake in the immediate aftermath of the shootings. The 13 second shooting that resulted in four deaths and nine woundings could have been followed by an even more tragic and bloody confrontation. The nervous and fearful Guardsmen retreated back to the Commons, facing a large and hostile crowd which realized that the Guard had live ammunition and had used it to kill and wound a large number of people. In their intense anger, many demonstrators were willing to risk their own lives to attack the Guardsmen, and there can be little doubt that the Guard would have opened fire again, this time killing a much larger number of students.

Further tragedy was prevented by the actions of a number of Kent State University faculty marshals, who had organized hastily when trouble began several days earlier. Led by Professor Glenn Frank, the faculty members pleaded with National Guard leaders to allow them to talk with the demonstrators, and then they begged the students not to risk their lives by confronting the Guardsmen. After about twenty minutes of emotional pleading, the marshals convinced the students to leave the Commons.

Back at the site of the shootings, ambulances had arrived and emergency medical attention had been given to the students who had not died immediately. The ambulances formed a screaming procession as they rushed the victims of the shootings to the local hospital.

The University was ordered closed immediately, first by President Robert White and then indefinitely by Portage County Prosecutor Ronald Kane under an injunction from Common Pleas Judge Albert Caris. Classes did not resume until the Summer of 1970, and faculty members engaged in a wide variety of activities through the mail and off-campus meetings that enabled Kent State students to finish the semester.

WHAT IS THE STORY BEHIND THE PULITZER PRIZE WINNING PHOTO OF THE YOUNG WOMAN CRYING OUT IN HORROR OVER THE DYING BODY OF ONE OF THE STUDENTS?

A photograph of Mary Vecchio, a fourteen year old runaway, screaming over the body of Jeffery Miller appeared on the front pages of newspapers and magazines throughout the country, and the photographer, John Filo, was to win a Pulitzer Prize for the picture. The photo has taken on a life and importance of its own. The Mary Vecchio picture shows her on one knee screaming over Jeffrey Miller's body. Mary told one of us that she was calling for help because she felt she could do nothing (Personal Interview, 4/4/94). Miller is lying

on the tarmac of the Prentice Hall parking lot. One student is standing near the Miller body closer than Vecchio. Four students are seen in the immediate background.

John Filo, a Kent State photography major in 1970, continues to work as a professional newspaper photographer and editor. He was near the Prentice Hall parking lot when the Guard fired. He saw bullets hitting the ground, but he did not take cover because he thought the bullets were blanks. Of course, blanks cannot hit the ground.

WHAT WAS THE LONG-TERM FACULTY RESPONSE TO THE SHOOTINGS?

Three hours after the shootings Kent State closed and was not to open for six weeks as a viable university. When it resumed classes in the Summer of 1970, its faculty was charged with three new responsibilities, their residues remaining today.

First, University faculty had to bring aid and comfort to our own. This began earlier with faculty trying to finish the academic quarter with a reasonable amount of academic integrity. The University had closed about the time of mid-term examinations. However, the faculty voted before the week was out to help students complete the quarter in any way possible. Students were advised to study independently until they were contacted by individual professors. Most of the professors organized their completion of courses around papers, but many gave lectures in churches and in homes in the community of Kent and surrounding communities. For example, Norman Duffy, an award winning teacher, gave off-campus chemistry lectures and tutorial sessions in Kent and Cleveland. His graduate students made films of laboratory sessions and mailed them to students.

Beyond helping thousands of students finish their courses, there were 1900 students as well who needed help with graduation. Talking to students about courses allowed the faculty to do some counseling about the shootings, which helped the faculty as much in healing as it did students.

Second, the University faculty was called upon to conduct research about May 4, communicating the results of this research through teaching and traditional writing about the tragedy. Many responded and created a solid body of scholarship as well as an extremely useful archive contributing to a wide range of activities in Summer of 1970 including press interviews and the Scranton Commission.

Third, many saw as one of the faculty's challenges to develop alternative forms of protest and conflict resolution to help prevent tragedies such as the May 4 shootings and the killings at Jackson State ten days after Kent State.

WHAT ARE THE MOST IMPORTANT UNANSWERED QUESTIONS ABOUT THE MAY 4 SHOOTINGS?

Although we have attempted in this article to answer many of the most important and frequently asked questions about the May 4 shootings, our responses have sometimes been tentative because many important questions remain unanswered. It thus seems important to ask what are the most significant questions which yet remain unanswered about the May 4 events. These questions could serve as the basis for research projects by students who are interested in studying the shootings in greater detail.

1. Who was responsible for the violence in downtown Kent and on the Kent State campus in the three days prior to May 4? As an important part of this question, were "outside agitators" primarily responsible? Who was responsible for setting fire to the ROTC building?
2. Should the Guard have been called to Kent and Kent State University? Could local law enforcement personnel have handled any situations? Were the Guard properly trained for this type of assignment?
3. Did the Kent State University administration respond appropriately in their reactions to the demonstrations and with Ohio political officials and Guard officials?
4. Would the shootings have been avoided if the rally had not been banned? Did the banning of the rally violate First Amendment rights?
5. Did the Guardsmen conspire to shoot students when they huddled on the practice football field? If not, why did they fire? Were they justified in firing?
6. Who was ultimately responsible for the events of May 4, 1970?

WHY SHOULD WE STILL BE CONCERNED ABOUT MAY 4, 1970 AT KENT STATE?

The May 4 shootings at Kent State need to be remembered for several reasons. First, the shootings have come to symbolize a great American tragedy which occurred at the height of the Vietnam War era, a period in which the nation found itself deeply divided both politically and culturally. The poignant picture of Mary Vecchio kneeling in agony over Jeffrey Miller's body, for example, will remain forever as a reminder of the day when the Vietnam War came home to America. If the Kent State shootings will continue to be such a powerful symbol, then it is certainly important that Americans have a realistic view of the facts associated with this event. Second, May 4 at Kent State and the Vietnam War era remain controversial even today, and the need for healing continues to exist. Healing will not occur if events are either forgotten or distorted, and hence it is important to continue to search for the truth behind the events of May 4 at Kent State as well as the Vietnam War. As Robert McNamara (1995) stated in his recent book, United States policy toward Vietnam was " ...terribly wrong and we owe it to future generations to explain why." Third, and most importantly, May 4 at Kent State should be remembered in order that we can learn from the mistakes of the past. The Guardsmen in their signed statement at the end of the civil trials recognized that better ways have to be found to deal with these types of confrontations. This has probably already occurred in numerous situations where law enforcement officials have issued a caution to their troops to be careful because "we don't want another Kent State." Insofar as this has happened, lessons have been learned, and the deaths of four young Kent State students have not been in vain.

ANNOTATED BIBLIOGRAPHY

Bills, Scott. (1988). *Kent State/May 4: Echoes Through a Decade*. Second Edition. Kent, OH: Kent State University Press. This book provides town and gown reactions to May 4th. It has the best annotated bibliography available on the literature on the shootings.

Casale, Ottavio M. & Paskoff, Louis (Eds.) (1971). *The Kent Affair: Documents and Interpretations*. Boston: Houghton Mifflin. This is an early, useful volume which reproduces local and national newspaper articles on the shootings as well as radio and television broadcasts.

Davies, Peter. (1973). *The Truth About Kent State: A Challenge to the American Conscience.* New York: Farrar, Straus & Giroux. This is a detailed narrative and analysis of the events of May 4 and their aftermath. He argues that the Guard conspired to fire upon the students. 74 photographs are included.

Esszterhas, Joe & Roberts, Michael D. (1970). *Thirteen Seconds: Confrontation at Kent State.* New York: Dodd, Mead. A very quick publication by two Cleveland journalists who use interviews of students, faculty, and Guardsmen to provide a background and narrative of May 1970 events.

Grant, Edward J. & Hill, Michael (1974). *I Was There: What Really Went on at Kent State* . Lima, OH: C.S.S. Publishing Co. The only book written by members of the Ohio National Guard, the authors provide a view of the hostile environment in which the Guardsmen found themselves.

Hare, A. Paul (Ed.) (1973). *Kent State: The Nonviolent Response.* Haverford, PA: Center for Nonviolent Conflict Resolution. A series of articles by noted peace activist Paul Hare as well as many Kent State faculty members. The common theme is the search for nonviolent approaches to conflictual situations.

Hensley, Thomas R. (1981). *The Kent State Incident: Impact of Judicial Process on Public Attitudes.* Westport, CONN: Greenwood Press. This is a detailed examination of the legal aftermath of the shootings, focusing upon the impact of various legal proceedings on public attitudes about the shootings.

Hensley, Thomas R. and Lewis, Jerry M. (Eds.) (1978). *Kent State and May 4th: A Social Science Perspective.* Dubuque, IA: Kendall/Hunt. This collection brings together a number of previous articles on May 4 that were published in social science journals, but articles covering the Kent State litigation and the 1977 gymnasium controversy were written specifically for this volume. This book also contains the excellent analysis of the events of May 4th written by James Best.

Kelner, Joseph and Munves, James. (1980). *The Kent State Coverup.* New York: Harper and Row. Kelner was the chief legal counsel for the students and parents in the 1975 federal civil trial. He presents a harsh analysis of the handling of the trial by Judge Donald Young. The book has a strong bias, but it provides the only detailed analysis of this long and important trial.

Michener, James. (1971). *Kent State: What Happened and Why.* New York: Random House and Reader's Digest Books. This is undoubtedly the most widely read book on May 4th because of Michener's reputation and the wide publicity it received. The book suffers from being produced so quickly, however, containing numerous factual errors.

Payne, J. Gregory (1981). *Mayday: Kent State.* Dubuque, IA: Kendall/Hunt. The book provides a rather sketchy overview of the May 4 events, presents excerpts from letters written by participants in the events, and discusses

the made-for-TV movie on May 4 to which Payne served as a consultant.

Report of the President's Commission on Campus Unrest. (1970). Washington, D.C.: U.S. Government Printing Office. Reprint edition by Arno Press. This remains the best single source for understanding the events of May 4. The report examines not only the shootings at Kent State but also the student movement of the sixties and the shootings at Jackson State University. Excellent photographs are included.

Stone, I. F. (1971). *The Killings at Kent State: How Murder Went Unpunished.* New York: Review Book. This is a rather sketchy book written with a strongly held viewpoint that the Guardsmen committed murder.

Taylor, Stuart; Shuntlich, Richard; McGovern, Patrick; & Genther, Robert. (1971). *Violence at Kent State, May 1 to 4, 1970: The Student's Perspective.* New York: College Notes and Texts. A study of the perceptions, feelings, attitudes, and reactions of Kent State students based upon a questionnaire sent to all Kent State students shortly after the shootings. Seven thousand students responded, and although this is not a random sample, it has the best data available about the views of Kent State students about May 4.

Tompkins, Phillip K. and Anderson, Elaine Vanden Bout. (1971). *Communication Crisis at Kent State: A Case Study.* New York: Gordon & Breach. This book presents a harsh analysis of the communications problems that permeated the University during May 1970.

Warren, Bill (Ed.) (1970). *The Middle of the Country: The Events of May 4th As Seen by Students & Faculty at Kent State University.* A hastily compiled set of essays put together by a Kent State University sophomore containing various reactions to the shootings by Kent State students and faculty members.

ADDITIONAL REFERENCES

Best, James J. (1978). "Kent State: Answers and Questions" in Thomas R. Hensley and Jerry M. Lewis (Eds.) *Kent State and May 4th: A Social Science Perspective.* Dubuque, IA: Kendall/Hunt.

Haldeman, H.R. (1978). *The Ends of Power.* New York: Times Books.

McNamara, Robert. (1995). *In Retrospect: The Tragedy and Lessons of Vietnam.* New York: Times Books.

Norton, Mary Beth; Katzman, David M.; Escott, Paul D.; Chudacoff, Howard P.; Paterson, Thomas G.; & Tuttle, William M. (1994). *A People and a Nation: A History of the United States.* Fourth Edition. Boston: Houghton Mifflin.

ENDNOTES

1. In addition to the many books on the Kent State shootings, numerous reports, book chapters, and articles have been written. The most comprehensive and accurate commission investigation is *The Report of the President's Commission on Campus Unrest* (1970) chaired by William W. Scranton. An excelllent book chapter on the shootings is by James J. Best (1978). The most comprehensive bibliography on the shootings is in Bills (1988).

2. Professor Hensley, the co-author of this article, became aware of this reference to the Kent State shootings because his daughter, Sarah, was taking Advanced Placement United States History at Kent Roosevelt High School with Mr. Bruce Dzeda. We thank Mr. Dzeda for reading this article and offering his reactions, although he bears no responsibility for the ideas expressed in this article.

3. In addition to Guard officers and enlisted men, Governor James Rhodes was also a defendent in the civil trial and signed the statement.

SECTION II | THE LEGAL AFTERMATH

Jurors, court officials, Ohio National Guard members, and others at the shooting site during the federal criminal trial in November, 1974. Photo by Doug Moore.

INTRODUCTION

The two essays in this section by Thomas R. Hensley of the Kent State political science department provide analyses of the major legal activities which have arisen from the May 4th events. The purpose of the first essay is to provide an overview of the most important judicial developments which have stemmed from the shootings. The analysis looks initially at the major governmental investigations of the shootings, including the report of the Scranton Commission appointed by President Richard Nixon. The main portion of the analysis focuses upon the seven major grand jury investigations and trials which have occurred: the 1970 state grand jury investigation, the 1971 state criminal trial, the 1974 federal grand jury investigation, the 1974 federal criminal trial, the 1975 federal civil trial, the 1977 federal court of appeals case, and the 1978-1979 retrial of the federal civil case. This analysis is important because the legal aftermath of the shootings has involved the official, governmental attempts to answer many of the pressing questions which arose after the shootings, including the ultimate question of who was legally responsible for the events of May 4. The second essay asks the question of what effect did these legal activities have upon the opinions of Kent State University students. Separate analyses were undertaken of the 1975 federal civil trial and the federal civil retrial in 1978-1979 to determine if students' attitudes about responsibility for the shootings changed in response to the decisions of the federal court.

THE MAY FOURTH TRIALS

Thomas R. Hensley
Kent State University

Our analysis in the previous section of the events on Kent State's campus in May of 1970 makes it clear that widely varying attitudes existed concerning responsibility for the shootings. In the immediate aftermath of the shootings, judicial activities were initiated to determine this responsibility and to assess appropriate penalties against those responsible. These efforts resulted in one of the longest, costliest, and most complex set of courtroom struggles in American history. The litigative struggle stemming from the shootings spanned the decade of the 1970s, and the various cases involved the trial, appellate, and supreme courts of both Ohio and the United States.

This chapter will provide a detailed description of the activities associated with the seven major judicial investigations and trials that focused upon the events of May 4: the 1970 Special State Grand Jury investigation, the 1971 state criminal trial resulting from the Special State Grand Jury investigation, the 1973-1974 federal grand jury investigation, the 1974 federal criminal trial resulting from the federal grand jury decision, the 1975 federal civil trial, the 1977 federal court of appeals decision ordering a retrial of the 1975 case, and the 1978-1979 federal civil retrial. These judicial investigations and trials have been the official, authoritative forums for seeking answers to the major questions arising from the shootings, but it will also be necessary to discuss some of the nonjudicial investigations which immediately

followed the shootings, analyzing these in reference to their relationships to the grand jury investigations and the trials. Numerous other legal actions have stemmed from the events of May 4, but these will not be considered because they have not focused upon the question of who was responsible for the events which occurred on the Kent State campus on May 4.[1]

The analysis is based upon a variety of resources. One important source has been a thorough compilation of articles from the *Akron Beacon Journal* from May 4, 1970, through March of 1979. The *Beacon Journal* received a Pulitzer Prize for its reporting on the 1970 shootings, and its continuing coverage of the legal aftermath of the shootings has been excellent. A second important source involves legal documents, including briefs, trial transcripts, and court decisions. A variety of scholarly articles and papers dealing with various aspects of the Kent State trials have also been drawn upon heavily in the analysis.[2] Finally, both formal interviews and informal discussions with direct participants in the trials have provided useful insights.

NONJUDICIAL INVESTIGATIONS AND REPORTS

In the immediate aftermath of the shootings, a number of investigations were undertaken by both governmental and nongovernmental groups. The most important investigations were made by the Federal Bureau of Investigation, the President's Commission on Campus Unrest (commonly known as the Scranton Commission, named after its chairman, former Pennsylvania Governor William Scranton), and the Ohio Highway Patrol. Investigations were undertaken by a wide variety of other groups as well: the *Akron Beacon Journal*, the Inspector General's Office of the Ohio National Guard, the Special Kent State University Commission on Campus Violence, the Ohio Civil Liberties Union, the Ohio Council of Churches, the American Association of College and University Professors, and the Ohio Bureau of Investigation.

In this section, attention will focus upon the investigations and reports of the FBI, the Scranton Commission, and the Ohio Highway Patrol, for these have had the greatest impact on the subsequent judicial activities. The primary emphasis will be upon the most important findings of each of these reports and the significance of each report in the subsequent litigative proceedings.

Ohio State Highway Patrol

The first group to complete its investigation and file a report was the Ohio Highway Patrol. As reported in the *Akron Beacon Journal* on July 22, 1970, the Patrol's report, a 3,000 page document, was presented to Portage County Prosecutor Ronald Kane, who commented: "The patrol did a tremendous, thorough job. . . . It will be a terrible waste if this report can't be placed before a grand jury. . . ."[3] Little information has ever been revealed concerning the findings in this report, for it was labeled confidential for possible grand jury use. Although no conclusions were drawn in this report, it does seem apparent that it placed major responsibility for the shootings on the students. The *Beacon Journal* story stated that the report showed: "Between 2,500 and 3,000 students milling on the campus during the anti-war fracas. Remarkable photos marking several hundred as suspects and possible grand jury indictees."[4] The report was subsequently to become a major working document for the Special State Grand Jury which met in the fall of 1970 and issued indictments against twenty-five persons, mostly Kent State students.

Federal Bureau of Investigation

Within twenty-four hours of the shootings, FBI agents were on the Kent campus to gather evidence

for a report to be submitted to the U. S. Department of Justice. It is estimated that more than 100 agents were in Kent to conduct the investigations, which resulted in the issuance by the Justice Department in late July of 1970 of a 7,500 page report, accompanied by a ten page summary. The full report was not made public at the time, but highlights of the summary were reported by the *Akron Beacon Journal* on July 23, 1970,[5] and substantial excerpts were later published in the *New York Times* and the *Congressional Record*.[6]

It is important to list in some detail the most significant findings related to the events of May 4 which are contained in the Justice Department's Summary of the FBI Report, for these findings have played an important role in subsequent developments. They were utilized by the Scranton Commission in making its report on the May 4 shootings, they were cited continuously by those groups and individuals seeking a federal grand jury investigation, and they were utilized by the Justice Department in its decisions regarding the convening of a federal grand jury. It is therefore important to identify in detail the major conclusions of the Justice Department Summary.[7] The conclusions presented here are similar to those cited in several books and articles which have argued that National Guard members were responsible for the shootings.[8] It is important to note that the Summary does not specifically reach the conclusion that National Guard members were responsible for the shootings, and the Summary acknowledges that conflicting interpretations existed regarding the shootings.[9] Nonetheless, the clear thrust of the summary points toward Guard responsibility.

> Just prior to the time the Guard left its position on the practice field, members of Troop G were ordered to kneel and aim their weapons at the students in the parking lot south of Prentice Hall. They did so, but did not fire. One person, however, probably an officer, at this point did fire a pistol in the air. . . .
> The Guard was then ordered to regroup and move back up the hill past Taylor Hall.
> The crowd on top of the hill parted as the Guard advanced and allowed it to pass through, apparently without resistance. When the Guard reached the crest of Blanket Hill by the southeast corner of Taylor Hall at about 12:25 p.m., they faced the students following them and fired their weapons. Four students were killed and nine were wounded.

Six Guardsmen, including two sergeants and Captain Srp of Troop G, stated pointedly that the lives of the members of the Guard were not in danger and that it was not a shooting situation.

We have some reason to believe that the claim by the National Guard that their lives were endangered by the students was fabricated subsequent to the event. The apparent volunteering by some Guardsmen of the fact that their lives were not in danger gives rise to some suspicions.

(One Guardsman) admitted that his life was not in danger and he fired indiscriminately into the crowd. He further stated that the Guardsmen had gotten together after the shooting and decided to fabricate the story that they were in danger of serious bodily harm or death from the students.

Also, a chaplain of Troop G spoke with many members of the National Guard and stated that they were unable to explain to him why they fired their weapons.

No verbal warning was given to the students immediately prior to the time the Guardsmen fired.

There was no request by any Guardsmen that tear gas be used.

There was no request from any Guardsman for permission to fire his weapon.

No Guardsman claims he was hit with rocks immediately prior to the firing.

The Guardsmen were not surrounded.

There was no sniper.

The FBI has conducted an extensive search and has found nothing to indicate that any person other than a Guardsman fired a weapon.

At the time of the shooting, the National Guard clearly did not believe that they were being fired upon.

Each person who admits firing into the crowd has some degree of experience in riot control. None are novices.

A minimum of 54 shots were fired by a minimum of 29 of the 78 members of the National Guard at Taylor Hall in the space of approximately 11 seconds.

Five persons interviewed in Troop G, the group of Guardsmen closest to Taylor Hall, admit firing a total of eight shots into the crowd or at a specific student.

Some Guardsmen (unknown as yet) had to be physically restrained from continuing to fire their weapons.

Four students were killed, nine others were wounded, three seriously. Of the students who were killed, Jeff Miller's body was found 85-90 yards from the Guard, Allison Krause fell about 110 yards away, William Schroeder and Sandy Scheuer were approximately 130 yards from the Guard when they were shot.

Although both Miller and Krause had probably been in the front ranks of the demonstrators initially, neither was in a position to pose even a remote danger to the National Guard at the time of the firing. Sandy Scheuer, as best as we can determine, was going to a speech therapy class. We do not know whether Schroeder participated in any way in the confrontation that day.

No person shot was closer than 20 yards from the Guardsmen. One injured person was 37 yards away; another, 75 yards; another, 95 or 100 yards; another, 110 yards; another, 125 or 130 yards; another, 160 yards; and the other, 245 or 250 yards.

Seven students were shot from the side and four were shot from the rear.

Of the 13 Kent State students shot, none, so far as we know, were associated with either the disruption in Kent on Friday night, May 1, 1970, or the burning of the ROTC building on Saturday, May 2, 1970.

As far as we have been able to determine, Schroeder, Scheuer, Cleary, MacKenzie, Russell and Wrentmore were merely spectators to the confrontation.[10]

President's Commission on Campus Unrest

On Sunday, May 24, 1970, Herbert G. Klein, White House Communications Director, announced that President Richard Nixon had decided to appoint "a high-level commission . . . to investigate the slaying of four students at Kent State University by National Guardsmen."[11] The Commission, under the direction of former Pennsylvania Governor William Scranton, was directed to study campus unrest throughout the United States, with specific focus upon Kent State University and Jackson State University, where two students were killed by police on May 15, 1970.

Nixon's decision to convene the Commission remains a subject of speculation. Creating such a commission was hardly surprising. In the wake of national tragedies, commissions can serve as credible fact-finding agencies, can assure the general public that the government is "taking action," and can buy time while passions cool. The controversy which continues to surround the Scranton Commission's activities is the extent to which Nixon may have attempted to subvert the work of the

Commission, and, if he did, the motivations behind his actions. In December of 1978, Republican Senator Lowell Weicker of Connecticut called for a federal grand jury investigation of the Scranton Commission's report.[12] Weicker's action was based upon information supplied by Charles Thomas, a historian with the National Archives, and by the Military Audit Project, a Washington-based group concerned with improper U. S. military activities. This information suggested that federal government agents may have been on Kent State's campus prior to the shootings and may even have served as agent provocateurs, thus contributing to the shootings on May 4.[13] According to this scenario, Nixon attempted to subvert the work of the Commission through staff members who made certain that this information did not get to Commission members.[14] No action has been taken by the Justice Department, and Weicker did not press his request. These questions thus remain unanswered.

The Scranton Report was made public on September 26, 1970, and it found both students and the National Guard at fault in the Kent State shootings. Concerning student responsibility, the Commission concluded:

The conduct of many students and non-student protestors at Kent State on the first four days of May 1970 was plainly intolerable. We have said in our report, and we repeat: violence by students on or off campus can never be justified by any grievance, philosophy, or political idea. There can be no sanctuary or immunity from prosecution on the campus. Criminal acts by students must be treated as such wherever they occur and whatever their purpose. Those who wreaked havoc on the town of Kent, those who burned the ROTC building, those who attacked and stoned National Guardsmen, and all those who urged them on and applauded their deeds share the responsibility for the deaths and injuries of May 4.[15]

The actions of some students were violent and criminal and those of some others were dangerous, reckless, and irresponsible.[16]

Concerning National Guard responsibility for the tragedy, the Commission concluded:

The May 4th rally began as a peaceful assembly on the Commons—the traditional site of student assemblies. Even if the Guard had

authority to prohibit a peaceful gathering—a question which is at least debatable—the decision to disperse the noon rally was a serious error. The timing and manner of the dispersal were disastrous. Many students were legitimately in the area as they went to and from class. The rally was held during the crowded noontime lunch period. The rally was peaceful, and there was no apparent impending violence. Only when the Guard attempted to disperse the rally did some students react violently.[17]

The indiscriminate firing of rifles into a crowd of students and the deaths that followed were unnecessary, unwarranted, and inexcusable.[18]

The Guard fired amidst great turmoil and confusion engendered in part by their own activities. But the Guardsmen should not have been able to kill so easily in the first place. The general issuance of loaded weapons to law enforcement officers engaged in controlling disorders is never justified except in the case of armed resistance that trained sniper teams are unable to handle. This was not the case at Kent State, yet each Guardsman carried a loaded M-1 rifle.

The lesson is not new. The National Advisory Commission on Civil Disorders and the guidelines of the Department of the Army set it out explicitly.

No one would have died at Kent State if the lesson had been learned by the Ohio National Guard.

Even if the Guardsmen faced danger, it was not a danger which called for lethal force. The 61 shots by 28 Guardsmen certainly cannot be justified.[19]

In its final conclusions, the Commission offered no recommendations, but rather stated: "Our entire report attempts to define the lessons of Kent State, lessons that the Guard, police, students, faculty, university administrators, government at all levels, and the American people must learn—and begin at once, to act upon. We commend it to their attention."[20]

The true impact of the three major investigations on subsequent judicial processes is difficult to assess with a high degree of confidence. The secrecy surrounding both the Ohio Highway Patrol's report and the FBI report makes it impossible to determine their precise impact, although it seems clear that the Highway Patrol's report was an important resource for the Special State Grand Jury, and the FBI report was utilized by the Scranton Commission and by the Justice Department in determining whether to convene a federal grand jury. The Scranton Commission's report, on the other hand, appears to have had little impact on subsequent judicial proceedings, nor is there evidence that President Nixon gave serious attention to its plea to close the deep cleavages among generational groups in American society.

While these reports seem to have had varying impacts on the subsequent judicial proceedings, the reports certainly left unsettled the question of responsibility for the shootings. Fingers of guilt were pointed in many directions, but no individuals or groups emerged as being primarily responsible for the shootings. This judgment could only be made in the courts, and hence our attention shifts to an examination of the litigative proceedings stemming from the May 4 tragedy.

CRIMINAL TRIALS

The first set of litigative activities to be examined involves the 1970 Special State Grand Jury investigation; the 1971 state criminal trial, which stemmed from the State Grand Jury indictments; the 1973-1974 federal grand jury investigation; and the 1974 federal criminal trial, which resulted from the federal grand jury probe. These judicial activities are analyzed together because they involve criminal law rather than civil law; the judicial activities stemming from the May 4 shootings which involve civil law will be analyzed in the next section of this article. Given the centrality of this distinction, it is important to specify the basic differences between cases in civil and criminal law. A useful clarification of these differences is provided by Henry J. Abraham:

> A case at *criminal law* is invariably brought by and in the name of the legally constituted government, no matter at what level—national, state, or local—it may arise. Chiefly statutory in the United States, criminal law defines crimes against the public order and provides for appropriate punishment. Prosecution brought under it by the proper governmental authority involves an accusation that the defendant has violated a specific provision of the law, an infraction for which a penalty has normally been provided by statute.[21]

In contrast, Abraham notes:

> A case at *civil law* is normally one between private persons and/or private organizations, for civil law governs the relations between individuals and defines their legal rights. A party bringing suit under it seeks legal redress in a *personal interest*. . . yet while suits at civil law far more often than not are suits among private persons, the government, too, may conceivably be involved.[22] (Emphasis in original)

Special State Grand Jury

Shortly after May 4, Portage County Prosecutor Ronald Kane announced that he would probably call a grand jury to investigate the shootings. According to an *Akron Beacon Journal* story of May 21, 1970, "the grand jury probe was recommended by County Coroner Robert Sybert to determine if the fatalities should be classified as 'accidental or homicidal.'"[23]

Kane was faced with enormous problems because of the scope and expense which such a grand jury probe would entail. The investigation would be "the most massive legal undertaking in Portage County's history,"[24] involving thousands of pages of information compiled by investigatory agencies and testimony from hundreds of witnesses. The cost of carrying out this investigation would go far beyond the county's financial capabilities. Kane, therefore, sought a grant for $100,000 from the state of Ohio to help finance the probe.

Ohio Attorney General Paul Brown ruled in July that the state could not legally approve the financial request, however, and on August 3, 1970, Governor Rhodes announced that he had ordered Brown to head a Special State Grand Jury investigation of the May 4 shootings. The *Beacon Journal* story of August 3 reports that Rhodes wrote to Brown:

> The people of Ohio are entitled to know what, if any, criminal acts took place at Kent State and who should be charged with perpetrating them.
> Only a grant jury can diminish the half-formed and mis-informed commentary on Kent State that still is heard. Only a grand jury could say who should face prosecution and for what.[25]

The *Beacon Journal* story also stated:

> Rhodes directed Brown to investigate acts leading to or inducing the illegal and criminal

acts in any way associated with campus unrest that took place in Kent or on the Kent State campus between May 1 and 5.

Such illegal or criminal acts themselves.

The legality of official response to such acts and to the 'general temper and situation' prevailing in Kent and on the KSU campus during May 1-5. . . .[26]

A question which begs to be answered at this point is why Rhodes made the decision to convene the Special State Grand Jury. Insufficient evidence exists to provide answers to this question, but it is possible to examine some possible explanations. The governor, as quoted above, wrote that the people of Ohio were "entitled to know,"[27] and an aide of the governor stated: "The governor wants the facts come to light. . . ."[28] A factor which may have been important in the decision was pressure from the U. S. Department of Justice. The *Beacon Journal* reported in the August 3 story that:

Rhodes' announcement came just days after U. S. Attorney General John Mitchell said the federal government would step into the KSU prosecution and impanel a federal grand jury if Ohio officials failed to act.

Mitchell's statement indicated the federal government might prosecute both students and Guardsmen.

A Justice Department memorandum to Kane last month, signed by Jerris Leonard, head of the Justice Department civil rights division, said six Guardsmen could be prosecuted for their actions.

Mitchell said last week there are "apparent violations of federal law."[29]

A different interpretation is offered by the Reverend John Adams, who has argued that Rhodes directed the Ohio Attorney General to call the Special State Grand Jury as a response to the recently released "inculpatory reports of the FBI," seeking by this approach to obfuscate the truth of May 4.[30]

The fifteen member jury was impaneled on September 14, 1970, with testimony beginning on September 15 and concluding on October 8, with more than 300 witnesses being called. On October 16, the grand jury issued secret indictments against twenty-five persons—mostly Kent State students but including some non-students and one professor—on forty-three offenses. In addition, the grand jury

issued an eighteen-page report, which placed primary responsibility for the events of May 2-4 on the university administration; found some students and faculty to share responsibility for the events; criticized officers of the National Guard for their actions; and declared that the Guardsmen who fired their weapons were not subject to criminal prosecution. Concerning student and non-student activities, the report stated:

The incidents originating on North Water Street in Kent, Ohio, on Friday, May 1, 1970, and which spread to other parts of the downtown area and the University, constituted a riot.[31]

We find that the rally on the Commons on Saturday, May 2, 1970, which resulted in the burning of the R. O. T. C. building, constituted a riot. There can never exist any justification or valid excuse for such an act. The burning of this building and destruction of its contents were a deliberate criminal act committed by students and non-students. Nor did the rioters stop with the burning of the R. O. T. C. building. They also set fire to the archery shed and engaged in further acts of destruction and stoned the members of the National Guard as they entered Kent.

Arson is arson, whether committed on a college campus, or elsewhere. The fact that some of the participants were college students changes nothing, except perhaps to further aggravate the seriousness of the offense.[32]

The Grand Jury finds that the events of Sunday, May 3, 1970, on campus and at the corner of Lincoln Street and East Main Street in Kent, Ohio, constituted a riot.[33]

The gathering on the Commons on May 4, 1970, was in violation of the directive of May 3 issued by the University Vice President in charge of Student Affairs. We find that all the persons assembled were ordered to disperse on numerous occasions, but failed to do so. These orders, given by a Kent State University policeman, caused a violent reaction and the gathering quickly degenerated into a riotous mob. It is obvious that if the order to disperse had been heeded, there would not have been the consequences of that fateful day. Those who acted as participants and agitators are guilty of deliberate, criminal conduct. Those who were present as cheerleaders and onlookers, while not liable for criminal acts, must morally assume a part of the responsibility for what occurred.[34]

Turning its attention to the Guardsmen, the jury wrote:

It should be made clear that we do not condone all of the activities of the National Guard on the Kent State University campus on May 4, 1970. We find, however, that those members of the National Guard who were present on the hill adjacent to Taylor Hall on May 4, 1970, fired their weapons in the honest and sincere belief and under circumstances which would have logically caused them to believe that they would suffer serious bodily injury had they not done so. They are not, therefore, subject to criminal prosecution under the laws of this state for any death or injury resulting therefrom.[35]

The circumstances present at the time indicated that 74 men surrounded by several hundred hostile rioters were forced to retreat back up the hill toward Taylor Hall under a constant barrage of rocks and other flying objects accompanied by a constant flow of obscenities and chants as "KILL, KILL, KILL." Photographic evidence has established, beyond any doubt, that as the National Guardsmen approached the top of the hill adjacent to Taylor Hall, a large segment of the crowd surged up the hill, led by smaller groups of agitators approaching to within short distances of the rear ranks of the Guardsmen.

The testimony of the students and Guardsmen is clear that several members of the Guard were knocked to the ground or to their knees by the force of the objects thrown at them. Although some rioters claim that only a few rocks were thrown, the testimony of construction workers in the area has established that 200 bricks were taken from a nearby construction site. Various students were observed carrying rocks in sacks to the "rally;" others brought gas masks and other equipment. . . . There was additional evidence that advance planning had occurred in connection with the "rally" held at noon on May 4th.

It should be added, that although we understand and agree with the principle of law that words alone are never sufficient to justify the use of lethal force, the verbal abuse directed at the Guardsmen by students during the period in question represented a level of obscenity and vulgarity which we have never before witnessed.[36]

Concerning the National Guard officers, the report stated:

The fact that we have found those Guardsmen who fired their weapons acted in self-defense is not an endorsement by us of the manner in which those in command of the National Guard reacted. To the contrary, we have concluded that the group of Guardsmen who were ordered to disperse the crowd on the Commons were placed in an untenable and dangerous position.

The Grand Jury also concludes that the weapons issued to the National Guardsmen are not appropriate in quelling campus disorders.[37]

Primary responsibility for the shootings was attributed to the university administration by the jury, which wrote:

We find that the major responsibility for the incidents occurring on the Kent State University campus on May 2nd, 3rd, and 4th rests clearly with those persons who are charged with the administration of the University. To attempt to fix the sole blame for what happened during this period on the National Guard, the students or other participants would be inconceivable. The evidence presented to us has established that Kent State University was in such a state of disrepair, that it was totally incapable of reacting to the situation in any effective manner. We believe that it resulted from policies formulated and carried out by the University over a period of several years, the more obvious of which will be commented upon here.[38]

The administration at Kent State University has fostered an attitude of laxity, over-indulgence and permissiveness with its students and faculty to the extent that it can no longer regulate the activities of either and is particularly vulnerable to any pressure applied from radical elements within the student body or faculty.[39]

Finally, the faculty was also criticized by the report:

Among other persons sharing responsibility for the tragic consequences of May 4, 1970, there must be included the "23 concerned faculty of Kent State University. . . ."[40]

If the purpose of the authors was simply to express their resentment to the presence of the National Guard on campus, their timing could not have been worse. If their purpose was to further inflame an already tense situation, then it surely must have enjoyed some measure of success. In either case, their action exhibited an irresponsible act clearly not in the best interests of Kent State University.[41]

The indictments and report of the Special State Grand Jury stimulated intense and polarized reactions from the public and led to two major new chapters in the judicial history of the Kent State shootings. The most direct result was the state criminal trial, which was conducted more than a year later. The indictments and report also provided a major stimulus to efforts for convening a federal grand jury investigation of the shootings, for critics of the state grand jury saw glaring inconsistencies between the reports of the FBI and the Scranton Commission, on the one hand, and the conclusions of the state grand jury, on the other hand. It is the former of these results—the state criminal trial—to which attention will now turn; when the story of that trial is completed, the focus will shift to the efforts to convene a federal grand jury.

State Criminal Trial

The state criminal trials did not begin until November 22, 1971, because of a lengthy appeal process stemming directly from the indictments and report of the grand jury. Lawyers for the "Kent 25" filed suits in late October and early November of 1970 with the U. S. District Court to have the grand jury's report destroyed and to overturn the indictments. Responding to these suits, Judge William K. Thomas on January 28, 1971, ordered that the report be expunged and destroyed, because "The Report irreparably injures, and as long as it remains in effect, the Report will continue to irreparably injure, as particularized, the rights of the indicted plaintiffs and of other persons similarly situated on whose behalf this action is brought,"[42] but he allowed the indictments to stand. Further appeal to the Sixth U. S. Circuit Court of Appeals failed to alter Judge Thomas' decisions, for the court upheld his rulings on the report and indictments.[43] A final appeal to the United States Supreme Court also failed when the Court on November 19, 1971, refused to halt the start of the trials of the "Kent 25."

State prosecuting attorneys experienced difficulties from the very beginning of the trial. The first defendant was convicted by the jury of interfering with a fireman but was not convicted on three other charges of arson, assaulting a fireman at the ROTC fire on May 2, and first-degree riot. The prosecution requested that charges be dismissed against the second defendant after four witnesses were called. The third and fourth defendants both pleaded guilty to first-degree riot, but the fifth defendant was ordered acquitted by Common Pleas Judge Edwin Jones on the basis of a lack of evidence and "a great possibility that some of the defendant's rights under the 14th Amendment were not necessarily observed."[44]

At this point, on December 7, 1971, sixteen days after the first defendant went on trial, special state prosecutor John Hayward issued a dramatic request for dismissal of charges against the remaining twenty defendants because of a lack of evidence. While the decision by the state surprised many, Ohio Attorney General William Brown revealed in an interview after the trial that he realized in June that many of the cases would have to be dropped: "the only evidence against [the fifth defendant] was her own statement to the grant jury, said Brown. 'And the cases were arranged according to their strength,' Brown added to illustrate how little evidence the state had in the remainder of the cases."[45] The reason the state pursued the cases as long as it did, Brown said, was that "we had an ethical and moral responsibility to go as far as we could . . . but if you don't have the evidence, you don't go to court."[46]

In the immediate aftermath of the state criminal trials, public reaction was once again both strong and divided, with students expressing support for the results and Kent townspeople generally opposing the outcome. Opponents of the state grand jury saw the results of the trials as vindicating their earlier criticism. This viewpoint was expressed clearly by former U. S. Senator from Ohio, Stephen Young:

> I am pleased but not surprised. I have repeatedly stated that the indictments were a fakery and a fraud from the outset.
> The purpose of the state grand jury in the first place was to whitewash Rhodes. . . .[47]

This view was also articulated by Benson Wolman, executive director of the Ohio chapter of the American Civil Liberties Union, who was quoted as saying that the dismissal request "exposes how outrageous the original action was. The flimsiness of the charges against the defendants . . . indicates, I think, what a fraud supposed Portage County justice really is."[48] It is interesting to note that in the front page news story on the request for the dismissals, the *Beacon Journal* writers stated that one of the major effects of the request was that it "further discredits the work of the special state grand jury that indicted 25 persons for 43 offenses."[49] Robert Balyeat and Perry Dickinson, two of the three special prosecutors for the grand jury investigation, defended their work and that of the grand jury, however. Balyeat said he was "'a little bit surprised,' explaining that he knew of no 'general problems as far as evidence was concerned.'"[50] Dickinson called the decision of the state prosecutors "surprising," stating that the grand jury

> evidently had sufficient evidence to indict these people. I think we had good cases. From the information I had I thought the cases were worthy of prosecution. There was sufficient evidence to go forward.[51]

None of the members of the state grand jury who were contacted by the *Beacon Journal* had any comment on the developments.[52]

The contradiction between the grand jury's indictments and the results of the subsequent criminal trials made it clear that responsibility for the shootings would not be resolved through criminal proceedings in the Ohio court system. Criminal law remedies remained a possibility at the federal level, however, and it is to this facet of the litigative proceedings that we now turn our attention.

Federal Grand Jury

Of all the various stages of the litigative process which have developed from the May 4 shootings, the greatest amount of attention by scholars and journalists has been given to the quest for a federal grand jury investigation and the results of the grand jury's investigation.[53] During a four-year period from 1970 to 1974, a number of major developments occurred: in early 1971 the U. S. Justice Department announced it would not convene a federal grand jury; in mid-1973 the Justice Department reopened its investigation of the shootings; in December of 1973 a federal grand jury was convened; and in March, 1974, indictments were issued against eight enlisted men of the Ohio National Guard. These events constitute a fascinating pattern of agonized decisions, conflicting opinions within the ranks of the Justice Department, extensive pressures on the department by the general public and by members of Congress, and reversals of earlier decisions.

Throughout the entire process, strong suspicions arose constantly of "political" motives behind "legal" decisions. On May 4, 1978, those suspicions

were confirmed. On that day NBC-TV news revealed the existence of a 1970 memorandum from White House aide John Ehrlichman to Attorney General John Mitchell. The memo, marked "EYES ONLY," read:

> The Tuesday, November 17, *Evening Star* at page A-7, reporting Jerry Leonard's backgrounder today (the 17th) says:
>
>> "During the discussions with reporters today, the Justice Department official also said no decision has been made as to whether to seek a Federal grand jury to investigate the May killings of four students by National Guard troops at Kent State University."
>
> In your office the other afternoon I showed you the President's memorandum on this subject and it was my understanding that you understood that the President had decided that no such grand jury would be sought. Will you please ask Mr. Leonard to advise the President by letter or memorandum that he fully understands the President's instruction in this regard?[54]

Why did Nixon issue this order?[55] Charles Thomas, the historian with the National Archives, believes it was because Nixon wanted to conceal the presence of federal agent provocateurs on the Kent State campus prior to the shootings.[56] A less sinister explanation is that Nixon did not want to give further publicity to this tragic result of his Vietnam War decisions. Nixon may have been especially concerned about a statement by Attorney General John Mitchell in July of 1970, indicating that FBI and Justice Department findings pointed to the apparent violations of federal law and the possibility of federal grand jury indictments against Ohio National Guard members.[57] Unfortunately we do not have a definitive answer to the question of why Nixon ordered no federal grand jury investigation. Our analysis of this aspect of the Kent State trials must therefore proceed with a recognition that an important piece of the puzzle is missing.

The issue of convening a federal grand jury arose immediately after the shootings, because the next day the FBI began its massive investigation for the Justice Department, which would use the FBI report to determine the need for a federal grand jury. According to a copyrighted story by David Hess which appeared in the *Akron Beacon Journal* on

May 20, 1975, the initial reaction to the FBI report came from Robert A. Murphy, then deputy chief of the Civil Rights Division, Criminal Section, U. S. Department of Justice, with whom the report was filed. In an internal departmental memorandum of June 19, 1970, Murphy, the chief federal investigator in the case, is reported to have stated that he did "not believe any legal grounds existed to prosecute guards, officers, or state officials on *criminal* charges."[58] (Emphasis added) Hess quotes Murphy directly from the memo: "'Although their conduct showed fool-hardiness and negligence, such is not the stuff of which specific intent is made.'"[59]

In a November 25, 1970 memo to Jerris Leonard, assistant attorney general in charge of the Civil Rights Division, Murphy did argue for the possibility of pursuing a civil case against the entire Ohio National Guard. The memo was "a rather long and complicated legal brief outlining the rationale for a civil suit."[60] Portions of the brief read:

Criminal sanctions imposed upon the individual Guardsmen who fired their weapons at Kent State are not an adequate remedy. . . .

National Guardsmen act under the close supervision of their superior officers whom we feel share responsibility for the shooting at Kent State.

These officers, by their decisions and their actions, placed their men in a difficult situation and they promptly lost control of both the situation and the men.[61]

Hess reports that Murphy concluded: "Since the purpose of the federal law 'is clearly to protect against incidents such as Kent State and to forestall their occurrence,'. . . the case called for some civil court action designed to enjoin the Guard from using tactics and procedures that might lead to another confrontation."[62]

Murphy's arguments were ultimately rejected by his immediate superior, K. William O'Connor, and by Leonard, although the memos involved "show an undisguised contempt for the quality of leadership exercised by high-ranking state and Guard officials and university leaders."[63] In a memo to Leonard dated March 9, 1971, O'Connor agreed that individual Guardsmen could not be criminally prosecuted. O'Connor's position was that there did not exist proof, beyond a reasonable doubt, concerning which Guardsmen shot the students; FBI ballistics reports "were absolutely inconclusive in establishing which Guardsman shot which weapon at which demonstrator. . . ."[64] Furthermore, O'Connor argued, it would be most difficult to prove that there was intent by the Guardsmen to deprive the students of their rights, as the law requires. O'Connor did, however, find grave fault, although not legal responsibility under criminal law, with National Guard and university officials.

Youthful, poorly trained, ill-equipped, and poorly led National Guardsmen . . . were placed in a confrontation with student elements engaged in protest of a national policy.

The entire university leadership was incapable of making decisions which might have averted the deaths and injuries of May 4.

Command responsibility of the National Guard units was in the hands of an incompetent who was later discharged.[65]

Finally, O'Connor wrote: "The injury to the country cannot be undone by anyone.... The only fruit of prosecution now would be the revival of the divisive forces which rent the nation in May 1970...."[66]

In addition to recommending against prosecution of enlisted Guardsmen, O'Connor rejected Murphy's argument for pursuing a civil suit against the Ohio National Guard as a whole. O'Connor's argument was that the changes in Guard procedures which could be sought in a civil suit had already been made by the National Guard.[67]

The question must be raised here about the impact of Ehrlichman's "eyes only" memo to Mitchell, ordering that no grand jury should be impaneled. Unfortunately, we do not know how far down the orders went from Mitchell to torpedo the grand jury investigation. Murphy has rejected the charge of improper intrusions. In a 1975 interview in the *Akron Beacon Journal* with reporter John Dunphy, Murphy stated:

You know people have theorized because of Watergate and other reasons that somehow or other there was corrupt influence on closing the case and I don't agree with that.

I thought it should have gone to the grand jury, but I don't know of any . . . there's nothing in our files and I don't know of any influence to get the case closed . . . closed by the White House.[68]

An analysis of the legal reasoning behind his memos lends support to Murphy's argument. As subsequent events were to reveal, the evidence was not present for successful criminal action against the Guardsmen. Quite clearly, however, Mitchell and Leonard were involved in grave improprieties. Leaders of the U. S. Justice Department were leading the obstruction of justice.

The first public announcement concerning the question of convening a federal grand jury came in a *Washington Post* story on March 21, 1971, in which it was reported that the Justice Department had decided reluctantly to recommend to Attorney General John Mitchell that a federal grand jury should not be convened because of the reasons identified by O'Connor in his memorandum to Leonard.[69] The reactions which arose to this story created strong pressures on the Justice Department, and Mitchell's official announcement that there would be no federal grand jury probe did not come until August 13, 1971.

These pressures are described in detail elsewhere,[70] so they can be summarized here. The most important leader in these activities was Reverend John Adams of the Office of the Department of Law, Justice, and Community Relations of the Board of Christian Social Concerns of the United Methodist Church. Working through the Civil Liberties Task Force of the Washington Inter-Religious Staff Council, Adams led an extensive effort "to research the issue and to bring every appropriate influence to bear upon those who were in the strategic positions of authority in the federal and state governments."[71] One of the most important results of these efforts was the publication of a 226-page study by Peter Davies, a New York insurance broker who had been deeply involved in researching the May 4 shootings. In his study—"An Appeal for Justice"[72]—Davies advanced the thesis that certain Guardsmen had conspired a few minutes before the shooting to fire upon the students.[73] This report was distributed, under the auspices of the Department of Law, Justice and Community Relations of the Board of Christian Social Concerns of the United Methodist Church, to the U. S. Department of Justice on June 21, 1971. After a month when no acknowledgment or response was forthcoming,[74] the study was released to the news media on July 23, 1971.[75] In addition to the activities led by Adams, the parents of the four dead students and the wounded students made appeals for the convening of a federal grand jury;[76] the Ohio chapter of the American Civil Liberties Union

provided some support for these efforts;[77] and nineteen Congressmen, led by William Moorhead, Democrat of Pennsylvania, also called for a federal grand jury probe.[78] All of these efforts met with failure, however, when Attorney General Mitchell announced on August 13 that the Justice Department had decided against convening a federal grand jury to investigate the shootings.

Reaction to Mitchell's announcement was, of course, intense and polarized, as all previous reactions to major developments had been. For the purposes of this study, attention needs to be focused upon the reactions of opponents of the decision, who continued to struggle for two more years before finally gaining a victory with the Justice Department's decision to reopen consideration of the case in August of 1973.

The parents of the dead students and the wounded students continued their quest, speaking out on the issue in various forums and filing suit on October 12, 1972, in an effort to compel a federal grand jury investigation;[79] this was dismissed in January of 1973 on the grounds that the court "could not interfere in a matter of discretion lying within the authority of the Federal prosecutor."[80] Kent State University students presented two petitions to the federal government; the first, containing more than 10,000 Kent State student signatures, was presented to the White House on October 21, 1971, and the second, with some 50,000 signatures, was presented on May 11, 1973, to the Justice Department. The official response to both petitions was negative. The results of the state criminal trials also led to revived calls for a federal grand jury.[81] Various religious groups also continued to press for a federal grand jury, and again John Adams was a leader in the efforts. Also during this period of time, Peter Davies published his book, *The Truth About Kent State: A Challenge to the American Conscience*;[82] and a movie entitled "Kent State 1970" was produced, based upon the Davies book and narrated by E. G. Marshall. Finally, both the House and Senate Judiciary committees exerted pressures on the Justice Department.[83]

All of these activities did not alter the decision of Mitchell nor did the government's position change when Mitchell was succeeded by Richard Kleindienst. But with Kleindienst's resignation, the linking of both Mitchell and Kleindienst to the Watergate scandal, and the new appointment of Elliot Richardson to the position of attorney general in April of 1973, new directions began to emerge in the Justice Department, leading to an announcement on August 3, 1973, that the case would be formally reopened. In making the announcement, J. Stanley Pottinger, assistant attorney general in charge of the Civil Rights Division, indicated that the decision did not reflect upon the integrity or probity of Mitchell; rather the decision was made in order to answer the gnawing doubts and questions in the public mind and "make sure that the department knows as much as can possibly be learned as to whether there were violations of Federal law."[84] Pottinger cautioned, however, that the decision to reopen the file "does not mean we have reason to believe the prior decision to discontinue active investigation was wrong or made for improper reasons, nor does it mean that we think that the additional inquiry is likely to lead to a different prosecutive judgment."[85]

Although the evidence is not strong as to why this important reversal was made by the Justice Department, bits and pieces of information can be put together to suggest the reasons. It appears that Pottinger played the key role, for he was responsible for initiating a fresh examination of the Kent State shootings after taking office in January, 1973.[86] The central role of Pottinger was emphasized by Robert Murphy in his 1975 interview by John Dunphy of the *Beacon Journal*:

Q Can you give a running summary of what transpired within the Justice Department from the time former Atty. Gen. John Mitchell closed the case in August 1971 until the time former Atty. Gen. Elliot Richardson opened it in August 1973?

A Not much happened between the time it was closed and reopened. The reason why it was reopened has been dealt with on one or two other occasions by Pottinger. But he said as the third anniversary of the shootings was coming up and he—having just become assistant attorney general and having received inquiries and knowing nothing about it since he was not in the Justice Department—he started to ask me and others, "What's this all about?" He became interested in it and finally went to Richardson.

Q Did Peter Davies' appeal in June, 1971, charging conspiracy on the part of the Guardsmen, or the petition for a grand jury submitted by the Kent State students have any effect on reopening the case?

A No, I don't think either one had anything to do with the case being reconsidered, frankly.

(Davies is a New Yorker who wrote a book on Kent State.)

Q Are you saying it was Pottinger's inquisitiveness that led to it?

A Yes, I think the inquiries of whatever kind and nature that Mr. Pottinger got sparked his curiosity.[87]

Murphy's statements give rise to the question of what inquiries sparked Pottinger's curiosity. The evidence here is slender at best, but Pottinger's own statement to Bill Moyers in an interview is perhaps instructive:

Moyers: Pottinger admits that part of the reason for re-opening Kent State was the persistence of private citizens.

What impressed you about the people who were coming in, saying; "Re-open the case?"

Mr. Pottinger: I think, most of all, it was a degree of intense concern—not to punish anyone. It didn't seem to be a vindictive kind of petition—it was: A "Can we find the truth? Can we discover the truth? There are so many questions unanswered." I think that's got to impress anybody who works on an incident of this magnitude.[88]

Pottinger's word choice suggests that it was contact with people like Reverend John Adams, Arthur Krause, and others deeply and personally affected by the tragedy who may have had this impact upon Pottinger.

Unquestionably, many other factors need to be included in explaining the final decision to reopen the case. In a press interview, Pottinger cited a number of possible reasons: The rash of lawsuits stemming from the shootings, the books written on the subject, continuous congressional inquiries, student petitions, pressure from the press.[89] Pottinger also stated, "We have concluded there are some areas into which an additional inquiry is desirable,"[90] implying that new evidence would be examined.

During the fall of 1973, activities proceeded on two main fronts, one investigative and one political. On the investigative front, Robert Murphy, chief of the civil rights criminal section who had originally recommended Guardsmen prosecution in 1970, was appointed by Pottinger as the head of the new investigation. According to an *Akron Beacon Journal* story on October 25, 1973,

> Murphy assembled a five-man team, two of whom are in Ohio now, to sift through old evidence, including state and local law enforcement reports, a State grand jury transcript, ballistics data, films, and a voluminous FBI reports (sic).
>
> Murphy and the team also are interviewing scores of witnesses and others close to the case in an apparent effort to expand on old evidence and develop new.
>
> Accounts of these interviews indicate that Murphy is determined to build a strong evidentiary case to uphold a recommendation that the case go to a grand jury.[91]

On the political front, considerable controversy arose over the appointment of Ohio Senator William Saxbe to replace Richardson as Attorney General when the latter resigned over a conflict with Richard Nixon stemming from the Watergate affair. Saxbe was at the time an inactive Ohio National Guard Colonel and a longtime friend of Ohio Governor Rhodes, and Saxbe indicated he might shut down the Kent State investigation if he were confirmed.[92]

Despite the controversy that arose over Saxbe's nomination and subsequent confirmation, the investigation proceeded unencumbered, and on December 12, 1973, Pottinger announced that a federal grand jury would investigate the Kent State shootings. On December 18, a twenty-three member jury was sworn in by U. S. District Court Chief Judge Frank Battisti, and a four-lawyer team headed by Murphy began presenting evidence to the grand jury. The lengthy and complicated probe—Murphy called it "one of the most complicated civil rights cases ever conducted"[93]—involved 39 sessions and lasted three-and-one-half months, during which time the jury heard from 173 witnesses including most of the 28 Guardsmen who fired weapons.[94]

A process that had begun almost four years before came to an end on March 29, 1974, when the federal grand jury handed down indictments against eight Guardsmen in three separate counts.[95] Five Guardsmen were named in one felony civil rights count, being charged with aiding and abetting each other and with willfully assaulting and intimidating the dead and wounded students by firing M-1 rifles and

did thereby willfully deprive said persons of the right secured and protected by the Constitution and laws of the United States not to be deprived of liberty without due process of law; and death resulted to the said Allison Krause, Jeffrey Miller, Sandra Scheuer, and William Schroeder from such deprivation.[96]

Three Guardsmen were named in two additional misdemeanor civil rights counts, one Guardsman being charged with "willfully discharging a loaded .45 caliber automatic pistol" and two Guardsmen being charged with "willfully discharging loaded 12 gauge shotguns" at the dead and wounded students and "did thereby willfully deprive said persons of the rights secured and protected by the Constitution and laws of the United States not to be deprived of liberty without due process of law."[97] The five indicted on the felony count faced a possible sentence of life imprisonment if they were convicted, and the three charged with misdemeanors faced maximum sentences of one year in jail and a $1,000 fine or both if convicted.

Public reaction to the decision of the grand jury was predictably strong and divided. Critics of the decision expressed both surprise and bitterness. Republican Senator Robert Taft told reporters that he was "'mildly surprised' at the indictments. 'I said before that I didn't think there was the basis for any indictable offenses. . . .'"[98] Paul Brown, Ohio Attorney General in May 1970, commented, "On the evidence which we had available to us, our grand jury decided not to indict any Guardsmen and I agree with their refusal to indict."[99] The bitterness felt by many was expressed by Major John I. Martin, a Guard leader on the Kent State campus on May 4: "These young men have civil rights, too. . . . I'm wondering if anybody is looking after them."[100] Reaction by supporters of the decision was rather varied. For many of the parents and wounded students, the decision served to reaffirm their shaken confidence in the American judicial system. Sandy Scheuer's father stated: "Justice works very, very slowly. But this shows we still have a civilized country."[101] Dean Kahler, one of the wounded students, expressed a similar view: "I think it reassures the faith I have in our system of justice. If you had asked me about it yesterday, I would have said no."[102] Another frequently mentioned viewpoint was that of basic support for the decision but disappointment that those in charge of the Guardsmen were not indicted. Democratic

Representative John Seiberling of the Kent-Akron area told reporters: "Morally, at least, people much higher than those Guardsmen have a responsibility for what happened. . . ."[103] Former Senator Stephen Young was even more adamant: "At least some semblance of justice is being meted out, even if they didn't indict Rhodes and those generals." Young continued, "(Rhodes) came there (to Kent) screaming and pounding on the table and demanding law and order, running scared because he was trailing behind Congressman Taft in the primary election. He caused the deaths of the students."[104] This same general viewpoint was taken by two wounded students, Alan Canfora and Tom Grace: "In the final analysis, the few triggermen must bear the blame for these deaths. . . . At the same time, the blame must also be shared equally by their superior officers, former Governor Rhodes and Richard Nixon."[105]

Federal Criminal Trial

Ironically, the federal criminal trial that had taken four and one-half years to begin lasted only ten days when, on November 9, 1974, U. S. Federal District Judge Frank Battisti acquitted the eight former national Guardsmen of charges, ruling that the federal government had failed to prove its case beyond a reasonable doubt.

A set of complex motions was initiated almost immediately after the grand jury handed down its indictments, thus delaying the start of the trial until late October of 1974. In the opening statement to the twelve-member jury, chief government prosecutor Robert Murphy admitted that there was no ballistic evidence to link any of the defendants to the weapons fired on May 4, but he told the jury that the government would prove its case on the basis of Guardsmen statements to the FBI and the Ohio Highway Patrol. Murphy also told the jury:

> The evidence will show there was no massive rush of students toward the Guard.
> We will prove to you that the Guardsmen were not surrounded at the time of the shootings; that no student was within 60 feet of the Guard at the time of the shooting; that only about 15 students who were within as much as 50 yards of the Guard were moving toward the Guard, and that the Guard was in its best and safest position, that is, high ground.
> And we will prove to you that the firing was indiscriminate and unjustified. . . .[106]

Ten days and thirty-three witnesses later, Judge Battisti's acquittal of the Guardsmen meant that the government had not succeeded in producing evidence sufficient to establish its contentions. In concluding his opinion, Battisti emphasized the limited scope of his ruling. He stressed that the relevant statue—Section 242 of Title 18 of the U. S. Code—required that the government establish beyond a reasonable doubt that the Guardsmen were possessed of *specific intent* to deprive students of their constitutional and federal rights. Specific intent is enormously difficult to establish, for it requires either explicit testimony about the defendants' motivation or the existence of extremely obvious circumstances. An example of such circumstances cited by Battisti was a case in which two police officers clamped a bicycle lock around a suspect's testicles to persuade him to confess to a crime. The government prosecutors had neither direct testimony from the Guardsmen nor such obvious circumstances to show specific intent. While the lack of evidence required acquittal of the Guardsmen, Battisti emphasized that the decision did not hold that the Guardsmen were justified in shooting.

> . . . it must be clearly understood that the conduct both of the Guardsmen who fired, and of the Guard and state officials who placed these Guardsmen in the situation . . . is neither approved nor vindicated by this opinion.

> The events at Kent State University were made up of a series of tragic blunders and mistakes of judgment. It is vital that state and National Guard officials not regard this decision as authorizing or approving the use of force against unarmed demonstrators, whatever the occasion or the issues involved. Such use of force is, and was, deplorable.[107]

This dramatic, mid-trial decision brought to an end the lengthy criminal law activities associated with the May 4 shootings, for prosecution at both the state and federal levels had now failed. The judicial proceedings were far from over, however, for looming on the immediate horizon was a massive federal civil case.

CIVIL TRIALS

The decision in the federal criminal trial was a disappointment for the wounded students, the parents of the dead students, and their supporters, while the outcome was a source of deep satisfaction for the Guardsmen and their supporters. Reaction to the verdict was muted, however, because of the widespread awareness that the issue of responsibility for the shootings would receive its final judgment through a pending federal civil case. This trial would for the first time place the enlisted Guardsmen, Guard officers, Governor Rhodes, and former Kent State President White as defendants against the wounded students and the parents, and few restrictions would be placed on the evidence brought into the trial. After five years of struggle, the plaintiffs were to have their day in court, their opportunity to establish who was really responsible for the shootings. The plaintiffs' day in court was to last for nearly four years.

The 1975 Federal Civil Trial

The pursuit of civil suits by the parents of the four dead students and the nine wounded students began shortly after the shootings occurred. These suits followed two general lines: suing the state of Ohio and its officers, and suing the various officials and Guardsmen in their individual capacities. The former approach did not prove successful; for after a lengthy struggle through Ohio state courts, the U. S. Supreme Court in 1973 refused to hear the case of *Krause v. Ohio*,[108] thus in effect upholding the doctrine of sovereign immunity, which basically is the principle that a sovereign entity cannot be sued without its consent. The second approach was to prove more fruitful for the plaintiffs, despite a series of initial setbacks. The attempt to sue officials and Guardsmen in their individual capacities was unsuccessful at the state level in a series of suits initiated at the lowest court levels and ultimately appealed to the Ohio Supreme Court, which ruled that the doctrine of sovereign immunity protected the state officials and Guardsmen from being sued.

A parallel effort to bring the suits before the federal courts under federal civil rights actions and federal wrongful death and personal injury actions was to prove successful, however. The suits were rejected in federal district court in mid-1971 when the late Judge James C. Cornnell upheld the doctrine of sovereign immunity, ruling that the state of Ohio could not be sued without its consent. By a 2-1 vote, the U. S. Sixth Circuit Court of Appeals in Cincinnati in late 1972 upheld the lower court's ruling.[109] However, a further appeal to the U. S. Supreme court reversed the two previous decisions. Speaking for a unanimous Court in *Scheuer v. Rhodes*,[110] Chief Justice Warren Burger ruled on April 17, 1974 that the doctrine of sovereign immunity was not absolute and that the federal district court should hear the plaintiff's claim.

> The Eleventh Amendment to the Constitution of the United States provides: "The judicial power of the United States shall not be construed to extend to any suit in law or equity, commenced or prosecuted against one of the United States by citizens of another State. . . ."
>
> However, since *Ex parte Young* . . . it has been settled that the Eleventh Amendment provides no shield for a state official confronted by a claim that he had deprived another of a federal right under color of state law.
>
> While it is clear that the doctrine of *Ex parte Young* is of no aid to a plaintiff seeking damages from the public treasury, . . . damages against individual defendants are a permissible remedy in some circumstances notwithstanding the fact that they hold public office.[111]

Following the Supreme Court's decision, the U. S. Sixth Circuit Court of Appeals remanded the suits back to the federal district court for hearing, and in July, 1974 Judge Donald Young of Toledo was assigned to hear the suits. The trial date was finally set for May, 1975, by Judge Young in order to allow the conclusion of the federal criminal trial stemming from the federal grand jury indictments and also to allow attorneys adequate time to prepare for the complex trial. During the pretrial period, Judge Young also determined that all of the suits would be heard in one trial,[112] thus placing the parents and the wounded students as plaintiffs against Governor Rhodes, former Kent State President White, former Ohio National Guard Adjutant General Sylvester Del Corso, National Guard officers, and enlisted Guardsmen as defendants.[113] Finally, Judge Young decided that the trial would proceed in two parts; the first segment would focus on the liability of the defendants, and, if liability were to be established, the second part of the trial would focus on the determination of damages.

Perhaps the most interesting and important pretrial development involved a conflict among lawyers for the plaintiffs, which resulted in an eleventh hour change in the head of the lawyers' team. Originally the plaintiffs' lawyers were to be headed by former U. S. Attorney General Ramsey Clark. Disagreements between Clark and Cleveland lawyer Steven Sindell led to Clark's withdrawal from the case in mid-May, just before jury selection began.[114] Clark was replaced by Joseph Kelner of New York, who had been involved for four years as the attorney for Mrs. Elaine Holstein, mother of Jeffrey Miller. Speculation arose following the trial as to the adverse effects on the plaintiffs' cases of this last minute change. Most observers believed that the plaintiffs' attorneys were poorly organized and were badly out-shown by the defendants' lawyers.[115]

The 1975 federal civil trial of *Krause v. Rhodes* was of a magnitude and significance that defy easy description. An enormous amount of money was potentially at stake, $46 million. The sheer length of the trial, which lasted fifteen weeks, made it "one of the longest courtroom dramas in the history of American law," and the complexity of the issues led Judge Young to conclude that it may have been the most difficult civil case for a jury in the history of the American legal system.[116] The jury was faced with the testimony of 101 witnesses, resulting in a trial transcript of over 12,000 pages; it was presented with seventy-six pages of legal instructions from Judge Young; and it was faced with at least 500 individual verdicts.[117] As the trial progressed, one juror was assaulted and threatened,[118] while Kelner, chief counsel for the plaintiffs, received three separate threats to "lay off the defendants, or we'll get you. . . ."[119] The significance of the trial was underscored by attorneys for both the defendants and the plaintiffs in closing statements. Kelner told the jurors: "I dare say that the case, perhaps, has no rival in its importance in the history of American justice."[120] Charles Brown, defense attorney, placed this perspective on the trial: "Ladies and gentlemen, in this historic case, you are not only the conscience of the community, you are the conscience of the United States of America."[121]

The jury's basic decisions, as set forth by Judge Young in his 76 pages of instruction given on August 23, 1975, centered on the following issues raised by the plaintiffs:

1. Did the defendants "knowingly subject the plaintiffs to the deprivation of the following rights and privileges secured and protected to them by the Constitution and laws of the United States, namely the right to assemble peaceably and petition for redress of grievances; their right not to be deprived of life or liberty without due process of law; the right not to suffer cruel and unusual punishment; and the right to protection against excessive government force?"[122]

2. Did the shootings by defendants constitute "assault and battery by the defendants upon the persons of the plaintiffs or the plaintiffs descendants?"[123]

3. Were the injuries and deaths from the shootings "the result of the willful or wanton misconduct or of the negligence of some or all of the defendants?"[124]

After five days of deliberation, the jury of six men and six women issued their verdict late in the afternoon of August 27: "We the jury, on the issues joined, find in favor of all the defendants and against the plaintiffs. . . ."[125] By a vote of 9-3 the jury decided that none of the thirteen plaintiffs had been denied their civil rights nor had they been victims of the violation of state laws relating to assault and battery and negligence. Subsequent interviews with two of the jurors suggested: the jury was convinced from the outset that Rhodes was not liable, but more disagreement existed concerning the other defendants;[126] especially critical pieces of evidence were a blurry film of the shootings and two sound tapes recorded a few seconds before the shooting containing chants of "Charge! Charge!" and "Lay down your guns. You're surrounded. Go home;"[127] and the jury may have believed responsibility for the disturbance lay with the students because of evidence that some students brought gas masks and rocks to the noon rally.[128] One jury member, Ellen Gaskalla, stated furthermore that Judge Young's decision to group the defendants into five groups—Rhodes, White, Del Corso, nine Guard officers, and seventeen enlisted men—"made a difference in people's minds."[129] According to a Cleveland *Plain Dealer* story:

> The jurors tended to feel that they had to find in favor of or against all of the men in each group, Mrs. Gasdalla said. She said she would have preferred considering the Guardsmen "more on an individual basis."

The Guardsmen were discussed individually, she said, but the judge's instructions as to these two groups influenced the voting.[130]

Reactions to the decision by plaintiffs and defendants alike were more intense than after any previous judicial decision, reflecting the tensions and uncertainties of the prolonged trial. All the deeply personal emotions which had been building for over five years poured forth as the jury's decision was announced. Cries from student plaintiffs of "Murderers!" "This is an outrage! There's no justice!" nearly drowned the voice of the court clerk as he read the verdicts.[131] Mrs. Scheuer, tears streaming down her face, cried, "They're still murderers!"[132] For some of the defendants, the tears were those of joy rather than sorrow; one National Guardsman, who heard the verdict over his car radio, said, "My emotions took over. I just pulled to the side of the road and cried like a baby I was so happy."[133] In general, however, a sense of deep relief rather than joy seems to have characterized the feelings of the Guardsmen. Lawrence Shafer's reaction was typical: "I hope it's the end. It's hard to tell how long I've been hoping that."[134] Other defendants saw the verdict not only as a personal exoneration, but also as a victory for American justice; former Guard officer Sylvester Del Corso called the verdicts "a great day for justice and law enforcement in this country."[135] Former Portage County Prosecutor Ron Kane echoed these sentiments, calling the trial and verdict "democracy in its purest form."[136] In stark contrast, Allison Krause's father, reflecting the views of the plaintiffs, despaired over the jury's verdict:

> They don't understand what the Constitution is about.
> They have just destroyed the most wonderful document ever made by man. Thanks to them, murder by the state is correct. The Constitution does not protect anyone against armed barbarians.[137]

Responses by the general public formed a much more ambiguous pattern. The local newspaper of Kent, the *Record Courier*, reported that "public reaction from residents around Portage County, with few exceptions indicated approval of the verdict. . . ."[138] The next day, however, the *Akron Beacon Journal* reported the results of phone calls received in response to their "Action Line" daily opinion poll, which had asked the question "Do you agree with the verdict of the Kent State jury?" The second largest response in the history of the poll—1,900 calls—resulted in a majority of 51 percent answering "no."[139]

1977 Appellate Case

Little question existed in the minds of the parents, students, and their lawyers that they would appeal the case. The only questions that had to be resolved were, what lawyers would be involved in the appeals case, and what issues would be focused upon in the appeal? Sanford Rosen, a San Francisco lawyer with longstanding ties with the American Civil Liberties Union, was selected to head the team of lawyers for the parents and students. Joining him were Nicholas Waranoff and Amitai Schwartz of San Francisco; three lawyers associated with the American Civil Liberties Union of Ohio foundation, Nelson Karl, Michael Geltner, and Clyde Ellis; and David Engdahl of the University of Colorado. The team of lawyers was confronted with a massive task, for their basic working document—the 1975 civil trial transcript—was approximately 13,000 pages, and over 100 possible avenues of legal appeal had to be researched and discussed before the written brief could be prepared and filed with the 6th U. S. Circuit Court of Appeals in Cincinnati.

After almost one and one-half years of work, the brief for the parents and wounded students was filed on May 3, 1976. In the brief, six major issues were presented for review:

I. Does the absence of substantial evidence to support the verdict require reversal of judgments?
II. Where a juror has been threatened and assaulted before deliberations, did the court err by telling the jury that the court took the treat seriously, and by refusing to voir dire the threatened juror or any other juror?
III. Were the jury instructions needlessly intricate, confusing, and obfuscatory?
IV. Whether prejudicial errors in the (charge) require reversal?
V. Whether numerous rulings concerning the conduct of the trial and the admissibility of evidence deprived plaintiffs of a fair trial?
VI. Whether the trial court erroneously refused to allow plaintiffs to use at trial federal grand jury testimony of the defendants?[140]

Oral arguments occurred in Cincinnati on June 21, 1977, with Rosen representing the students and parents. The issue in which the three-judge panel showed the most interest was Judge Young's handling of the threat to the juror. Rosen emphasized the arguments on this issue raised in the written brief:

On Wednesday, August 20, 1975 (two days before the jury went out), the trial court informed counsel that one of the jurors had been threatened, physically assaulted and told that he had better not vote the wrong way. The person making the threats was unidentified and neither his bias nor the identity of the threatened juror was revealed to counsel. The court decided to sequester the jury for its deliberations, and to inform the jury of the reason for sequestration.[141]

The judge cleared the courtroom and, over plaintiffs' strenuous objections, delivered a terrifying speech:

"I am very much troubled and disturbed by information that has come to my ears that threats have been made to at least one of your number in an attempt to influence your decision in this case.
I was brought up in an old school that threats of the type that were made are not to be ignored and not to be taken lightly.
There have been times when I have ignored such threats and I have blood on my hands and it is not easy to carry blood on your hands for ignoring things, and I don't propose to have it happen again if I can avoid it."[142]

On August 22, the judge said that he was not going to excuse the juror. He gave as his reason his assumption (he never interrogated the juror) that the juror would not consider the threats, and said that it was not the juror's fault and he or she had tried to do the right thing. This failure to question the juror was error.[143]

. . . the prejudice resulting from the trial court's action is patent. His "blood on my hands" speech and his refusal to question either the threatened juror or other jurors about the impact upon them of the threat result in a presumption of prejudice that was not overcome. Hence the judgments must be reversed.[144]

The appeals court on September 12, 1977 concluded that a new trial must be held. The court offered the following rationale for its decision:

The Supreme Court laid down the following rule in *Mattox v. United States*, 1892: Private communications, possibly prejudicial, between jurors and third persons or witnesses or the officers in charge are absolutely forbidden and invalidate the verdict, at least unless their harmlessness is made to appear.

The intrusion in this case represents an attempt to pervert our system of justice at its very heart. No litigant should be required to accept the verdict of a jury which has been subjected to such an intrusion in the absence of a hearing and determination that no probability exists that the jury's deliberations or verdict would be affected. Although we are reluctant to do so, particularly in face of the obvious good faith efforts of the trial judge to deal with a most difficult problem which arose near the end of an exhausting trial, we conclude that reversal for a new trial is required.[145]

The court made some important additional rulings in the case as well. The opinion stated that all claims against former Kent State President Robert White should be dropped because he had no control over the National Guard. The court also dismissed the claim of the plaintiffs that their right of peaceable assembly had been denied on May 4, 1970:

It is settled that violent demonstrations do not enjoy First Amendment protection. The plaintiff's argument is . . . "prior restraint" is never justified and the authorities must always indulge the presumption that the next assembly will be peaceful no matter how violent the preceding ones have been. That is not the law, particularly in a school or college setting.[146]

Finally, the court also ruled that it was permissible to use federal grand jury testimony which had not been allowed in the earlier trial.

The decision of the federal appellate court thus opened the door for a second federal civil trial over the May 4 shootings. No jury decision was ever to be announced in this second civil trial, however, for an out-of-court settlement was reached in mid-trial.

The 1979 Federal Civil Trial

Negotiating an out-of-court settlement is rarely an easy task, and the complexities of the May 4 civil trial seemed to present insurmountable barriers to such a solution. Common agreement had to be reached among thirteen plaintiffs and twenty-eight defendants. Not only did a monetary settlement have to be set, but also the wording of a statement by the defendants had to be made acceptable to all involved. Further, the source of the monetary settlement was to be the state of Ohio, and this required the involvement of the state legislature. And all of this had to be accomplished in a case of great emotional intensity and symbolic significance. This Gordian knot was to be untied by Judge William K. Thomas. Our concern in this section is to describe the process by which the settlement was reached, analyze the reasons why the plaintiffs and defendants agreed to the terms of the settlement, and survey reactions to the outcome of the case.

Initial attempts to reach an out-of-court settlement were unsuccessful by Judge Donald Young, the trial judge in the 1975 civil case who had been assigned the retrial of the case. The plaintiffs had criticized Young sharply for his handling of the 1975 case,[147] and he was not able to gain the confidence of the plaintiffs or their lawyers as he tried to achieve a settlement. In September of 1978 Young announced that he was stepping down from the case because of his inability to achieve a settlement. In a statement concerning his withdrawal from the case, Young was critical of the plaintiffs. He suggested that they should settle for about $380,000, the amount the state had allocated for the retrial, and further noted:

> I realize that settlement for so small a sum would not be very palatable to the plaintiffs, but something is better than nothing.
>
> I do not believe that the plaintiffs can ever win these cases, no matter how often they are tried or retried.[148]

With the assignment of Judge Thomas to the case in late September of 1978, new possibilities for a settlement emerged. Thomas did not bear the stigmatism from the 1975 civil trial, and the plaintiffs remembered with favor his ruling in 1971 to expunge the report of the Special State Grand Jury. Both sides were impressed by the abilities and dedication of Thomas, and an agreement slowly began to emerge on the financial terms and the wording of the statement. By the time the trial was ready to begin in December, terms of the settlement had been reached. The wording of the statement had been the most difficult part of the settlement, but getting the financial issue resolved took the longest period of time. The $675,000 was to be paid by the state of Ohio, and this unprecedented action required approval by the State Controlling Board, which was controlled by state Democratic legislators who were initially uncertain about the financial arrangements.[149] Questions were raised about the legality of the Board paying such a settlement, the potential liability of individual Board members if suits were brought against them, the type of precedent that might be set, and the reactions that voters might have to the settlement.[150] When the Controlling Board met on December 19 to consider the proposal, a motion was passed 5-2 to postpone action indefinitely, with the four Democrats all voting for postponement. This action was taken not only because of doubts about the legality, precedent, and political acceptability of the settlement, but also because of poor communication. Democratic legislators had not had time to discuss the settlement in the hectic closing days prior to the holiday break, leaving the Democrats on the Board with little party guidance. Further, the Board began its meeting at 12:30 p.m., unaware until then that they had to approve the funds by 1:30 when the trial was scheduled to begin. The failure of the Board to approve the funds meant the trial had to commence. The trial lasted only a few days in December, however, for after opening statements were given and two witnesses were called, Judge Thomas recessed the trial on December 21. The reason given was to provide time for the judge to deal with matters relating to a strike by independent steel truckers, but the recess also allowed time for the Board to reconsider its decision.

While the chances for reaching an out-of-court settlement did not look good, several developments during the holiday period altered the situation. Ohio Attorney General William J. Brown provided assurances to the legislators that they had the authority to approve such a payment. The concern of Democrats about adverse public reaction appears to have been calmed by a series of editorials in major Ohio newspapers which expressed their support for the settlement.[151] Thus, when Democratic legislators caucused on January 3, 1979 to discuss the political acceptability of the settlement, agreement was reached to support the allocation of funds. On January 4 the Board approved the payment by a vote of 6-1.

With the monetary settlement approved, Judge Thomas was able to announce on January 4 the full terms of the settlement. The plaintiffs would receive $675,000, divided as follows:

Dean Kahler, $350,000
Joseph Lewis, $42,500
Thomas Grace, $37,500
Donald MacKenzie, $27,500
John Cleary, $22,500
Alan Canfora, $15,000
Douglas Wrentmore, $15,000
Robert Stamps, $15,000
James Russell, $15,000
Parents of the four slain students, $15,000 each
Attorneys' fees and expenses, $75,000

The statement signed by the twenty-eight defendants read:

> In retrospect, the tragedy of May 4, 1970 should not have occurred. The students may have believed that they were right in continuing their mass protest in response to the Cambodian invasion, even though this protest followed the posting and reading by the university of an order to ban rallies and an order to disperse. These orders have since been determined by the Sixth Circuit Court of Appeals to have been lawful.
>
> Some of the Guardsmen on Blanket Hill, fearful and anxious from prior events, may have believed in their own minds that their lives were in danger. Hindsight suggests that another method would have resolved the confrontation. Better ways must be found to deal with such confrontation.
>
> We devoutly wish that a means had been found to avoid the May 4 events culminating in the Guard shootings and the irreversible deaths and injuries. We deeply regret those events and are profoundly saddened by the deaths of four students and the wounding of nine others which resulted. We hope that the agreement to end this litigation will help to assuage the tragic memories regarding that sad day.[152]

Finally, the plaintiffs agreed to end all litigation against the defendants stemming from the May 4 shootings.

Why did the plaintiffs and the defendants agree to these terms? Looking first at the plaintiffs, a public statement issued after the settlement by the parents of the slain students reasoned that the basic objectives they sought over the long legal struggle had been "accomplished to the greatest extent possible under present law. . . ."[153] The five objectives identified were:

1. Insofar as possible, to hold the State of Ohio accountable for the actions of its officials and agents in the event of May 4, 1970.
2. To demonstrate that the excessive use of force by the agents of government would be met by a formidable citizen challenge.
3. To exhaustively utilize the judicial system in the United States and demonstrate to an understandably skeptical generation that the system can work when extraordinary pressure is applied to it, as in this case.
4. To assert that the human rights of American citizens, particularly those citizens in dissent of governmental policies, must be effected and protected.
5. To obtain sufficient financial support for Mr. Dean Kahler, one of the victims of the shooting, that he may have a modicum of security as he spends the rest of his life in a wheelchair.[154]

Each of these objectives was important for the plaintiffs, but they are not sufficient for understanding the decision to accept the settlement. A fundamental stimulus was the fear of losing the case. The plaintiffs' chief attorney, Sanford Rosen, described the trial outcome as a "crapshoot."[155] This was probably too optimistic. It was unlikely that any jury selected would have been initially sympathetic to the parents and students. For example, the Kent State Jury Project,[156] involving random telephoning of registered voters in Northeast Ohio, found that a majority of the respondents rejected the plaintiffs' basic argument, that the Guardsmen fired upon the students without provocation.[157] Jury selection in the 1979 trial reinforced strongly the situation facing the plaintiffs. Thirty-three persons were excused from jury duty because of fixed opinions in the case. Thirty of the thirty-three were prejudiced against the plaintiffs.[158] Even assuming that twelve truly impartial jurors were selected, a most unlikely probability, the plaintiffs still faced enormous obstacles. The 1975 jury had voted 9-3 against the plaintiffs, and Rosen and his colleagues had no major new evidence to introduce. Most critically, the plaintiffs' attorneys still lacked the major piece of evidence they needed, an explanation as to why the Guardsmen fired. Rosen in his opening statement to the jury admitted "we do not know. . . ."[159] But lawyers for the defendants had an answer. The Guard fired because they were in serious danger of injury or death from the riotous students.

Even assuming the plaintiffs could win the case, a careful examination of the implications of winning pushed the plaintiffs toward accepting the out-of-court settlement. How much money would a jury return in damages in a case like this? Rosen believed that $40,000 would probably be the best that the plaintiffs could receive, with the exception of Dean Kahler.[160] By the time the costs were deducted, plaintiffs could well have received less than they received through the out-of-court settlement. In an interview after the trial, Judge Thomas did not challenge Rosen's assessment, and he stressed the difficulty in predicting a jury's decisions about damages in a civil rights case.[161] A further consideration was whether the plaintiffs would ever get their money if a jury awarded damages against the defendants. While Rhodes probably had the wealth to pay any damages, could the enlisted Guardsmen meet their financial obligations if damages were assessed against them? Garnishment of their wages would certainly be a slow process for the plaintiffs to receive their damages. Yet a final consideration had to be taken into account: winning the case posed many problems for the plaintiffs. A victory would have undoubtedly resulted in an appeal by the defendants. This would have meant additional years of litigation with its attendant costs and personal anguish. Also, there was always the possibility of having the victory turned into defeat on appeal.

The decision by the plaintiffs to accept the terms of the settlement was thus an eminently reasonable one. The advantages accruing from an acceptance of the settlement were substantial, especially in light of the likelihood of losing the case and the questionable advantages even of winning the case. Yet it was not an easy decision, for acceptance of the decision meant that neither Rhodes nor Guard officers and enlisted men would ever be held legally responsible for their actions.

But why did the defendants agree to the terms of the settlement? While the defendants probably felt they would win, there was always a possibility that they could lose. Even if they did win, the defendants knew that this meant more appeals and thus the continued prolonging of the litigation which had already covered nearly a decade. The enticement of ending the litigation forever was a powerful force. Furthermore, the terms of the settlement meant that all of the defendants would be freed of any personal financial liability. Finally, the wording of the statement did not require the admission of guilt or liability for the shootings. Thus, the defendants also found that the benefits of the settlement far outweighed its disadvantages.

Reactions to the settlement varied widely. Plaintiffs, defendants, and their lawyers expressed basic satisfaction with the settlement, but their respective interpretations of the meaning of the settlement were in sharp conflict. Rosen argued that the students and parents achieved "a great victory. It is an unprecedented settlement. Never before has a government apologized and paid money for injuries and deaths it caused."[162] Defendants' lawyers viewed the settlement in quite different terms. When asked if the settlement was an apology, Burton Fulton replied, "I don't read it as an apology, but as an expression of grievance. It is an acknowledgment that a tragedy occurred."[163] Plaintiff Arthur Krause and defendant Sylvester Del Corso expressed similarly opposing interpretations. Krause stated: "Everyone in the world knows that a monetary settlement is not made unless there is guilt and liability involved."[164] Del Corso argued "there is no apology"[165] and further "this is no admission of liability."[166]

Several plaintiffs and defendants spoke primarily in terms of the great emotional stress associated with the long ordeal. Defendant Lawrence Shafer expressed a widely held feeling: "I'm glad it's over with."[167] Plaintiff Dean Kahler stated: "I hope some day I'll be able to go to sleep and spend eternity in peace. Now, I don't feel that."[168] The somber mood of the plaintiffs was reflected in the remarks of Jeffrey Miller's mother: "My initial thought (about a settlement) was, I'm not satisfied; I'm upset, I'm horrified. But I realized that nothing would satisfy me. I wanted the impossible. I wanted Jeffrey back."[169]

Reaction from the general public was quite mixed. Some supporters of the plaintiffs expressed satisfaction with the settlement; one student observed, "It seemed as much as we could have hoped for."[170] Others sympathetic to the students and parents were critical of the outcome. Greg Rambo, who had led the petition drive for a federal grand jury, told reporters: "I'm disappointed that after eight years of struggle, it should end like this."[171] Joseph Kelner, chief counsel for the plaintiffs in 1975, stated, "I'm stunned at the utterly inadequate amount of money that has been paid. I feel that justice has not been served."[172] A view that was expressed by several individuals was disappointment that the out-of-court settlement meant there would be no opportunity to resolve the many unanswered questions about the shootings. The most prevalent reaction, however, seems to have been one of relief. Bob Tomsho, campus reporter for the *Record Courier* paper of Kent, observed: "Many people, both on the campus and in the community, are hesitant to discuss the shootings. Most of those who will, express relief that another episode in the tragedy is behind us."[173]

Unanimous support for the settlement came from the three major newspapers of Northeast Ohio, the Akron *Beacon Journal,*[174] the *Cleveland Plain Dealer,*[175] and *The Cleveland Press.*[176]The editorial in the Beacon Journal stated some common themes:

> . . . debate as to who was guilty of what will doubtless continue as long as memory of that tragic day persists.
>
> But Thursday's out-of-court settlement . . . should at least put an end to painful judicial probing of the old wounds and help the long, slow process of healing.
>
> And the terms of the settlement perhaps come as close to "justice" as any neutral observer could hope for.[177]

CONCLUSIONS

While the May 4 trials spanned the decade of the 1970s, no clear judgments emerged from these extensive legal activities about who was responsible for the shootings. A state grand jury investigation and state criminal trial resulted in three protesters being found guilty of charges relating to the burning of the ROTC building on May 2, but twenty-two of the indictees were not convicted. Members of the Ohio National Guard were acquitted in a federal criminal trial. Guard officers, Guard enlisted men, Governor Rhodes, and Kent State President White were found not liable for damages in a 1975 federal civil suit, and no legal liability was established for

any defendants in the 1979 out-of-court settlement of the retrial of the 1975 civil suit. The court proceedings have thus failed to establish who was responsible for the May 4 shootings, although several decisions have exonerated people from responsibility.

Does this mean that the American court system failed in regard to the Kent State May 4 tragedy? The best answer seems to be "no." It is probably asking too much of the court system to provide a definitive answer to a complex set of events such as those associated with May 4. The American court system is basically organized to deal with disputes between two persons who have a specific legal issue in contention. The system is not structured to deal effectively with confusing, unpredictable situations involving thousands of people. Nonetheless, the courts did provide some answers. The decision of the federal district court was that none of the Guardsmen were criminally liable, and in the 1975 federal civil trial all of the defendants were exonerated. The 1979 out-of-court settlement in the federal civil trial seems to capture best the complex and ambiguous legal issues surrounding May 4, however. The defendants were not found legally responsible, but they did sign a statement of regret, and the parents and wounded students did receive a considerable amont of money. Each side could make a valid claim that their position was vindicated.

ENDNOTES

1. The legal actions not considered in this paper include a false arrest action brought by former Kent State University student body president Craig Morgan and others against KSU and Kent city police officers; the judicial decisions to close Kent State after the shootings and then to reopen the university; a suit filed by the American Civil Liberties Union involving the search of KSU dorms after the shootings; a suit on the constitutionality of Ohio's "Campus Riot Act"; contempt cases involving state grand jury prosecutor Seabury Ford and KSU professor Glenn Frank for violating a "gag" rule relating to the state grand jury probe; a suit by Ohio National Guard Sergeant Myron Pryor against Peter Davies and others regarding his book which suggested Pryor was a central figure in an Ohio National Guard conspiracy to punish the students; a suit filed by three former KSU students involving the training and weapons given Ohio National Guardsmen; a CBS suit against Donald Young's "gag" rule in the 1975 federal civil trial; and finally, the numerous cases stemming from the 1977 controversy over building a gymnasium annex on part of the area where students and Guardsmen confronted each other in 1970.

2. The most important scholarly research on the Kent State trials has been done by David Engdahl: "Immunity and Accountability for Positive Governmental Wrongs," *University of Colorado Law Review* 44, 1 (1972); "The Legal Background and Aftermath of the Kent State Tragedy," *Cleveland State Law Review* 22, 1 (Winter 1973): 3-25; "The Legislative History of the Law Revision Center, a Comprehensive Study of the Use of Military Troops in Civil Disorders, with Proposals for Legislative Reform," *University of Colorado Law Review* 42 (1972); and "Soldiers, Riots, and Revolution: The Law and History of Military Troops in Civil Disorders," *Iowa Law Review* 57, 1 (October 1971). Other useful articles include John P. Adams, "Kent State: Justice and Morality," *Cleveland State Law Review* 22, 1 (Winter 1973): 26-47; Robert Howarth, "Sovereign Immunity—An argument Pro," *Cleveland State Law Review* 22, 1 (Winter 1973): 48-55; Gordon Keller, "Middle America Against the University: The Kent State Grand Jury," *The Humanist* 31 (March/April 1973): 28-29; Jerry M. Lewis, "The Quest for a Federal Grand Jury," in Hensley and Lewis, eds., *Kent State and May 4th: A Social Science Perspective*, Dubuque, IA: Kendall/ Hunt, pp. 59-65; Steve Sindell, "Sovereign Immunity—An argument Con," *Cleveland State Law Review* 22, 1 (Winter 1973): 55-71; and Judge William K. Thomas, "Jury Selection in the Highly Publicized Case," *Columbus Bar Association Journal* 35, 5 (May 1979): 3-4 ff. An important book on the 1975 civil trial is Joseph Kelner and James Munves, *The Kent State Coverup*, New York: Harper and Row, 1980.

3. *Akron Beacon Journal*, 22 July 1970, p. A1.

4. *Ibid.*

5. *Akron Beacon Journal*, 23 July 1970, p. A1.

6. *New York Times*, 31 October 1970, p. 15. The Justice Department Summary of the FBI Report can also be found in chapter 4 of I. F. Stone, *The Killings at Kent State: How Murder Went Unpunished* (New York: New York Review Book, 1971) and in Ottavio Casale and Louis Paskoff, eds., *The Kent Affair: Documents and Interpretations* (Boston: Houghton Mifflin Co., 1971), pp. 119-26.

7. The full summary appears in *Congressional Record* 119, 1 (January 3, 1973 to January 16, 1973): 1113-19.

8. For example, I. F. Stone, *The Killings at Kent State: How Murder Went Unpunished* (New York: New York Review Book, 1971), chapter 4; Peter Davies; *The Truth About Kent State: A Challenge to the American Conscience* (New York: Farrar, Straus, and Giroux, 1973), Appendix III; and Engdahl, "The Legal Background and Aftermath of the Kent State Tragedy," 19-21.

9. For example, the summary states: "As with the Guardsmen the students tell a conflicting story of what happened just prior to the shootings. A few students claim that a mass of students who had been following the Guard on its retreat to Taylor Hall from the practice football field suddenly "charged" the Guardsmen hurling rocks. These students allege in general that the Guard was justified in firing because otherwise they might have been overrun by the onrushing mob."

10. *Congressional Record*, 119, 113-19.

11. *Akron Beacon Journal*, 25 August 1970, p.A1.

12. See *Kent Record Courier*, 22 December 1978, pp.1,5.

13. See Charles Thomas, "The Kent State Massacre: Blood on Whose Hands?" *Gallery* 7,5 (April 1977): 98.

14. *Ibid.*, p. 104.

15. The President's Commission on Campus Unrest, *The Kent State Tragedy* (Washington, D. C.: U. S. Government Printing Office, 1970), p.87.

16. *Ibid.*, p. 90.

17. *Ibid.*, p.89.

18. *Ibid.*, p.90.

19. *Ibid.*, p. 91.

20. *Ibid.*, pp. 91-92.

21. Henry J. Abraham, *The Judicial Process*, 3rd ed., (New York: Oxford University Press, 1975), p. 22.

22. *Ibid.*

23. *Akron Beacon Journal*, 21 May 1970, p. A10

24. *Akron Beacon Journal*, 29 June 1970, p. B1.

25. *Akron Beacon Journal*, 3 August 1970, p. A1.

26. *Ibid.*

27. *Ibid.*

28. *Ibid.*

29. *Ibid.*

30. Adams, "Kent State – Justice and Morality," p. 29.

31. "Report of the Special Grand Jury," Supplemental Order, Portage County Court of Common Pleas, October 15, 1970, p. 6.

32. *Ibid.*

33. *Ibid.*, p. 8.

34. *Ibid.*, pp. 8-9.

35. *Ibid.*, p. 10.

36. *Ibid.*, pp. 10-11.

37. *Ibid.*, pp. 11-12.

38. *Ibid.*, p. 14.

39. *Ibid.*, p. 14.

40. *Ibid.*, p. 12. The twenty-three faculty issued a statement on May 3 which was sharply critical of Governor Rhodes and President Nixon.

41. *Ibid.*, p.13.

42. *Hammond v. Brown*, 323 F. Supp. 326, at 357.

43. *Hammond v. Brown*, 323 F. Supp. 326 aff'd, 450 F. 2d 480.

44. *Akron Beacon Journal*, 8 December 1971, p. A1.

45. *Ibid.*

46. *Ibid.*

47. *Akron Beacon Journal*, 8 December 1971, p. A1.

48. *Ibid.*

49. *Akron Beacon Journal*, 8 December 1971, p. A1. *Beacon Journal* reporters have attempted to strike a balanced, neutral ground in all of their reporting.

50. *Akron Beacon Journal,* 8 December 1971, p. A18.

51. *Ibid.*

52. *Ibid.*

53. Two useful studies are by Adams, "Kent State—Justice and Morality" and Lewis, "The Quest for a Federal Grand Jury." Two very important interview were conducted by *Akron Beacon Journal* reporters John Dunphy and David Hess with Justice Department official Robert Murphy and published on 4 May 1975 and 20 May 1975.

54. *Akron Beacon Journal*, 5 May 1978, p. A14.

55. Unfortunately, the Nixon memo itself has never been made public.

56. Thomas, "The Kent State Massacre," p. 104. Thomas did not know about the existence of the memo when he wrote

his article, but its appearance provided confirming proof to Thomas of Nixon's activities and motivations.

57. See *Akron Beacon Journal*, 3 August 1970, p. A1.

58. *Akron Beacon Journal*, 20 May 1975, p. A1

59. *Akron Beacon Journal*, 20 May 1975, p. A5. Specific intent would have to be established beyond a reasonable doubt in such a federal criminal trial.

60. *Ibid.*

61. *Ibid.*

62. *Ibid.* See also *Akron Beacon Journal*, 20 March 1977, p. A16.

63. *Akron Beacon Journal,* 20 May 1975, p. A1.

64. *Akron Beacon Journal,* 20 May 1975, p. A5.

65. *Ibid.*

66. *Ibid.*

67. *Ibid.*

68. *Akron Beacon Journal*, 4 May 1975, p. A8.

69. Adams, "Kent State – Justice and Morality," pp. 32-33.

70. Adams, "Kent State – Justice and Morality" and Lewis, "The Quest for a Federal Grand Jury."

71. Adams, "Kent State – Justice and Morality," p. 36.

72. Davies, "An Appeal for Justice," *Congressional Record*, (22 July 1971), E8143-58.

73. Adams states that Davies's involvement stemmed from a meeting on 17 May 1971, involving himself, Cleveland attorney Steven Sindell, and Deputy Attorney General Richard Kleindeinst in which the question of possible conspiracy was discussed. In that meeting, "Surprisingly, the Deputy Attorney General did not dismiss the suggestion and conceded that the Civil Rights Division had not explored this possibility at all. When I urged that any decision about a federal grand jury be delayed long enough for us to submit material concerning Michener's veiled hints of the more serious wrong-doing than deprivation of civil rights without due process of law, Kleindeinst readily agreed." This encouragement from the Justice Department led Adams to call upon Davies, for Davies had been involved in researching the question for almost a year. Adams, "Kent State—Justice and Morality," p. 40.

74. *Ibid.,* p. 41.

75. *Ibid.*

76. Lewis, "The Quest for a Federal Grand Jury," p. 12.

77. *Ibid.,* p. 8.

78. *Akron Beacon Journal,* 16 October 1971, p. A3.

79. *Schroeder et al. v. Kleindeinst*, Civ. Action No. 2048-72 (D.D.C.).

80. *Akron Beacon Journal*, 17 January 1973, p. C14.

81. Calls for a federal grand jury came from such diverse sources as former Senator Steven Young, a longtime critic of the state grand jury, and the *Akron Beacon Journal*, which has tried to steer a middle ground in its reporting. Cf. *Akron Beacon Journal*, 8 December 1971, pp. A6 and A18.

82. Davies, *The Truth About Kent State.*

83. *Akron Beacon Journal*, 1 August 1973, p. A11.

84. *Akron Beacon Journal*, 8 August 1973, p. A1

85. *Ibid.*, p. A2.

86. *Akron Beacon Journal,* 13 June 1973, p. A1.

87. *Akron Beacon Journal,* 4 May 1975, p. A8.

88. Lewis, "The Quest for a Federal Grand Jury," pp. 1-2, citing Bill Moyers, "Kent State: Struggle for Justice," (Transcript) (New York: Educational Broadcasting Corporation, 1974).

89. *Akron Beacon Journal*, 4 August 1973, p. A2.

90. *Ibid.*, pp. A2, A6.

91. *Akron Beacon Journal*, 25 November 1973, p. D3.

92. *Akron Beacon Journal*, 4 November 1973.

93. *Akron Beacon Journal* , 30 March 1974, p. A6.

94. *Ibid.* pp. A2, A6

95. Murphy stated that it was only these eight Guardsmen who fired in the direction or at human beings on May 4. *Akron Beacon Journal*, 30 October 1974, p. C1.

96. *United States v. Shafer,* Indictment, p. 1. They were charged with violating Section 242 of Title 18, U. S. Code, which provides:
    Whoever, under color of any law, statute, ordinance, regulation or custom, willfully subjects any inhabitant of any State, Territory or District to the deprivation of any rights, privileges, or immunities secured or protected by the Constitution or laws of the United States,. . . shall be fined not more than $1,000 or imprisoned not more than one year, or both; and if death results, they shall be subject to imprisonment for any term of years or life.

97. *Ibid.*, pp. 2,3. These three Guardsmen were also charged with violating Section 242 of Title 18, U. S. Code.

98. *Akron Beacon Journal,* 30 March 1974, p. A6.

99. *Ibid.*

100. *Ibid.*

101. *Ibid.*

102. *Ibid.*

103. *Akron Beacon Journal,* 30 March 1974, p. A1.

104. *Akron Beacon Journal*, 30 March 1974, pp. A1 and A6. Rhodes had earlier declared that the grand jury probe was an attempt to smear his reputation. Cf. *Akron Beacon Journal*, 10 February 1974, p. C4.

105. *Akron Beacon Journal*, 30 March 1974, p. A6.

106. *Akron Beacon Journal,* 30 October 1974, p. C1.

107. *United States v. Shafer,* 384 F. Supp. 496 (1974), at 503.

108. *Krause v. Ohio*, Civil No. 884,042 (Cuyahoga County, Ohio, C. P., Nov. 17, 1970); 28 Ohio App. 2d 1, 274 N.E. 2d 231 (1971), *rev'd,* 31 Ohio St. 2d 132, 285 N.E. 2d 736 (1972), *appeal dismissed,* 41 U. S. L. W. 3329 (U. S. Dec. 12, 1972) (No. 22), *petition for rehearing dismissed,* 22 Jan. 1973.

109. *Krause v. Rhodes*, 471 F. 2d 430 (6th Cir. 1972).

110. *Scheuer v. Rhodes* 416 U.S. 232 (1974).

111. *Scheurer v. Rhodes* 416 U.S. 232 (1974), at 237, 238.

112. Thirteen separate suits were actually involved, filed by each of the parents of the dead students and the nine wounded students. Each suit was further directed at each of the officials, officers, and enlisted men individually.

113. Although there were originally fifty-three defendants, charges were dropped against many of the enlisted men, reducing the final number of defendants to twenty-nine.

114. *Akron Beacon Journal*, 10 June 1975, p. B2.

115. See, for example, *Akron Beacon Journal,* 31 August 1975, p. A2. In Kelner's book, heavy responsibility for the plaintiff's defeat is placed on Judge Donald Young's handling of the trial.

116. *The Cleveland Press,* 28 August 1975, p. B6.

117. See note 112 above. Judge Young, however, placed the defendants into five groups to simplify the process. The significance of this decision is mentioned below.

118. *Akron Beacon Journal,* 22 August 1975, p. A1.

119. *Akron Beacon Journal,* 20 August 1975, p. D6.

120. Trial Transcript, *Krause v. Rhodes,* 390 F. Supp. 1072 (N.D. Ohio 1975), p. 12,189.

121. *Ibid.,* p. 12,361.

122. *Ibid.* p. 12,445.

123. *Ibid.* p. 12,469.

124. *Ibid.* p. 12,473.

125. *Akron Beacon Journal,* 28 August 1975, p. A1.

126. *The Cleveland Press,* 29 August 1975, p. A1.

127. *The Cleveland Press,* 29 August 1975, p. A16.

128. *Cleveland Plain Dealer,* 30 August 1975, p. 13A.

129. *Plain Dealer,* 30 August 1975., p. 13A.

130. *Ibid.*

131. *Akron Beacon Journal,* 28 August 1975, p. A1.

132. *Ibid.*

133. *Akron Beacon Journal,* 28 August 1975, p. A1.

134. *Ibid.*

135. *Akron Beacon Journal,* 28 August 1975, p. A11.

136. *Record Courier,* 28 August 1975, p. A11.

137. *Plain Dealer,* 28 August 1975, p. 17A.

138. *Record Courier,* 28 August 1975, p. A1.

139. *Akron Beacon Journal,* 29 August 1975, p. A1.

140. Brief for Appellants at 1, 2, *Krause v. Rhodes,* 390 F. Supp. 1072 (N.D. Ohio, 1975), on appeal.

141. *Ibid.,* p.88.

142. *Ibid.,* p. 89.

143. *Ibid.* p. 91.

144. *Ibid.,* pp. 96, 97.

145. *Krause v. Rhodes,* 570 F. 2d 563 (6th Cir. 1977), at 567, 570.

146. *Ibid.,* at 570-71.

147. The plaintiffs believed that many of Young's decisions as well as his general demeanor, showed favoritism to the defendants. The incident cited most frequently was Young's addressing governor James Rhodes as "Your Excellency" when Rhodes took the witness stand. See Trial Transcript, *Krause v. Rhodes,* 390 F. Supp. 1072 (N.D. Ohio, 1975), p. 8786.

148. *Akron Beacon Journal,* 22, September 1978, p. A1.

149. The State Controlling Board of Ohio is a seven-person group which is empowered to release funds which the state legislature has appropriated and to make certain transfers of funds. The Board was composed of six legislators, four Democrats and two Republicans, and a representative of the Ohio Office of Budget and Management. The latter is appointed by the governor. Interestingly, Governor Rhodes had appointed Robert F. Howarth, Jr., to the Board, and Howarth had been an attorney for Rhodes in the earlier state court cases over the May 4 shootings.

150. Specific concern of the Democratic legislators was the potential reaction against a payment which would free Republican Governor Rhodes from any personal financial liability.

151. Editorials favoring the settlement appeared in several of Ohio's major newspapers, and after the settlement Judge Thomas expressed his appreciation to the papers for their editorial positions. See *The Cleveland Press,* 6 January 1979, p. B2; *Record Courier,* 8 January 1979, p. 4; and *The Plain Dealer,* 7 January 1979, p. A27.

152. Statement issued in Cleveland, Ohio, January 4, 1979, by the defendants in the federal civil trial. This statement was printed in many of the major newspapers in the northeast Ohio area.

153. Statement issued in Cleveland, Ohio, January 4, 1979, by the parents of the students killed at Kent State University on 4 May 1970.

154. *Ibid.*

155. Interview with Sanford Rosen on 4 May 1979 by Thomas R. Hensley.

156. This was a project, led by Columbia University sociologists, seeking to provide valuable data on potential jurors for attorneys for the plaintiffs.

157. *Akron Beacon Journal,* 12 December 1978, p. B2.

158. Thomas, "Jury Selection in the Highly Publicized Case," p. 8.

159. *Akron Beacon Journal,* 20 December 1978, p. B1.

160. Interview with Sanford Rosen on 4 May 1979 by Thomas R. Hensley.

161. Interview with Judge William K. Thomas on 19 July 1979 by Thomas R. Hensley.

162. *Plain Dealer,* 5 January 1979, p. A1.

163. *Ibid.*

164. *Record Courier,* 5 January 1979, p. 11.

165. *Plain Dealer,* 5 January 1979, p. A8.

166. *Daily Kent Stater,* 5 January 1979, p. 1.

167. *Akron Beacon Journal,* 5 January 1979, p. A1.

168. *Record Courier,* 5 January 1979, p.11.

169. *Ibid.*

170. *Daily Kent Stater,* 5 January 1979, p. 1.

171. *Daily Kent Stater,* 5 January 1979, p. 11.

172. *Akron Beacon Journal,* 5 January 1979, p. A12.

173. *Record Courier,* 12 January 1979, p. 4.

174. *Akron Beacon Journal,* 5 January 1979, p. A6.

175. *Plain Dealer,* 5 January 1979, p. A8.

176. *The Cleveland Press,* 5 January 1979, p. A8.

177. *Akron Beacon Journal,* 5 January 1979, p. A6.

The Impact of Judicial Decisions on Attitudes of an Attentive Public: The Kent State Trials

Thomas R. Hensley
Kent State University

Attitude change is an important subject of interest to social scientists. Every discipline within the social sciences is concerned with the issue of how people's attitudes undergo change. One area which has not been given much attention, however, is the effect of judicial decisions upon public attitudes. While numerous public opinion studies of courts and judicial decisions can be found (see Goldman and Jahnige [1976: Chapter 4] for a review), only one major study has been published in which an attentive public's attitudes have been studied before and after a judicial decision to assess the change in attitudes as a result of the decision (Muir, 1967).

The judicial activities stemming from the May 4, 1970 shootings at Kent State University have provided a unique opportunity to study the impact of judicial decisions on the attitudes of an attentive public, Kent State University students. We will examine two decisions: the decision of a federal district court jury in 1975 finding neither public officials nor members of the Ohio National Guard liable for damages from the shootings, and a 1979 out-of-court settlement in a retrial of the 1975 federal district court civil case. For both of these cases, we will be examining attitude change in regard to (1) attitudes toward responsibility for the shootings, (2) attitudes toward the specific judicial structure, and (3) attitudes toward the American judicial system. The theoretical framework for the analysis will be based on both cognitive consistency theory and judicial support theory, and an experimental design/analysis of variance approach will be utilized to analyze the data.

Legal Aftermath of the May 4 Shootings

Many analyses have been written of the May 4 shootings at Kent State University, e.g., Michener (1971), Davies (1973), and Hensley and Lewis (1978), where four students were killed and nine students were wounded by members of the Ohio National Guard, which had been called to Kent and the Kent State campus because of protest disturbances following U. S. military incursions into Cambodia as part of the Vietnam War. Because these events have been widely discussed, only a brief review of selected events will be presented here.

In the immediate aftermath of the shootings, responsibility for the shootings was attributed to

Reprinted from *Sociological Focus*, 13:3 (August 1980) pp. 273-91 by permission of the North Central Sociological Association.

I wish to thank a number of people who made significant contributions to this study: James J. Best, Steven R. Brown, Marlyn G. Heller, Jerry M. Lewis, and Judith W. Reid.

many groups and individuals. Some placed the blame on radical protestors, both student and non-student. Others blamed the Ohio National Guard, with both Guard officers and Guard enlisted men being singled out for blame. Higher political figures—Ohio Governor James Rhodes, Vice President Spiro Agnew, and President Richard Nixon—were also identified by some as bearing heavy responsibility for the shootings. University administrators, faculty members, and the general student body were also mentioned by some as being responsible. These widely varying perceptions of responsibility in the immediate aftermath of the shootings were mirrored in the deluge of reports, books, and articles on the shootings which followed in the years after the shootings.

The authoritative determination of responsibility for the shootings eventually fell upon the federal judicial system, where both federal criminal and civil cases emerged in the '70s. The initial federal action involved the convening of a federal grand jury in December of 1973. The grand jury met for three months, and in March of 1974 the grand jury returned indictments against eight enlisted men of the Ohio National Guard. In the federal criminal trial in the fall of 1974, all eight were ordered acquitted at mid-trial by the judge for lack of sufficient evidence to establish proof beyond a reasonable doubt of their guilt. Throughout the summer of 1975, a massive federal civil trial was held in which the parents of the four slain students and the nine wounded students brought a $50 million damage suit against Ohio Governor Rhodes, 1970 president of Kent State Robert White, and Ohio National Guard officers and enlisted men. In late August of 1975, the jury voted 9-3 that none of the defendants were liable for damages. This case was appealed, and in the fall of 1977 the Sixth U. S. Court of Appeals ruled that a new trial had to be held because the trial judge in the 1975 case had improperly handled a threat to a juror. The new civil trial resulted in an out-of-court settlement directed by Judge William K. Thomas, who announced the terms of the settlement on January 4, 1979. The settlement provided for the parents and the wounded students to receive $675,000 and for a statement of regret signed by the 28 defendants.

COGNITIVE CONSISTENCY AND JUDICIAL SUPPORT THEORY

The central question posed in this study is about the impact of the decisions of authoritative judicial structures upon people's attitudes. More specifically, when a decision is made in a controversial case, do people, when they disagree with the decision, change their attitude on the issue to conform with the decision? Or do they maintain their attitude toward the issue and change their opinion of the judicial structure? If individuals lower their evaluations of a specific judicial structure, does this also carry over into a more negative attitude about the general judicial system, or is this more general attitude relatively stable?

A framework for examining these questions is provided by cognitive consistency theory and judicial support theory. The former provides the general model for studying attitude change, while the latter allows us to set forth specific hypotheses. Cognitive consistency theory[1] postulates that attitude change can occur when an individual's attitudes are in conflict; this conflict produces a psychological state of dissonance which can be reduced by changing one of the dissonance-producing attitudes, thereby achieving attitude consistency or balance.

These ideas can be used in studying the impact of the May 4 civil trials on the attitudes of Kent State students. From four diagrams in Figure 1, we see that students in diagrams (1) and (4) would find themselves in dissonance producing situations following a judicial decision on the May 4 shootings. In (1) a student believed before the trial that the National Guard was responsible for the shootings and, at the same time, had high support for the specific judicial structure involved in the case. However, the court ruled that the National Guard was not responsible for the shootings, thus conflicting with the student's attitude regarding responsibility. In (4) dissonance also exists. This student did not believe the National Guard was responsible and was not supportive of the court, yet the court's decision conforms with the student's belief about responsibility for the shootings. As in (1), dissonance could be reduced or eliminated by changing either attitude toward the court or attitude toward responsibility for the shootings. A student in either situations (2) or (3) should not experience dissonance. In (2) the student believes the National

Guard was responsible, thereby disagreeing with the court's decision. But the student's attitude toward the court was negative and, as a result, he or she is not surprised by a decision which is disagreeable. In (3) the student believes the National Guard was not responsible and is supportive of the court, which makes the "right" decision—that the Guard was not responsible—and hence no dissonance arises.

Figure 1. The Four Possible Situations of Attitude Consistency/Dissonance Immediately Following an Authorative Decision by a Legal Structure

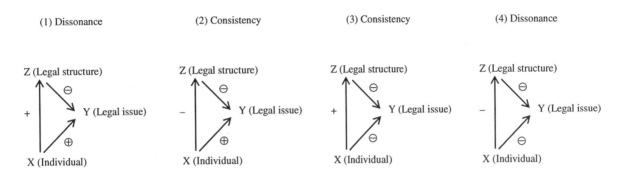

⊖ Position that the Guard was not responsible for the shootings

⊕ Position that the Guard was responsible for the shootings

− Negative attitude toward the legal structure

+ Positive attitude toward the legal structure

The analysis to this point has dealt with specific support, i.e., support for a specific judicial structure involved in a controversial decision. This logic can be extended in a straightforward manner to diffuse or general support for the entire judicial system. One merely substitutes "judicial system" for "legal structure" in Figure 1.

In the two dissonance producing situations, the individual can change one of two attitudes to eliminate or reduce dissonance. Which attitude will change? Cognitive consistency theory posits that the attitude held least strongly will be the one most likely to change. This provides relatively little guidance to us, however, because we have no reliable or valid direct measure of which attitude people hold most strongly. For assistance we must look to the scholarly research on judicial support.

Easton states that political support can be classified as either diffuse or specific. Diffuse support consists of those "strong ties of loyalty and affection" held by members of a political system "independent of any specific rewards which the member may feel he obtains from belonging to the system" (Easton, 1965: 125). In contrast, specific support involves satisfactions which members of the political system experience in regard to particular demands to which the system has responded. Thus, specific support involves perceptions of benefits stemming from particular decisions and policies of the political system. Both diffuse and specific support can be directed toward persons, groups, goals, ideas, or institutions of the political system.

Easton suggests that diffuse support is generally stable and constant, while specific support is more susceptible to change. When demands are not met, "discontent and disaffection may be stimulated," and specific support may decline; but "whatever the grievances a member expresses, he may still remain fundamentally true to the system" (Easton, 1965: 126). Specific support is thus more likely to vary because it is responsive to the daily actions of political actors and institutions, while diffuse support is unlikely to be affected by any one action or short term series of actions.

Easton's work has provided the stimulus for a substantial amount of research on judicial support, and the vast majority of studies have confirmed the original propositions. Empirically based studies of specific judicial support by Murphy, et al. (1973), Miller and Scheflin (1967), Casey (1976), and Lehne and Reynolds (1978) have found that public attitudes on issues do not change easily regardless of a court's decision, but support for courts is affected by the public's agreement or disagreement with decisions. None of these studies were before and after studies, however, and the only study which has used a before-after design—Muir's (1967) analysis of the impact of school prayer decisions—found significant attitude change on the prayer issue, conforming to the Supreme Court's decisions. Further, attitude change toward the Supreme Court tended to increase.

What, then, are we to conclude about possible changes in Kent State students' attitudes regarding responsibility for the shootings and specific judicial support? With a certain degree of caution, we offer the following hypotheses:

H_1: Students will not significantly alter their attitudes about responsibility for the shootings in response to the decision of an authoritative judicial structure.

H_2: Students who are placed in a situation of cognitive dissonance following a decision of an authoritative judicial structure will significantly change their attitude toward the judicial structure. More precisely,

H_{2a}: If dissonant students disagree with the decision, they will significantly lower their support.

H_{2b}: If dissonant students agree with the decision, they will significantly increase their support.

What about diffuse support? Easton's original formulation posits that diffuse support is stable and not susceptible to change in the short run. Most research has focused on the Supreme Court, and the general pattern revealed by the research, e.g., Murphy, et al. (1973), Casey (1976), Sarat (1975), Rodgers and Lewis (1974), and Engstrom and Giles (1972), is consistent with Easton's formulation. While individuals may disagree with specific decisions of the Court, their general belief in the legitimacy and fairness of the Court does not change quickly. While this research suggests we should not expect change to occur in diffuse support attitudes, a study by Rodgers and Hansen (1974) raises some doubts about the validity of this line of argument. Rogers and Hansen were interested in what happens when a general principle of law in which one believes—which they define as diffuse support—comes into conflict with a specific action which happens to be a violation of that principle. In studying the issue of Amish parents in Iowa

violating the law by not sending their children to public schools, they found that a sample of Iowa citizens did not change their attitude about the specific issue of the right of Amish parents to educate their children as they saw fit, but rather altered their diffuse support attitude concerning behavior in compliance with the law. As with specific support, then, our literature review leaves us in a somewhat uncertain position. The weight of the literature leads us, however, to the following hypothesis:

H_3: Students will not significantly alter their diffuse support for the judicial system in response to the decision of a judicial structure, regardless of the outcome of the decision.

METHODOLOGY

The research design for the study is a "one-group, pretest-posttest study" (Campbell and Stanley, 1963). For both of the cases under analysis, we selected before the decisions were announced a random sample of Kent State University students to whom we mailed questionnaires designed to measure the attitudes in which we were interested. After the respective decisions in the two cases, we sent follow-up questionnaires to those students who had responded to the first round, measuring the same attitudes measured in the first round. Although this design is superior to the *ex post facto* designs used in almost all previous studies of judicial impact on public opinion, it must be recognized that a one-group, before and after study is not the strongest possible design. Among its weaknesses are the potential effects of reactions to the survey instrument; the effects of history, i.e., the impact of events other than the judicial decision; the question of whether a single after measurement coincides with the period in which change actually occurred, if it did; and most importantly, the lack of control of extraneous variables associated with students in our respective samples, because we could not randomly assign students to various "treatment effects" or to control groups (see Campbell and Stanley [1963: 5-12] for a fuller discussion of these weaknesses). These potential problems require caution in the interpretation of our results.

An analysis of variance approach is used in analyzing the data. A rather substantial body of literature has developed regarding statistical procedures for analyzing attitude change: see, for example, Cronbach and Furby (1790), Farley and Newkirk (1977), and Linn and Slinde (1977). One option favored by some is the use of multiple regression analysis, and we have utilized this technique in an earlier study of the 1974 federal grand jury investigation (Best and Hensley, 1978) as well as in another study of attitude change (Hensley and Sell, 1977). For the purposes of this research, however, an analysis of variance strategy seems most useful and appropriate. Analysis of variance allows us to test our hypotheses more directly than multiple regression, for the structuring of the variables in analysis of variance corresponds precisely to the logical structure of dissonance theory as presented above. In addition, analysis of variance is intuitively easier to understand than multiple regression analysis, because with analysis of variance we can discuss most of the data analysis results in terms of simple means. Our analysis is based on the work of Roger Kirk (1968), whose book is a sophisticated exposition of the use of analysis of variance in association with a wide variety of experimental research designs. Using Kirk's terminology, we will be using to test most of the hypotheses analysis of variance for a split-plot design (also called repeated measures design) or,

more technically, a factorial design with block-treatment confounding (Kirk, 1968: Chapter 8).

A final area of methodological concern involves questionnaire construction and sampling procedures. The questionnaires used for the two cases were similar. With each before questionnaire, we were concerned primarily with measuring students' attitudes about responsibility for the shootings, support for the specific judicial structure, and support for the American judicial system. We also sought a variety of demographic information. Each after questionnaire was sent to those students who responded to the before questionnaire, and the second questionnaire contained similar questions regarding the three attitudes. In the after questionnaires we also asked the students about their agreement or disagreement with a variety of comments taken from the newspapers after the decisions.

Our sample for the 1975 federal civil trial consisted of 500 students selected randomly from the Kent State Student Directory. We increased our sample size to 600 for the 1978-79 trial. We received 222 first round responses in 1975 and 312 first round responses in 1978-79. For the after questionnaires, we received 135 responses in 1975, and 184 in 1979. While our response rate for both rounds is only

Table 1. Comparison of Student Samples in Spring 1975 and Fall 1978 with the Respective Kent State University Student Bodies on Selected Characteristics.

CHARACTERISTICS*	SPRING 1975		FALL 1978	
	SAMPLE	STUDENT BODY	SAMPLE	STUDENT BODY
Sex				
Male	53%	53%	48%	49%
Female	47%	47%	52%	51%
Total	100%	100%	100%	100%
Class				
Freshman	13%	22%	14%	25%
Sophomore	16%	19%	13%	17%
Junior	12%	20%	19%	17%
Senior	35%	23%	23%	17%
Graduate Student	24%	17%	30%	24%
Total	100%	101%	99%	100%

* Totals do not add to 100% because of rounding error.

about 30 percent, significant numbers of the non-respondents can be attributed to the failure of the questionnaires to reach students rather that students' failure to respond, for the Kent State Registrar's Office estimates that accurate addresses may be missing for as many one-third of the students. Despite the return rate problems, Table 1 reveals that for each of the surveys our samples are generally reflective of the Kent State student body on the characteristics of gender and class standing.

THE 1975 FEDERAL CIVIL TRIAL

The 1975 federal civil trial over the May 4 shootings was one of the longest, costliest, and most complex civil cases in American history. After a trial that stretched over the entire summer of 1975, the jury decided 9-3 that none of the defendants—Ohio Governor Rhodes, former Kent State President Robert White, Ohio National Guard officers, and Ohio National Guard enlisted men—were liable for damages. What impact did this decision have upon Kent State students' attitudes toward responsibility for the shootings, toward the federal district court, and toward the American judicial system?

Looking first at students' attitudes regarding responsibility for the shootings, we seek to test the following hypothesis:

H_1: Students will not significantly alter their attitudes about responsibility for the shootings in response to the decision of an authoritative judicial structure.

In examining Table 2, which contains the mean responsibility scores[2] before and after the 1975 trial, we find that remarkably little change occurred in students' perceptions of responsibility for any of the individuals or groups. The mean scores for each of the defendants—Rhodes, White, Guard officers, and Guard enlisted men—declined slightly, but analysis of variance reveals that none of these changes were statistically significant at the .05 level, used throughout this study. We can thus accept Hypothesis 1 for the 1975 Kent State civil trial: students did not change their attitudes about responsibility for the shootings to conform to the authoritative decision of the federal district court.

Did students' attitudes toward the federal district court undergo change? Cognitive consistency theory and judicial support theory lead us to believe that we should expect significant attitude change in specific support for those students placed in a dissonant condition by the decision. We hypothesized that:

Table 2. Mean Scores of Kent State Students' Perceptions of Responsibility for the May 4 Shootings Before and After the 1975 Federal Civil Trial

INDIVIDUALS AND GROUPS	MEAN RESPONSIBILITY SCORES*	
	BEFORE 1975 TRIAL	AFTER 1975 TRIAL
Guard Officers	3.41	3.33
Rhodes	3.41	3.37
Non-student radicals	3.15	3.15
Radical students	3.02	3.14
Guard enlisted men	2.82	2.74
White	2.73	2.70
Nixon	2.50	2.49
K. S. U. administrators	2.28	2.30
Agnew	1.95	1.88
K. S. U. faculty	1.64	1.67
Non-radical students	1.55	1.54

* Responsibility scores can range from 4 (very responsible) to 1 (not responsible).

H_2: Students who are placed in a situation of cognitive dissonance following a decision of an authoritative judicial structure will significantly change their attitude toward the judicial structure. More precisely,

H_{2a}: If dissonant students disagree with the decision, they will significantly lower their support.

H_{2b}: If dissonant students agree with the decision, they will significantly increase their support.

An examination of Tables 3 and 4 leads us to accept these hypotheses. Significant changes occurred in students' support for the federal district court; and students who agreed with the decision of the court increased their support for the court, while those students who disagreed with the court's verdict decreased their support for the court to a significant degree. Looking first at table 3, we see the mean support scores[3] for two groups of students, those who viewed the National Guard as responsible for

the shootings and those who did not hold the Guard responsible.[4]

Those who viewed the Guard as responsible for the shootings showed a decrease in support from a 3.87 before the decision to a mean of 3.42 after the decision, while those students who did not believe the Guard was responsible increased their support scores from a mean of 4.06 to 4.54. Table 4 provides a more formalized testing of these differences through analysis of variance. We are interested in testing the interaction effects, for we are hypothesizing that attitudes of specific support will change significantly based upon students' agreement or disagreement with the outcome of the trial[5]. We see in Table 4 that our general hypothesis is confirmed, for the overall interaction effect is statistically significant. Further, when we apply Fisher's least significant difference test[6] to both groups of students, we find both Hypotheses 2a and 2b confirmed.

Table 3. Students' Mean Specific Support Scores for the Federal District Court Before and After the 1975 Trial

ATTITUDE TOWARD GUARD RESPONSIBILITY	SPECIFIC JUDICIAL SUPPORT SCORES*	
	BEFORE THE DECISION	AFTER THE DECISION
Guard Responsible (N = 92)	$\bar{x} = 3.87$	$\bar{x} = 3.42$
Guard Not Responsible (N = 35)	$\bar{x} = 4.06$	$\bar{x} = 4.54$

*Specific support scores can range from a low of 2 to a high of 6.

Table 4. Analysis of Variance Table for Students' Specific Judicial Support Scores Before and After the 1975 Federal Civil Trial

SOURCE	df	MS	F	P
Between subjects				
A (Responsibility)	1	31.76	13.91	.001
Error	124	2.28		
Within subjects				
B (Time)	1	2.29	2.91	.089
A x B (Interaction)	1	10.20	12.96	.001
Error	124	.79		

Our final concern is with the impact of the 1975 decision on students' diffuse support attitudes toward the American judicial system. General support for the judicial system is thought to be deeply ingrained and hence not susceptible to easy change, and thus we examine the following hypothesis:

H$_3$: Students will not significantly alter their diffuse support for the judicial system in response to the decision of a judicial structure, regardless of the outcome of the decision.

The data to test this hypothesis appear in Tables 5 and 6. They lead us to accept the hypothesis: students' attitudes concerning diffuse support for the American judicial system did not alter significantly as a result of the decision of the jury in the 1975 May 4 civil trial. Looking first at Table 5, it can be seen that diffuse support scores[7] for students who believed the Guard was responsible shifted only slightly, dropping from a mean of 8.67 before the trial to a mean of 8.53 after the trial. A somewhat larger change can be observed for the students who did not believe the National Guard was responsible. The mean diffuse support score for these students

increased from 9.66 to 10.14. Thus, we do see some shifts in mean support scores, but they are rather small shifts, and analysis of variance results as shown in Table 6 reveal that these differences are not large enough to be statistically significant. Hence, we accept Hypothesis 3 that students' diffuse support scores did not change significantly.[8]

THE 1979 FEDERAL CIVIL TRIAL

The contrast between the ending of the first May 4 civil trial in 1975 and the culmination of the second civil trial in 1979 could hardly have been more stark. The 1975 trial outcome was a clear victory for Governor Rhodes and members of the Ohio National Guard, and it was a bitter defeat for the parents and wounded students. The 1979 civil trial lacked any such clarity of outcome. All 13 plaintiffs received financial awards and a statement of regret from the defendants. But none of the defendants personally had to pay any money, and the statement of regret did not explicitly contain any admission of guilt or liability.

Table 5. Students' Mean Diffuse Support Scores for the American Judicial System Before and After the 1975 Federal Civil Trial

ATTITUDE TOWARD GUARD RESPONSIBILITY	DIFFUSE JUDICIAL SUPPORT SCORES*	
	BEFORE THE DECISION	AFTER THE DECISION
Guard Responsible (N = 95)	$\bar{x} = 8.67$	$\bar{x} = 8.53$
Guard Not Responsible (N = 35)	$\bar{x} = 9.66$	$\bar{x} = 10.14$

*Diffuse support scores can range from a low of 3 to a high of 15.

Table 6. Analysis of Variance Table for Students' Diffuse Judicial Support Scores Before and After the 1975 Federal Civil Trial

SOURCE	df	MS	F	P
Between subjects				
A (Responsibility)	1	86.45	13.37	.001
Error	124	6.46		
Within subjects				
B (Time)	1	.03	.02	.891
A x B (Interaction)	1	5.13	2.53	.109
Error	124	2.01		

The unexpected, ambiguous, and controversial out-of-court settlement in January of 1979 provided another opportunity to analyze the impact of an authoritative judicial decision on attitudes of an attentive public toward a specific controversial issue, a specific court, and the American judicial system. We shall test the same hypotheses examined in connection with the 1975 trial.

We begin with the hypothesis that Kent State students' attitudes about responsibility for the shootings were not affected by the settlement:

> H_1: Students will not significantly alter their attitudes about responsibility for the shootings in response to the decision of an authoritative judicial structure.

Table 7, which contains the mean scores of students' perceptions of responsibility before and after the settlement, reveals that no noticeable differences exist in students' attitudes toward responsibility for the shootings. For all of the individuals and groups, the before and after scores are remarkably close. Analysis of variance provides statistical confirmation that none of the changes were significant, and hence we can accept Hypothesis H_1 for the 1979 federal civil trial.

Having established that students' attitudes toward responsibility for the shootings did not change significantly, we can now turn our attention to the question of whether attitudes of students toward the federal district court underwent significant changes. Cognitive consistency theory leads us to believe that such changes may have occurred for those students who were placed in a dissonant condition by the outcome of the case. Our specific hypotheses are:

> H_2: Students who are placed in a situation of cognitive dissonance following a decision of an authoritative judicial structure will significantly change their attitude toward the judicial structure. More precisely,
> H_{2a}: If dissonant students disagree with the decision, they will significantly lower their support.
> H_{2b}: If dissonant students agree with the decision, they will significantly increase their support.

Unique methodological problems arise when we try to test these hypotheses. In studying the 1975 trial, the outcome of the decision was clear in regard to responsibility for the shooting. It was therefore an easy matter to determine if students' attitudes regarding responsibility for the shootings were in agreement with the decision. The 1979 out-of-court settlement, however, was highly ambiguous in regard to the question of the defendants' responsibility. Hence, before we can look at changes in specific support, we first need to determine how students perceived the outcome of the settlement, for

Table 7. Mean Scores of Kent State Students' Perceptions of Responsibility for the May 4 Shootings Before and After the 1979 Federal Civil Trial

INDIVIDUALS AND GROUPS	MEAN RESPONSIBILITY SCORES*	
	BEFORE 1979 TRIAL	AFTER 1979 TRIAL
Non-student radicals	3.52	3.41
Radical students	3.37	3.36
Guard officers	3.27	3.26
Rhodes	3.12	3.14
Guard enlisted men	2.74	2.61
White	2.40	2.43
Nixon	2.22	2.27
K. S. U. administrators	2.15	2.19
Agnew	1.75	1.74
K. S. U. faculty	1.51	1.50
Non-radical students	1.38	1.32

*Responsibility scores can range from 4 (very responsible) to 1 (not responsible).

only then can we determine if a student's views on responsibility were in agreement or disagreement with the outcome. Specifically, we need to assess which students perceived the settlement as finding the defendants responsible for the shootings and which students viewed the outcome as not placing responsibility on the defendants. We did this by factor analyzing a number of newspaper statements about the settlement which we included in our after questionnaire. From this we were able to select two questions from which we built a scale enabling us to classify students into three groups: those who perceived the settlement as finding the Guard responsible, those who perceived it as finding the Guard not responsible, and those who were uncertain.[9]

The results of this classification procedure can be seen in Table 8, which contains the before and after mean scores on specific support[10] for each group of students. Six groups of students are represented in Table 8, based upon the students' attitude toward Guard responsibility[11] and perceptions of the outcome of the settlement. According to Hypothesis 2a, dissonant students in disagreement with the decision should lower their support for the court significantly. Two groups of students need to be examined in this context: (a) those who viewed the Guard as responsible and perceived the settlement as finding the Guard not responsible; and (2) those who viewed the Guard as not responsible but perceived the settlement as

finding the Guard responsible. The former group did lower its support quite substantially, from a mean of 4.50 before the settlement to a mean of 3.40 after the settlement. The latter group showed an increase in support, however, from a mean of 3.88 to 4.41.

Before using analysis of variance to accept or reject Hypothesis 2a, we can look at Hypothesis 2b by examining the mean scores of those groups which were in agreement with the outcome. Hypothesis 2b predicts that dissonant students who agreed with the decision will increase their support for the court. Two groups were in agreement with the outcome: (1) those students who felt the Guard was responsible and viewed the settlement as finding the Guard responsible; and (2) those who felt the Guard was not responsible and perceived the settlement in the same way. Neither of these two groups increased their support; both groups showed nearly identical, slight decreases.

Turning now to formal hypothesis testing, we see in Table 9 that the overall interaction effect was not significant.[12] We can, however, test the before and after scores for each group separately.[13] Using Fisher's least significant difference test, we find that: (1) we reject H2b for both groups; (2) we reject H2a for those students who held the Guard as not responsible and viewed the settlement as finding the Guard responsible; and (3) we accept H2a for the group that viewed the Guard as responsible but saw the settlement as finding the Guard not responsible.

Table 8. Students' Mean Specific Support Scores for the Federal District Court Before and After the 1979 Trial

ATTITUDE TOWARD GUARD RESPONSIBILITY*	PERCEPTIONS OF OUTCOME OF THE SETTLEMENT	SPECIFIC JUDICIAL SUPPORT SCORES	
		BEFORE THE SETTLEMENT	AFTER THE SETTLEMENT
Guard Responsible (N = 99)	Guard Responsible (N = 45)	$\bar{x} = 4.20$	$\bar{x} = 3.98$
	Uncertain (N = 44)	$\bar{x} = 3.93$	$\bar{x} = 3.82$
	Guard Not Responsible (N = 10)	$\bar{x} = 4.50$	$\bar{x} = 3.40$
Guard Not Responsible (N = 53)	Guard Responsible (N = 17)	$\bar{x} = 3.88$	$\bar{x} = 4.41$
	Uncertain (N = 18)	$\bar{x} = 4.18$	$\bar{x} = 3.71$
	Guard Not Responsible (N = 18)	$\bar{x} = 4.22$	$\bar{x} = 4.00$

*Specific support scores can range from a low of 2 to a high of 6.

Table 9. Analysis of Variance Table for Students' Specific Support for the Federal District Court Before and After the 1979 Civil Trial

SOURCE	df	MS	F	P
Between subjects				
A (Responsibility)	1	.512	.317	.581
B (Perceptions of Outcome)	2	.838	.519	.602
A X B (Interaction)	2	.062	.038	.963
Error	145	1.610		
Within subjects				
C (Time)	1	4.019	5.429	.020
A X C (Interaction)	1	2.545	3.437	.062
B X C (Interaction)	2	3.139	4.240	.016
A X B X C (Interaction)	2	2.176	2.939	.054
Error	145	.740		

We now shift our attention to an analysis of changes in students' attitudes toward the American judicial system. Our analysis of the 1975 trial data led us to accept the hypothesis that no significant change would occur in students' diffuse support, and hence we expect this hypothesis to be confirmed again in regard to the 1979 trial:

H_3: Students will not significantly alter their diffuse support for the American judicial system in response to the decision of an authoritative judicial structure, regardless of the outcome of the case.

An examination of mean scores in Table 10 and the analysis of variance in Table 11 leads to the clear conclusion that students' diffuse support for the American judicial system did not undergo significant change. Examining the mean diffuse support scores[14] in Table 10, we see rather small changes in the before and after scores for each of the six groups of students. Table 11 reveals that the overall interaction effect is not significant, and none of the simple main effects proved to be statistically significant.[15] Thus, we can accept Hypothesis 3 that students did not significantly alter their support for the American judicial system in the aftermath of the 1979 out-of-court settlement of the Kent State civil trial.

Table 10. Students' Mean Diffuse Judicial Support Scores for the American Judicial System Before and After the 1979 Trial

ATTITUDE TOWARD GUARD RESPONSIBILITY*	PERCEPTIONS OF OUTCOME OF THE SETTLEMENT	SPECIFIC JUDICIAL SUPPORT SCORES	
		BEFORE THE SETTLEMENT	AFTER THE SETTLEMENT
Guard Responsible (N = 99)	Guard Responsible (N = 44)	$\bar{x} = 8.95$	$\bar{x} = 9.07$
	Uncertain (N = 48)	$\bar{x} = 9.25$	$\bar{x} = 9.42$
	Guard Not Responsible (N = 10)	$\bar{x} = 9.10$	$\bar{x} = 8.70$
Guard Not Responsible (N = 53)	Guard Responsible (N = 17)	$\bar{x} = 9.29$	$\bar{x} = 9.29$
	Uncertain (N = 18)	$\bar{x} = 9.89$	$\bar{x} = 9.33$
	Guard Not Responsible (N = 14)	$\bar{x} = 10.50$	$\bar{x} = 10.64$

*Diffuse support scores can range from a low of 3 to a high of 15.

Table 11. Analysis of Variance Table for Students' Diffuse Judicial Support Scores Before and After the 1979 Trial

SOURCE	df	MS	F	P
Between subjects				
A (Responsibility)	1	30.250	4.972	.026
B (Perceptions of Outcome)	2	6.210	1.021	.364
A X B (Interaction)	2	11.752	1.932	.146
Error	145	6.083		
Within subjects				
C (Time)	1	.430	.240	.631
A X C (Interaction)	1	.130	.073	.784
B X C (Interaction)	2	.309	.173	.843
A X B X C (Interaction)	2	1.823	1.017	.365
Error	145	1.792		

CONCLUSIONS

This study has been concerned with the question of what impact judicial decisions have upon the attitudes of an attentive public. The results of the analysis of the 1975 and 1979 civil trials concerning the May 4, 1970, shootings at Kent State provide some reasonably clear answers. Kent State students' attitudes about responsibility for the shootings did not change to conform with the decisions of authoritative judicial structures. Attitude change was frequently observed, however, for those students who were placed in a dissonant situation by a decision and who disagreed with the decision; the pattern for these students was a significant lowering of support for the judicial structure issuing the decision. No significant changes were found in diffuse support attitudes toward the American judicial system. These results are thus quite different from those of a somewhat similar study concerning the school prayer cases which concluded: "Can law change deep-rooted attitudes? Of course it can. . . . Judiciously used, law can and does manipulate our deep-rooted attitudes, our personalities" (Muir, 1967: 138). The results of the present study, as well as a number of other studies on attitudes and the judicial process, suggest that Muir's conclusions give too much influence to the courts' abilities to change attitudes about social issues. At least in the short run, the courts seem to have limited influence on people's attitudes about controversial issues, and the courts risk losing support in controversial cases.

ENDNOTES

1. Social psychologists generally identify four distinctive approaches to attitude change: functional, learning, consistency, and social judgement/involvement. The cognitive consistency approach encompasses several more specific theories, including Fritz Heider's balance theory, Charles Osgood and Percy Tanenbaum's congruity theory, and Leon Festinger's cognitive dissonance theory. Despite differences among these theories, there are strong commonalities among them, and we will be focusing upon elements common to all of them. Two studies drawn upon substantially in this section are Wagner and Sherwood (1969) and Manheim (1975).

2. Students were asked to rank the 11 individuals and groups on a four-point responsibility scale ranging from very responsible to not responsible.

3. Specific support scores for the federal district court were measured by asking students both before and after the trial (1) whether the federal district court is (was) an appropriate place to decide responsibility for the shootings and (2) whether the trial will be (was) fair and unbiased. Students could answer yes, undecided, or no to each question. These questions, which loaded together in a factor analysis which we ran to test scale validity, were added together to give us a six-point scale of specific support, six being the highest score and two being the lowest score.

4. The National Guard was selected because the vast majority of the defendants were Guard officers and enlisted men. The classifications of Guard responsibility were created in the following manner. We assigned values from one through four to the rankings of not responsible to very responsible, respectively, for both the Guard officers and enlisted men. For each student, we summed their scores of responsibility for both the officers and enlisted men. Students could thus have scores ranging from two (neither group was responsible) to eight (both groups were very responsible). Students who had scores of six, seven, or eight were classified as considering the Guard responsible,

while students who had scores of five or below were classified as viewing the Guard as not responsible.

5. When interaction is present, tests of main effects (in Table 4, Responsibility and Time) are not usually of substantive interest to the researcher.

6. When a significant overall interaction effect has been found, then it is permissible to examine "simple main effects," i.e., the before and after scores of subgroups within the sample. Fisher's least significant difference test is an especially appropriate statistic allowing us to test these simple main effects. See Kirk (1968: 263-66) for a discussion of simple main effects. A good discussion of Fisher's least significant difference test can be found in Kirk (1968: 87-88) as well as in Carmer and Swanson (1973).

7. Diffuse support scores for the American judicial system were measured through the use of three questions asked both before and after the 1975 trial: (1) "Ordinarily, the average person in America will get a just trial;" (2) "Most juries do just what the judge and prosecutor tell them to do;" and (3) "Wealthy and well-known people are less likely to be convicted than someone like me." Five-point scales from strongly agree to strongly disagree were used with each statement. Students scores on each of these statements, which loaded together on a factor analysis we ran to test scale validity, were added together to give a diffuse support scale which ranged from 3 (lowest) to 15 (highest).

8. Tests of simple main effects also were not significant. Technically, however, such tests are not appropriate, for they should only be undertaken when the overall interaction is significant or when one has hypothesized *a priori* that specific simple main effects will be significant.

9. Again we selected the National Guard because all of the defendants except Rhodes in the 1978-79 trial were members of the Guard. The two questions which emerged on the "responsibility factor" were: (1) "The defendants' statement is an admission of moral responsibility and the compensation is an acknowledgment of legal liability" and (2) "Although there was no admission of guilt from the defendants, the settlement itself implies that those who acted for the state bore some responsibility for the tragedy." Students responded to each statement by indicating on a one-to-seven scale whether they agreed or disagreed with the statements. A score of one was given for strongly agree and a seven was given for strongly disagree. To determine if students believed the settlement found the defendants responsible for the shootings, we summed the two scores for each student, giving us a scale from 2 (strongly agreed that the settlement established the defendants' responsibility) to 14(strongly disagreed that the settlement established defendants' responsibility). We then divided the scale into three categories of Guard responsible, uncertain, and Guard not responsible.

10. We determined specific judicial support scores in the same manner as was done for the 1975 data.

11. Responsibility scores were determined in the same manner as was done for the 1975 data.

12. The overall interaction effect (A X B X C) was nearly significant at .056.

13. Even if the overall interaction effect is not significant, it is permissible to test simple main effects if you have hypothesized such effects *a priori*.

14. Diffuse support scores were determined in the same manner as with the 1975 data.

15. Technically, tests of simple main effects are not appropriate because we accepted our hypothesis of no significant overall interaction effect and did not hypothesize *a priori* any significant simple main effects.

REFERENCES

Best, James J. and Thomas R. Hensley, 1977 "Causes and consequences of student perceptions of responsibility for the 1970 Kent State shootings." *Heuristics* 8: 30-52.

Campbell, Donald T. and Julian C. Stanley,1963 *Experimental and Quasi-Experimental Designs for Research.* Chicago: Rand McNally.

Carmer, S.G. and M.R. Swanson, 1973 "An evaluation of ten multiple comparison procedures by Monte Carlo methods." *Journal of the American Statistical Association* 68: 66-74

Casey, Gregory, 1976 "Popular perceptions of Supreme Court rulings." *American Politics Quarterly* 4: 3-45.

Cronbach, L.J. and L. Furby, 1970 "How we should measure change – or should we?" *Psychological Bulletin* 74: 68-80

Davies, Peter, 1973 *The Truth About Kent State: A Challenge to the American Conscience.* New York: Farrar, Straus, Giroux.

Easton, David, 1965 *A Framework for Political Analysis.* Englewood Cliffs, N.J.: Prentice-Hall.

Engstrom, R. and M. Giles, 1972 "Expectations and images: A note on diffuse support for legal institutions." *Law and Society Review* 6: 631-36.

Farley, L.T. and M.G. Newkirk, 1977 "Measuring attitude change in political science courses." *Teaching Political Science* 4: 185-98.

Goldman, Sheldon and Thomas Jahnige, 1976 *The Federal Courts as a Political System.* Second edition. New York: Harper and Row.

Hensley, Thomas and Jerry M. Lewis, 1978 *Kent State and May 4th: A Social Science Perspective.* Dubuque, Iowa: Kendall/Hunt.

Hensley, Thomas and Deborah K. Sell, 1977 "A study-abroad program: An examination of impacts on student attitudes." *Teaching Politcal Science* 6:387-412.

Kirk, Roger, E., 1968 *Experimental Design: Procedures for the Behavioral Sciences.* Belmont, California: Brooks/Cole.

Lehne, Richard and John Reynolds, 1978 "The impact of judicial activism on public opinion." *American Journal of Political Science* 22:896-904.

Linn, R. J. and J.A. Slinde, 1977 "The determination of the significance of change between pre- and post-testing periods." *Review of Educational Research* 47: 121-50.

Manheim, Jarol B., 1975 *The Politics Within: A Primer in Political Attitudes and Behavior.* Englewood Cliffs, N.J.: Prentice-Hall.

Michener, James, 1971 *Kent State: What Happened and Why.* New York: Random House.

Miller, A.S. and A.W. Scheflin, 1967 "The Power of the Supreme Court in the Age of the Positive State: A Preliminary Excursus." *Duke Law Journal* (April): 273-320.

Muir, William, 1967 *Prayer in the Public Schools: Law and Attitude Change.* Chicago: University of Chicago Press.

Murphy, Walter, Joseph Tanenhaus, and Daniel Kastner, 1973 *Public Evaluations of Constitutional Courts: Alternative Explanations.* Beverly Hills, California: Sage Publications.

Rodgers, Harrell and Roger Hansen, 1974 "The rule of law and legal efficacy: Private values vs. general standards." *Western Political Quarterly* 27: 387-94.

Sarat, Austin, 1975 "Support for the legal system: An analysis of knowledge, attitudes, and behavior." *American Politics Quarterly* 3:3-24.

Wagner, Richard and John Sherwood (eds.), 1969 *The Study of Attitude Change.* Belmont, California: Wadsworth.

SECTION III

MAY 4 AND ITS IMPACT: A SOCIOLOGICAL PERSPECTIVE

Ohio National Guardsmen firing tear gas and then advancing on students who had gathered at the Victory Bell on the Commons to protest the Vietnam War and the presence of the Guard on campus. Photo by Doug Moore.

INTRODUCTION

The essays in this section provide a sociological analysis of the events of May 4 and afterward. The first essay by Jerry M. Lewis is an intensive case analysis, using Smelser's model of collective behavior, of the two and one-half hour period on May 4, 1970, leading up to and including the shootings. Lewis argues that all the conditions specified by Smelser for a hostile outburst were present that day. This essay should be compared with the study by the same author in Section IV of this volume which uses Smelser's model to examine the May 4th Coalition and "Tent City."

The next two essays should be considered as a group. Both describe the impact of the shootings and the possible effect of them on the "radicalization" of students. Raymond J. Adamek, who is a member of the Kent

State University sociology department, and Lewis look at the impact of social control violence in terms of whether it radicalized or pacified those students directly exposed to it.

The last article by Lewis uses Griswold's theory of culture to analyze the wide-spread impact of the famous photograph of Mary Vecchio screaming over the body of one of the slain students, Jeffrey Miller.

A Study of the Kent State Incident Using Smelser's Theory of Collective Behavior[1]

Jerry M. Lewis
Kent State University

This paper applies the theoretical model of collective behavior developed by Neil J. Smelser (1962) to data derived from diverse sources dealing with the events at Kent State University. In particular, it focuses on a period of 2-1/2 hours (11:00 a.m. to 1:30 p.m.) on May 4, 1970, as it looks at the events leading to and surrounding the killing of four undergraduate students and the wounding of nine other students.

Much has been written in efforts to understand this great tragedy which stimulated the first national student strike in the history of American education. Few other episodes of collective behavior have been so widely written about as this event. However, much of the work has been of a popular variety and there has been very little systematic behavioral analysis done.

This study begins with an exegesis on Smelser's model of collective behavior. This model is currently the only viable general theory of collective behavior available to sociologists. Therefore, this study provides an opportunity for integrating a large body of data on a collective behavior episode with the only detailed theory available.

Theory of Collective Behavior

This system of thought is based on a set of concepts and propositions which can be used to order all variations in collective behavior, which Smelser ((1962:8) defines "...as mobilization on the basis of a belief which redefines social action."

The basic theoretical component of the general theory is taken from economic variables. Smelser (1964:91) sees the processes of collective behavior as a value-added action. He thinks that this approach is useful as a way of ordering

determinants in a scale from general to specific. Each determinant is seen as logically—though not necessarily temporally—prior to the next. Each determinant is seen as operating within the scope established by the prior, more general determinant. Each determinant is viewed as a necessary but not a sufficient condition for the occurrence of an episode of collective behavior; taken together the necessary conditions constitute the sufficient condition for its occurrence.

The five determinants of collective behavior are labeled: structural conduciveness, structural strain,

Reprinted from *Sociological Inquiry*, 42:2 (1972) pp. 87-96 by permission of Alpha Kappa Delta International Sociology Honor Society.

growth of a generalized hostile belief, mobilization of participants for action, operation of social control.[2]

My analysis of determinants focuses on what Smelser calls a hostile outburst. In his analysis of collective behavior he seldom speaks of crowds per se but refers to such events as hostile outbursts. These phenomena are defined as "...mobilization for action under a hostile belief." Smelser (1962:226) writes that "...participants in an outburst must be bent on attacking someone considered responsible for a disturbing state of affairs." My analysis focuses on the students who directed hostility, primarily through verbal attacks, at the Guard during the 2-1/2 hour period on May 4, 1970.

Structural Conduciveness

The first necessary condition is called structural conduciveness and refers to situations generated by the social structure that provides a range of possibilities within which a hostile outburst can occur. Structural conduciveness suggests that social conditions are permissive for an occurrence of a hostile outburst. For example, race riots until the sixties have usually been between white majorities and black minorities.

Smelser feels that structural conduciveness should be analyzed in terms of three variables which he calls (a) the structure of responsibility, (b) the presence or absence of channels for expressing grievances, (c) facilitation of communication among the aggrieved. He (1962:241) argues that the variables which determine conduciveness are general and they simply "...indicate the possibility of hostile outbursts, no matter what kind of strain confronts an aggrieved group."

Structural Strain

This determinant describes conditions of strain which fall within conditions of conduciveness. The strain is particularly at the level of norms and values in the pre-crowd situation according to Quarantelli and Hundley's (1970:541) interpretations of Smelser's (1962) arguments. Strain is in itself not enough to cause an outburst. Rather, it contributes its "value" to the eventual outcome if an outburst does occur.

Growth of a Generalized Hostile Belief

In all episodes of collective behavior, beliefs prepare participants for the ensuing action. Hostile beliefs grow in a five stage value-added process of (Smelser, 1962:102) ambiguity, anxiety, assignment of responsibility to agents, a desire to punish or restrict the responsible agent, and a generalized belief in omnipotence. Further, a generalized hostile belief spreads through the action of the precipitating factors. Smelser (1962:249) writes:

> The precipitating factor for the hostile outburst channels generalized beliefs into specific fears, antagonisms, and hopes. In analyzing the events that precipitate hostile outbursts, it is more important to consider their context than to reason from their content.

In addition, the precipitating factors can have certain specific effects in supporting the general conditions of conduciveness, strain, and spread of the hostile belief. These effects (Smelser, 1962:249-252) are: (1) confirmation of existing fears and hatreds; (2) introduction of new deprivation; (3) reduction of opportunities for peaceful protest; (4) indication of "failure" and the assignment of responsibility.[3]

Mobilization of Participants for Action

In regard to this determinant Smelser (1962:253) writes,

> The final stage of the value-added process that results in a hostile outburst is the actual mobilization and organization of action. It does not occur, however, unless the other determinants—conduciveness, strain, and a belief that has crystallized and spread—are present.

The variables which provide an ordering of the mobilization process are called (a) leadership, (b) the organization of outburst, and (c) spread of the hostile outburst.

Leadership can come in the form of events, individuals, or organizations, all of which provide a model to follow the outburst action. The organization of the outburst depends on (a) the degree of pre-existing structures and (b) the actions of the social control agencies. The latter variable describes the rapidity and effectiveness of the social control agencies in countering the outburst.

The analysis of the spread of a hostile outburst falls into two categories. Smelser (1962:259) says that any hostile outburst can be looked at as having a real and derived phase. The real or initial phase results from the build-up on conditions prior to the beginning of the outburst. In the derived phase, however, the hostility may become unrelated to the conditions giving rise to the initial outburst.

The Control of Hostile Outbursts

This determinant is not like the others, but rather is a counterdeterminant. Smelser writes (1964:92) that the exercise of force can be in the form of

> counterdeterminants of a preventive sort (dealing with conduciveness and strain) and counterdeterminants which appear only when the collective episode has made its appearance.

THE EVENTS OF APRIL 30 - MAY 4, 1970[4]

The announcement by President Nixon that troops had been sent into Cambodia is a useful starting place for describing the events leading to the deaths of four Kent students. However, these five days should be placed in a larger context. Kent State had a fairly active anti-war movement. In October, 1969, 4,000 students and faculty participated in an anti-war march. In November, a large delegation of undergraduates went to the Washington, D.C. anti-war rally. The general feeling among the activists, both liberal and radical, was that the war was winding down. Students were becoming increasingly concerned about ecology and black problems.

The Nixon announcement hit with an impact. On Friday, May 1st, two rallies were held. At the first, a group of graduate students buried a copy of the Constitution which they declared had been "murdered" by the act of sending troops in to Cambodia. Later, black students held a rally to listen to black students from the Ohio State University talk about recent disturbances there. Both rallies were short and peaceful.

Later that evening trouble started with some young people gathering in the streets about 11:00 p.m. yelling anti-war chants and throwing bottles. Some people in the bars along the "strip" came out and joined them. Police arrived in riot gear and then demonstrators in the crowd of about 500 started breaking store and office windows and also throwing rocks and bottles at the police. Police moved them all back toward campus, four blocks away down the main street. There the crowd was dispersed with tear gas. Calm was restored by 2:00 a.m. There were two reasons people were on the streets. First, it was hot and the bars were overcrowded and uncomfortable. Secondly, about one hour and a half after the street actions had started, the city police shut the bars down and put a lot of angry people onto the street. One owner told me that the police over-reacted and should never have closed the bars down. While there is no question that the city police were undermanned, he felt a better tactic would have been to leave the people in the bars.

Some people awoke Saturday feeling considerable concern about the past evening's events. Rumors about Weathermen and weapons being on campus and a few threats made to downtown merchants to put up antiwar signs inflamed feelings. To my knowledge, the rumor about Weathermen was never substantiated, nor was the rumor about guns being used by students, nor were any threats against merchants carried out. The campus was calm.

About 8:00 p.m. that evening a crowd began to gather on the University Commons, a central meeting place for student political activities. Around 8:20 p.m. a crowd of 300 to 500 left the Commons and milled around the campus, moving first to dorms then to classroom buildings and finally back to the Commons. It had grown to about 1,000 to 1,200 by this time. There were never any plans for violence articulated, and it is my feeling that the majority of students just wanted to see what was going to happen. There was a carnival spirit with many couples in the crowd. When the crowd returned to the Commons, the ROTC building, an old barracks structure, became the center of attraction. Rocks were thrown at it. Someone tried to light a curtain through a broken window using paper matches. The fire didn't take. Another tried a burning piece of paper, but the curtain only smoldered. Then someone brought a rag soaked in the gas tank of a parked motorcycle. That got the wall burning. The Fire Department came. Their hoses were cut. The firemen almost put out the fire but apparently were rattled and packed up fast. The riot squad of the campus arrived in helmets and gas masks and were pelted by rocks. Tear gas was fired at the crowd. The crowd dispersed in several directions. Most returned to dorms or continued to observe, but a few individuals moved across the Commons and burned a small shed. The ROTC blaze flared again and by the time fire trucks returned, it was out of control.

The National Guard moved onto campus about 9:30 p.m. Unknown to the faculty marshals or students, they had been in Kent since 7:00 p.m. The mayor of Kent had decided to call in the National Guard because of rumors about Weathermen and guns, the threats, and the damage done on Friday night. The Guard took over the campus, often refusing freedom of movement to top university officials.

Sunday morning Governor James Rhodes arrived in Kent and met with University and local officials. He changed the Guard's orders from protecting property and lives to breaking up any assembly on campus whether it was peaceful or violent. He said every force of law and every weapon possible would be used, that no one was safe in Portage County, and added (*Akron Beacon Journal*, May 24, 1970) "I think we are up against the strongest, well-trained militant group that has ever assembled in America." Sunday evening there was a sit-in at a street intersection which was the first major confrontation between the Guard and students. It was dispersed by the Guard with no serious injuries occurring to students or Guard.

Monday students were angry, Guardsmen weary, town merchants short-tempered, and the running of the University was no longer the province of its officials.

Classes, for the most part, were held on Monday morning. Shortly before noon, a crowd began to gather on the Commons, a central meeting place for any group that wants to hold a rally.

Three separate categories of students could be identified on the Commons: *the active core, the cheerleaders, and the spectators*. I think it can be safely said that in any collective behavior situation, these three types are present. The core were those who carried out the action toward the Guard by gestures, yells, and the throwing of missiles. The cheerleaders were those students who yelled in support of the core and, on some occasions, yelled at the Guard itself. The spectators simply observed what was going on.

The core stood around the victory bell yelling at the Guard who were protecting the burned-down ROTC building. The cheerleaders and the spectators were concentrated primarily on Taylor Hill and nearby dorms which are both on the edge of the Commons.

About noon, warning was given for the crowd to disperse because they were in violation of an order which was against any form of assembly. Shortly after the warning was given, the Guard began, through the use of tear gas, to move the crowd. The students divided into several sectors. One group went to dorms near Taylor Hall; another went down onto the football practice field; and a third (the group I was with) went down into the Taylor Hall parking lot near Prentice Hall.

By any collective behavior definition, the crowd had been widely dispersed and broken up. After helping spectators who had been gassed, I stood at the edge of the parking lot and watched the skirmish between the students and soldiers on the football practice field. About 70 soldiers had followed the students to the practice football field, and the students engaged them by throwing some rocks but mostly clods of dirt. Soldiers in turn lobbed tear gas at the students. A few of the canisters were thrown back at the Guard. Most of the students gathered were just watching and yelling taunts at the Guard and support for those returning the canisters to the soldiers. The interaction between the Guard and students was almost choreographed, and one had the feeling that a sporting event was in progress.

The Guard turned and marched in formation to the top of Taylor Hall hill. When they reached the top, the firing began, resulting in the death of four students and the wounding of nine others. Five hours later, the University was closed by the University President and court injunction, and most of the students had left campus.

ANALYSIS OF MAY 4, 1970

This analysis uses the Smelser model to order the data relative to the events of May 4, 1970 at Kent State University.

1. Structural Conduciveness

What were the conditions that were generated by the social structure which were permissive for the hostile outburst?

The structure of responsibility. This variable revolves around the assigning of blame. Prior to the confrontation on Monday, students had been dealing with law enforcement figures and the Guard for three days. The Scranton Commission (1970:243) notes,

> The pattern established on Friday night was to recur throughout the weekend: there were disorderly incidents; authorities could not or did not respond in time to apprehend those responsible or to stop the incidents in their early stages; the disorder grew; the police action, when it came, involved bystanders as well as participants; and, finally, the students drew together in the conviction that they were being arbitrarily harassed.

Continuing this theme, the Commission (1970:253) reports:

> As the ROTC building burned, the pattern of the previous night was repeated — authorities arrived at the scene of an incident too late to apprehend the participants, then swept up the bystanders and the participants together in their response. Students who had nothing to do with burning the building—who were not even in the area at the time of the fire—resented being gassed and ordered about by armed men. Many students returning to the campus on Sunday after a weekend at home were first surprised at the Guard's presence, then irritated when its orders interfered with their activities. Student resentment of the Guard continued to grow during the next two days.

By Monday, the students had strong feelings that the Guard had invaded their campus turf and particularly the Commons. On Monday, the first view of troops most students had as they arrived at the Commons was the Guard formed into a skirmish line with the major concentration of troops in front of the burned ROTC building. Students felt they had a right to be on the Commons and the Guard was saying symbolically that they did not have this right.

The Scranton Report (1970:267) notes:

> Many students felt that the campus was their "turf." Unclear about the authority vested in the Guard by the governor, or indifferent to it, some also felt their constitutional right to free assembly was being infringed upon. As they saw it, they had been ordered to disperse at a time when no rocks had been thrown and no other violence had been committed. Many told interviewers later, "We weren't doing anything."

Michener (1971:327) writes:

> At 11:00 in the morning of a bright, sunny day, students began collecting on the Commons as their 9:55-10:45 classes ended. They came casually at first, then in larger numbers when some of their 11:00-11:50 classes dismissed early because the confusion on campus made it too difficult to teach. Many students wandered by, as they always did, to check on what might be happening. Another set of classes, 12:05-12:55, would soon convene, and it was traditional for students who were involved either in leaving one class or heading for another to use the Commons as their walkway. Without question, they had a right to be on the Commons. But were they entitled to be there on this day? A state of emergency had been declared by Mayor Satrom, presumably outlawing any unusual gatherings. Classes would meet, and that was about all. Yet testimony from students is overwhelming that they believed their campus to be operating as usual. On Friday a rally had been openly announced for Monday noon, and invitations to attend it had been circulated on succeeding days; in fact, announcements for this rally had been scrawled on certain blackboards and were seen by students when they reported for classes on Monday.

Along with the invasion of the turf, the Guard also represented a clear symbol of the Vietnam war on campus. Anti-war feeling had been high in the Fall, and this presence of the Guard heightened feelings already regenerated by Nixon's announcement on Cambodia. The Guard was defined by the active core, gathered around the Victory Bell and their supporting cheerleaders, as the source of the trouble. The core began interacting with the Guard through the use of symbols. One form was chanting such as:

> "One, two, three, four"
> "stop your fucking war"
> "Seig Heil, Sieg Heil"
> "Pigs off campus, Pigs off campus"
> "Strike, Strike, Strike"

The chanting, along with related gestures, continued until just before noon when the crowd around the bell was told to disperse.

The presence or absence of channels of communication. By noon Monday, students and faculty had been dealing with the Guard *per se* for about 40 hours when the order to disperse came. A jeep carrying three Guardsmen and one campus policeman drove near the active core, and the policeman gave the order in several forms. The students attempted to drown out the order and threw a few rocks at the jeep although none hit the officer or the Guardsmen.[5] The jeep withdrew and within three minutes after the order had been given to disperse, the Guard moved on the students with bayonets and tear gas.[6] The tear gas was also directed towards the cheerleaders and the spectators. Consequently, communication channels were rapidly closed after it became clear that the Guard wanted the students to leave the Commons. Since the Guard was in charge, no other channels were available. If the marshals had wanted to try to negotiate between the active core and the Guard, they would have had no opportunity to do so. It is interesting to note that after the shootings, the Guard officers allowed time for negotiations of the kind that should have gone on at this point.

Communication among the aggrieved. The Commons, about seven acres, combines natural settings with buildings to form an amphitheater in the center of Kent's campus. The Commons is a traditional gathering place for students as well as a crosswalk area for students moving between dorms and classrooms. As the students gathered, the active core formed around the bell; the cheerleaders were near them on Taylor Hill; and the spectators gathered further up the hill and on the surrounding buildings. Communication among students was facilitated by the fact that the various roles of the students were clearly delineated. Secondly, the focal point of the Guard around the ROTC building made it quite easy for the active core to direct its action toward the Guard. Thirdly, most of the students had heard about the rally and come either to protest or to observe a protest.

Summary. Smelser suggests that the conditions of conduciveness were quite general. This study finds that conditions were highly conducive for a hostile outburst. First, blame was easily assigned to the Guard because of the pattern of continuing interaction that had occurred over the past three

days. In addition, the Guard represented the resurgence of anti-war feeling that had had a long history at Kent. Secondly, because the Guard controlled the campus, they effectively shut down communication after the order to disperse had been given. Thirdly, communication was facilitated by the fact that many students came to the rally with certain expectations about the place of the rally and the potential content of the rally, expectations that had developed not only during the days immediate to May 4th, but in context of political and student traditions at Kent.

2. Structural Strain

What were the conditions of strain that were the basis for this hostile outburst?

Strain in norms and values. As has been noted above, the major source of strain was the presence of the Guard on the students' turf. Interaction between Guard and the students had occurred on the Commons on the previous Saturday, but in a context of an event, the burning of the ROTC building, that the general student body saw as an unjustified act (Taylor *et al.*, 1971:36). Monday represented a different situation. Students in the active core were gathering for a political rally to protest the Guard's presence. Other students were there to observe. They were ordered to leave (see above) but they felt they had a right to stay. Consequently there was normative strain, being told to leave from a traditional gathering place, the challenge in regard to the right of assembly.

The strain, however, was not one-sided. The Commanding General of the Guard believed that the students knew that the university had declared the rally illegal. One study (Tompkins and Anderson, 1971:43) notes that 56% of the students did know the rally was illegal. Another (Taylor, *et al.*, 1971:101) states that 67% of the students did know the rally was prohibited. When students began to gather, the Commanding General, according to Michener (1971:328) was

> astonished to see so many students proceeding as if the rally were still authorized. The crowd was growing larger every minute. He saw about 600 students massing not far from his troops and became justifiably concerned. Giving a clear order, he commanded that the students be dispersed. This order was given before any rocks had been thrown.

The Guard officer saw this as a direct challenge to authority. Consequently, a clear situation of value strain was present.

Summary. There was strain present on both sides. The fact that the Guard and the students presented themselves to each other in symbolic modes indicates that there was considerable need to reconstitute the social environment.

3. Growth and Spread of a Generalized Hostile Belief

Were there variables present that combined to generate hostile beliefs? What place did the precipitating factors have in spreading hostile beliefs?

Ambiguity. This condition was present on May 4th. Students were confused as to the legal status of the rally (see above). That is, whether the rally was prohibited or not, and if it was prohibited, by whom—the university or the National Guard? Even after the order to disperse had been clearly given, the situation remained ambiguous. Many students felt that the officer who gave the request to leave was asking, not ordering, and consequently this increased the confusion.[7]

Anxiety. This analyst did not discover anxiety as generated by ambiguity. As the crowd formed on the Commons there were internal feelings of anger among some students and feelings of curiosity among many students. The Scranton Report (1970:265) indicates:

> Shortly before noon, students began to ring the Victory Bell. Two generalized emotions seem to have prevailed among the 2,000 or so young persons who were now on or near the Commons. One was a vague feeling that something worth watching or participating in would occur, that something was going to happen and the Guard would respond. The other was antipathy to the Guard, bitter in some cases, accompanied by the feeling that the Guard, although fully backed by official pronouncements, was somehow "trespassing" on the students' own territory.

The third condition Smelser postulates is the assigning of responsibility to the agent that is the cause of the more general and diffuse feelings of ambiguity and anxiety. The students clearly assigned responsibility to the Guard rather than the university administration. However, it was not because of general feelings of ambiguity and anxiety but rather

feelings of hostility towards the presence of the Guard on the Commons. It is quite possible that those students who had feelings of anxiety did not go to the rally. Seventy-eight percent of the students knew about the rally (Taylor, *et al.*, 1971:100). Therefore, it is quite plausible that many students made a decision not to go. Further, the decision could well have been made because of feelings of anxiety.[8]

The fourth and fifth variables under this rubric can analytically be combined in this analysis. The active core felt a strong desire to punish (fourth variable) the Guard. As the interaction progressed the students felt an exaggerated sense of omnipotence (fifth variable) in terms of their power to drive the Guard from the Commons. In regard to the fourth variable, Taylor *et al.* (1971:101) write that 57% of the students felt the purpose of the rally was to protest the presence of the Guard on campus. This figure is based on a general sample of Kent's students and would probably be much higher for those who actually attended the rally.

On the fifth variable, the feelings of power began to develop as the interaction between the Guard and the students progressed. The statements that followed describe the feelings of some students, and captures the general mood.

About five to ten minutes before the shootings, the Guard drove a group of students on to the practice football field.

> Student #1 (Eszterhaus and Roberts, 1970:157)—"The students began to realize that the National Guard had maneuvered themselves into a partially enclosed area and were, in a sense, encircled."
> Student #2 (Eszterhaus and Roberts, 1970:157)—"They couldn't pursue and they couldn't contain. The students started gaining the upper hand for the first time, and they knew it."

When the Guard realized they were trapped, at least 16 Guardsmen knelt and formed a skirmish line and pointed their M-1 rifles at students in the parking lot (Michener, 1971:338). Students began to yell (Ezsterhaus and Roberts, 1970:159) "Shoot, Shoot, Shoot."

> Student #1 (Ezsterhaus and Roberts, 1970:159)—"Those Guardsmen who had not assumed the kneeling position seemed to be milling around in no particular formation and

began to take a few steps towards Taylor Hall. Some interpreted it as a withdrawal."

As the withdrawal began:

> Student #3 (Eszterhaus and Roberts, 1970:159)—"They walked at a pretty fast pace. Then they started running. *Everybody started screaming because it was like we'd won.*"

Ignorance also facilitated these feelings of bravado. The students knew that the Guardsmen had unsheathed bayonets and were willing to use them as they had on the two previous evenings. However, the vast majority were unaware that the M-1's were loaded. Taylor *et al.* (1971:109) report that 27% of the total sample knew the Guard had live ammunition and that 10% said the Guard would fire at students. When they analyzed their data in terms of the patterns of participation, as reflected in Table 1, a striking finding is evident. The participants more than any other group thought they were safe. These members of the active core knew they could be gassed and bayoneted, but they clearly thought they were safe from lethal fire. Consequently, they felt they could express themselves in a manner appropriate to the force being used against them.[10]

Precipitating factors. There were two precipitating factors which contributed to the growth and spread of the hostile belief. First, the call for the rally on Monday that was first put out at the Friday rallies. Secondly, the action of the Guard in making a stand in front of the burned ROTC building. Smelser (1962:249) says that the principal function of the precipitating factor is to make specific the hostile belief. This happened when the students came to the Commons. The desire to either participate in or observe a rally combined with the presentation of the Guard focused the two hostile beliefs which set the stage for action. The two precipitating factors all had the effects noted above. The call for the rally brought the students to the Commons. The stance of the Guard focused matters to a point of confrontation. Consequently, existing fears were confirmed; new deprivation was introduced; peaceful protest opportunities were reduced; and assignment of blame was made by the students and the Guard to each other.

Summary. This analysis suggests that four of the five variables that make up the generation of hostile beliefs combined on Monday May 4th to create deep and widespread hostility toward the Guard. This, coupled with two clear precipitating factors, brought the Guard and the students into a confrontation.

4. Mobilization for Action

What variables were present that shaped the mobilization of the students to carry out a hostile outburst against the Guard?

Leadership. This variable refers to the degree of formal organization present in the outburst. Whether there were leaders present on May 4th is a source of considerable dispute.

The Scranton Report makes no mention of leadership either from individuals or groups. Michener suggests there may have been some planning in terms of the continual ringing of the bell but does not prove it. My own observations indicated no formal leadership from either groups or individuals. However, Smelser (1962:254) suggests that "events" can serve as models of leadership. The chanting of the active core, while based on neither a formal group or individual leader, served to channel the verbal action of the entire body of students toward the Guard. In addition, the Guard provided leadership when they announced to the core that the rally was illegal.[11]

Table 1. Did you think that the National Guard would fire on students?

	ALL STUDENTS	PARTICIPANTS	OBSERVERS	NONATTENDERS
(a) yes	10%	0.9%	6%	14%
(b) no	74%	94%	81%	64%
(c) uncertain	16%	5%	13%	22%
N* =	6,921	541	2,156	3,666

*The subtotals do not equal the total N because the authors exclude two categories of responses from their analysis – those who checked the "counter-demonstrate" or the "other" responses for going to the rally. (Taylor *et al.*, 1971: 109)

Organization of the hostile outburst. This variable depends on preexisting crowd structure, ecological factors, and the manner in which social control agencies contain the demonstration.

The analysis of the pre-existing crowd structure combines naturally with ecological factors in this case. The Commons represented a natural gathering area because of its tradition as a political arena. Further, it is easy to get to and from dormitories and classrooms. The presence of students moving back and forth across the Commons on a day that classes were normally being held created a fairly organized pre-crowd structure in a clearly defined ecological space. The discussion of social control is deferred until the next section following Smelser's procedure of analysis.

The shape of the hostility divided into the two phases that Smelser described. In the initial phase, students confronted the Guard as they protected the burned ROTC building. During this phase, no attempt was made to move on the Guard by the students. The active core maintained at least a 100 yard distance from the Guard for slightly over a half hour. The expressing of hostility came primarily in the form of very strong language and gestures.

The derived phase began when the Guard chased the students on to the practice football field. The interaction moved from a conversation of gestures to a mode of a sporting event. The Scranton Report (1970:267) noted:

> Tear gas canisters were still flying back and forth; after the Guard would shoot a canister, students sometimes would pick it up and lob it back at the Guardsmen. In some cases, guardsmen would pick up the same canister and throw it at the students. Some among the crowd came to regard the situation as a game–"a tennis match" one called it–and cheered each exchange of tear gas canisters.

Summary. This analysis shows that all the variables that contribute to mobilizing participants to action were present on May 4th.

5. The Control of Hostile Outbursts

What was the effect of the social control agent as a counter-determinant after the hostile outburst had begun? The fundamental question in looking at social control deals with the manner in which force is applied at the scene of the outburst. Smelser (1962:267) after examining the literature on riot control, suggests four principles for the control of hostile outbursts. Using these principles is helpful in understanding, in part, why the Guard directed its hostility towards students.

The first principle is the prevention of communication so beliefs cannot be disseminated. The Guard, until it fired, never acted in a manner that would have interrupted the communication among the various groups of students on the Commons. The Guard kept themselves as the focal point, and students kept dividing into the active core, the cheerleaders, and the spectators.

Secondly, social control forces should prevent interaction between leaders and followers. This is, in this case, an extension of the first point. While there were no leaders *per se*, many journalists, lawyers, and scholars have questioned why the Guard did not move in and arrest (they had the power) those members of the active core who remained around the bell after the gassing began.

Thirdly, social forces should never bluff force. As noted earlier, this happened when the Guard knelt during the derived phase of the interaction when both the Guard and students "played" the game of throwing tear gas. One writer (Davies, 1971:107) has proposed a theory that elements of the Guard may have developed a plan to fire at the students at this point. While this story has not been proven, there is no question that some soldiers were operating outside the chain of command at this point. This bluffing action may have been taken because of the hostility felt by these men toward students.

Fourthly, Smelser suggests that the social control forces should avoid entering into controversies with the crowd. However, in the Kent case it would have been impossible for the Guard to avoid entering into the conflict. The Guard was the source of the problem. The fact that their actions kept them at the focal point of attention maintained a high level of hostility on both sides throughout the period of interaction.

Summary. The Guard ineffectively applied force throughout the period leading to the shootings. In almost all their actions, rather than serving as a counterdeterminant, they acted as precipitating factors in keeping the hostility at a level equal to and higher than before the outburst began.

One additional comment seems in order. Throughout the study I concentrated primarily on the students' action as a hostile outburst. The question of viewing the Guards' behavior as a hostile outburst could be legitimately raised. The reason I did not do this is that there is simply not very much information available on the Guard. Only two Guardsmen (both general officers) testified before the Scranton Commission. Further, until the Davies Report (1971) was issued, only the FBI and the Guard reports contained the names of the Guardsmen who had fired their weapons. Neither of these reports was available to the general public. Therefore, given the paucity of attitudinal and demographic data available to me, I felt the Guardsmen's actions could best be understood as social control behavior placed in a more general analysis of the students' actions.

EVALUATION OF SMELSER'S THEORY

It seems appropriate to conclude with an evaluation of Smelser's ideas. This study has taken Smelser's general theory of collective behavior and applied it to the data dealing with the killings at Kent State University on May 4th, 1970. In general, the analysis found all the conditions were present which the theory specifies as being necessary for the development of a hostile outburst. The theory was found to be extremely useful in organizing the large body of information that has been generated by the Kent State episode.

The reactions of other writers in dealing with Smelser's theoretical work has been mixed. Quarantelli and Hundley (1969:552) note that Smelser's work represents an effort "far beyond any previous scholar [in that] he had advanced a set of propositions that are at least partly testable." They conclude, however, that their data on a student protest in Columbus, Ohio do not support the argument that the understanding of a hostile outburst requires "...the postulation of a generalized belief and the mobilization-for-action condition" (Quarantelli and Hundley, 1969:550).[12]

Milgram and Toch (1969:562) suggest that the major value of Smelser's theory is its ability to organize a large body of data but they question its predictive value. It may be that Smelser's ideas are only applicable to large sets of data about events related to an episode of collective behavior—a situation that does not seem to be present in other studies (Quarantelli and Hundley, 1969; Milgram and Toch, 1969) that used his theory.

Couch (1968:310) has noted that collective behavior discussions are often formed in deviant behavior perspectives. He (Couch, 1968:322) argues that a social systems approach is a more fruitful way of looking at crowds and serves to challenge the stereotype that crowd behavior is pathological and bizarre. I was persuaded by this argument and felt along with Couch (1968:310) that Smelser's work represented the only general theory of collective behavior that addressed itself to social system questions.

There was only one key aspect of the events that could not be handled by the model and that was the role of internal social control as illustrated by the activities of the faculty and student marshals.

Smelser sees social control agents as external to the participants in the outburst. He (1962:262) writes,

> Why is it, then, that those agencies who control the ultimate deterrent to hostile expression and which are in principle stronger than the perpetrators of any outburst, sometimes do not prevent hostile outbursts?
>
> We shall examine the question on two levels—first, the behavior of the *authorities* who are responsible for deciding to control the outburst, and second, the behavior of those who *implement* these decisions on the spot, i.e., the police, military, etc.

At Kent, faculty and student marshals played a very complex role in the drama. In particular, a few faculty marshals were responsible for both getting students to clear the Commons after the shootings and preventing the Guard from charging the students before they cleared the area (Michener, 1971:399-408; Scranton Report, 1970:278-279). It may be that the same questions that govern the understanding of social control agents (above) are also pertinent to internal social control agents. Future theoretical work by Smelser and others needs to address itself to the problem of marshals and their place in the social control of hostile outbursts on college campuses. This is true, as well, for other third party conflict resolution activities such as youth patrols (Knopf, 1969; Marx and Archer, 1971) in the black community.

REFERENCES

Brown R. 1965. *Social Psychology*. New York: The Free Press

Couch, C. 1968. "Collective behavior: An examination of some stereotypes," *Social Problems*, 15:3 (Winter): 310-322.

Davies, P. 1971. *Kent State: An appeal for justice.* (Mimeographed.)

Eszterhaus, J. and M.D. Roberts. 1970. *13 Seconds: Confrontation at Kent State.* New York: Dodd, Mead.

_____, 1970. *The Report of the President's Commission on Campus Unrest.* Washington D.C.: U.S. Government Printing Office.

Knopf, T. 1969. *Youth Patrols: An Experiment in Community Participation.* Waltham, Mass.: (Lemberg Center for the Study of Violence, Brandeis University.)

Lukas, J.A. 1970. "Study says killing of four at Kent State, not Cambodia, set of national student strike," *The New York Times* (June 24, 1970). New York Times Publishing Company.

Marx, Gary T. and D. Archer, 1971. "Citizen involvement in the law enforcement process." *American Behavioral Scientist*, 15 (Sept.-Oct.):52-72.

Michener, J. 1971. *Kent State: What Happened and Why.* New York: Random House and Reader's Digest Press Book.

Milgram, Stanley and Hans Toch. 1969. "Collective behavior: Crowds and social movements." Pp. 507-610, G. Lindzey and E. Aronson (eds.), *The Handbook of Social Psychology.* Reading, Massachusetts: Addison-Wesley.

Quarantelli, E.L. and J.R. Hundley, Jr., 1969. "A test of some propositions about crowd formation and behavior." Pp. 538-554 in Robert R. Evans (ed.), *Readings in Collective Behavior.* Chicago: Rand McNally.

Smelser, N. 1962. Theory of Collective Behavior. New York: The Free Press.

_____. 1964. "Theoretical issues of scope and problems." Pp. 89-104 in Robert R. Evans (ed.), *Readings in Collective Behavior.* Chicago: Rand McNally, 1969.

Taylor, S., R. Shuntich, P. McGovern and R. Genthner. 1971. *Violence at Kent State: The Student's Perspective.* New York: College Notes and Texts.

Tompkins, P.K. and E. Vanden Bout Andersen. 1971. *Communications Crisis at Kent State.* New York: Gorden and Breach.

ENDNOTES

1. This study was supported by a National Institute of Mental Health Grant, R01 MH17421- 02SP. I am indebted to A. Paul Hare of Haverford College and my colleague Elliott Rudwick both of whom have encouraged me in this effort. In addition, my colleagues Ray Adamek, Denny Benson, Diane Lewis, Tom Lough, Richard O'Toole and Eugene Wenninger made many helpful comments.

2. Originally Smelser listed six determinants. However, he (1964:92) revised his formulation to make the precipitating events a sub-category of the growth of a generalized belief.

3. I omitted the last two effects from Smelser's list because they are illustrations of types of precipitating factors rather than illustrations of the effects of the factors.

4. I was present for most of the campus events described in the paper and was on the Commons as a faculty peace marshal on Monday, May 4th. When the Guard fired I was in the parking lot where several students were killed or wounded. This narrative is based on my experiences and the narrative in *The Report of the President's Commission on Campus Unrest* (Scranton Report).

5. I was present at this time and saw no rocks hit any of the four passengers. Michener (1971:329) also comes to this conclusion.

6. An earlier order had been given at 11:49 a.m. but this had not been heard by the students as it was given some distance from where the active core was stationed.

7. I interpreted the order as a request not a demand mainly because the order, while quite clearly given, was presented in several forms, including the request "to go home to your dorms." Michener (1971:329) also notes the confusion.

8. I am grateful to Professor Adamek for this suggestion.

9. Photographic evidence indicates the Guard did not run. The emphasis is mine.

10. It should be noted that there is a possibility of distortion due to *ex post facto* self-justification on the part of the students.

11. I am indebted to Professors Adamek and O'Toole for these insights.

12. While Quarantelli and Hundley's work does not completely support Smelser, their effort represents a major contribution in that they developed the first useful paradigm for applying Smelser's rather complex theoretical scheme to hard data.

SOCIAL CONTROL VIOLENCE AND RADICALIZATION: THE KENT STATE CASE

Raymond J. Adamek
Jerry M. Lewis
Kent State University

ABSTRACT

This study explores two popular hypotheses as to the effects of the employment of excessive social control force on student demonstrators. One hypothesis suggests that experiencing social control violence will tend to radicalize students, while the other suggests that it will pacify them. A questionnaire survey of the entire student body and interviews with 233 Kent State University undergraduates measuring their attitudes towards violence, and the impact of the May 4, 1970 killings on their political outlooks, indicate that radicalization is positively associated with the experience of social control violence.

Since the early 1960's, protests and demonstrations have become a more and more common occurrence in American life. Starting with civil rights demonstrations in the South, these tactics have most recently been employed on college campuses to espouse a variety of causes. Fully one-third of the colleges and universities in the United States were the scene of demonstrations following the Cambodian incursion and the Kent State killings in May of 1970 (Braungart and Braungart, 1971). Moreover, a recent survey by the American Council on Education suggests that the freshmen of the 1971-72 academic year are "more prone to dissent than their predecessors" (Jacobsen, 1972). Reactions to the escalation of the war in April and May of 1972 indicate that the antiwar movement is not dead, as some have suggested, although it does seem to have diminished in scope.

Student activism has become the object of increasing concern and research by various educators and social scientists. To date, most of the research has focused on the differential socioeconomic, academic, psychological, and family characteristics of "activists" and "nonactivists" (see, for example, the works reviewed in Braungart, 1971; Foster and Long, 1970; Horn and Knott, 1971), or on the differential characteristics of educational institutions which were or were not the locales for student demonstrations (Astin, 1970; Blau and Slaughter, 1971; Kahn and Bowers, 1970; Peterson, 1966,

This is an explanded and revised version of a paper presented at the annual meeting of the American Sociological Association, New Orleans, August 1972. The authors wish to thank Stuart Taylor *et al.* for permission to use their data.

Reprinted from *Social Forces*, 51:3 (March 1973) pp. 342-347 by permission of the University of North Carolina Press and the Southern Sociological Society.

1968; Sasajima et al., 1968; Scott and El-Assal, 1969). Aron (1971; 1972) has investigated various components of student political ideology, and their relationship to different types of activism. Relatively little research, however, has focused on the effects which the actions of social control agents (police, National Guardsmen, et al.) have on student demonstrators and others, particularly where such control has involved the use of excessive force.[1] This research hiatus exists in spite of the fact that various activist groups have advocated confrontation as a political technique to provoke social control agents to violence in order to radicalize both those involved in the confrontation and the general population.

There appear to be two hypotheses regarding the use of social control violence. One might be termed the "radicalization" hypothesis and suggests that when severe force is used against demonstrators they will become radicalized in their attitudes and behavior. That is, their political orientation will generally move to the left, they will increasingly come to question the legitimacy of existing governmental institutions and processes, and they will be more accepting of the use of violence as a political technique to achieve change. The second hypothesis might be termed the "pacification" hypothesis and suggests that the use of severe force by social control agents is effective in stopping demonstrations, demoralizing demonstrators, and deterring further expressions of dissent. While no major studies have focused on these hypotheses as their central concern, a few have touched on them.

In his study of the "Columbia Crisis" in the spring of 1968, Barton (1968) found that the use of excessive police force against demonstrators had the effect of increasing the sympathy of faculty and students for the tactics (a sit-in and general strike) employed by the demonstrators. The police action had less of an effect on faculty and students' attitudes regarding the six demands of the demonstrators, although here too the slight change noted was favorable to the dissidents. Kornberg and Brehm (1971) report a similar increase in the sympathy of students (but not faculty) for demonstrators' tactics (sit-in) after police violence at Duke University. They also report greater sympathy for the demonstrators' demands after the police action. Finally, Wysong and Walum (1971), in the only longitudinal study of those mentioned, report police violence in the Spring 1970 disruptions at Ohio State University had the effect of

intensifying and sustaining the protect activism of those predisposed to such activism (predisposition measured by attitude toward draft evasion) and of increasing the protest activism of those not predisposed to such activism.

In contrast to these studies, which measured attitudes shortly after the incidents in question, the present article, focusing on the two hypotheses mentioned above, takes as its central concern the long-range impact of social control violence on demonstrators' attitudes. In particular, it attempts to determine whether the violence used by National Guardsmen at Kent State University in May 1970, resulting in the deaths of four students and the wounding of nine others, had a generally radicalizing or pacifying effect on student opinions.[2]

THE STUDY

As a part of a larger study on student culture and ideology being conducted at several universities, we interviewed Kent State University undergraduates in April and May of 1971, one year after the shootings.[3] A probability sample was drawn from the 1970-71 student directory. The data reported below are based upon the response of 233 undergraduates, a 70 percent response rate. Data provided by the University Registrar on three variables, sex, academic class, and college, indicated a fair degree of correspondence between the sample distribution and the undergraduate student body. The major differences (all 10 percent or less) were the underrepresentation of males and of students enrolled in the College of Education, and the overrepresentation of students enrolled in the College of Fine and Professional Arts. Interviews were conducted by junior and senior undergraduates enrolled in two sociology courses, and by a sociology graduate assistant.

ANALYSIS AND FINDINGS

To evaluate the hypotheses discussed above, we first turn to a survey completed by colleagues in the Psychology Department at Kent State six weeks after the killings. Stuart Taylor et al. (1971) found that participating in the May 4 rally made Kent's students "much more violence oriented" and "more likely to participate in demonstrations" (see Tables 1

Table 1. Response of Kent Students to the Question: "Have the KSU events made you more or less violence oriented than you were before the events?" by Degree of Participation at May 4 Rally (in percent)*

RESPONSES	PARTICIPANTS	OBSERVERS	NON-ATTENDERS
Much more	27	8	6
Somewhat more	34	26	15
No change	20	36	48
Somewhat less	9	10	9
Much less	10	20	22
(N)	(109)	(433)	(887)

Gamma = .23

*Adapted and recalculated from Taylor et al. (1971:153). These data are based on a random subsample drawn by those authors from over 7,000 respondents.

Table 2. Response of Kent Students to the Question: "Because of the KSU events would you be more or less likely to participate in demonstrations?" by Degree of Participation at May 4 Rally (in percent)*

RESPONSES	PARTICIPANTS	OBSERVERS	NON-ATTENDERS
More likely	81	43	25
No change	15	34	38
Less likely	4	23	37
(N)	(109)	(433)	(894)

Gamma = .45

*Adapted and recalculated from Taylor et al. (1971:153).

and 2). These data clearly favor the radicalization hypothesis for participants, and also to a lesser extent, for those students who said they were only observers at the rally. A pacification effect was more characteristic of the nonattenders, the end result appearing to be a greater polarization of the student body. One might expect the radicalization of the demonstrators to be short-lived, the result of the shock of an incident involving extreme social control violence. Our own data, gathered one year after the incident, bear on this question.

In attempting to isolate the impact of the use of social control violence on demonstrators' attitudes, we will present two sets of comparisons. The first involves a contrast of the attitudes of 64 students who reported that they had "engaged in protest or demonstration which involved direct confrontation with police, National Guard, or some such authority, and which spilled over into violence," with the opinions of 169 others who indicated they had not engaged in such a confrontation. Interview data

indicated that most of the 64 students were referring to confrontation with the Guard during May 2-4, 1970.[4] However, to ensure that we were aware of the degree of social control violence employed, and to get at the salience of the shooting incident itself, we made a second comparison.

From the 64 students who indicated they had engaged in violent confrontation with authorities, out data allowed us to isolate 30 who were definitely referring to the May 4 rally.[5] We contrasted their replies to several opinion items with those of 30 other students who had not participated in any confrontation with authorities involving violence. The latter were matched on an individual basis with the May 4 participants on the following variables: sex, college major, father's political views, mother's political views, Hollingshead's (1957) two factor social class index, religion, and college grade point average.[6] Because of the small pool from which we had to draw (n = 169), with the exception of sex, the matching could not be exact across all levels of each variable. However, chi-square tests indicated no significant differences between the two groups on matched variables with the exception of grade point average. Whereas 20 percent of the participants had GPAs of 3.0 or above, 43 percent of the controls fell in this category (p<.01). In addition to the above variables, the 30 May 4 participants proved not to differ significantly from their controls on the following: race, age, size of hometown, home state, academic class, father's and mother's educational levels, father's and mother's disciplinary style, and father's occupation. They did differ significantly (p<.05) in their political views. Sixty-nine percent of the May 4 participants classified themselves as radicals, radical-liberals, or liberals, compared to 28 percent of their matched controls. The May 4 participants were also significantly (p<.01) more likely to have engaged in various protest activities such as attending protest rallies and meetings, marching or picketing on behalf of a cause, engaging in civil disobedience, and participating in nonviolent confrontation with authorities. Finally, while about three-fifths of both groups' mothers were housewives, the controls' working mothers were concentrated in professional, technical and higher white-collar occupations, while the participants' mothers were concentrated in clerical and sales jobs (p< .05).

The 64 students who had participated in violent confrontation with authorities were also fairly similar to the 169 students who had not participated in such confrontations. Of the 21 variables mentioned above, the two groups differed significantly on 8, however, including their own political views, sex, age, academic class, religion, grade point average, and protest activity. Compared to the other students, the 64 participants were more likely to be more liberal in their political views, to have mothers who were more liberal, to be males, to be 19-22 rather than older or younger, to be upperclassmen rather than freshmen, to be Jewish, to have grade point averages between C and B rather than higher or lower, and to have engaged in various protest activities.

The items on which we contrasted the above groups were categorized into four constellations of attitudes towards violence. One constellation concerns the attitudes of students toward general categories of violence users. A second constellation concerns attitudes towards specific events involving violence. The third constellation concerns attitudes

towards various strategies to achieve political change, including violence. The fourth constellation concerns attitudes toward specific techniques of social protest — some violent, others not. Our findings are presented in summary form in Chart 1.

Like the Taylor *et al.* (1971) data, these findings tend to support the radicalization hypothesis. Within each attitude constellation, those students who have been subjected to social control violence are more likely to hold favorable opinions toward violence and its employment as a means of social protest to achieve change. Indeed, the relationships appear strongest where the most drastic tactics are suggested. This is true even of the May 4 participants and their controls, who are quite like one another except for their experience with social control violence. Conversely, there is little support here for the hypothesis that social control violence generally demoralizes demonstrators or pacifies them.

Thus far, our data have merely shown a relationship between participation in violent confrontation with agents of social control and attitudes favorable toward violence. They have not demonstrated radicalization on a before-after causal basis, although Taylor *et al.* (1971) data strongly imply such a relationship (see Tables 1 and 2). To approach such a design, we compared the responses of the 30 May 4 participants and their matched controls to some open-ended items which allowed us to classify them as: (1) having changed their political outlook as a result of the May 4 incident; (2) having their previous outlook strengthened by the May 4 incident; or (3) not having their political outlook affected by the May 4 incident. The results are presented in Table 3.

These data indicate that the political outlooks of two-thirds of the participants were either changed or strengthened as a result of the May 4 incident. Seventeen of these 20 students indicated that they had "moved to the left," become "more liberal," "more anti-government," or less accepting of existing governmental institutions and processes. The direction of change of the political outlooks of 3 of these students could not be definitely determined from their responses. One-third of the nonparticipant controls also indicated that their political outlooks were affected by the event. Six of these 10 respondents indicated they had become more liberal, 1 indicated he had become more conservative, and again the responses of 3 others did not permit specification of the direction of change. Thus, of the 30 students (participants and controls) who indicated that the May 4 confrontation had some effect on them, at least 77 percent were radicalized in the sense in which we have used this term.7 In

Chart 1. If a Kent State Student Has Participated in a Confrontation Where Social Control Violence Occurred He Is More Likely To:

	64 PARTICIPANTS VS. 169 NON-PARTICIPANTS (GAMMA)	30 MAY 4 PARTICIPANTS VS. CONTROLS (GAMMA)
Constellation I: Attitudes Toward Violence Users		
1. approve of the activities of radical or revolutionary students.	.63*	.57
2. have sympathy for urban rioters.	.52	.51
Constellation II: Attitudes Toward Specific Events		
3. be sympathetic with the bombings at Oakland and the University of Wisconsin.	.53	.59
4. believe that police raids on the Black Panthers constitute political repression.	.51	.52
Constellation III: Attitudes Toward Political Strategies		
5. not advocate participation in political parties to sponsor candidates to bring about change.	.56	.51
6. advocate planning and working for a revolution to change the entire system.	.53	.26†
7. approve of the use of violence to bring about change in society.	.50	.55
8. believe real progress comes only when a mass of aroused people defy authority and demand immediate change.	.42	.39
9. believe that if a man's beliefs are in conflict with the law, he is justified in defying that law to get it changed.	.37	.19‡
Constellation IV: Attitudes Toward Protest Techniques		
10. condone destruction of university property.	.80	.80
11. condone the seizure of private or secret files.	.77	.73
12. feel sympathetic towards the destruction of draft board files.	.59	.69
13. condone strikes.		
14. advocate direct confrontation with violence to get desired changes.	.57	.77
15. condone boycotts.		
16. condone sit-ins in classroom facilities.	.51	.29
17. advocate nonviolent demonstrations and resistance to precipitate faster changes.	.38	.53
18. not advocate educating voters to vote for desired changes.	.39	.33
19. condone sit-ins in administration building.	.32	.24

*Gammas indicate the strength of the relationships between the degree of social control violence respondents experienced and their expressed attitudes. Gammas are significant at p < .001 unless otherwise noted.
†p<.01
‡p<.02

Table 3. Self-reported Impact of May 4 Confrontation on the Political Outlook of Rally Participants and Matched Controls

MAY 4 CONFRONTATION WITH GUARD WAS:	PARTICIPANTS		CONTROLS	
	N	%	N	%
Significant in changing political outlook	9	30	3	10
Significant in strengthening outlook	11	37	7	23
Not mentioned as affecting outlook	10	33	20	67
Total	30	100	30	100

$\chi^2 = 7.2$; df = 2; p<.05.

summary, these data again run counter to the hypothesis that social control violence is likely to demoralize or pacify demonstrators. Rather, such violence appears to radicalize those who are confronted by it.

DISCUSSION

In evaluating our study, two things should be kept in mind. First, the research design was not experimental, since no "before" measures of attitudes were obtained. Rather, we relied primarily upon self-reported changes in attitude to assess the impact of social control violence. Furthermore, the Taylor *et al.* (1971:107) data, gathered closest to the event, suggest that self- selection was an important factor in determining who participated in the May 4 confrontation. While self-identified "radicals" made up 4 percent of all students, they constituted 28 percent of the rally participants. Corresponding figures for self-identified "liberals" were 39 percent and 64 percent, respectively. Our own data on the 30 participants and their controls, gathered one year after the incident, also suggest that participants were more radical prior to the event.

Recognizing the weaknesses in the research design, and the fact that many of the May 4 participants were predisposed to (further) radicalization, we would still hold that the major conclusion to be drawn from our data is that the extreme social control force applied by the National Guard radicalized the students most directly involved. Our data do not support the pacification hypothesis.

REFERENCES

Aron, W.S. 1971. "Ideology and Behavior as Components of Radicalism." Paper presented at the annual meeting of the American Sociological Association, Denver.

_____. 1972. "Political Radicalism: Ideology and Behavior Among Students at the University of Chicago." Unpublished Ph.D. dissertation abstract, University of Chicago.

Astin, A. 1970. "Determinants of Student Activism." In Julian Foster and Durward Long (eds.), *Protest! Student Activism in America.* New York: Morrow.

Barton, A.H. 1968. "The Columbia Crisis: Campus, Vietnam, and the Ghetto." *Public Opinion Quarterly* 32 (Fall): 333-351.

Blau, P.M., and E.L. Slaughter. 1971. "Institutional Conditions and Student Demonstrations." *Social Problems* 18 (Spring): 475-487.

Braungart, R.G. 1971. "Family Status, Socialization, and Student Politics: A Multivariate Analysis." *American Journal of Sociology* 77 (July): 108-130.

Braungart, R.G., and M.M. Braungart, 1971. "Administration, Faculty, and Student Reactions to Campus Unrest." Paper presented at the annual meeting of the American Sociological Association, Denver.

Foster, Julian, and Durward Long (eds.) 1970. *Protest! Student Activism in America.* New York. Morrow.

Hayden, Tom. 1967. *Rebellion in Newark: Official Violence and Ghetto Response.* New York: Random House.

Hollingshead, August. 1957. *Two Factor Index of Social Position.* New Haven: Yale (mimeo).

Horn, J.L. and P.D. Knott. 1971. "Activist Youth of the 1960's: Summary and Prognosis." *Science* 171 (March):977-985.

Jacobsen, R.L. 1972. "Freshmen Reported More Protest Prone Than Predecessors." *The Chronicle of Higher Education* 6(January 10):4.

Kahn, R.M. and W.J. Bowers. 1970. "The Social Context of the Rank-and-File Student Activist." *Sociology of Education* 43 (Winter): 38-55.

Kornberg, A., and M.L. Brehm. 1971. "Ideology, Institutional Identification and Campus Activism." *Social Forces* 49(March):445-459.

Lewis, J.M. 1972. "A Study of the Kent State Incident Using Smelser's Theory of Collective Behavior." *Sociological Inquiry* 42(Spring):87-96.

Peterson, Richard E. 1966. *The Scope of Organized Student Protest in 1964-65*. Princeton: Educational Testing Service.

_____. 1968. *The Scope of Organized Student Protest in 1967-68*. Princeton: Educational Testing Service.

Raine, W.J. 1970. "The Perception of Police Brutality in South Central Los Angeles." In Nathan E. Cohen (ed.), *The Los Angeles Riots*. New York: Praeger.

Sasajima, M., J.A. Davis, and R.E. Peterson. 1968. "Organized Student Protest and Institutional Climate." *American Education Research Journal* 5(May):291-304.

Scott, J.W., and M. El-Assal. 1969. "Multiversity, University Size, University Quality and Student Protest: An Empirical Study." *American Sociological Review* 34(October):702-709.

Scranton, William. 1970. *The Report of the President's Commission on Campus Unrest*. Washington: Government Printing Office.

Taylor, Stuart, Richard Shuntich, Patrick McGovern, and Robert Genthner. 1971. *Violence at Kent State: The Students' Perspective*. New York: College Notes and Texts.

Wysong, J.A., and L.R. Walum. 1971. "The Dynamics of Dissent: Student Radicalization in a Campus Crisis." Paper presented at the spring symposium on Conflict and Change in Contemporary America, The Ohio State University.

ENDNOTES

1. We are speaking here of relatively rigorous empirical research. Narrative accounts of several disruptions have included evaluations of the impact of social control violence on demonstrators and others. See, for example, Foster and Long (1970:414-415) and Hayden (1967:59). Raine (1970) has investigated the relationship between perception and experience of police brutality on an individual basis (as opposed to mass confrontations) and participation and attitudes toward the 1965 Watts riots. In general, his findings are similar to those reported below.

2. The general facts of this incident are well known. For more details see Scranton (1970). Lewis (1972) offers a sociological interpretation of the event.

3. We are indebted to William S. Aron, University of Chicago, who developed the questionnaire used in this study.

4. Two students were not registered at Kent State University during the Spring Quarter, 1970, and therefore were undoubtedly referring to other incidents. A few of the Kent State students may also have been referring to incidents other than those occurring in Kent from May 2–4, 1970.

5. The quality of the data varied by the extent to which different interviewers followed instructions to probe on certain items. Although interview content suggested that the vast majority of the other 34 respondents were referring to the May 4 confrontation, we decided to include in this category only those students whom the interviewers had recorded as having specifically mentioned the May 4 confrontation when they responded to this item.

6. These variables have been found to be significantly related to students' political outlooks and protest activities in various studies. See, for example, Braungart (1971), Foster and Long (1970) and Horn and Knott (1971).

7. We should note that one-third of the participants and two-thirds of the controls did not mention the event as having been significant in causing their political outlook to change or be strengthened.

SOCIAL CONTROL VIOLENCE AND RADICALIZATION: BEHAVIORAL DATA

Raymond J. Adamek
Jerry M. Lewis
Kent State University

ABSTRACT

Utilizing self-reports of Kent State students' protest and socio-political activity before and after May 4, 1970, this study evaluates the plausibility of two hypotheses. The radicalization hypothesis suggests that exposure to extreme social control violence, such as that employed by National Guardsmen on Kent's campus, would lead to greater protest activity. The pacification hypothesis suggests that protest activity would decrease after exposure to social control violence, to be replaced by inactivity, or by "more acceptable" socio-political activity. The data support the radicalization hypothesis.

Student activism has become the object of increasing concern and research by various educators and social scientists. To date, most of the research has focused on the differential socio-economic, academic, psychological and family characteristics of "activists" and "non-activists" (see, for example, the works reviewed in Foster and Long, 1970; Horn and Knott, 1971; Braungart, 1971), or on the differential characteristics of educational institutions which were or were not the locales for student demonstrations (Peterson, 1966, 1968; Sasajima, et al., 1968; Scott and El-Assal, 1969; Astin, 1970; Kahn and Bowers, 1970; Blau and Slaughter, 1971). Aron (1971, 1972) has investigated various components of student political ideology, and their relationship to different types of activism. Relatively little research, however, has focused on the effects which the actions of social control agents (police, National Guardsmen) have on student demonstrators, and others, particularly where such control has involved excessive use of force.[1] This research hiatus exists in spite of the fact that some activist groups have advocated confrontation as a political technique to provoke social control agents to violence in order to radicalize both those involved in the confrontation and the general population.

There appear to be two hypotheses regarding the use of social control violence. One might be termed the "radicalization" hypothesis and suggests that when severe force is used against demonstrators, they will become radicalized in their attitudes and behavior. Their political orientation will generally move to the left, they will increasingly come to question the legitimacy of existing governmental institutions and processes, they will be more

This study was supported by the Office for Research and the Department of Sociology and Anthropology, Kent State University, Kent, Ohio. A shorter version of this paper was presented at the annual meeting of the American Sociological Association in Montreal, August 1974.

accepting of the use of violence as a political technique to achieve change, and they will become more politically active. The second, or "pacification" hypothesis, suggests that the use of severe force by social control agents is effective in stopping demonstrations, demoralizing demonstrators, and deterring further expressions of dissent or transforming them into more acceptable types of socio-political activity. While no major studies have focused on these hypotheses as their central concern, a few have touched on them.

Barton (1968) found that the use of excessive police force against demonstrators at Columbia University increased the sympathy of faculty and students for the tactics (a sit-in and a general strike) employed by the demonstrators. The police action had less effect on faculty and students' attitudes regarding the six demands of the demonstrators, although here too the slight change noted was favorable to the dissidents. Kornberg and Brehm (1971) report a similar increase in the sympathy of students (but not faculty) for demonstrators' tactics (sit-in) after police violence at Duke University. They also report greater sympathy for the demonstrators' demands after police action. Wysong and Walum (1971) reported that police violence in the spring 1970 disruptions at the Ohio State University intensified and sustained the protest activism of those already predisposed and increased the protest activism of others.

We have investigated the impact of the Kent State killings on those students present at the campus rally on May 4, 1970. Our data indicated that as far as student *attitudes* were concerned, the first hypothesis was more plausible. That is, in general, the attitudes of those students most directly involved in the incident were radicalized. (Adamek and Lewis, 1973).

THE PRESENT STUDY

Two years after the fatal shootings at Kent State, a large-scale non-violent sit-in took place outside the R.O.T.C. offices on Kent's campus following an anti-war rally on the Commons. This demonstration provided the impetus and opportunity for us to gather data regarding students' protest and political *behavior*, and to continue our studies of the long-range impact of social control violence. We wanted to contrast the social characteristics and activist careers of those students who chose to be arrested to

dramatize their commitment to the anti-war movement vis-a-vis those students who did not sit-in to arrest. Interviews were completed with 116 (89%) of the 129 persons arrested at the sit-in utilizing a questionnaire developed from our previous (1973) study.[2] The same instrument was mailed to a random sample of juniors and seniors registered at Kent State during the Spring (1972) Quarter. The latter were most likely to have been on campus during May of 1970. Two hundred and seventy-three respondents (55%) returned a usable mail questionnaire.[3] An analysis of the social characteristics and activist careers of the 116 sit-in participants and the 273 non-participants is given elsewhere (Lewis and Adamek, 1974). We will contrast the protest and socio-political activity of a subsample of these respondents, that is, those students (N = 124) who were enrolled[4] at Kent in the spring of 1970 and who indicated they had gone to the May 4 rally either to demonstrate or to observe, and those (N = 84) who were enrolled but indicated they did not go to the rally. In order to determine the impact of the May 4 shootings on behavior, we asked our respondents to indicate how many times they had engaged in various *protest* and *socio-political* activities before and after that date. Thirty-one of these 208 students were arrestees. They constituted 23.4 percent of the 124 May 4 rally attenders, and 2.4 percent of the 84 non-attenders. Although the arrestees were not randomly sampled, they are included in this study since our primary focus is on persons who have experienced social control violence, and they added to our N in this category.

FINDINGS

Utilizing chi-square analysis, the 124 students present at the rally were contrasted with the 84 absent from the rally on the basis of twenty-three socio-demographic variables. The two groups did not differ significantly (p>.05) on the following variables: race, age, year in school, academic major, fathers' and mothers' religion, religion the respondents were raised under, current religious preference, employment status, degree of financial dependence on parents, primary source of educational funding, grade point average, father's political views, father's and mother's occupation, father's and mother's education, Hollingshead's two factor index of social class, and parents' estimated combined annual income. The two groups did differ significantly (p<.05) in that those present at the rally were more likely to be males, attend church less frequently, and to describe their own and their mothers' political views as radical or liberal. Overall, the two groups were quite similar.

Table 1 indicates the mean frequency with which our respondents reported they had engaged in various protest activities before and after May 4, 1970. In general, students who attended the rally on May 4, 1970 were engaged in more protest activities than those who were absent both before and after May 4. This was true for every category of protest activity, from the most mild, to the most severe. Moreover, within groups over time, we see that those at the rally reported they had engaged in each of the six categories of protest activity from three to six times more often *after* May 4, while those who were not at the rally reported appreciably increased activity in only one category, a rather mild form of protest activity–attending a rally or public protest meeting.

The increased protest activism of those exposed to the extreme social control violence of May 4 was, furthermore, a general phenomenon. With the exception of the civil-disobedience arrest and the violent-confrontation categories, half or more of those who attended the rally reported that their protest activities increased in each of the other four categories after May 4. In contrast, in 5 of 6 categories less than 20% of those not at the rally reported increased activity after May 4.

These data are more consonant with the radicalization hypothesis. Students who attended the rally on May 4, 1970 were relatively more activist than those who did not attend. Having experienced the social control violence on May 4, they generally became even more active than those who did not attend, and more active than they themselves had been prior to May 4. Those who did not attend the rally remained relatively inactive.

Table 2 focuses on the socio-political activism of our respondents. The activities included here reflect support for various social-action welfare groups, or attempts to affect political change "within the system." Both groups of respondents report less activity of this type than protest activity. In general, those who attended the rally were more active than those who did not in each of the five categories, both before and after May 4. Rally attenders became substantially more active after May 4 than they were

Table 1. Mean Frequencies with Which Students Present and Absent from the Rally on May 4, 1970 Engaged in Various Protest Activities Before and After That Date

PROTEST ACTIVITY	BEFORE 4 MAY 1970		AFTER 4 MAY 1970	
	PRESENT (N)(123-124)	ABSENT (84)	PRESENT (122-124)	ABSENT (83)
Attended a rally or public meeting protesting public policy	4.34	1.28	13.74	3.08
Engaged in picketing or marching on behalf of a cause	1.84	.74	6.42	.89
Engaged in some form of civil disobedience but were not arrested	.41	.17	1.76	.11
Engaged in civil disobedience leading to arrest or jail	.06	.01	.36	.02
Engaged in nonviolent confrontation with authorities	.88	.13	2.67	.08
Engaged in violent confrontation with authorities	.71	.14	2.41	.04

Table 2. Mean Frequencies with Which Students Present and Absent from the Rally on May 4, 1970 Engaged in Various Socio-Political Activities Before and After That Date

SOCIO-POLITICAL ACTIVITY	BEFORE 4 MAY 1970		AFTER 4 MAY 1970	
	PRESENT (N)(123-124)	ABSENT (82-83)	PRESENT (124)	ABSENT (83)
Worked on a project designed to help people who are poor or disadvantaged	2.22	.95	2.79	2.06
Worked actively in support of a cause by canvassing, leafleting, petitioning	1.76	.59	4.63	1.81
Served as an officer of a social action organization	.30	.28	.35	.34
Worked full-time for social cause or social action organization	.32	.17	.30	.13
Worked in a political campaign	.36	.29	.36	.17

before in only one category–canvassing, leafleting and petitioning. Interestingly enough, depending upon content, this socio-political activity might also be considered a protest activity. Those who did not attend the May 4 rally also reported an increase in canvassing, leafleting and petitioning of about the same magnitude, as well as an increased tendency to work on projects designed to help the poor and disadvantaged.

These data again tend to support, or at least do not contradict, the radicalization hypothesis, while they offer little support for the pacification hypothesis. Students who were subjected to the social control violence of May 4, 1970 generally maintained their previous levels of socio-political activity, and significantly increased such activity in one instance. Moreover, considering Tables 1 and 2 together, we find no evidence that protest-active students were pacified in the sense that they transformed their protest activity into more acceptable (and safer) vehicles for achieving social change. Rather, they *increased* their protest activity while maintaining their socio-political activity at the same level.[5]

Following the strategy adopted in our earlier paper (Adamek and Lewis, 1973), in order to isolate the impact of the May 4 incident more rigorously, we undertook a case by case matching of rally attenders and non-attenders on the following variables: sex, race, academic major, perception of fathers' and mothers' political position, social class, grade point average, religion raised under, and protest and socio-political activity levels prior to May 4.[6] This process yielded 18 pairs of matched respondents. Although matching could not be exact across all levels of each variable, chi-square analysis indicated that the two groups did not differ significantly from one another on these variables, nor on any of the other socio-demographic variables mentioned above. A comparison of the mean frequencies with which these two groups participated in protest and socio-political activities is given in Table 3.

Since the two groups were matched on the frequency of activities prior to May 4, there were no significant differences between them at that point in time, as would be expected. Focusing on protest activism first, we note that those present at the May 4 rally engaged in significantly more rallies, pickets and marches, and confrontations after May 4 than those who were absent, and were also slightly more active in the civil disobedience categories. Moreover, rally attenders were substantially more active after May 4 than they were before in 4 of 6 protest categories (the civil disobedience categories again being the exception). Those absent from the rally, on the other hand, did not substantially increase in any category of protest activity, with the possible exception of the most mild form of protest– attending rallies or protest meetings, where they registered a two-fold increase in frequency, compared to almost a ten-fold increase for rally attenders.

The increase in protest activism among rally attenders was again a fairly general phenomenon. Sixty percent or more of the 18 rally attenders became more active in the first two categories after May 4, with 11-39% becoming more active in the other four categories. In contrast, in every category except attending rallies and protest meetings, where 39% became more active after May 4, less than 12% of the 18 non-attenders became more active.

The data on socio-political activism indicate that the 18 matched attenders did not differ substantially from the non-attenders either before or after May 4, except that non-attenders were more likely to be working on projects for the poor and disadvantaged before the rally, and attenders were more active than non-attenders in such activities as canvassing after the rally. Rally attenders were at least slightly more active than non-attenders in all but one socio-political activity after May 4.[7] Comparing within groups across time, rally attenders were more active after May 4 than they were before in every category, although appreciably so in only one (canvassing, leafleting). The pattern over time for the 18 who did not attend the rally was inconsistent, and in no case were the differences substantial. The data from the matched samples thus reinforce our findings for the larger sample.

In summary, those who were subject to the social control violence on May 4, 1970 reported substantially increased activism in the two year period after that date. This was particularly true of all categories of *protest* activism, which would indicate that they had been radicalized by their experience. Those who were not subject to the social control violence of May 4 generally reported that they had only maintained their previously low levels of activism. In the few categories where their activism increased, it was either of the socio-political variety, or the most mild form of protest activity.

While the major concern of this paper is with the effects of social control violence on reported behavior, we did gather some data on attitude change. Before being asked to indicate the extent of their protest and political activism, our respondents were asked, in two open-ended questions, "whether any significant changing or strengthening...has occurred in the development of your political outlook," and, if so, "what was significant in causing your outlook to change or be strengthened." Sixty-six percent of the 124 students present at the May 4 rally spontaneously mentioned "May 4" or "Kent State" to the latter question, as opposed to 46 percent of the 84 students absent from the rally ($X^2 = 7.99$, p<.01). These data are elaborated in Table 4.

Table 3. Mean Frequencies with Which 18 Matched Students Present and 18 Matches Students Absent from the Rally on May 4, 1970 Engaged in Various Activities Before and After That Date

	BEFORE 4 MAY 1970		AFTER 4 MAY 1970	
PROTEST ACTIVITY	**PRESENT**	**ABSENT**	**PRESENT**	**ABSENT**
Attend rally/protest meeting	1.17	1.17	10.11	2.33
Picket or march	.22	.22	2.28	.28
Civil disobedience–not arrested	0	0	.44	.11
Arrested for civil disobedience	0	0	.11	0
Nonviolent confrontation	.06	.06	.89	.11
Violent confrontation	.11	.06	.94	0
SOCIO-POLITICAL ACTIVITY				
Work on project for poor	.33	1.11	.67	.56
Canvass, leaflet, petition	.11	.28	1.50	.33
Served as officer	.11	.17	.17	.28
Worked full-time for social cause	.11	.11	.17	.06
Work in political campaign	.11	.06	.17	0

Thirty-one point seven percent of the students present on May 4 indicated they were radicalized in the sense the term is used in this paper, while only 7.3 percent said their political outlooks became more apathetic, cynical, or frustrated, which might be indicative of "pacification." Fewer of the students absent from the May 4 rally indicated that they were radicalized, although their political outlooks also generally moved to the left.

The results of our attitude study (Adamek and Lewis, 1973) conducted one year after the May 4, 1970 incident, together with other data gathered in this study (Lewis and Adamek, 1974) and the present analysis argue that the general effect of the use of social control violence by the National Guard was to radicalize rather than pacify the attitudes and behavior of the students most directly affected by it. That is, they became more accepting of the use of violence, moved to the left in their political attitudes (Adamek and Lewis, 1973), and became more politically and protest active.

It is true that since the ideological content of the students' *behavior* cannot be directly determined from our present questionnaire items, one might argue that the increased activism we observed might have been in *support* of "the establishment." Our previous findings on attitudes, the political context of this period, and the fact that students most directly affected by the Guard's action on May 4, 1970 were over-represented in one "leftist" protest, however, make this unlikely to be true of any substantial number of our respondents.

The concept of radicalization, of course, need not carry the present connotation of "leftist." In a society where social control agents represent a leftist government, violence on their part might "radicalize" the attitudes and behavior of those affected by making them more right-wing in orientation.

We should also point out that we have been speaking only of the effects of the sporadic and situational application of social control violence. In a society where social control agents employ excessive force regularly in response to almost all expressions of dissent, public "pacification" and apathy might well result.

DISCUSSION

The results of our research, and that of Barton (1968), Kornberg and Brehm (1971) and Wysong and Walum (1971), as well as several narrative accounts of incidents involving social control violence, appear to agree that such violence generally has a radicalizing effect on participants. Moreover, our research indicates this radicalization is relatively long-lived.

From the standpoint of those agencies charged with "maintaining the system," the lesson would seem to be to avoid the use of excessive force in quelling disturbances, since this is likely to turn those involved against the system. What constitutes excessive force is less clear, however, and is ultimately defined by demonstrators, spectators and

Table 4. Nature of Change in Political Outlook Reported by Those Present and Absent from May 4 Rally Who Indicated May 4 Was Significant in Changing Their Outlook

NATURE OF CHANGE	PRESENT		ABSENT	
	N	%	N	%
More radical; anti-establishment	23	28.0	5	12.8
More politically active	3	3.7	3	7.7
More liberal	32	39.0	24	61.5
More middle-road; conservative	3	3.7	1	2.6
More apathetic; cynical; frustrated	6	7.3	0	0.0
More opposed to violence	4	4.9	0	0.0
Not discernable	11	13.4	6	15.4
Total	82	100.0	39	100.0

others, not by the social control agents themselves. Social control agents face a difficult dilemma adapting to a rapidly changing situation. If they utilize too little force, demonstrators may achieve their aims, or counter-demonstrators may begin to "take the law into their own hands."[8] If they employ too much force, the demonstrators' activities may be halted temporarily, but they apparently gain more adherents.

The dilemmas posed by the use of force are not limited to the social control agents alone, however. Foster and Long (1970:419-446) have analyzed the responses of educational institutions to student disruptions, and their ramifications. Calling in off-campus forces, they note, is attractive because it helps to insure protection of life and property, may demoralize all but "the most ferocious activists," and may lay the groundwork for the punishment of demonstrators through the courts. However, they note, this course has potentially high costs. The presence of outside forces is inflammatory, expensive, and an admission that the university cannot control its own affairs. Police or National Guard intervention also runs counter to academic traditions. Moreover, by inviting off-campus social control agents on the scene, the university makes itself accountable for their actions. Yet such forces often act quite autonomously once on the scene, and so the university may not actually control their actions. Finally, to the extent that university communities constitute distinct subcultures, outside social control agents are operating in an unfamiliar environment, and may commit tactical errors which have negative consequences for all concerned.

All of these negative consequences appeared at Kent State. The presence of the Guard on campus was certainly inflammatory, and was the major issue precipitating the noon rally culminating in four deaths (see Taylor, *et al.*, 1971:101). Students who perhaps could have cynically accepted the Cambodian "incursion" were incensed at the Guard's invasion and occupation of their campus. The costs incurred as a consequence of the actions of these forces are incalculable, either in monetary or other terms, but included the loss of life and limb, disruption of the academic year, student and faculty disillusionment and consternation, and severely damaged relations with the local community, the state legislature, and prospective students. Once on the campus, and particularly in developing "field" situations, the Guard acted quite autonomously,

although out of its element. Tactical decisions were made on the basis of ignorance of the University's formal and informal structure and norms. The commanding officer on the Commons indicated he thought the crowds were swelling because the students were on a noon lunch break, and that if he could only disperse them temporarily, they would return to classes at one o'clock (Akron Beacon Journal, 1970). In fact, the University holds classes throughout the lunch hour. In any case, students felt the issues at hand were serious enough to warrant skipping classes, something the Guard officer apparently did not consider in developing his plan of action. As the situation developed, the Guard also appeared to misread the mood and intent of the crowd. While the students were genuinely outraged at the Guard's presence and the prohibition against even peaceful assemblies, they were at the same time playing a confrontation game. Since the Guard did not fully comprehend this paradoxically light-hearted mood, they could not respond to it, but rather persisted in their dead-serious military frame of reference (Scranton 1970:289).

For student activists, confrontation tactics which precipitate the use of social control force also present various dilemmas. Lipsky (1968) has suggested that those who utilize protest as a political tool must deal with at least four constituencies: the target group, e.g., those who are able to make the changes or grant the concessions desired; the general public, whom the demonstrators hope to radicalize; individuals of various persuasions whom they hope to weld together to help press their demands; third parties, who normally interact with the target group, and who can bring pressure to bear on it to make the desired changes. Protest politics is not always the best way to deal simultaneously and effectively with these constituencies. Moreover, demonstrators themselves run the risk of injury, imprisonment, and death.

Quite often everybody loses and nobody gains when massive social control force is introduced into a social conflict situation. Greater efforts should be made by sociologists to explore alternative means of dealing with such situations. The use of "third party" forces holds some promise (Knopf, 1969; Lewis, 1971; Marx and Archer, 1971).

The paucity of research on the effects of social control violence on demonstrators and others is somewhat surprising, although understandable when the design problems are considered. To date, the few "hard" empirical studies available have generally focused on attitude change over a short time period. Almost none have dealt with the effects that incidents involving social control violence have on behavior. Yet such studies are important if we are fully to understand the genesis and development of protest behavior among students and other populations. Several scholars (Derber and Flacks, 1967; Dunlap, 1970; Aron, 1972) have recognized that earlier studies focusing on social background variables are of limited utility in explaining why some students are radicalized and others are not. Although a start has been made, we need more sophisticated studies of the effects of university milieu on student activism. Peer group relations have also been relatively neglected, although Barton (1968:347) has suggested that peer networks were important in sustaining the radicalism generated by police violence at Columbia. Finally, as Aron (1972) has suggested and our research indicates, more attention needs to be given to individuals' "reactions to formative situational variables," such as incidents involving social control violence.

REFERENCES

Adamek, Raymond J. and Jerry M.. Lewis. 1973. "Social control violence and radicalization: the Kent State case." *Social Forces* 51(March): 342-347.

Akron Beacon Journal. 1970. Testimony of Major General Robert Canterbury before the Commission. (August 21):A9.

Aron, William S. 1969. "The culture and ideology of youth." Mimeographed questionnaire. Community and Family Study Center, University of Chicago.

_____. 1971. "Ideology and behavior as components of radicalism." Paper presented at the 66th Annual Meeting of the American Sociological Association, Denver.

_____. 1972. "Political radicalism–ideology and behavior among students at the University of Chicago." Ph.D. dissertation abstract, University of Chicago.

Astin, Alexander. 1970. "Determinants of student activism." Pp. 89-101 in Julian Foster and Durward Long (eds.), *Protest! Student Activism in America*. New York: William Morrow.

Barton, Allen H. 1968. "The Columbia crisis: campus, Vietnam, and the ghetto." *Public Opinion Quarterly*, 32(Fall):333-351.

Blau, Peter M., and Ellen L. Slaughter. 1971. "Institutional conditions and student demonstrations." *Social Problems* 18(Spring):475-487.

Braungart, Richard G. 1971. "Family status, socialization, and student politics: a multivariate analysis." *American Journal of Sociology* 77(July):108-130.

Brzezinski, Zbigniew. 1968. "Revolution and counter-revolution (but not necessarily about Columbia)." *The New Republic* 158(June 1):23-25.

Derber, Charles, and Richard Flacks. 1967. "An exploration of the value system of radical student activists and their parents." Paper presented at the Annual Meeting of the American Sociological Association, San Francisco.

Dunlap, Riley. 1970. "Radical and conservative student activists: a comparison of family backgrounds." *Pacific Sociological Review* 13(Summer):171-181.

Foster, Julian, and Durward Long (eds.). 1970. *Protest! Student Activism in America*. New York: William Morrow.

Hayen, Tom. 1967. *Rebellion in Newark: Official Violence and Ghetto Response*. New York: Random House.

Horn, John L., and Paul D. Knott. 1971. "Activist youth of the 1960's: summary and prognosis." *Science* 171 (March): 977-985.

Kahn, Roger M., and William J. Bowers. 1970. "The social context of the rank-and-file student activist." *Sociology of Education* 43(Winter): 38-55.

Knopf, Terry Ann. 1969. *Youth Patrols: An Experiment in Community Participation*. Waltham: Brandeis University.

Kornberg, Alan, and Mary L. Brehm. 1971. "Ideology, institutional identification and campus activism." *Social Forces* 49(March): 445-459.

Lewis, Jerry M. 1971. "Faculty marshals and student dissent." Report #55, Center for Nonviolent Conflict Resolution, Haverford College, Haverford, Pennsylvania.

Lewis, Jerry M., and Raymond J. Adamek. 1974. "Anti-R.O.T.C. sit-in: a sociological analysis." *The Sociological Quarterly* 15(Autumn):542-547.

Lipsky, Michael. 1968. "Protest as a political resource." *The American Political Science Review* 62(December): 1144-1158.

Marx, Gary T., and Dane Archer. 1971. "Citizen involvement in the law enforcement process: the case of community police patrols." *American Behavioral Scientist* 15 (September/October): 52-72.

Peterson, Richard E. 1966. *The Scope of Organized Student Protest in 1964-1965*. Princeton: Educational Testing Service.

_____. 1968. *The Scope of Organized Student Protest in 1967-1968*. Princeton: Educational Testing Service.

Raine, Walter J. 1970. "The perception of police brutality in South Central Los Angeles," in Nathan E. Cohen (ed.), *The Los Angeles Riots*. New York: Praeger.

Sasajima, Masu, Junius A. Davis, and Richard E. Peterson. 1968. "Organized student protest and institutional climate." *American Educational Research Journal* 5(May): 291-304.

Scott, Joseph W., and Mohamed El-Assal. 1969. "Multiversity, university size, university quality and student protest: an empirical study." *American Sociological Review* 34(October):702-709.

Scranton, William. 1970. *The Report of the President's Commission on Campus Unrest.* Washington: United States Government Printing Office.

Taylor, Stuart, Richard Shuntich, Patrick McGovern, and Robert Genthner. 1971. *Violence at Kent State: The Students' Perspective.* New York: College Notes and Texts.

Wysong, Jere A., and Laurel R. Walum. 1971. "The dynamics of dissent: student radicalization in a campus crisis." Paper delivered at the Spring Symposium on Conflict and Change in Contemporary America, May 13-14, 1971, The Ohio State University.

ENDNOTES

1. We are speaking here of relatively rigorous empirical research. Narrative accounts of several disruptions have included evaluations of the impact of social control violence on demonstrators and others. See, for example, Hayden (1967:59), and Foster and Long (1970:414-415). Raine (1970) has investigated the relationship between perception and experience of police brutality on an individual basis (as opposed to mass confrontations) and participation in and attitudes toward the 1965 Watts riots. In general, his findings are similar to those reported below.

2. This questionnaire was developed by Aron (1969), to whom we are indebted.

3. To determine whether a bias appeared in who returned questionnaires and who did not, we cross-tabulated the time the questionnaires were returned with three variables. No significant differences were found between the time respondents returned their questionnaires and their purpose in attending the May 4, 1970 rally (to participate, to observe, enrolled but did not go, not enrolled and did not go), nor between the time their questionnaires were returned and the level of their protest activity, either before or after May 4, 1970.

4. Four of these students indicated they were not enrolled in the spring of 1970 but did attend the rally. These students were enrolled in the spring of 1972, and were retained in the analysis.

5. Since this study combines two groups of students who were drawn from different universes (31 students from the 129 sit-in participants, and 177 from the random sample of juniors and seniors), we "ran" Tables 1 and 2 separately for these two groups to see if the basic findings would hold. They did. Although the sit-in arrestees were generally more active both before and after May 4 than the 177 students who were not arrested, that May 4 incident had the same impact on both groups. That is, arrestees present at the May 4 rally increased their protest and socio-political activity in 10 of 11 categories after May 4, while arrestees absent from the May 4 rally increased their activity in only 6 of 11 categories; non-arrestees present at the May 4 rally increased their protest and socio-political activity in 9 of 11 categories after May 4, while non-arrestees absent from the May 4 rally increased their activity in only 5 of 11 categories. (Control tables available from authors on request.)

6. These variables are significantly related to students' political outlooks and protest activities in various studies. See, for example, Foster and Long (1970), Horn and Knott (1971), and Braungart (1971).

7. Even in this one category (serving as an officer in a social action organization), a comparison of the *medians* of the two groups indicates that rally attenders were more active.

8. Brzezinski (1968) has suggested that the authorities' best bet is to come down hard and fast on "revolutionaries," isolate them from any audience that might become radicalized, remove them from the scene for the duration, and then grant reforms to neutralize their more moderate supporters. While this strategy may be effective, it is obviously quite conservative, and easier said than done.

THE ANTI-VIETNAM WAR PIETA

Jerry M. Lewis
Kent State University

INTRODUCTION

This essay looks at the cultural impact of a photograph taken on May 4, 1970 during an anti-National Guard demonstration at Kent State University. This picture has had a continuing impact on perspectives of the Vietnam War as well as the 1960s.

Using aspects of Wendy Griswold's (1987) methodological framework, I examine the short- and long-term impact of a photograph of Mary Vecchio,[1] an anti-National Guard demonstrator, screaming over the body of Jeffrey Miller, a student killed at Kent State University. This photograph, which I call the "anti-Vietnam War pieta," has become part of the culture of the Vietnam era and the more encompassing 1960s.

I begin with an overview of Griswold's approach to cultural analysis. Second, I place the photograph in the cultural context (brief) that it occurred. Third, I describe the picture in detail. Lastly, I interpret the picture using Griswold's approach to cultural analysis.

Wendy Griswold has written widely on the sociology of culture. She laid out her approach to cultural analysis in an essay (1987) entitled, "A

Methodological Framework for the Sociology of Culture." In the essay she provides an elaborate framework or protocol for doing cultural sociology. The core components are designed to assist the analyst with the difficulties of making sense of an important cultural object. The framework has five core components including the artist's intention, the reception of the cultural item over time and space, the comprehension of the cultural item using genres, the explanation of the cultural item in its social contexts, and the validation of the analysis of the cultural item. Each of these components as well as the sub-components is discussed in more detail in the analysis section of the study. I do not have an independent section for validation as I attempt to do this throughout the analysis.

A CULTURAL BRIEF[2]

In *The Ends of Power*, H. R. Haldeman (1978), a top aide to President Richard Nixon, said that the shootings at Kent State began the slide into Watergate, eventually destroying the Nixon administration. This is an illustration of the national importance of the tragedy which began on May 4,

This is a revised version of a paper presented at the annual meeting of the American Sociological Association in Los Angeles, California in August, 1994. I wish to thank Stanford Gregory, Diane L. Lewis and Susan Rogers for substantive and editorial comments on the paper. I am grateful for the work of my research assistants Barbara Fischer, Paula DiGiorgio and Julie Anderson on this project.

1970 with the deaths of four students and wounding of nine others by the Ohio National Guard.

The Vietnam War

In the Vietnam era, a better term in my view than the '60s, the dominant issue was the controversy over the War. It was a natural catalyst for students in its power to implicate students into activism because of the War's pervasiveness, emotional impact, and growing protest culture. The pervasiveness of the War is expressed in the idea that Vietnam was America's first television war. But it was *more* than television, as an examination of era newspapers shows. Beyond the media, the Vietnam War affected many Americans. A neighbor, friend, or loved one could have been killed, injured, missing in action, or a prisoner of war.

The Vietnam War generated powerful emotional responses particularly to events. It did not start out that way. For many years it was seen as a dirty little war in a faraway place. But 1968 changed all this. Powerful media images brought us the attack on the American embassy during the Tet offensive, and the execution of a prisoner on the streets of Saigon.

Later in 1968, the drama of antiwar conflict was brought into living rooms with the confrontations between antiwar demonstrators and the Chicago police during the Democratic National Convention. These images evoked an emotional response which found expression on college campuses through rallies and teach-ins.

Lastly, the activism of the Vietnam War era was encouraged and sustained by a developing protest culture. In particular, the values of activism were reinforced by the antiwar movement culture. The peace sign was everywhere--on walls, shirts, and placards at rallies. Music of the era also supported protest values. Thus, the Vietnam War was a natural issue for the college student with its pervasiveness, emotionality, and protest culture. In looking back, one wonders why more students were not involved in antiwar activities.

May 4, 1970

A national tragedy began on May 4, 1970 at Kent State University with the killing of four students and wounding of nine others by the Ohio National Guard. In 1970, I was an assistant professor of sociology at Kent State University, having come to Kent in 1966. In late April 1970, the United States invaded Cambodia and widened the War. This sparked protest throughout the United States. Two days after the Cambodian invasion, on a Saturday evening, the Ohio National Guard came on campus because an R.O.T.C. building was attacked and burned to the ground. Protests continued through Sunday.

Shortly before noon Monday, May 4, I went to the Commons--a wide open grassy area--as a Faculty Marshal to observe the rally held to protest the presence of the Ohio National Guard on campus. I moved on to the Commons and passed students who had been gathering around the Victory Bell for the past hour. I watched the crowd for about fifteen minutes when the National Guard moved against the students, driving them off the Commons with a tear gas attack. Students responded very angrily to the attack, which did little more than provoke them. The Guard continued to advance on students and drove them over a hill as they moved to a practice football field. A few minutes later I looked up and saw the Guard retracing their steps from the parking lot over the hill to the Commons. As they got to the top of the hill, twenty-eight of the more than seventy Guardsmen fired their rifles. Many Guardsmen fired into the air or the ground. However, a small portion fired into the crowd below killing four Kent State students and wounding nine others. I was standing twenty yards from where Sandy Scheuer was killed, but took cover when the firing began. My experiences are typical of many that day including Mary Vecchio and John Filo, the photographer who took the picture.

AN ANALYSIS OF THE ANTI-VIETNAM WAR PIETA

The Artist's Intentions

Studying a cultural object (which is any item that has shared significance embodied in form) begins with an examination of the artist's intentions. The artist that creates a cultural object has intentions which can be subjected to a cultural analysis. Griswold (1987: 7-8) proposes that the analyst constructs a brief ". . . which is a list of constraints and influences, clustered by their sources and types, that together constitute the artist's probable intention." The brief includes such things as the artist's immediate circumstances, training and experience, community expectations, physical media, and aesthetic conditions.

John Filo

John Filo, a Kent State photography major in 1970, won a Pulitzer Prize and other awards for his now famous picture of Mary Vecchio. He continues to work in journalism today. He was near the Prentice Hall parking lot when the Guard fired but was closer to the National Guard than I was. He told me that he saw bullets hitting the ground, but did not take cover because he thought the bullets were blanks. Of course, blanks can't hit the ground. Filo took the film to a small paper in Tarentum, Pennsylvania, *The Valley Daily News and Daily Dispatch,* because he was concerned about the possibility of the FBI or other agencies taking his film.

John Filo, the photographer, was acting as a news professional even though he was student at the time. He said in a 1990 interview that immediately after the firing had stopped, "I thought, I've got to get out of here. Then I said, Wait a minute. What am I doing? You say you're a journalist, let it go." (Bush, 1990, p. 6) For example, he thought it was essential that he get his pictures out of the Kent area in order to escape the clutches of the Federal Bureau of Investigation. There had been persistent rumors that the FBI had been confiscating camera and film over the weekend. John drove the back roads of Pennsylvania to Tarentum to have the picture published saying to the editor who he knew from previous work that he thought he had some good pictures. "At the time, I was paranoid" (Bush, 1990, p. 6). Commenting on the consequences of the shootings, Filo (Payne, 1981, p. 119) said: "I had a tremendously rough time readjusting just to home life after that day. I am talking about dealing with people on a day to day at any level." In the 1981 film *Kent State* he recreated his experiences of the shootings and taking the picture (Payne, 1981, p.154)

The Valley Daily News of Tarentum published the picture as well as putting it on the Associated Press wire service. John won the Pulitzer. John was trained as a photo-journalism major. Clearly he knew that it was important to take his camera to the demonstration. He also understood how to frame the picture. He clearly was courageous, which probably cannot be trained but is certainly an important factor in the values of a news photographer.

Mary Vecchio

Mary Vecchio was a 14 year-old run away when she left her parents' Florida home in 1970. She eventually found her way to Kent, arriving on the campus May 1, 1970, four days before the shootings and leaving immediately afterward for Indianapolis (Personal interview, 4/4/94). Soon after the picture was published in *Newsweek*, she was tracked down by the Federal Bureau of Investigation and returned to her home. The picture had an immediate impact on the Vecchio family, said Mary Vecchio. Within three years her family had received more than 50,000 letters, most of them hostile (Leingang, 1994:1).

Vecchio was a self-described antiwar activist. What kind of activist was she? There were three ways that students got involved in the antiwar movement. First, there were the core activists who did most of the work of organizing rallies, writing pamphlets, sending letters to newspapers and so forth. Next were the secondary activists, who were interested, did a little work, but for the most part just lent the movement moral support. Lastly were "event participants" (rally attenders), whose main responsibility was to show up at programs and demonstrations such as large rallies and teach-ins. I would put Vecchio in the latter category. She said (Leingang, 1994, p. 1), "I just came to protest the War. It was something I had to do. When I got to campus, I met people by the Victory Bell [on May 4, 1970] and then the National Guard came."

The Pieta and Its Reception

Moving from the artist's intentions, the analyst turns his or her concerns to the reception of the object over time and space. Here the cultural sociologist looks at the impact of the cultural item in terms of the number of interpretations, popularity as measured by immediate esteem, impacts on other cultural items, endurance over time, and canonization by elites.

In this section of the paper, I look at five issues that flow from Griswold's theoretical model of reception. These include interpretation, market success, influence on other cultural objects, canonization, and endurance.

Interpretation

The Mary Vecchio picture shows her on one knee screaming over Jeffrey Miller's body. Mary told me that she was calling for help because she felt she could do nothing (Personal Interview, 4/4/94). Miller is lying on the tarmac of the Prentice Hall parking lot. One student is standing near Miller's body closer than Vecchio. Four students are seen in the immediate background.

The first general reaction to the picture has to do with the "outside agitator" myth. Because Mary Vecchio was not a student, many people including the public, antiwar activists and writers, political commentators, and scholars have concluded that there were many outsiders on campus. This does not seem to be the case. For example, all those students killed or wounded on May 4 were registered students. In addition, all those who were indicted for activities on May 1-4 were officially tied to the university as students or in one case, a faculty.

Another widespread interpretation of the picture was one suggesting that it describes America's agony over the Vietnam War. It became a metaphor for a very troubled society.

Market Success

In considering market success, Griswold argues that the analysis should look at the popularity and immediate impact of the cultural item. She sees the impact of the item as a measure of the esteem it has been awarded. The immediate impact of the picture was quite evident, with the strongest and widest impact resulting from its use on the cover of 5/18/70 *Newsweek*, which came out shortly after the shooting. Kim Sorvig (1990, p. 6), in *To Heal Kent State*, writes about this early attention to "The Picture:"

> John Filo's version of The Picture was on the front pages of many U.S. newspapers; two weeks later, blazoned with the title "Nixon's Home Front," it was the cover of *Newsweek*. There was no escaping it and no way to avoid reacting to it, whether in grief or in anger or both. Even if you had successfully ignored the manifest griefs and horrors of the preceding decade, you responded to The Picture. It summarized so much.

Impact on Other Cultural Objects and Endurance

For the analysis of the Mary Vecchio picture, the categories of impact and endurance can be grouped

together. The impact on other cultural objects as well as endurance allows the analyst to look at the breath and depth of a cultural item's influence. To convey this to the reader, I am going to examine the various ways that the picture was used during the 20th anniversary of May 4.

Using the original picture as published in the *Valley Daily News* as a baseline, it is possible to describe several forms of the picture in a range of media over time. The first type, which I call the exemplar, is a reproduction of the original photograph published in the *Valley Daily News*. The exemplar can be identified in the following manner. It has Jeffery Miller and Mary Vecchio in the center with five students clearly identifiable in the background. One of these students is closer to Jeffery Miller's body than Mary Vecchio. The exemplar was published in 1990 primarily with an AP story by George Esper (For example, Winona Minn. *Daily News*, 4/29/90, p. 1E). The largest form of the exemplar was in the *Daily News* with the picture 11 1/2 inches wide by seven inches high. The smallest form of the exemplar in the newspaper sample appeared in the Lisbon, Ohio *The Morning Journal*, (5/4/90 no page) with a width of 4 1/2 inches and a height of 3 inches. Seventy-seven percent of the pictures in the newspaper sample used the exemplar.

The next form of the picture I call the modified exemplar. This form of the picture is cropped in such as manner that a student is left out on either the far left or right of the picture. Typically it is the student on the left. The modified exemplar often appears at major anniversaries. An example of the largest form of the modified exemplar appeared in the Pittsburgh, PA, *Pittsburgh Press* (May 4, 1990, B1) It was eight inches wide by 7 1/4 inches high. The smallest form was 4 inches wide by 3 1/2 inches wide (Pittsburgh Pa, *Post Gazette*, 5/4/90, p.1). The modified exemplar represented 12% of the newspaper sample. Thus, two forms of the picture, the exemplar and the modified exemplar, represented 89% of the newspaper sample.

The next form of the picture is the truncated exemplar. This form of the picture has from three to zero students in the background. As students drop out of the picture, the focus increasingly is on Jeffery Miller's body and Mary Vecchio's face. The truncated exemplar ranges from 5 1/2 inches wide by 4 inches high (USA TODAY, 5/1/90, p. 1) to 3 inches by 3 inches in the Detroit, Mich., *Free Press* (5/4/90, p.1F)

The fourth type of use of the picture is as a drawing. It is a representational drawing that approximates the picture and is typically found in collages about May 4, student activism, or the 60's.(Cleveland, Oh., *Plain Dealer*, 5/4/90, p. 1). It is usually in the form of a truncated exemplar and smaller than the original. For example, in a 1990 story about May 4 and student activism, aspects of the picture are part of a collage of protest activities including a demonstration against apartheid. A 60's example may be found in the center of the book cover for Jules Archer's *The Incredible Sixties* (1986). It is a representational drawing of Jeffery Miller and Mary Vecchio.

The fifth type of use of the picture is as a political cartoon. Here the picture is clearly not representational but retains most of the characteristics of the Pieta picture. The cartoonist Skelly used the picture as a political statement attacking the killings in Beirut. This picture appeared in Singapore's *The Straits Times* (1991, p. 24), but it was originally published in the *San Diego Union*. It shows a "Mary Vecchio" figure in 1970 and similar figure in Beirut in 1990.

Another use of the cartoon format was by Oliphant (Universal Press Syndicate, 5/11/94). In a political cartoon, he has a man dressed in a business suit with a brief case asking Mary Vecchio, "Pardon me miss, did something important happen here?" The little bird character, in the lower right corner, asks, "Is there an MBA in the house?" The implication of the cartoon is that college campuses do not care about May 4, the Kent State killings, or student activism. Interestingly, Oliphant incorrectly attributes the picture to Doug Moore who, in 1970, was Kent State University's chief photographer. My guess is that Oliphant based his cartoon on an earlier *Newsweek* picture (May 7, 1990, p. 27) that cited Moore not Filo as the photographer. *Newsweek*'s mistake is particularly important because it was the publication that originally spread the picture around the world. The attribution in the original usage was correct.

The cartoon moves the full distance from the exemplar of the Filo photograph. This is an abstract pieta in that it retains only enough detail to link it to the content of the original photograph. The last three forms of the picture, "truncated exemplar,

representational drawing and cartoon," represented 11% of the 1990 newspaper sample.

Canonization

James Michener, a self-described art expert, described Mary Vecchio as the girl with the Delacroix face. He wrote about the picture (Michener, 1971, pp. 544-555) that, "The photograph was the epitome of grief, the perfect symbol of a university youth in turmoil." A colleague of mine, Ben Bassham, who is an art historian, said that he agrees with Michener's interpretation that the picture has the qualities that Delacroix attempted to capture in his paintings of women.

Kim Sorvig, who is a landscape architect, commented on the power of the picture as I have noted above. He based his entire proposal for the 1986 memorial competition on the picture (Sorvig, 1990).

The picture's canonization continued with the 20th anniversary of May 4 in 1990. The picture was used in a variety of ways associated with this anniversary. I identified 450 photographs used to illustrate over 500 stories related to the 1990 anniversary. These were clipped from newspapers throughout the United States. The period examined spanned April 4, 1990 to May 28, 1990. Six photographs account for 81 per cent of all the photographs. In rank order they are: the Memorial (18%), the Mary Vecchio picture (17%), photographs of the National Guard in May of 1970 (13%), photos of the slain students (12%), the annual vigil on the site of the shootings (11%) and Dean Kahler, the most seriously wounded of the students, in a wheelchair on the site (10%). Thus, we see that after twenty years the picture is still very much a part of the media culture associated with May 4.

Comprehension of the Anti-Vietnam War Pieta

The Griswold framework points to the comprehension of cultural objects using a genre approach. The cultural analyst comprehends an object, says Griswold, by apperception or interpreting the new cultural object using what is already known (Griswold, 1987:17). This process of apperception is facilitated by the using of genre which are classifications of similarities and differences often based on powerful exemplars.

Under comprehension, the analyst is directed by Griswold's model to interpret the characteristics of the cultural object through scientific reasoning, particularly replication. She suggests that the cultural analyst look at the cultural object by using ideas of genre. Griswold writes, "Comprehension entails apperception, the interpretation of a new object in terms of what is already known" (Griswold, 1987, p. 17). Genre is the key to this analytic process, argues Griswold. She (Griswold, 1987, p. 17) writes, "Making generic distinctions involves sorting, seeing the similarities in different literary objects, abstracting the common elements from a welter of particular variations."

Three genres are germane to this analysis. First are the artistic works known as the Pieta. Second are pictures related to war. Third are pictures related to the Vietnam War.

Pieta

Most people experience the Pieta by viewing the photograph. The Pieta of Michelangelo was commissioned on August 25, 1498 by the Cardinal of San Donigi. At the time, Michelangelo was an unknown artist. However, The Pieta was not an unknown image to worshipers of the time. Many artists had used it. Robert Coughlan (1966, p. 76) writes:

> Until the 15th Century, the theme of the pieta belonged almost exclusively to the artists of the northern Europe, whose gruesome figure of Jesus and Mary, mainly of wood, seemed designed to shock worshipers into awareness of Christ's sacrifice.

Michelangelo's Pieta dramatically shifted the conventions by portraying the dead Christ as ". . . still alive, His veins distended by the pulse of life . . ." (Coughlan 1966, p. 74). Mary, who was often portrayed in agony in her sorrow, is depicted with physical and spiritual beauty showing her grief with her left hand.

Both the Pieta and the Mary Vecchio photographs are framed as pyramids with the top being the heads of two Mary's while the bases are the earth for the Pieta and the parking lot for Jeffrey Miller. The Mary Vecchio picture shows the shock and horror of the shootings at Kent State by the look on Mary's face. Next, her upraised hands, as if in prayer, capture the sorrow of the moment. Mary expresses her grief over the death of her son, not in her face but with her hand.

Jeffrey Miller is seen lying on his stomach while the Christ lies on his back cradled by Mary. Jeffrey Miller's vitality before the moment of the shooting is illustrated by the blood on the Prentice Hall parking lot, while the Christ's blood is seen in his pulsing veins.

Both are outdoor scenes. The Pieta has dirt at the feet of Mary, while the Vecchio picture is in a parking lot.

There are differences. Michelangelo's Pieta has no one else in the frame--only Mary and Jesus; the Kent State picture shows others present. The student standing near Jeffrey Miller is closer to his body than is Mary Vecchio.

War Photographs

Since the Civil War, photographers have captured the tragedy and drama of American wars. The picture of the dead on the sunken road after the battle of Antietam is one example. World War I pictures show the desolation of the land by trench warfare.

World War II had many powerful images including the pictures of the D-Day invasion on the beaches of Normandy, many of which we revisited during the 50th anniversary activities. The kiss celebrating V-J Day and the raising of the flag on the island of Iwo Jima are two more important World War II photographs.

It is the last photograph that I want to address in this analysis of genre. The Iwo Jima picture shows a squad of six marines raising the flag on Mt. Suribachi. The picture, by Associated Press photographer Joe Rosenthal, won him a Pulitzer Prize. It also had many other impacts. The picture prompted paintings, statues, reprints, coins, and stamps. The massive memorial to marines built in Washington, D.C. was based on the picture. Ironically, the picture was not of the first American flag raised on Iwo Jima, but the second. Two marine squadrons were sent up Mt. Suribachi in an attempt to raise the spirits of those who were still fighting below. The first squadron up the mountain planted a small flag. Although photographers were present as both squadrons went up the mountain, it was the second squadron that presented a more dramatic flag-raising ceremony as they replaced the first smaller flag with a second, larger one.

Vietnam War Pictures

The Vietnam war provided pictures that had enormous national impact including General Nguyen Ngoc Loan's execution of a prisoner during the Tet Offensive in 1968; the Mylai village massacre in 1969; and the Vietnamese girl who was napalmed in June of 1972 (Wilson, 1972, p. 6). But, ironically, the most powerful picture of the Vietnam era was taken in middle America at Kent State University in Ohio. For a compelling comparative analysis see Linda White's (1995) master's thesis, "Two Photographs that Changed America," dealing with the execution and Vecchio pictures.

Explanation of the Anti-Vietnam War Pieta

After comprehending a cultural object, the analyst attempts to explain it by linking the object to the external world. Explanation is the core activity of the sociologist of culture. The explanation of a cultural object requires that the analyst place it in a social context. This social context Griswold (1987: pp. 25-26) begins with categories, groups, and mentalities that are intermediate between the social agent and the large society. The analyst concludes by investigating local sensibilities, proximate and remote social and cultural experiences.

Griswold suggests that the explanation of a cultural project is based on a five-stage process beginning with agents, who are influenced by what she calls "mentalities" (the second stage) based on categories and/or group influences. The third stage directs the analyst to look at the impact of art work on local sensibilities. This third stage is shaped by forces that are analyzed in the fourth stage, particularly the economic, political, and cultural experiences of the people in question. This is labeled the proximate stage of social and cultural experience. The last or fifth stage fits the art work into a larger institutional framework, which Griswold labels the remote social and cultural stage. The analysis begins with the agents and their mentalities who use the picture.

Agents and Mentalities

It is possible, suggests Griswold (1987, pp. 24-25), to identify many types of actors who interact with the cultural object and to construct a structure of intention (brief). Types of actors range from cultural producers such as artists to mediators such as editors to recipients such as audiences. In the case of a well known cultural object such as the Mary Vecchio picture, the task set for the analyst can be a daunting one. It is possible to identify several distinct types of agents using the "Pieta" photograph. First, there are cultural producers, who built on it for their own artist purposes. Second are the mediators, in a variety of media, who use the picture for a considerable range of editorial reasons. Lastly are the audiences for these media, who have distinct reasons for paying attention to the picture.

Earlier, the types of use of the picture were noted, including sculptures, cartoons, and abstractions illustrating news and magazine stories. Kim Sorvig's (1990) submission noted above serves as an exemplar for the artistic use of the picture. Editors of magazines, newspapers, and television shows have, as mediators, used the picture in a variety of ways. However, four basic uses stand out. First, there is the use to illustrate stories related to the May 4 shootings at Kent State and its aftermath. Second, the picture is employed to illustrate some aspect of the story related to the Vietnam War. For example, ABC's "Good Morning, America" (4/25/94) used the picture to show the linkage between President Richard Nixon's administration and the Kent State University killings.

A third utilization of the picture by agents is illustrating material related to the culture of the sixties. For example, Jules Archer's (1986) *The Incredible Sixties* includes a drawing of the "Pieta" as part of a collage of sixties representations located in the center of the dust cover just above a drawing of Martin Luther King. Interestingly, there is no mention of the picture anywhere else in the book including the opening chapter that deals with the Kent State shootings. John Filo is credited on the back of the dust cover. Lastly, the picture is used to date a certain period.

Without interview data one cannot be completely certain why the picture was used, but it is possible to suggest some directions of inquiry. The emotion of the Mary Vecchio picture captures the passion of the anti-Vietnam War conflict for audiences who see this cultural object. In addition, the picture shows the costs of political activism.

But, perhaps the best reason lies in the emotional power of the picture. We see

Michelangelo's Pieta in the Filo photograph. The most emotional of all sculptures teaches us why the Mary Vecchio picture has had such a long cultural life.

Impact on Public Opinion Cultures

The Griswold model points to questions that require the analyst to take account of the distribution of influences that shape how particular groups related to a cultural object. Griswold argues that one must be aware of local sensibilities that are shaped by temporal and spatial considerations. The temporal and spatial considerations are defined as proximate and remote cultural experiences. According to Griswold, this means the degree of connection that groups have with cultural items. She suggests (personal conversation on June, 23, 1994) that this perspective is similar to Erving Goffman's (1974) framing. The understanding and interest in a cultural object likely have some type of differential distribution. Though the cultural object under analysis in this paper--the Pieta--was rapidly distributed by popular culture and news sources nationally and internationally, it is possible to suggest a temporal-spatial configuration.

The public opinion process for a powerful cultural object is a complex interaction located geographically and temporally between people and mass media. It is possible to treat the cultural object as a dependent or independent variable. As an independent variable the analysis looks at the impact of the cultural object on various audiences. As a dependent variable one examines how these audiences seek out the cultural object.

Treating the picture as an independent variable influencing various public opinion cultures, it is possible to identify five different cultures. One can use the imagery of a stone dropped in a pond, with the picture as the stone. The widening ripples represent various public opinion regions including local, Northeast Ohio, Midwest, national, and international region.

Though the starting point of Kent State controversies is always the same, the shootings on May 4, 1970, the formation of opinions, and the construction of social reality are strikingly different in each of these public opinion regions.

In the local public opinion region (primarily the City of Kent where Kent State University is located) the reaction involves one of the more powerful concerns that local residents had and have about

May 4: the presence of outside agitators. After the picture was released, it was discovered that Mary Vecchio was not a Kent State student and this fed rumors of outside agitators even thought Miss Vecchio had been on campus for only a few days before the shooting and left immediately after. As Rudwick and Meier (1972) noted, rumors of outsiders on campus were rife in the days before shootings. This was likely true on most college campuses. The picture reinforced these views and continues to do so today.

In the next public opinion region, Northeast Ohio, which encompasses the home county of Kent State and its six adjoining counties, the debate shifts from substantive issue about the shootings to questions about the University. That is, how could the University allow these things to happen on its campus? The picture generates negative images about the university and its faculty and students. There is a certain amount of blaming the victim here.

The involvement of the university and its students is illustrated by responses to a survey (N=385) I conducted in 1976. Seventy-four percent of undergraduates responded "strongly agree" or "agree" to the question, "I am often asked about the May 4, 1970 events simply because I am a Kent State student." Since most Kent State undergraduates still come from Northeast Ohio, these data suggest that the controversies at the university are still very much on the minds of the residents of the Northeast Ohio public opinion region.

Moving to the next large region, the Midwest, the character of the public opinion process contrasts sharply with the others just examined. As opposed to these regions just examined, the primary source of information about Kent State is the mass media. For the most part the media outside the Northeast Ohio region tended to cover the most dramatic aspects of the May 4 story. Consequently, the picture is often used in ways not directly connected to May 4. The picture is often shown with very little in-depth follow up. It is used in the ways noted earlier to illustrate a story about Kent State or the sixties. This leads to confusion about what actually happened at Kent State on May 4, 1970.

At the national level, the problem of fleeting images is linked to the importance of television as Americans' basic source of news. The average network television news story is rarely longer than 90 seconds and emphasizes the visually interesting.

Therefore, the considerable power of the Mary Vecchio picture is very useful because it is visually efficient. However, the result for the national audience is often confusion about what happened on May 4 because so little information is provided. This is particularly true for the issue of the outsider agitator. At the international level, all the problems of the national level are compounded with the confusion about the cultural context of the incident

CONCLUSIONS

Why has the Mary Vecchio picture had such staying power over the years? This analysis, based on the theoretical model proposed by Wendy Griswold, suggests three reasons. First, and perhaps most important, it is a very strong image comparable to the photograph of one of the most important pieces in the history of art—Michelangelo's Pieta. The beauty, agony, and power of both images force one to struggle with the issues that compelled the creation of the art in the first place—the death of the Jesus and the shootings at Kent State. Second, the picture lends itself to a variety of uses ranging from illustrative photographs of the both the anti-Vietnam War culture as well as the more encompassing 1960s to political pins and brochures. Third, it captures perhaps more than any other photograph the agony of American society's experience with the Vietnam War.

REFERENCES

Archer, J. 1986. *The Incredible Sixties*. San Diego: Harcourt Brace Jovanovich.

Bush, B. 1990. "20 years later, one photo still says it all." Springfield, Illinois: *The State Journal-Register* (May 4, 1990): 1, 6.

Coughlan, and The Editors of Time-Life Books. 1966. New York: Time Incorporated.

Goffman, E. 1974. *Frame Analysis*. New York: Harper and Row.

Goldman, V. 1993. *The Power of Photography*. New York: Abbeville Publishing Group.

Griswold, W. 1986. *Renaissance Revivals: City Comedy and Revenge Tragedy in the London Theatre 1576-1980*. Chicago: University of Chicago Press.

Griswold, W. 1987. "A Methodological Framework for the Sociology of Culture." *Sociological Methodology*. Vol.17:1-35.

Haldeman, H. R. 1978. *The Ends of Power*. New York: Times Books.

Leingang, M. T. 1994. "Subject of famous May 4 photograph returns to bury past." *Daily Kent Stater* (April 5):1,12.

Lewis, J. M. "Interview with Mary Vecchio." Kent, Ohio. Kent State University, 4/4/94.

Michener, James. 1971. *Kent State: What Happened and Why*. New York: Random House and Reader's Digest Books.

Payne, J. Gregory. 1981. *Mayday: Kent State*. Dubuque, Iowa: Kendall/Hunt.

Rudwick, E. and A. Meier. 1972. "The Kent State Affair" *Sociological Inquiry*. Vol.42:81-86.

Sorvig, K. 1990. *To Heal Kent State*. Philadelphia: Worldview Press.

White, L. 1995. *Two Photographs that Changed America: The Pulitzer Images of Eddie Adams and John Filo*. Master's Thesis. Athens Ohio: Ohio University.

Wilson, J. 1989. "Photographer, famous photo's subject hold reunion in Havana, Cuba" *News Photographer*. (November): 6-7.

ENDNOTES

1. Mary Vecchio now uses her married name. However, I will continue to refer to her using her family name because it is so associated with the picture.
2. Aspects of this section have been previously published in *American History Illustrated* (June, 1990) and *Crowd Management* (April-June, 1995).

THE GYM ISSUE

A meeting of the May 4th Coalition at Tent City in July, 1977. Photo by Doug Moore.

INTRODUCTION

On May 4, 1977 a new controversy arose on Kent State's campus over the decision to build a new Health, Physical Education and Recreation facility on an area north of Memorial Gymnasium which included portions of the land where students and Guardsmen confronted each other on May 4, 1970. This conflict grew from a local controversy into one of national significance involving Congress, the White House, and the Supreme Court. It dominated life on the Kent State campus during spring, summer, and fall of 1977, and its effects continued for many years.

The first essay by Thomas R. Hensley on the gym controversy is similar in scope and purpose to his essay on the Kent State trials in Section II of this book. Originally written in 1977, he has attempted to present an overview of the conflict. discussing the historical development of the dispute as well as the strategies and activities of the two major sides in the controversy, a student-based group called the May 4th Coalition and the university's board of trustees. Jerry M. Lewis' essay on a particular aspect of the controversy, the Tent City period, is a further application of Smelser's theory of collective behavior and should be compared with his earlier analysis in this book of the events of May 4th using Smelser's model. The third essay by Hensley applies Janis' theory of "groupthink" to the 1977 gymnasium controversey in an attempt to explain the refusal of the board of trustees not only to reconsider their decision about where to build the gym facility but also to discuss the issue with the May 4th Coalition.

KENT STATE 1977: THE STRUGGLE TO MOVE THE GYM

Thomas R. Hensley
Kent State University

INTRODUCTION

It is nearly noon. Tension grips the Kent State campus. Nobody knows exactly what is going to happen, but it is clear that the potential for tragedy is present. Protestors, student and non-student, gather in increasingly large numbers around the Victory Bell on the Kent State Commons, the traditional gathering place for rallies, but officials have declared the rally to be illegal. Law enforcement personnel, under orders to break up any rally, nervously face the demonstrators across the Commons. While substantially outnumbered by the protestors, the law enforcement men are well-equipped, weapons are loaded, and tear gas is ready. An order is read to the demonstrators that they must disperse because the rally has been banned, but in the confusion few protestors hear the order and it is apparent that the demonstrators are not going to leave.

This is not a description of May 4, 1970. Rather, this is a description of October 22, 1977 at Kent State University. Kent State University, where in the immediate aftermath of the 1970 shootings, President Robert I. White declared: "This is where it happened; this is where it ends and shall never happen again."[1]

Fortunately, the replaying of the 1970 confrontation on the Commons did not lead to the same tragic results that occurred in 1970. During that fall afternoon in 1977, however, demonstrators and law enforcement personnel were engaged in continuous confrontations. Members of the Portage County Sheriff's Office dispersed protestors by riding their horses into the crowds, and tear gas covered several areas of the campus. Kent State had once again become thrust into statewide and national attention, and the deep and jagged wounds of 1970, which had been so slow to heal, had been ripped open again. The immediate cause of the new era of confrontation was the construction of a Health, Physical Education, and Recreation facility on an area where part of the 1970 confrontation occurred. The issues went much deeper than the building of one facility, however, for the ideological and generational cleavages of the Vietnam era had reemerged on the Kent State campus.

This is an expanded version of a paper presented at the 1978 annual meeting of the Ohio Association of Economists and Political Scientists.

I wish to express my appreciation to a number of people who read an earlier version of this manuscript: John Begala, Dennis Carey, Carter Dodge, Bob Hart, John Hendrikson, George Janik, Betty Kirschner, Jerry M. Lewis, Todd McFarren, Joyce Quirk, Michael Schwartz, and Richard Taylor. It is important to note that all interpretations are mine and are not necessarily shared by the readers above.

This analysis seeks to describe and explain the series of events which plunged Kent State University once again into a deep crisis. In addition to telling an important story in Kent State history, this article sets the foundation for the two theoretical articles which follow in this section of the book.

Sources

A wide variety of sources will be drawn upon in this study. I personally observed most of the major events which occurred in connection with the controversy, and I talked informally on almost a daily basis with a wide variety of people about these events. In addition, I collected the newspaper articles on these events appearing in the three major local newspapers, the *Daily Kent Stater*, the *Record-Courier*, and the *Akron Beacon Journal*. Another important data source was the countless leaflets which flooded the Kent State campus during the controversy. A wide variety of inter-university memos were also been made available to me, and these frequently proved insightful. Because of the involvement of local, state, and federal courts in this controversy, court documents constituted yet another valuable data resource. The minutes of the meetings of the Kent State Board of Trustees were also useful. Several of my students prepared insightful papers analyzing aspects of the Blanket Hill controversy.[2] Finally, tape recorded interviews with a number of key participants were invaluable in helping me to analyze these events. Lengthy interviews were held with trustee Joyce Quirk; Dr. Michael Schwartz, who served as interim president of the university during part of July and August of 1977; State Representative John Begala, who played a major third party role throughout the summer; Dr. Dave Luban, an active member of the protest group, the May 4th Coalition; John Henrikson, a Kent State student who was active in the coalition during the spring and summer; and trustee Robert Baumgardner.[3]

The Problem of Objectivity

It is necessary to acknowledge the problem facing any author writing about a controversial event—objectivity. I do not claim *to be* objective in my treatment, but I do claim that I have *tried to be* objective. The reader will be the ultimate judge of my success or failure. It does seem important for me to offer here my personal views which developed as the controversy unfolded during the spring and summer months, views which I am certain affected to some extent my research and writing during the fall of 1977. At the beginning of the controversy in May, while I was generally supportive of the concerns of the May 4th Coalition, I could not view the gymnasium addition controversy as being a truly fundamental moral issue. Gradually during the late spring, I came to the viewpoint that the choice of the site was a bad decision for a variety of historical, moral, and ecological reasons, and I hoped that the trustees would change their decision. By late spring and early summer, it became apparent to me that the protest movement would not go away, and that the costs to the university in building the facility would far outweigh the costs of finding an alternative site. When it finally became crystal clear in late August that the trustees were determined not to change the site, I felt that they had made a grave error but at this point I felt that there was no viable choice but to acquiesce in the decision. My views have changed somewhat during my intensive analysis of the controversy, and my current views will be presented in the concluding section of the study.

Organization

The analysis will be divided into six major sections. The first will be an effort to define the sides in the controversy and to provide some insights about the major actors in the controversy. The next section will provide a description of the historical planning and development of the HPER facility. With this background established, the following three sections will focus upon a detailed analysis of the specific events in the controversy. This analysis will be organized chronologically according to three distinct time periods: May 4, 1977 to May 12, 1977, when the protest group, the May 4th Coalition, was created; May 12, 1977 to July 12, 1977, the period in which this coalition created a "Tent City" on the KSU campus as the symbol of their protest; and July 13 to September 19, 1977, the two month period in which construction was suspended while litigation was being pursued by the coalition as they sought to preserve the site. Following a brief epilogue covering the fall period after construction resumed on September 19, I will in the final section summarize the analysis of the earlier sections and offer my personal views on the controversy.

THE KEY ACTORS

Introduction

One of the most difficult problems in analyzing this controversy is understanding who were the major decision makers in the controversy. This is especially true for the May 4th Coalition, whose nebulous structure and fluid membership make the group impervious to neat definition. The problems are not much less severe in identifying the real decision makers for the university, for Kent State lacked clearly defined leadership during this entire time period. Subsequent analysis demands a clarification of the key sides and actors in the controversy, however, despite the problems in the attempt.

The May 4th Coalition

The May 4th Coalition can perhaps best be described as a loose association of individuals who shared at least one common concern: preventing the HPER facility from being built on the site of the shootings of May 4, 1970, with the site being defined as the entire area where the Guard and students confronted each other during the period when the Guard broke up the noon rally and fired upon the students. Beyond this it is difficult to characterize the coalition in an easy manner. Meetings of the coalition throughout the spring and summer were open, and anyone in attendance was allowed to participate in discussions and to vote. No "officers" or "leaders" were ever selected; when conditions required that committees be formed or representatives selected for particular tasks, persons were selected on an ad hoc basis for that function only. Thus, the coalition was a group without membership requirements and without permanently elected leaders or representatives. It was unlike anything that had ever been seen on Kent's campus. Coalition members themselves took great pride in the unique qualities of their organization, and many saw their "constructive anarchism" or "ultimate participatory democracy" as a potential landmark development in the history of social movements.

It is important to note also that the coalition underwent substantial changes throughout the spring and summer months in terms of active participants. Although a number of people were active throughout the entire spring and summer, substantial numbers of people dropped out along the way and, similarly, many new recruits joined the coalition throughout this period. The fluctuations in membership were due to many factors; personal problems, job requirements, disagreements over tactics and decision making procedures, fear of the consequences of future arrests, and sheer exhaustion seem to have been the major factors for people dropping out of active participation. New recruits appear to have been attracted to the coalition because of support for its cause, identification with and support for a broader radical movement, and a desire to be where the action is. In terms of actual numbers, a typical coalition meeting—and they were held daily—would draw from 100 to 200 people, and the rallies would attract from 500 to 1500 supporters.

The University Leadership

Just as the decision making structure and processes of the coalition defy easy description, so too does the university's decision making process during this period. Prior to and during the controversy, the university was in the midst of a deep leadership crisis, with no single person or group clearly in charge of decision making. As a result, a substantial number of persons were involved in making decisions; but nearly every decision was a reaction to events which appeared largely beyond the direct control of the university leaders, for in a leadership vacuum long range or short range planning does not get accomplished. An understanding of the university's decision making process requires an overview of these major actors and the positions in which they found themselves.

The evidence seems rather clear that Kent State President Glenn Olds, who assumed the position in 1971, had lost effective control over university decision making by the end of the 1975-1976 academic year. Olds had done an effective job in his initial years of healing many of the wounds which the university suffered in the aftermath of the May 4th shootings. Gradually, however, the faculty came to the view that Olds' leadership in the academic sector was inadequate, and in the spring of 1976, the faculty voted in favor of collective bargaining over the pleas of Olds and also gave Olds a public vote of "no confidence." Olds was also experiencing problems within the administrative ranks of the university. Michael Schwartz, who was to become interim president for a month and one-half in the summer of 1977 after Olds left Kent State, has observed:

I came here in March of 1976, and it didn't take very long to see that the president was in fact not running the university. He was literally unable to make a decision, and it was an administrator's nightmare because you didn't get decisions made except in the most simple matters. It also became pretty obvious early on to me that it was members of the board—not the whole board—who were then running the university, making the big decisions in most of the important areas....[4]

A series of tumultuous events at the start of the 1976-1977 year led to the resignation of Olds in November of 1976. The two most widely publicized developments, both involving the College of Business Administration, concerned (1) allegations that university resources were being used to assist a private economic advising corporation composed of several faculty and administrators from the Business College and (2) allegations that several Business College faculty had improperly accepted gifts and expense-paid trips to Puerto Rico from a Ph.D. student in the College.

Against the backdrop of all these problems which had mounted during the recent months, Olds' resignation made the leadership vacuum even more severe, and some trustees felt even more compelled to try to fill the leadership void.[5]

Throughout the 1976-1977 academic year, then, several of the trustees were closely involved in the day-to-day management of a troubled university. The faculty was thoroughly disenchanted with the management of the university; and as collective bargaining efforts broke down in the spring of 1977, faculty attacks on the trustees became increasingly harsh and a strike vote was taken to force the trustees back to the bargaining table. Throughout the academic year efforts to resolve the controversies within the Business College met with little success, and by the end of the year several members of the College, including the Dean, resigned their positions. In addition, severe conflicts within the top ranks of the administration became public when Olds recommended to the trustees that some senior vice presidents be released, and the trustees passed a resolution putting all senior vice presidents on renewable one-month contracts. Finally, projected student enrollments for the coming fall were down approximately 10 percent, creating the possibility of further financial difficulties in the near future for the university, whose financial problems had been even further compounded by a record breaking cold winter.

During 1976-1977, then, Kent State University was a school facing difficult problems of great significance with no effective leadership. Olds observed in an interview as he prepared to leave Kent State:

It's been an absolutely atypical, almost absurd year, and that trend is catastrophic because no board can run a university. . . . The president has to.[6]

Yet the president was not running Kent State; and trustees, people with no experience in directly administrating a university and with their own demanding careers to pursue, saw themselves facing the necessity of directly conducting the major affairs of the university. Nearly overwhelmed by a baffling array of problems—an angry faculty potentially on the verge of striking, unresolved allegations about scandals within the Business College, deep conflicts within the upper echelons of the administration, major financial problems, potentially declining enrollments—the trustees were to find their greatest problem yet to emerge.

PLANNING AND DEVELOPMENT OF THE HPER FACILITY

Planning for the Health, Physical Education and Recreation facility spanned a period of more than one and one-half decades. Because many of the issues which arose in the spring and summer of 1977 centered around the historical planning and development of the HPER facility, it is important to identify precisely the major stages in this lengthy process.[7]

The facility was first formally proposed in December in 1962 when a document entitled "Building Plans, School of Health, Physical Education and Recreation" was given to the university's architect Gae Russo by the School of Health, Physical Education and Recreation, which had worked with the School's Space Planning Council. It was not until the 1967-1969 biennium that the proposed facility was included in the university's capital improvements requests to the Ohio Board of Regents. This request was included in the university's requests for each of the next four biennia as well: 1969-1971, 1971-1973, 1973-1975, and 1975-1977. The Board of Regents tabled the requests in 1969-1971, 1971-1973, and 1973-1975, but the facility was finally approved for the 1975-1977 biennium when the regents authorized a total of $6 million for the project. This included $500,000 for the demolition of an old Physiology Laboratory and Wills Gymnasium, the women's gymnasium which had already been condemned by state officials, as well as $500,000 for architects' fees and engineers' fees. The facility was to be a combination instructional, research, office, and recreational building which would include five regular classrooms, three seminar rooms, a large lecture hall, forty-five offices, three research laboratories, eight handball courts, two dance studios, two gymnasiums, a swimming pool, and a variety of other facilities.[8]

While approval by the Board of Regents did not come until 1975, serious planning for the facility occurred throughout the sixties and early seventies. During the period between 1963 and 1969, the Long Range Planning Committee of the Division of Health, Physical Education, Recreation and Athletics considered many different sites for the facility. In the late sixties land at the corner of Allerton and Summit Streets was purchased by the university, and on October 20, 1969, the Long Range Planning Committee recommended this site for the facility.[9] On April 16, 1970, a different site was recommended by the HPER Space Planning Committee, which proposed that the facility be built north of the current Memorial Gymnasium[10] and it was this site which was specified in the plans which the School sent to the Board of Regents in early 1974.[11] Opposition was expressed to the location, however, by Olds in a memo dated March 4, 1974 to Dean Carl Erickson of the School of Health, Physical Education and Recreation:

> Thank you for your memo of 15 February. I was remarking that the physical education facility is still our top priority.
>
> I think you know I am personally opposed to the location recommended and would be happy to discuss this with you and your colleagues and/or any others at the appropriate time.
>
> We will certainly be pressing for this new facility in the new biennium.[12]

Erickson responded to Olds in a memo dated April 30, 1974, explaining in detail the reasons why the location north of Memorial Gymnasium was chosen. Nine specific reasons were identified by Erickson; these need to be presented in detail because of their centrality to the subsequent conflict.

1. The space at the north end of Memorial Gym which we call the Memorial "U" should be included in future planning as we currently have three erected walls which we can incorporate into our future building.
2. Our plan is not to utilize a great amount of the area north of the building as we recommend that the new unit be attached to the Memorial Gym Building, go north a limited distance and then project eastward with the entrance on Midway Drive, without removing any currently standing trees. By utilizing this space, we can conserve on the cost for heating lines, utilities, locker and shower room space, etc.
3. The present area provides adequate parking which would eliminate the development of a future parking area if the building was located elsewhere.
4. By having the facility in this area it will provide accessibility to students to attend their classes on a one-hour schedule rather than a three-hour schedule. If the facility is to be moved to the outskirts of the campus, the students must take the bus to get there which means that they must plan for a free hour before the class period to get there and a free hour after the class period to return to the campus for other classes.
5. The central location is now considered the University Center and has become the center for student activity. An addition to our building will enhance additional participation in student activity.
6. The facility, by being in the center of the campus, will centralize the location of the faculty and for the first time bring all units together.
7. The students participating in intramural programs have indicated that they want it located centrally on campus and not on the outskirts.
8. We are concerned about state subsidy, student credit hours, productivity, etc. If the facility is moved to the outskirts of the campus, I can foresee a very significant decline in student enrollment in the physical education basic instruction program and student participation in the intramural and campus recreation program.

9. Having all units centrally located in the middle of the campus enhances student advising, counseling and, also, the recruiting of new students.[13]

Erickson's arguments for the location proved to be persuasive, for in a responding memo of May 8, 1974, Olds wrote:

> I have your memorandum of April 30 and its helpful summary on the question of the location of the Physical Education Facility. My objection to the placement of anything more in the center of the campus turned on the critical problem of space utilization. I gather from your memorandum, however, that you do not plan to preempt that whole field and link it so tidily with the present Memorial Building that it will constitute one continuous facility.

> With that understanding, and with the possibility that it would not alter as dramatically as I felt, I would be willing, certainly, to modify my view and to consider more responsively than I was willing to do in our last conversation, the prospect of the consummation of that location.[14]

Following state approval of funds for the facility in March of 1975, the next major developments occurred in June of 1975 as university representatives prepared to present their specific plans for the facility to the Board of Regents. In a memo of June 13 to Vice President for Administration Walter Bruska, University Architect Russo presented the following recommendation on behalf of himself and the Department of Health, Physical Education and Recreation:

> Since the capital funds for this project are limited, it will be necessary to utilize existing facilities in Memorial Gym in order to avoid the duplication necessitated by a separate facility. We are therefore recommending the new structure be an addition to the North end of Memorial Gym. This would also allow for a unification of all H. P. E. and R. programs, since Wills Gym and the Physiology Lab are to be demolished as a part of this project. Building costs could be minimized since this location is close to all utility lines. The loss of the North playfield is not serious since we are presently preparing additional fields between Midway Drive and Tri-Towers and the new building includes a large field house for those activities.[15]

On June 27, 1975 Bruska responded to Russo:

> This is to inform you that the President and Vice Presidents have discussed your recommendation requesting the site location for the projected new HPE&R and Nursing School buildings.

> We have approved the site locations which you have recommended. The following suggestions were made that I would ask you to keep in mind in establishing the exact site and the layout for the buildings:

> Re: HPE&R—Attempt to retain as much of the playing field and open vista—north of Memorial Gymnasium, as possible.[16]

In response to Bruska's expressed concern over the amount of area to be utilized, Russo wrote to Bruska on July 3, 1975:

> No more of the area next to the existing Memorial Gym will be taken by the New H. P. E. & R. Building than is absolutely necessary. You should be aware, however, that the area required is likely to be somewhat larger than that occupied by the existing building simply on the basis of square footage. . . .[17]

A memo from Russo to Erickson a short time later—July 18, 1975—provides insight into the precise location envisioned by the university officials at this time. Attached to the memo was a copy of the building program for the facility which was to be mailed shortly to the Board of Regents for approval as well as a site map. The site map indicated that the facility would extend straight back from Memorial Gymnasium. While the site was designated only in rough form, it clearly would not cut into the Blanket Hill area at all, would not be near the Prentice Hall parking lot, and would occupy much less than half of the practice football field.[18]

In September of 1975 the Richard Fleishman Architects firm of Cleveland was selected by a university committee to design the building. Throughout the latter part of 1975 and the early part of 1976, many meetings were held between the architects from the Fleischman firm, University Architect Russo, and the HPER Space Planning Council. On June 18, 1976 the preliminary plans, specifications, and cost estimates were approved by the State Architects' office. After further modifications and subsequent state approval, Fleischman and Erickson were prepared to present the plans to the Board of Trustees at their November 11, 1976 meeting. This would be the first time that all the trustees had been officially involved in the development of the new facility.[19]

It was at this meeting that student concern over the location of the building was first formally expressed.[20] An article in the *Daily Kent Stater* on November 3, 1976 indicated that the proposed facility could cover part of the area where the May 4th confrontation occurred, and a *Stater* article the next day indicated that the trustees would be considering plans for the HPER building at their next meeting.[21] On November 9, members of the Student Caucus,[22] the May 4th Task Force,[23] and other interested students met to draw up a list of concerns about the location of the facility to be presented to the trustees. At the trustee meeting on the 11th, about forty students were in attendance, and Scott Marburger, Student Caucus executive secretary, and Nancy Grim, a caucus representative, presented six student concerns to the trustees:

1. Lack of adequate student input on all levels of the decision making process;
2. Insufficient justification of the currently proposed facility;
3. Destruction of the natural beauty of the area;
4. Possible alteration of the May 4th site, raising legal and historical questions;
5. Need for complete and exhaustive consideration of alternative sites;
6. Intended source of operating and maintenance costs of the proposed facility.[24]

The minutes of the trustees' meeting indicate that some of these concerns were shared by the trustees, but ultimately they voted unanimously to approve the building progress report, which meant that final completion of the plans could proceed. A number of reasons seem to explain the trustees' decision. At this point, the trustees unquestionably found the arguments presented by Erickson and Fleischman to be more convincing than student arguments, and there was little reason to think that student concern over this issue would develop much further. Second, the trustees saw themselves as being locked into a decision to approve the plans, even at this early stage in the controversy. Well over a decade of work had gone into the development of

plans for the facility, and substantial costs had already been committed in architectural fees. A third factor of significance was that the HPER facility was simply not a major concern of key decision makers during this time period, for the minds of Olds and Janik were preoccupied with the surprise announcement that was to capture the next day's headlines: the resignation of Olds.[25] Ironically, Olds, reflecting upon his tenure as Kent State president in his letter of resignation, stated: "Except for those permanent losses of life and disabilities never to be regained, the human and public effects of 1970 have been virtually healed. . . ."[26]

MAY 4TH - MAY 12TH: BIRTH OF THE MAY 4TH COALITION

Events Prior to May 4th

As May 4th, 1977 approached, there were few preliminary rumblings of the impending volcanic eruptions which were to grip Kent State University. Several days of extensive commemorative activities were planned, but these events were basically similar to those which had been carried out in previous observances of the 1970 shootings: movies and art displays; a candlelight walk around the campus on the evening of May 3rd, followed by an all-night silent vigil at the places where the four students were killed; and a program of speakers, recalling the events of 1970 and reflecting upon their past, present, and future significance. The major new event planned for May 4, 1977 was a planned march involving as many as 5000 persons through portions of Kent, the first such march since 1970.

The weeks leading up to May 4, 1977 were not without controversy, however. Members of the May 4 Task Force, as well as reporters and editors of the *Daily Kent Stater*, criticized university administrators for their neglect and callousness toward the events of May 4.[27] Among the specific complaints were the failure of the administration to cancel classes for all or part of May 4th; the refusal to consider renaming four campus buildings after the students who were killed; the conversion of Hyde Park from an area dedicated to free speech into a parking lot;[28] the plans to build the gymnasium addition on part of the area where the 1970 confrontation occurred; and a proposal to cut the budget of the Center for Peaceful Change which was created in the aftermath of May 4, 1970 as an "enduring, living, educational memorial to serve students, now and in the future, and to penetrate the full significance of May 4. . . ."[29] The primary focus of controversy was the issue of the cancellation of classes. Students had picketed the administration building, and a strike was called by the May 4th Strike Committee.[30] In addition, a ceremony was held on May 3rd outside the library naming four campus buildings after the slain students. Concern over the HPER facility was of decidedly secondary importance during this time, although on the morning of May 4th, the May 4th Strike Committee sponsored a workshop in the Student Center Governance Chambers on stopping the proposed gym.

Despite these controversies, the general mood on the campus and in the city was calm. When the May 4 Task Force announced that they were planning the march in Kent, the general reaction among Kent residents was one of indifference. Kent City Council members reported that they had received no complaints from Kent residents. Councilman Ted Sapp expressed the general view of Council members: "Residents won't make much of it. . . . It's been quite awhile since May 4. Most people are pretty apathetic about everything, anyway."[31] A dissenting view was expressed by Councilman Dal Hardesty, who was quoted as saying: "Most of the clowns they [the Task Force] are bringing on campus should be ignored. It's a shame money is being spent to bring rabble like these people to speak."[32] Hardesty said he "wouldn't want any part of the bunch of stinking clowns they brought in at KSU."[33] But Hardesty also noted, "People in the city, if they reacted at all, will just be disgusted. They [the speakers] won't be nearly as effective in getting a rabble going as they were in 1970."[34] A telephone survey of a random sample of Kent State students conducted by the *Daily Kent Stater* revealed that while a majority of students were going to participate in observing the day, they were not going to boycott all of their classes for the day. Sixty-four percent of the students surveyed said they would be attending classes, while 30 percent stated they would not attend and 5 percent were undecided. A majority of those surveyed—61 percent—did indicate that they would attend at least one of the events planned for the day.[35] For the university's trustees, it would be business as usual; a meeting was to be held at four o'clock that afternoon to consider names of the final candidates for president of the university. While the meeting was held, it was not to be a day for business as usual.[36]

May 4, 1977: Rockwell Sit-In

The candlelight march began about 11 p.m. on May 3rd and was estimated to involve 1000 persons, the largest turnout since 1971. It was a solemn and moving event for those participating. Reflecting on the size and the mood of the group, Professor Jerry Lewis, one of the organizers, reflected, "It's taken on an appropriate religious meaning rather than a political meaning."[37] Among those most touched by the observance was Sandy Scheuer's mother, who attended for the first time: "'I'm sorry we weren't here before. We didn't know that this still mattered here.'"[38]

The activities for May 4th began around noon in Memorial Gymnasium, for the inclement weather made it undesirable to meet on the Commons. A crowd of approximately 3000 packed the gymnasium to hear a variety of speakers, the most famous being comedian and activist Dick Gregory, radical lawyer William Kunstler, and Vietnam veteran and author Ron Kovic. The mood of the speeches during the day was noticeably different than it had been in past years, where the focus had been primarily upon paying tribute to the slain students and analyzing the causes and lessons of the tragedy. Most speakers saw these causes as resting in the very nature of American society, a society which students were challenged to change. This general challenge to change America usually drew polite applause. While the speeches of 1977 also stressed the theme of the persisting, deep-rooted problems of America which gave rise to the May 4th shootings, a sense of surging energy began to swell as the speakers addressed concrete local issues which had recently arisen, specifically the question of the future of the Center for Peaceful Change and the decision to build the gymnasium addition near the site of the shootings. Kovic, Kunstler, and Gregory brought the crowd to its feet time and time again, roaring its approval of their pleas to prevent construction of the gym. Kovic ignited the crowd with his challenge: "If they try to build that gym, if they try to hide that truth, then they're going to have to bury 1000 students in the cement that they pour."[39] Kunstler added to the electricity surging through the crowd by appealing to the audience to "lie down in front of the bulldozers"[40] if they start construction and promising to return to defend anyone jailed in trying to halt construction of the gym addition. Gregory also talked about the gym issue by assuring the crowd that "there are a lot of people out there watching you and depending on you to win your struggle,"[41] and he promised to fast without solid food until the project was halted.

Energized by the dynamic oratory of the afternoon, a crowd of approximately 1500 people participated in the march which followed the afternoon's speeches. Following the march, word spread that the trustees were meeting in Rockwell Hall, the administration building. Approximately 200 protestors, almost all Kent State students, entered the building in the late afternoon chanting "Stop the Gym." Finding themselves locked out of the trustees' conference room, the protestors occupied part of the second floor and demanded to meet with university officials. Eventually both Olds and trustee chairman Janik appeared before the protestors to listen to their concerns and to explain the positions of the university. Dissatisfied with the responses of Olds and Janik but uncertain about what to do, the group continued to occupy the building until about 1:00 a.m. During this time, a variety of strategies were discussed, and eventually a list of eight demands was developed by the newly born May 4th Coalition.

The demands were: (1) *Justice!* The Kent State University administration must officially acknowledge the injustice of the Kent State massacre of May 4, 1970. (2) *Move the Gym!* The new HPER building (gym) must *not* be built on the site of the shootings of May 4, 1970, and in the future, no construction or alteration of the site must be permitted. (3) *Keep the CPC!* The status of the Center for Peaceful Change must be maintained as it is as an all-university program. (4) *No 'business as usual' on May 4!* Henceforth May 4 must be set aside as a day of remembrance and education about the Kent State massacre; and the regular activities of the University must be cancelled every May 4 hereafter. (5) *Name the buildings!* The four buildings which have been named after the four slain students must be officially recognized: The business building is William Schroeder Hall; the art building is Allison Krause Hall; the library is Jeffrey Miller Memorial Library; the music and speech building is Sandra Scheuer Music and Speech Center. (6) *Amnesty for May 4, 1977!* Amnesty must be given to all students, faculty, and staff who commemorated May 4, 1977 and are threatened with reprisals of any kind. (7)

Support UFPA! The administration must reopen negotiations in good faith with the United Faculty Professional Association. (8) *No reprisals for the sit-in!* The university must guarantee that no administrative, academic, or legal actions will be taken against participants in the May 4, 1977 Rockwell Hall occupation and sit-in, either now or in the future.[42]

Following the formulation of the demands, the protestors left the building and held a brief public conference, primarily for the benefit of the media. Spokesperson Dean Kahler, who was wounded and permanently paralyzed in the 1970 shootings, read a statement which included the list of demands that the protestors wanted to be placed on the agenda of the next trustee meeting, scheduled for May 12. Before dispersing, an announcement was also made concerning a rally which would be held the next night and another rally which would occur on May 12 to coincide with the trustees' meeting.

What were the results of the Rockwell sit-in? The most obvious concrete results were the list of eight demands set forth by the coalition, which Janik agreed to discuss with representatives of the coalition on May 6th. Also, a steering committee was selected to develop further the goals and strategies of the coalition. While these tangible results were significant, of far greater importance was the genesis of a new student movement which not only came to dominate life on the Kent State campus but also spread across the nation, involving students from dozens of other campuses and eventually many non-student radicals as well. The movement had its foundation cast firmly in local issues, all of which centered around perceptions of administration and trustee insensitivity to and lack of genuine concern about the events of May 4th. No amount of explanation from university leaders was going to alter these deeply held attitudes which had been building for several years. The evidence was overwhelming to the coalition members: the failure to cancel classes, the lack of positive responses to the request to name four buildings after the slain students, the announcement just before May 4th of possible changes in the program of the Center for Peaceful Change, the decision to build the physical education facility on the site of the May 4th confrontation, and, as a final act of callousness, the conduct of a trustee business meeting on May 4th. For the coalition, the time of grudging acquiescence was over; a new period of protest was born.

While the protest had its basis in local issues, some members of the coalition felt that something much larger was occurring. Protestors were well aware that local and area newspapers, radio stations, and television stations were covering the event extensively, and that the national media had also picked up the story. Knowing that they had captured the media's attention, believing deeply in the justness of their causes, and turned on by the excitement of the protest, some members of the group sensed that the long-latent student protest movement of the Vietnam era had been reincarnated at Kent State. Ron Kovic seemed to express the view of many in the group: "For seven years we've been intimidated and frightened, but we've been reborn."[43] Stokely Carmichael, who had spoken on campus earlier in the evening, also sensed this view of the significance of the night's activities: "Right now history is being made."[44] The next night, assuring a large crowd that "the whole world is watching," Kovic yelled, "Let the world record that we have begun a new cause, a new movement, that we have wanted and waited for seven years."[45] It is unclear how many believed this, but it seems clear that some students thought this might be true and, feeding upon this belief, saw themselves as destined to win their struggles.

May 5th-May 12th

The steering committee selected during the Rockwell sit-in met the next day, May 5th, and made several major policy decisions, including (1) the demands formulated the night before were not negotiable, although the coalition members would answer questions from Janik about the demands; (2) unspecified affirmative actions would be taken if the demands were not met; and (3) Janik would be asked to place the demands as the first item on the trustees' agenda and to allow more than one coalition member to speak.

That evening the first formal meeting of the coalition was held in the Kiva with about 500 people in attendance. During the lengthy meeting, the group approved the decisions of the steering committee and selected nine persons to meet with Janik the next day to discuss their demands. Also, plans were made for a mass rally on the day of the trustees' meeting. By 11:00 p.m. the meeting had lost more than half of the audience, but a fiery speech by Kovic ignited the remaining people who marched through the campus yelling to students in the dorms "Join us," "Stop the gym," and "The people, united, will never be defeated." Approximately 2000 gathered in the Student Center plaza area, listening and applauding impromptu speeches until about 1:00 a.m. Again, as on the night before, a feeling of purpose and power energized the newly created coalition.

At its meeting with Janik on May 6th, the coalition presented a resolution containing the eight demands to Janik who said he would present the resolution to the trustees at their meeting and would allow coalition spokespersons to present during the informational part of the meeting their views on four of the demands: changing the gym site, changing the status of the Center for Peaceful Change, cancelling classes on May 4th, and renaming four campus buildings after the slain students.[46]

An estimated 1500 persons gathered on the Commons on May 12 prior to the trustees' meeting, and, after hearing from a few speakers, marched to the Student Center plaza to show support for the eight demands. The Kiva was packed to capacity, and several hundred persons were forced to wait outside where the proceedings were broadcast.

During the course of the lengthy meeting, Olds and the trustees addressed each of the eight demands, agreeing with four of them, sending two of them to committees for further examination, and rejecting two. The demands which were supported involved maintaining the full university status of the Center for Peaceful Change; no reprisals for the Rockwell sit-in, which Olds labeled an "extended seminar;" no punishment for anyone missing classes on May 4; and reopening negotiations with UFPA, which the trustees said they had done by approving a faculty salary agreement earlier in the meeting. The demands of naming the buildings and cancelling regular university activities every May 4 to make it a day of remembrance and education were sent to special university committees for study and decisions. On the issue of officially acknowledging the injustice of the May 4th shootings, the trustees argued that this would not be appropriate because the case was still in litigation. Finally, discussion focused upon the critical issue of the HPER facility, for the trustees were to decide at that meeting whether to approve the awarding of construction contracts for the proposed facility to the low bidders. Bob Hart presented the views of the coalition's demand to move the facility, and the reply was negative.

At this point Hart proclaimed: "The demands are obviously not being met. The coalition will no longer participate in this travesty."[47] With this statement, about 300 coalition members walked out of the meeting. After a brief walk through the dormitory areas where they failed to gain many more supporters, the group gathered on the practice football field north of Memorial Gymnasium where the new facility would be located. A tent appeared and the cry went up to "take the hill;" tents were pitched on Blanket Hill, a beautiful tree-filled area where Guardsmen marched in 1970 just prior to shooting and where a portion of the new gym would be built. Tent City was founded. Approximately sixty people slept on the hill that first night, vowing not to leave until the demand to "move the gym" was met.

In the meantime, the trustees were voting 8-1 to approve awarding of the low bids. David Dix was the lone dissenter. Dix argued that while he favored the site in principle, he felt that the trustees could spend two more weeks going over the plans with the students in the hope of creating greater understanding and harmony. For the rest of the trustees, the reasons for their decision appeared to them to be logical and responsible. The university had gone through normal decision making procedures in planning for the facility, it would not touch upon the area where any students were killed or wounded in 1970, the facility would not interfere with the ongoing legal process, the reasons for choosing this location were eminently logical, several hundred thousand dollars had already been committed to the project, and any delay might jeopardize the chances of getting the money from the state. In addition, the trustees felt that they had responded as positively as was possible to the set of eight demands, and they had listened to student concerns on both November 11, 1976 and May 12, 1977, the only times students had asked to appear before the board on this issue. Despite all this, however, the protestors persisted in their demand and then stormed out of the meeting when they didn't get their way. Thus, the trustees saw themselves as having only one possible decision, to proceed with the project.

The expectation on the part of the trustees at this time seems to have been that the issues were basically resolved, and they could now focus their attention on the other pressing issues which had commanded their constant attention throughout the year. But a short distance away, the new community of Tent City was being created, and this encampment was to provide the stimulus for developments which would plunge the university into its deepest crisis since 1970.

MAY 12TH - JULY 12TH: TENT CITY

Introduction and Overview

Tent City was in existence for sixty-two days, from its establishment on May 12, 1977 until July 12, 1977, when 193 persons occupying Blanket Hill were arrested and all tents and other camping equipment were impounded by the law enforcement agents. During this period a small, local protest mushroomed into a controversy which became a focal point of state and national attention. Despite the intensive amount of activities during this period, however, no agreements for resolving the controversy were reached between the coalition and the trustees. Indeed, throughout this entire two-month period, neither the trustees nor Olds ever met officially with the coalition in an attempt to resolve their differences. The reason for this was deceptively simple: the two sides were firmly committed to positions which were fundamentally incompatible. The coalition demanded that the HPER facility must not be built on any land where the National Guard and students confronted each other on May 4, 1970, and the majority of the trustees believed there was no acceptable alternative to locating the facility on portions of the site of the 1970 shootings. Thus, neither side believed there was anything which could be usefully discussed.

Compounding these fundamental differences in viewpoints were attitudes of distrust and misunderstanding on both sides. The majority of the trustees had little initial understanding of the movement with which they were confronted, although the deep intensity and commitment of coalition members and their imaginative and sophisticated abilities to mobilize support for their cause became apparent later to the trustees. In the early stages, however, most trustees did not know how to interpret this movement. Was it the 1977 version of streaking, the year's faddish "spring fling" for students? Or was it the beginning of a new radical movement which presented a potentially serious challenge to the university?[48] These remained unanswered questions, for few trustees and major university administrators made serious efforts to understand the dynamics of the Tent City movement.[49] The coalition, on the other hand, had little respect or trust for most members of the board and administration because of past interactions, and little empathy existed for the position in which the trustees found themselves.

The early polarization of positions, the lack of understanding of each side by the other, and the high levels of mistrust were most unfortunate developments, for the initial six weeks of the Tent City period presented the only time period when compromise might have occurred. The contracts for the facility became legally binding in late June,[50] and after this date, any attempts by the trustees to change the site would have potentially confronted both the university as an institution and the trustees as individuals with substantial legal suits. Hence, because no serious attempts at accommodation emerged from either side before this date, from June 28 on the realistic chances for negotiation were gone.[51]

Strategies and Activities of the Coalition.

The Tent City period was characterized by creative, sophisticated, and effective activities of the coalition which impressed even the leadership of the university. For example, trustee Dr. James Fleming remarked after a board meeting in July, just before the arrests which ended Tent City: "I think their protest has been very effective. . . ."[52] What was the position that the coalition took toward the site, what was the basic strategy of the coalition during this period, and how did they seek to implement their strategy?

The view of the coalition concerning the importance of maintaining the site was set forth in detail in a position paper issued on June 23, 1977.

The antiwar movement of the late 1960's and early 1970's was the largest student movement this country has seen, a major part of American history. Kent State was a major turning point of the movement.

The Kent State Murders of May 4, 1970 were not merely a tragic incident frozen in the past. That this is not only an episode in the history of KSU, but a continuing symbol all over America and the world, is indicated by the letters of solidarity which come in every year. It was a

major turning point of the struggle against the war in Vietnam. It is an outrageous abridgement of the right to free and public expression. The continuing cover-up and denials by the KSU administration state and federal governments [sic] smolders like Watergate and the Korean bribery scandals, destroying the facade of "public trust."

Kent State is obligated to preserve Blanket Hill and the playing field as they were in 1970.

For the past seven years the KSU administration has worked hard to distort the facts, confuse the issues, and bury the history of May 4, 1970. The natural extension of this policy is to literally bury the site of the shootings under a sprawling building. But Kent State is obligated to preserve this site, as Boston must preserve the site of the Boston Massacre.

The destruction of this area would be a confirmation of the bloody suppression of free expression on May 4, 1970. The preservation of this site is essential to carry the lessons of "Kent State" to future generations.[53]

The basic strategy of the coalition centered around two premises: (1) it would be ineffective to attempt to convince the administration and trustees to change the site through logical arguments relating to moral, historical, and ecological concerns[54] and (2) therefore, it was necessary to work to create such enormous pressures on the trustees that there would be no choice but to build the facility on another site. In creating these pressures, the coalition perceived their major source of strength as being the university's Achilles' heel, its concern over a badly tarnished public image. If the coalition could sustain wide-spread attention to their struggle through the media, then real pressure would build on the trustees who wished to avoid further publicity about May 4th related protest. The coalition also felt that tremendous pressure could be placed on the trustees through the continuous use of threats about escalated protest—e.g., stopping the bulldozers with hundreds or thousands of bodies and forcing the university into arresting hundreds of protestors if they tried to end Tent City. Thus, the primary strategy for the coalition during this period became that of keeping constant media attention on the protest and posing the threat of escalating conflict; this strategy, it was reasoned, would create enormous public image problems for the university, and the trustees would therefore be forced to alter their decision on the location of the facility.

Operating from this basic strategy, the task was therefore one of generating these pressures. No leaf was left unturned in the coalition's tireless efforts. Coalition members appeared in classes to explain their position to students and faculty. Leaflets criticizing the trustees and administration, explaining the coalition's position, and announcing coalition activities flooded the campus on almost a daily basis. In another attempt to isolate the university leadership, coalition members talked with contractors for the building and with labor groups, emphasizing that the coalition was not opposed to building an HPER facility but only to building a facility on this site. Benefit concerts were held frequently to build support and to generate financial support for the movement. Intensive research was undertaken on the development of plans for the facility in the hope that irregularities could be discovered and publicized. A major rally was held on June 4, at which both Dick Gregory and William Kunstler spoke, encouraging the coalition to continue its struggle. Black students' support was sought through linking the Kent State and Jackson State tragedies as well as through expressing support in the spring for demands by the Kent State Black United Students for a larger share of the monies allocated student organizations. Many letters were sent to the university and area newspapers expressing the position of the coalition. T-shirts and bumper stickers proclaiming messages such as "Remember Kent State; Move the Gym" began to appear.

On the political front, efforts were directed at legislative, executive, and judicial authorities. Coalition members picketed area Congressman John Seiberling's office in mid-May and in late June also picketed Governor James Rhodes during a trip to Portage County. In addition, coalition members sought the involvement of the area's State Representative John Begala as well as intervention from the White House. The political avenue explored most fully during this period was the judicial system in the hope that grounds could be found for seeking an injunction to prevent construction. Although a number of bases for such an injunction were considered, injunctive action was not taken in this period because lawyers did not believe there was any chance of securing a favorable court response.

Underlying and sustaining all efforts during this period was the physical reality of Tent City, whose importance to the coalition's cause cannot be overstated. "Tentropolis" was a powerfully visible symbol to coalition members and to observers of the belief that the land was indeed sacred and belonged to "the people." As such, Tent City was a great attraction to the news media,[55] which fed directly into the coalition's strategy. The "canvas campus" also served an invaluable function in facilitating the development of close personal ties and a deep sense of solidarity among many coalition members. And finally, the physical presence of Tent City served as a constant reminder to university officials of the dilemma they ultimately faced: move the gym or face nationwide publicity once again over student protest.

Strategies and Activities of University Officials

The position of the majority of the trustees throughout this period never waivered. They continued to believe that they had made the only reasonable decision available to them, and the examination of alternatives which occurred before the June 24th date served to reinforce their position that the gym had to be built on the chosen site. The basic alternative which was given most serious consideration was the possibility of rotating the facility about 35 or 40 feet away from the Blanket Hill area. Olds directed University Architect Ted Curtis to examine this alternative, but Curtis' study led him to the conclusion that the costs involved in the rotation outweighed the benefits which could be gained. Coalition response to Curtis' report made it clear that even if the recommendation would have been to rotate the facility, the proposal would not have met the concerns of the coalition to preserve the entire area. In the meantime, Vice President Richard Dunn had been exploring with legislative leaders the possibility of securing additional funds to alter the site of the facility, and he received indications that the legislature would not provide any money for this purpose.[56]

Given these conditions, the strategy of the university leadership throughout the period was basically one of maintaining a low profile, hoping that this would minimize adverse publicity and that the protest would die out as a variety of factors took their toll on the protestors: unpleasant weather, the ending of the regular academic year, sheer exhaustion as the days wore on, and the threat of arrest if occupation of the hill continued. It was recognized that ultimately it might become necessary to arrest the protestors, but this would not have to occur until after the contracts became final on June 24 and the contractors could actually begin construction.

A variety of other activities were also initiated in attempts to prove the concern of university officials for the tragedy of May 4, to alter the opinions of coalition members regarding the appropriateness of the site, and to build public support for the decision to build on the chosen site. One of the earliest of these efforts was the publication of a proposal by Vice President Fay Biles originally set forth in January, 1977 that a small memorial chapel be constructed "near the area where the four (students) were killed, using only the expertise of our own schools and departments."[57] While this proposal received initial support from some coalition members, it came to be rejected as the coalition developed the position that they wanted the entire area left untouched, just as it was in 1970.[58]

Several members of the administration—most notably Dean of Student Affairs Richard Bredemeier and University Architect Ted Curtis—met several times with coalition members, and several trustees visited Tent City. Another activity by the administration during the period involved the preparation of a "Fact and Issue File" prepared under the direction of Anthony May, Director of Communications, and sent to various news editors, assignment editors, and editorial writers in an attempt to provide wide publicity of the university's positions on the controversy.

In discussing the strategies and activities of university officials, it is vitally important to discuss the deep divisions which existed within the Board of Trustees. Two members of the board, Joyce Quirk and David Dix, announced their public opposition to the site at a trustee meeting on June 9. Quirk stated:

> This is an admission of neglect of my part of not knowing in advance what specifically was involved in the gymnasium project before I voted in November and May. I have spent some time recently at the area where the building is to go and agree with some that it is indeed a poor choice for the gym. I am disappointed that this board has not taken steps to communicate with the concerned students and faculty on this matter. I made a mistake in voting initially to approve the plans in November and the bids in May.

> The possibility of considering alternatives for this site might indeed be costly but in the long run the historical and aesthetic losses in my estimation might prove even higher.[59]

Dix had also reached the conclusion that the proposed site was a bad choice:

> We made a mistake and the sooner we recognize it the better off we are going to be.
> I think we have proven ourselves insensitive to [the event of May 4th.]
> We need the facility. . . but we cannot ignore the worst thing that ever happened to the Kent community and the University, I think that is what we are doing.
> I have thought about it and I cannot accept it. It goes against my conscience.[60]

At this important meeting, where the trustees also elected Dr. Brage Golding, then president of San Diego State University, as the new president, Quirk introduced a resolution that the trustees reconsider the decision about the site of the facility. Dix seconded this motion, but Robert Blakemore then moved to table the motion "until the tents—and everything on the hill—are removed and at that time I will be very happy to join in discussion on the motion."[61] Quirk's motion was never removed from the table.

Interestingly, Blakemore joined Quirk and Dix in expressing public opposition to the site a month later when speaking before the Akron Kiwanis Club. Blakemore rejected the coalition argument that the site should be preserved because of its significance in regard to the May 4th tragedy, but he observed: "One of their objections is that the site has a lot of natural beauty, and they're right. It's too attractive a site to be used for a gym."[62]

The Arrests of July 12

Once the contracts became legally binding on June 24, a confrontation on Blanket Hill was fast approaching. With the contracts becoming final, construction could now begin, and the protestors would have to leave voluntarily or be subject to arrest. No formal meetings had been held between the trustees and the coalition, and both were adamant in their positions. Olds announced the position of the university officials: "I will ask the students to leave the hill peacefully. If they do not, we will go the route of obtaining an injunction from the court."[63] The coalition, having struggled for so long, was determined not to leave Blanket Hill voluntarily. The tactic which emerged was to send out an appeal throughout the nation for all supporters to come to Blanket Hill where protestors would lock arms and legs to resist removal or arrest in a non-violent manner.

As the day of confrontation came closer, tension rose on campus. A concern about the possibility of violence was widespread. These fears were heightened by a loud and emotional clash between Olds and 100 coalition supporters on July 6. The protestors, growing increasingly anxious about when the arrest would occur, decided to march to Rockwell Hall to form a picket line. Upon arriving at Rockwell, the demonstrators were met by Olds. During the approximately forty minute impromptu confrontation, the emotions which had been building for nearly two months spilled forth as "hoots, catcalls, and obscenities greeted much of what Olds said."[64] After being shouted down several times, Olds retreated into Rockwell. Visibly shaken, Olds told reporters:

> I didn't dream I would see an eye-for-an-eye, tooth-for-a-tooth atmosphere on campus as I did just a while ago. I've worked as hard as I know how to avert it. But I see some of the same events happening as happened before.[65]

With tensions running high and the possibility of a serious confrontation looming, a number of last-ditch efforts were made to seek a way out of the conflict. None of the efforts were to prove successful, however. The two persons who initiated the greatest efforts were trustee Joyce Quirk and State Representative John Begala.[66]

Quirk had been working tirelessly throughout the period with a wide variety of individuals and groups to affect some type of resolution of the conflict. Faced with the unwillingness of a majority of board members to have a meeting to reconsider the site location, Quirk had initiated efforts to involve professional mediators in the controversy. Through a variety of personal contacts, Quirk and others were eventually able to bring the controversy to the attention of White House staff member Midge Constanza, and on July 7 Quirk proposed that both sides request non-binding federal mediation to seek a way out of the conflict. Neither side made such a request prior to the arrests, however.

Begala had also been involved in a continuous series of efforts to resolve differences in the controversy, and as tensions heightened in early July he received calls expressing concern that "all hell could break loose." Deeply concerned about the situation in his own town and at his own university, Begala went to Lieutenant Governor Richard Celeste to inform Celeste about the situation and seek his advice on what could be done. Celeste said that he would talk to Senate majority leader Oliver Ocasek about the problem, and the next day Begala received a call from Ocasek to come to his office to talk about the controversy. At that meeting Ocasek told Begala that he would support an additional appropriation of $750,000 or $1 million or more to rotate the gym, and he told Begala that this could be made public. The question of how to go about affecting the change was also discussed, and the possibility of seeking a change order arose, for this allows alterations to be made in contracts without any rebidding.[67] State Senator Marcus Roberto, another area legislator, then became involved with Begala in trying to find a way out of the controversy, and both went to discuss the matter with the speaker of the House of Representatives, Vernal Riffe. Riffe's initial position was negative, for he felt that the trustees were firmly committed to putting the gym on the site they had designated and that the legislature had no business telling the university where to put its buildings. After considerable pleading, Begala and Roberto extracted a commitment from Riffe: if the trustees would pass a resolution requesting the state legislature for money to change the gym site, then he would consider the possibility of appropriating funds.[68]

When Begala informed university officials of the developments, Janik, Johnston, and Dunn flew to Columbus to meet with state officials. During the discussions, Janik and Johnston learned that a change order could not be issued because of the amount of money that was involved.[69] They thus took the stand that they were not in a position where they could pass a resolution asking for state aid to change the location, for they would be hit by law suits regardless of which way they went. If they did try to affect the change through a change order, then they could be subjected to suits from the next lowest bidder. If they went the route of rebidding the contracts, then Arnes and a host of other contractors could bring suit. In addition, the trustees did not receive a firm commitment from Riffe that he would support such legislation, only that he would consider it.

Begala's interpretation of the situation was that the problems faced by the trustees could have been resolved, despite these difficulties. Begala felt that the chances of getting funding from the legislature were good at this point, and careful writing of the legislation could have eliminated the possibility of law suits.

> We could have taken care of the situation if we'd have had the cooperation from the [university] administration. We could have appropriated the additional money and given the money to Bucky Arnes or we could have passed legislation saying that because of the situation an emergency exists that there would be no bids involved and that Bucky Arnes would get the contract for the gym. As far as I can tell we could have done either of those.[70]

Janik and Johnston did not completely reject the possibility of asking the trustees to pass such a resolution. They returned to Kent and asked Center for Peaceful Change faculty member Dennis Carey to approach the coalition about the rotation plan. The coalition turned down the proposal; only a complete change of the site for the gym would be acceptable. Thus, Begala's initiatives met resistance from the trustees and opposition from the coalition.

With the situation clearly at an impasse, the trustees on July 10 authorized Olds to initiate legal action to prevent the protestors from occupying Blanket Hill or from obstructing or interfering with the construction of the facility. The motion was filed on July 11 by university attorneys with Portage County Common Pleas Judge Joseph Kainrad. Later that same day Kainrad issued a temporary restraining order directing the removal of the protestors and their facilities but also directing the university to refrain from beginning any construction until he heard arguments from both sides at a July 21 hearing on the question of whether a permanent injunction should be issued.

The time of decision had finally arrived for members of the coalition. About 250 coalition members met at the Student Center on the evening of the 11th, and an overwhelming majority voted to defy the court order by not leaving when ordered and instead to be arrested.

On the morning of July 12, nearly 1000 people, including national news media personnel, were on or near Blanket Hill, anxiously awaiting the long-anticipated arrests. Following a reading of an order to disperse, unarmed Kent State University police arrested 193 persons including Mr. and Mrs. Martin Scheuer, parents of slain student Sandy Scheuer, and Mr. and Mrs. Albert Canfora, parents of wounded student Alan Canfora.[71] The fears of violence never materialized as the police untangled arms and legs and either led, carried, or dragged protestors to waiting buses. Robert Apt of the American Civil Liberties Union expressed the view of most observers when he called it "the most amazing demonstration of restraint on both sides I have ever seen."[72]

Analysis of the Tent City Period

The Tent City period has to be considered a great success for the coalition. While they did not succeed in forcing the trustees to change the site, they had made remarkable gains. They had succeeded in turning a local protest into a national issue, and in so doing they had been able to create support from many important individuals and groups for their basic goal of preserving the site. The reasons behind the support for the coalition goal were many and varied. Some people were very impressed by the commitment, the ingenuity, and the discipline shown by the coalition. Others were convinced by the arguments which the coalition had publicized so well in regard to the historical, moral, and ecological importance of the site. Finally, many people now saw no end to the conflict unless the trustees agreed to move the facility, and these people believed that the costs to the university of continuous, escalating conflict would far outweigh the costs of changing the site. For whatever mixture of reasons, the coalition during this period had been able to gain substantial student and faculty support;[73] three trustees had reversed their earlier position and were now opposed to the site; and involvement by the White House, the Department of Interior, members of Congress, and members of the Ohio legislature was to occur in the next few weeks. Furthermore, the Tent City period had generated deep commitments from many coalition members who were prepared to devote their entire energies to this cause, and their efforts succeeded in attracting many new recruits to their ranks. It was to become apparent fairly soon, however, that the elimination of Tent City was to create severe problems for the coalition.

July 13th - September 19th: The Legal Struggle

Overview of the Period

The two month period following the elimination of Tent City was dominated by efforts of the coalition to use the courts to prevent or delay construction of the HPER facility on the designated site. Against the backdrop of continuous litigative struggle, the controversy outside the courtrooms was characterized by escalating rhetoric, increasing polarization of both campus and community, increasingly militant coalition tactics, and progressively harsher responses by law enforcement authorities.

Throughout this entire period the majority of the trustees remained firmly committed to building the HPER facility on the chosen site, despite an enormous range of pressures which came to be placed on them. All of their previous beliefs remained: proper procedures had been followed all along, the facility would not cover the most important portions of the May 4th confrontation, the costs of changing the location were prohibitive, genuine responses had been made to all of the coalition's demands over which the trustees had control, there were no definite commitments from any source on additional funds to change the location, and massive lawsuits against the trustees in their official and private capacities could result from a decision to change the site. During the months of July and August, it appears that increasingly the majority of the trustees seemed to see the coalition as a radical, communist-oriented group, and they seemed to fear that a capitulation on the gym issue would stimulate continuous radical demands on the university and the trustees. Finally, personal resentments also seem to have developed among some trustees in reaction to the verbal abuse which they received from some coalition members. Thus, throughout the period the majority of the trustees remained firmly committed to their position and grew increasingly resentful of the seemingly countless attempts to pressure them into changing their decisions.

During this period, Dr. Michael Schwartz and Stephen Parisi emerged as important university decision makers in setting strategy for the university along with the trustees. Schwartz served as interim president from July 15 to September 1, and Parisi was the primary legal counsel for university officials. Schwartz did not feel that the site chosen for the HPER facility was the best location; but he did not believe that there had been any "cover-up," he believed the university needed strong administrative leadership, and he felt there was no way out of the decision to build on the chosen site. Schwartz saw the situation in the following terms:

> . . . . there is really no way you can sit down and . . . try to adjudicate in your office conflicting values when they are so rigidly held as they were. In the second place it seemed to me that we were faced with a situation that was in fact primarily legal more than anything else. The contractual obligations involved in this matter were complicated to say the least, and there was involved here enormous personal liability.[74]

Schwartz, Parisi, and the trustees therefore committed themselves to a strategy of allowing the courts to settle the controversy, for a judicial verdict would give them legitimacy and, in Schwartz' words, "I didn't see any way that we could not prevail."[75]

The internal dynamics of the coalition during this period differed dramatically from those of the trustees, for during the unfolding of the lengthy court battles in July, August, and September the unity of the Tent City period began to break down and eventually serious ruptures occurred among members of the coalition. It remains less than obvious even to coalition members why and how these divisions developed. Certainly no single reason stands out to explain the emergence of these divisions. Part of the problem facing the group was the elimination of Tent City. The coalition no longer had the benefit of its constant symbolic message nor its enhancement of close personal ties.[76] Sheer exhaustion also began to take its inevitable toll. As the weeks and months passed, energy levels began to decline for some, and the practical realities of school and jobs began to assert themselves. The lengthy meetings of the coalition which were held nearly every night also contributed to these problems. A further serious problem centered around the continuous debates and disagreements over the proper tactics to be utilized. While many shades of opinion existed, the most basic disagreement throughout the period involved the degree of militancy which was necessary to achieve the basic goal of preserving the site. As attempt after attempt to work "through the system" failed, the position of increasingly militant tactics began to appear as the only viable approach, but many coalition members could not support these tactics. Finally, serious problems also emerged concerning charges that the former democratic processes of the coalition were being undermined.

These pressures thus brought about substantial changes in the active participants in the coalition in the period following Tent City. Perhaps the most critical developments involved the Revolutionary Student Brigade, a Maoist oriented group. The Kent State RSB chapter had only a handful of students, but these students were among the most dedicated members of the coalition. Throughout the entire struggle the RSB members saw the gym issue as being symptomatic of the problems of American capitalist society.[77] By August the local RSB had begun to emerge as a potent force within the coalition[78] and had begun to develop plans with the national RSB headquarters for a convention at Kent State to found a National Communist Youth Organization. Increasing numbers of RSB members came to Kent to build this movement in mid and late August. Veteran coalition members who saw more militant tactics as the only viable approach for the coalition supported the views of the RSB members, and increasing numbers of longtime coalition members began to drift away from the group because of concerns about tactics and also because of a perceived breakdown in the former democratic basis of decision making as RSB members came increasingly to dominate the tactics committee.

Despite the internal divisions which arose within the coalition during this period, however, they did maintain their central strategy of the Tent City period of placing so much pressure on the trustees and other authorities that a decision to move the gym would have to be made. And again as in the Tent City period, the coalition experienced a wide range of successes in generating these pressures. Yet these pressures were never to result in a decision to move the gym.

The Common Pleas Court Period

In the immediate aftermath of the 193 arrests and the elimination of Tent City from Blanket Hill, the attention of both the trustees and the coalition focused upon the impending decision by Common Pleas Judge Kainrad on whether to place a permanent injunction on the protestors and to allow

the university to commence construction. Hearings began on July 21 and Kainrad issued his decision on July 25. Before turning to this decision, however, it is necessary to discuss the many significant developments which occurred outside the courtroom during this time period.

One of the most important developments was the intervention of Midge Constanza, a White House staff member. Constanza had been contacted about the Kent State controversy through efforts initiated earlier by trustee Joyce Quirk, and on July 14 Constanza talked by telephone with coalition leader Alan Canfora, Olds, and Janik, congratulating them on the handling of the arrests, expressing White House concern, and suggesting mediation to resolve the impasse.[79] Constanza invited representatives from both sides to come to Washington. Only July 19 and 20, Constanza arranged for meetings with coalition members[80] and university officials.[81] Also in attendance at these meeting were area congressman John Seiberling and representatives of Ohio Senators John Glenn and Howard Metzenbaum as well as representatives from the Department of Interior. While university officials had little enthusiasm for the efforts of Constanza, they reluctantly went along with a basic plan which emerged from the discussions to have a request made to the Department of Interior to initiate a study to determine if the site of the May 4 confrontation qualified as a national historic landmark. Supporters of the plan hoped that this could offer a number of possible avenues out of the conflict. First, if the study could be quickly completed, construction could be delayed and a resolution of the impasse could be reached. Second, there was hope that if the area was declared a national historical site, then the federal government might be able to provide funds to compensate the university for not building the facility on the disputed site. On July 25, Secretary of Interior Cecil Andrus announced that in response to a joint request from Metzenbaum and Seiberling, he was ordering a historical site study of the area of campus where the confrontation occurred on May 4th. The hopes of an immediate decision and for federal compensation never materialized, however, for Andrus indicated that the study would take eight months to complete and no commitments of federal funds were ever made to university officials.[82]

During this period between the arrests on Blanket Hill on July 12th and Judge Kainrad's decision on the 25th, conflict between the administration and faculty broke into the open as significant numbers of faculty took public positions in opposition to the building site. On July 20 and 21, a faculty/community "watch" was held at the site to express support for changing the location. Statements strongly critical of the administration and trustees were read at the beginning of the twenty-four hour watch, which ultimately involved approximately 200 persons including 75 faculty members. In addition, the faculty union, the United Faculty Professional Association, made a decision to enter into the court case on the side of the coalition.[83] Administrative efforts to counteract faculty opposition to the location came from newly appointed interim president Michael Schwartz as well as from Vice President and Provost John Snyder. Schwartz sent a two page memo dated July 21 to all academic deans, explaining that "any alternatives are so potentially expensive that with declining enrollment we would be fiscally irresponsible to initiate any change" and asking the deans to "share this summary with the faculty."[84] On the 25th, Snyder called a meeting of all faculty at which he expressed his sympathy with many of the concerns of the protestors but emphasized that projected fall enrollments were down substantially, the protests were affecting enrollment, and "a 10 percent overall reduction in the student body will mean at least a 10 percent reduction in faculty."[85]

Support for building the facility on the chosen site also emerged during this time period when a prominent area citizen, Richard Larlham, announced that he was gathering signatures for petitions supporting the trustees' decision and seeking to close the university until gym construction was completed.[86] Larlham remained active throughout the conflict in trying to build and demonstrate public approval of the chosen site.

Throughout this period, the primary thrust of coalition activity was directed at protest activity which it was hoped would not only influence Judge Kainrad's decision but also convince the trustees that they had no acceptable alternative but to change the site. The basic vehicle for this was to be a national rally on July 22. Agreement emerged that open defiance of the temporary restraining order would occur, but long discussions arose over whether to march across the site or to reoccupy it as well as over the question of how many people would be involved in violating the court order. On the evening before the rally, the decision was made to

have 13 "symbolic" arrests, one for each student killed and wounded on May 4th.[87] The rally attracted about 500 persons, and after speeches and a march around campus, the designated individuals went onto the site, which had by now been roped off. Moments later, many other protestors swarmed onto the site, with about 150 persons eventually occupying the area for about twenty minutes. A small number of campus police were present taking photographs and videotape, but no arrests were made. Two days later, on the 24th, the coalition again tried to place pressure on Kainrad by overwhelmingly deciding to reoccupy the site once again if Kainrad ruled in favor of the university.

Kainrad issued his decision on the 25th, granting a permanent injunction against the coalition and removing the temporary restraining order against construction.

It is a fundamental principle of law that the courts should not interfere with the discretion of a legislative or governing body unless that body acts outside the law, without legal authority or their actions are so inequitable as to constitute a fraudulent abuse of discretion.

There has been no evidence presented to this court from which the court can conclude that the Board of Trustees was without legal authority in their determination to construct the H. P. E. R. Facility.

Section 3341.04 of the Ohio Revised Code delegates to the Board of Trustees of Kent State University the general power to govern and regulate the use of its property, including the grounds and facilities thereon.

There is no evidence to support the Coalition Defendants' contention that proper procedures were not followed in the awarding of the contracts to the successful contractor.

The Coalition Defendants by their written comments and news releases offered into evidence to the court, by their actions at the time of the Notice to Vacate, and by their actions after the issuance of the temporary restraining order, clearly convinced the Court that they are trespassers and intend to continue to trespass upon the premises, and that the Plaintiffs, due to the nature of such continuing trespass and the multiplicity of suits that would be required by law, are entitled to equitable relief from this Court.

One who seeks equity must come with clean hands and be prepared to do equity. These

Coalition Defendants do not comply with these standards.[88]

Construction Begins— Temporarily

Although events had been occurring at a dizzying speed in the days between the Blanket Hill arrests and Kainrad's decision, the next several days were to involve an even more rapid unfolding of major developments. The trustees' meeting of July 26 was the initial focal point of attention following Kainrad's decision. At their emergency session the trustees were faced with three new developments in the controversy: Kainrad had ruled in their favor, the Interior Department had announced within hours of Kainrad's decision that it was undertaking a study to determine if the area should be a national historical landmark, and the coalition had reaffirmed their threat to reoccupy the site if the trustees did not change their decision.[89] The emotionally tense meeting, held at one of Kent State's regional campuses, drew a large number of coalition supporters. After a two hour executive session, trustee chairman Janik announced that the board had voted to go ahead with construction. Quirk and Dix were the only trustees to favor a ten day delay in construction to examine more fully the implications of the Interior Department's decision. Coalition members were left angry and disillusioned by the decision. Their feelings were expressed in a prepared statement read by Greg Rambo:

> The board has spoken. Let the world note and history record that George Janik and Company have voted with the complete knowledge that their action will result in yet another confrontation on the KSU campus
>
> Once again another valuable lesson has been that the system does not work for us. We have but one course of action left for us. We shall reclaim our land.
>
> [The board's] malicious intent is well known and we have exposed these scoundrels for what they are. May they burn in hell.[90]

The decision of the board was not the only blow to the coalition on the 26th, however, for earlier in the day Portage County Sheriff Allen McKitrick filed arrest warrants for twenty-seven demonstrators who had reoccupied the site on July 22. This list included many of the coalition leaders. Roadblocks were set up to arrest several of the twenty-seven who

were returning to campus from the trustee meeting. Three persons were arrested that evening, and more than a dozen others turned themselves in the next morning. Bail was set at $2000.

The coalition now found itself in a battered and weakened condition. The trustees had not given in to the enormous pressures which the coalition had created, many of the leaders were in jail with large bails and serious arrest records facing them, the outlook in the courts was dismal at best, and sheer exhaustion was beginning to take a heavy toll. Under these conditions, disagreement and uncertainty increasingly characterized the coalition's actions. On the evening after the trustee's decision on the 26th, they decided to reoccupy the site on Thursday noon. But at their meeting on the next evening, the decision was reversed as they voted not to reoccupy the site until construction was actually ready to begin. A rally on Thursday noon was attended by about 300 persons, but a large number of those were faculty and student observers and media people who had anticipated some major developments. The rally turned out to be uneventful, involving only a few speeches and some picketing. Following a lengthy coalition meeting that night, however, the site was once again occupied as protestors scaled the newly constructed chain-link fence which had been built around the construction area. Sixty-one protestors were arrested that night and eight others the next day, including four Cleveland area clergymen.

Defeat seemed certain for the coalition at this point, for about 7:00 a.m. on the 29th, a few short hours after the last protestor had been carried away, construction equipment appeared on the site. Throughout the day, the heavy equipment rolled back and forth across the old practice football field directly north of Memorial Gym, preparing the ground for the actual construction. The only faint hope remaining for the coalition was in the courts, but, as expected, the appeal of Kainrad's decision by the coalition lawyers, which had been filed following the trustees' decision on the 26th, was turned down by the State Court of Appeals.[91]

The Federal District Court Period

Just as defeat appeared certain, however, yet another major development occurred: U. S. District Court Judge Thomas Lambros ordered a halt to construction in response to a legal brief which had been filed at 4:48 p.m. on Friday the 29th by coalition lawyer Tony Walsh. The brief, which had been dictated by William Kunstler to coalition member Chic Canfora, a former legal secretary, sought a "temporary restraining order, preliminary and permanent injunction restraining and enjoining defendants . . . from continuing construction at the scene until a decision has been reached by the Department of the Interior as to the declaration of the scene as a national historic site. . . ."[92] Lambros' surprise decision on Friday was followed on Monday, August 1 by another startling move when he ordered both sides to try to negotiate an out-of-court settlement of the dispute. We cannot be certain why Lambros acted as he did, but it was certainly a move which surprised even coalition lawyers who saw little basis for federal jurisdiction in the case. Among the reasons which have been suggested for Lambros' decision are: a concern about the conflict at the university and a desire to try to resolve the issue to prevent further harm to the school, support for the coalition's position, or a desire to further his own career by emerging as the person who was responsible for resolving the Kent State controversy.[93]

A week of intensive discussions followed Lambros' order to the parties to negotiate, but no realistic prospect ever existed for achieving a compromise agreement.[94] The position of the majority of the trustees and Schwartz was firmly set on placing the building on the chosen site, and there was a deep resentment at what was viewed as a second major, unwarranted federal intrusion into a matter over which the national government had no legitimate authority. The only potential compromise which the university leadership was willing to consider was a substantial rotation of the facility up to 300 feet away from Blanket Hill and away from much of the practice football field. The proposition contained, however, a number of explicit and implicit conditions: (1) this would be a recommendation to the trustees to consider, (2) the coalition would first have to drop all of its legal actions, (3) the contractor would have to be satisfied, and (4) the university would have to be provided with the additional money, estimated at $1.7 million, needed to rotate the facility. These conditions could not be accepted by the coalition because they would strip them of their ability to use the courts to challenge the university, there would be no guarantee at all that the facility would be rotated, and the facility would still cover portions of the

practice field. Further, no firm assurances ever emerged that the university could receive the additional funds. The coalition did not, of course, know the university's position during the negotiations. Initially optimistic over their chances of preserving the site, hopes turned to disillusionment as the negotiations dragged on for a week with no solution emerging despite the discussion of many alternatives and the efforts of U. S. Department of Justice mediator Richard Salem.

Negotiations reached an impasse a week after they had begun. Charges and countercharges were hurled back and forth by university and coalition leaders. Schwartz stated: "We went to court in good faith. But it requires two parties to negotiate, no matter how supportive of their cause. One must now begin to doubt the interests of the coalition in seeking a negotiated resolution of this issue."[95] Coalition representative and assistant philosophy professor Dave Luban replied: "Schwartz is simply not telling the truth. The university is talking out of sides of its mouth that haven't been invented yet."[96] The university, Luban argued, made no proposals in court but only "said "no" to everything."[97]

With the breakdown in negotiations, Lambros on August 9 issued a Memorandum Opinion and Order dismissing the coalition's motion on all grounds except the "claim of deprivation of the right to petition the Government for a redress of grievances."[98] The temporary restraining order was left in effect pending consideration of the right to petition issue, on which briefs were due by August 16.

During the period of court-ordered negotiations, another major development was simultaneously competing for front page space in the area newspapers beginning on August 2 when the banner headline of the *Akron Beacon Journal* proclaimed: "New KSU Chief Wants to Move Gym."[99] The story indicated that Golding had been visited at his cabin in Maine by trustees Quirk and Dix and Reverend John Adams[100] and after discussion with them Golding had decided to request the trustees to pass a resolution asking the legislature for money to relocate the HPER facility. Further, Golding was reported to have urged the three to involve trustees, coalition members, the families of the dead and wounded students, and community members in a drive to gain state financial support to change the site. It was probably inevitable that the president-elect could not avoid entanglement in the controversy prior to his formal assumption of duties on the first of September. The nature of his involvement was one which created a significant controversy within the larger crisis, however, for Golding was to deny on August 4 that he had made this commitment to request the trustees to pass such a resolution. Golding took the position that his discussion with Quirk, Dix, and Adams was to have been kept in total confidence and that he never advocated that the trustees formally request funds from the state legislature to move the building.[101] Adams then responded in a 42 page statement released on August 8 that he and the two trustees did not betray any trusts and did not make incorrect statements about Golding's position.[102]

Golding decided it was necessary to come to Kent to attempt to resolve the controversy which had arisen out of the Maine meeting and to see if the trustees still wanted him as president.[103] Golding thus found himself as a new president who not only was denied the traditional honeymoon period but also found himself in divorce court before the marriage was consummated. He arrived in Kent on Wednesday, August 10, the day after negotiations in federal court had broken off, and during his visit he met with each of the trustees as well as university administrators and coalition members Alan Canfora and Debbie Phipps. At the conclusion of his visit on Friday, August 12, Golding stated:

> Personally, I wish the gym had not been put there. I feel strongly enough about it that I think the trustees should make one last effort to respond to the feeling against the gym.[104]

Golding's request reportedly was that the trustees approach the legislature either through a formal resolution or through informal personal contacts.[105] On the same day, Schwartz and Dunn went to Columbus to talk to state legislative leaders. Schwartz later said, "These explorations have not been fruitful."[106]

Throughout the first two and one-half weeks in August the daily activities of the coalition received relatively little public attention. The papers focused instead upon the negotiations in federal district court, the controversy which had arisen over the Maine meeting, and Lambros' impending decision. This was to prove to be a critically important period for the coalition, however, and one characterized by contradictions. On the one hand, during this period there were continuing evidences of successes by the

coalition, for their efforts were resulting in numerous actions and statements by numerous individuals and groups which put great pressure on the trustees. On the other hand, serious internal divisions began to emerge within the coalition itself, leading eventually to serious breaks among the membership.

Evidence of the success of the coalition's efforts came from many directions. In early August Fireman's Fund American Insurance Company notified state officials that it would cancel the project's vandalism insurance on August 15, and subsequently eight other companies refused to take the policy. On August 4 Portage County Prosecutor John Plough announced that he was writing to the trustees and to the state legislators from the area urging that the gym be moved: "I think it is mindboggling the amount it could potentially cost the county if the gym is put in its present site and the construction lasts two or three years."[107] A story in the *Akron Beacon Journal* on August 8 indicated that state representative Michael Stinziano of Columbus had requested Janik to consider the possibility of scaling down the proposed facility and using the money saved with a smaller building to meet the costs which would be incurred by changing the plans. Stinziano asked the trustees to "seriously consider the offers that the Democratic (legislative) leadership has made to seek an answer to this conflict."[108] In addition, a result of the controversy stemming from the Maine meeting was that new efforts were launched by both sides to seek financial support from Columbus to change the site, although no concrete commitments emerged from these efforts.[109] On the national scene, noted columnist Joseph C. Harsch, writing in the *Christian Science Monitor* on August 4, observed:

> It seems to me that it is as insensitive for the authorities of Kent State and Ohio to try to obscure with a gymnasium the place where the four fell on the fourth of May, 1970, as it would be for Pennsylvania to put an office building where Pickett launched his charge at Gettysburg.[110]

While the efforts of the coalition had succeeded in stimulating all of these pressures, which built on the trustees, this was a difficult period for the coalition in terms of group solidarity. The basic conflicts arose over tactics, although many other problems challenged coalition unity.[111] In late July prior to Lambros' decision to intervene, the membership was sharply divided over whether or not to reoccupy the site, with many believing that a further violation of the court order would be ineffective and perhaps counterproductive. These people were criticized by more militant coalition members, many of whom were becoming increasingly radicalized because of the arrests and high bonds which had occurred on the 26th and 27th. When the sixty-one went over the fence in the early morning hours of the 29th and Judge Lambros ordered a halt to construction later the same day, this was viewed as clear proof of the validity of the more militant position, for a direct cause and effect relationship was perceived between the reoccupation and Lambros' decision. From this point on, the more militant coalition members began to dominate the movement, supported by new recruits who shared their tactical views. While many of the less militant members remained within the coalition throughout August and frequently exerted important influence on coalition activities, some did drop out and others searched for viable alternative tactics. The divisions were not to become publicly apparent until September.

Lambros' long awaited decision came on Wednesday, August 17 when he announced that he had found in favor of the university and that construction could therefore continue. In his opinion, Lambros rejected the coalition's claim that the university had violated their right to petition the government for redress of grievances, arguing "to further enjoin construction of this site on the basis of a right of plaintiff to petition the government for redress of grievances would, depending on one's viewpoint, either substitute the Court's judgment for the legislatively determined methods and procedures to declare a location a national historic site, or substitute the Courts' judgment for the judgment of the State of Ohio."[112] In regard to a variety of other claims made by the coalition in an amended complaint filed on August 12, Lambros found either a "lack of subject matter jurisdiction or failure to state claims upon which relief can be granted. . . ."[113] In reaching his decision on the 17th, Lambros did agree, however, to provide the coalition with a twenty-four hour period until he prepared his written opinion in which coalition lawyers could file an appeals brief with the U. S. 6th Circuit Court of Appeals.

Prospects of defeat once again loomed large for the coalition as two bulldozers were moved to the gym site within an hour after Lambros' decision. It was obvious, however, that the coalition was not going to stand by as construction began. As university attorney Parisi left the courthouse, one coalition member snarled at him: "You take a message back to your boss. You tell him if construction starts to just wait and see what happens."[114] At a meeting that night, the tactics committee avoided detailed proposals but discussion centered around "organized mass confusion."

The Appeals Period

Yet another surprising development was to come from Lambros, for on the next day his written opinion contained a nearly illegible, handwritten scrawl at the end of the opinion that "the temporary restraining order dissolved herein is restored during the pending of any appeal taken from this order."[115] Lambros' ruling thus opened the doors for coalition lawyers to appeal ultimately to the Supreme Court, a process which would delay construction for several more weeks. We do not know the reasons for Lambros' surprise decision to restore the temporary order, but two possibilities are (1) Lambros was deeply concerned about the possibility of serious confrontation and wanted to achieve further time for a possible compromise solution to be found and (2) the announcements immediately after Lambros' decision on the 17th by U. S. Senator James Abourezk and State Representative Les Brown that they would introduce legislation calling for a moratorium on the gym construction pending completion of the Interior study.[116]

The appeals process was to last for several weeks. During this period one last major attempt was made to bring about a trustee reconsideration of the decision on the site. This effort was initiated by interim president Schwartz as a follow-up to Golding's desire to have the trustees request financial assistance from the state legislature for moving the facility. Once again, however, no trustee action was to occur.

Although an initial attempt by Schwartz to convene a special meeting of the trustees for Sunday, August 14, did not succeed, the trustees did meet on Friday, August 19 in a special session, reportedly to consider a resolution drafted by Robert Blakemore which asked state legislators Roberto and Begala "to work on behalf of the university to find funds to move the gym."[117] At that meeting the trustees again went into executive session, and after two hours announced that they had decided by a 6-1 vote[118] to invite Roberto and Begala to meet with them on Wednesday, August 24. Discussion had arisen on a much stronger resolution which would have formally requested state aid in the dispute, but insufficient support existed for the resolution. Out of the trustee meeting on the 19th came a proposal which had not been given much serious attention before, a plan to change the university's laboratory school into a new HPER facility. The idea, suggested by Blakemore, aroused intense controversy during the week prior to the trustees' meeting on the 24th.

Begala, a graduate of the laboratory school, became the main proponent of the plan. He argued that the future of the University School was somewhat tenuous because of the high costs to the state of running the school, that the plan would not only allow for an HPER facility to be developed but also allow for penalties to be paid at no extra cost,[119] and that some solution had to be found because "the institution and the Kent community have suffered enough."[120] Begala stressed, however, that he would not move on the plan in Columbus unless the trustees passed a resolution requesting state assistance.

A wide variety of reactions arose to the plan. Both the area papers, the *Record-Courier* and the *Akron Beacon Journal*, took a position urging careful exploration of the proposal.[121] The May 4th Coalition did not take a stand on the plan, for their position had consistently been one of opposing the proposed site but not advocating any particular alternative. Loud opposition arose from parents of children attending the school as well as from members of the university's College of Education. One parent warned: "If they think the protestors are bad, wait until they see middle-aged parents protesting."[122] Contractor Bucky Arnes' reaction was unequivocal: "I think it's a bunch of crap."[123] Most importantly, however, there was no indication of support for the proposal from any of the trustees other than Blakemore, Dix, and Quirk. Baumgardner was quoted as saying:

> I think the majority (of the trustees) still feels it should be built where its proposed. I'm still behind the building 100 percent as it's proposed.
> The idea to use the University School came up a long time ago when the financial affairs

committee was considering the project. It's just not practical. We would have to convert the University School to a physical education facility and still have to put millions into the existing gym for renovations. We would be wasting a substantial amount of taxpayers' money—and that's who we're ultimately responsible to.[124]

Trustee opposition was made crystal clear at the meeting of the 26th when only Blakemore, Dix, and Quirk attended. After this non-meeting, there could be no question about the possibility of the majority of the trustees changing their minds to build on the chosen site. The only hope for the coalition to prevent construction now rested with the federal courts.

Despite temporary successes, the appeals efforts of the coalition lawyers ultimately failed. The 6th U. S. Circuit Court of Appeals handed down its decision on August 24th, ruling that the federal courts had no jurisdiction in the controversy. The appeals court did, however, order a further ten day delay in construction to allow the coalition lawyers to make their final appeal to the U. S. Supreme Court. While Supreme Court Justice Potter Stewart refused on September 3 to ban construction, a further appeal to Justice William Brennan did succeed when Brennan on September 6 granted the coalition's lawyers' request for a temporary stay on construction pending his hearing of arguments on the appeal. On September 8 Brennan rejected the coalition's arguments and lifted the temporary ban on construction. Tireless efforts by the coalition lawyers continued, but no new restraining orders on construction were issued. It was the end of the line, and the lawyers knew it. Tony Walsh told a reporter, "We're playing for time now. All we have left are tricks."[125]

Throughout the appellate period in late August and early September, the coalition continued its efforts to place pressure on the courts and the trustees, but internal conflicts were to destroy both the unity and effectiveness of the coalition. Tactically, a high point for the coalition was a rally on August 20 featuring Joan Baez, as an estimated 1500 persons filled the Commons for the rally, which was addressed by many of the parents of the dead and wounded students. Following the rally an estimated 600 persons marched to the Kent city police station to protest arrests of coalition members who had been jailed the night before, following a victory celebration at a local bar after Lambros' decision to prohibit construction pending further appeals.[126] While some other activities were initiated after the Baez rally,[127] basically the last days of August were occupied with planning for a fall offensive, for the coalition was now hopeful that construction would be delayed until classes began on September 12. With the influx of nearly 20,000 students back to the campus, combined with substantial outside support, it was felt that enormous opposition to the site location could be generated.

The coalition was never able to generate this broad base of support from returning Kent State students. Conflict over tactical decisions as well as decision making procedures resulted in permanent splits within the coalition. These conflicts in turn diverted coalition energies from building support among returning students, and the more militant tactics and rhetoric of the coalition resulted in harsh criticism by important student leaders and groups.

The conflicts among the members of the coalition were due to many factors, but the emergence of the Revolutionary Student Brigade as a dominant force within the coalition during this period is of central importance. Several reasons seem to account for this development. First as was mentioned earlier, most of the Kent RSB members had been with the coalition from its beginning stage, and this earned them a strong legitimacy, especially in the eyes of new recruits to the movement. Second, the RSB members had developed considerable administrative and organizational skills through their past activities on the Kent State campus. They knew the procedures to be followed in registering rallies, setting up informational booths, and undertaking a host of other administrative details which were central to coalition activities. A third factor involved the past successes of the RSB tactical positions. They had continually taken a hard line on the need for militant tactics. The validity of the RSB tactical position was seen to be proven by the events of July 29. As discussed above, on that day sixty-three demonstrators were arrested early in the morning for reoccupying the site, construction began in the early morning and lasted all day, and in the late afternoon Judge Lambros issued his decision halting construction. Most coalition members saw a cause and effect relationship between the act of violating the court order and the decision by Lambros. The correctness of the RSB line had been proven. As the local RSB rose to prominence within the coalition, they began to develop plans with the national Revolutionary Student Brigade headquarters for a fall convention at Kent State to found a National Communist Youth Organization. Substantial numbers of RSB members began to arrive in Kent in mid and late August to support this movement.

It is important to point out, however, that it is too simplistic to say simply that the RSB "took over the coalition." Many important leaders like Carter Dodge, Alan and Chic Canfora, and Greg Rambo were not members of the RSB, but they identified strongly with the commitment, skills, and tactical approaches of RSB members. It was probably the support which these leaders gave to the RSB that primarily accounted for the success which the RSB experienced within the coalition.

The growing internal problems which had confronted the coalition since the end of Tent City now threatened to rupture completely. Two areas of conflict were critical. One area involved the question of tactics. The increasingly larger RSB group and their supporters argued that given trustee and administration intransigence, the only viable tactics were those of increased militancy, including violations of court orders and possible destructive actions directed toward equipment and property. Many veteran coalition members agreed with this logic, but a substantial number of members believed that the tactics were either counterproductive or unacceptable. When confronted with challenges from more radical coalition members as to viable alternatives, however, the less militant members were unable to offer convincing alternatives. This struggle over tactics was compounded by an equally serious problem, the conduct of coalition meetings. Veterans coalition members had always prided themselves in the participatory democracy which had characterized coalition activities, but many individuals perceived that RSB members were subverting the democratic basis of coalition meetings.

> . . . many people believed decisions were being made *undemocratically* by "packing" meetings, dragging out the meetings until only the RSB supporters were present, picking the chairmen at the end of the meeting (when only RSB supporters were left), thus making the next meeting be tilted in favor of RSB. . . . [128]

As a result of these conflicts in late August some coalition members began to drift away from the group, and others remained within the coalition but sought to counteract the influence of the RSB and their supporters. John Herikson has observed:

> It was strange the way people locked into the coalition in August. They had gotten to the point where they felt they had devoted so much of their life or at least so much of their energy to the struggle that they couldn't leave now.[129]

As the beginning of the new school year approached, then, the position of the coalition was that militant tactics would be necessary given the intransigence of the trustees. Alan Canfora told a reporter the coalition was prepared to use "hit and run" tactics to prevent the beginning of construction and to disrupt the project if construction began. "A half-built gym might be a fitting memorial to what has happened here."[130] A rally on Labor Day, September 5, was attended by approximately 300 supporters, who marched to Golding's home on campus and had a brief confrontation with two campus policemen over the use of a power outlet on a campus building. Protestors were threatened with arrest but none occurred. On Sunday, September 11, the day before classes began, about 300 coalition supporters held another rally on campus. After three hours of demonstration, wire cutters were used to break down the chain-link fence around the site and about 125 protestors once again reoccupied the site. Police did not make arrests but took videotape for future arrests.

The actions of the coalition on the 11th seem to have been a critical turning point, for widespread criticism of coalition tactics emerged from various student groups. Student Caucus unanimously passed a resolution on September 13 stating that Caucus could not support any violent or destructive actions to relocate the facility but also urging that students work actively to change the site through non-violent means. The resolution was sponsored by Caucus member Georgiann Taylor "because of what happened Sunday."[131] Caucus member Rebecca Huntington criticized the leaders of the coalition:

> There has been a domination of the Coalition by certain political groups using the new HPER facility to impress their beliefs on other people.
> When the Coalition was founded it was supposed to be a diverse organization. Now

they're driving away people who were willing to use logical, nonviolent, sensible means to relocate the HPER facility.[132]

On Tuesday, September 13 the formal split of coalition ranks occurred when about 80 coalition members met separately from the coalition. Sam Murphy, an active member throughout the spring and summer, stated: "We're upset about an organization on campus, the Revolutionary Student Brigade, let's face it."[133] The group had issued a leaflet the day before stating their basic position: "A growing number of people committed to moving the gym now feel it has become necessary to explore alternatives to the organization and tactics of the May 4 Coalition."[134] Out of this meeting developed the new Blanket Hill Council.

The coalition's carefully built base of support on Kent State's campus had now crumbled. Internal divisions preoccupied the coalition during the critical days just before construction, and hence no successful efforts to generate broadbased support among KSU students was to materialize as the day of construction arrived. A predominant slogan of the coalition throughout the spring and summer had been, "The people, united, will never be defeated." This prophecy was never to be fully tested. The people had not remained united.

Construction began on the morning of Monday, September 19. Only a small handful of coalition members were present. Tears filled the eyes of many who watched the huge bulldozer rip into Blanket Hill. It seemed to those who had struggled for so long that the land itself was crying out in agony as the giant machine proceeded with its emotionless, efficient, powerful strokes. Construction of the gym had finally begun again, but it was not a moment of triumph for university leaders. Golding, confronted by a gym opponent, exclaimed in frustration: "God damn it, I'll say this for the 1000th time. I can't stop it."[135]

The lack of effective protest on September 19 when construction resumed in full did not mean that the protest against the gym site was over. Coalition members continued to work on a variety of fronts throughout the fall. The two major events were large national rallies on September 24 and October 22.

The rally on September 24 drew the largest crowd of any rally the coalition had ever sponsored. Estimates placed the crowd at about 3000 and most of the protestors were from other campuses. After a series of speeches on the Commons, the crowd marched through the campus, spray painting names and slogans on the four campus buildings which the coalition wanted to have named after the four slain students. The rally culminated with the breaking down of portions of the fence surrounding the construction site and the brief reoccupation of the site by approximately 100 people. Some rocks were thrown at police by demonstrators, but the police maintained a low profile throughout the day and only a few arrests occurred.

The university administration and law enforcement officials took a much different approach to the October 22 national rally. On the week prior to the rally, Golding sought and received from the Portage County Common Pleas Court a temporary restraining order against the May 4th Coalition, prohibiting "defendants and all persons acting in aid of, or in conjunction, or in concert with, any or all of them and to others to whom notice and knowledge of this order shall come" from holding any rallies, marches, or demonstrations on the Kent State campus unless two conditions were met:

a. A rally, march or demonstration sponsored by a registered campus organization which has complied with the applicable regulations and procedures of the Student Life Office of Kent State University and has executed a proper agreement with the Student Life Office of Kent State University, which agreement shall include accepting financial responsibility for the clean-up of any debris and the repair of any damage which might occur; and in addition,

b. The rally, march or demonstration takes place between the hours of 10:00 a.m. and 4:00 p.m., in the area south of Summit Street across the street from the Student Center Parking Lot, and bounded on the east by the new Campus Approach Road and on the west by the Asphalt Service Drive.[136]

Because the first condition was not met, all protest rallies became illegal. The strategy of the law enforcement officials was to present a large show of force on campus, lining the inside of the fence around the construction site and breaking up any gatherings banned by the temporary restraining order. Approximately 500 demonstrators were on campus for the rally. This was far fewer than had been anticipated, perhaps because of the messages sent out by the university to other schools warning about the consequences of participating in an illegal

rally. The vast majority of the protestors were again from outside Kent State, and for the first time the leaders were not from Kent State, probably because of the threat of serious charges which faced coalition leaders who had been arrested on previous occasions. As described at the beginning of this essay, the day was characterized by continuous confrontations, but no serious injuries and few arrests occurred.

In the aftermath of the October 22 rally, campus attention focused primarily upon the short term extension of the temporary restraining order which university officials received from the court, pending a hearing scheduled for November 10 on making the order a permanent injunction. Prior to the formal court hearing, however, university officials decided not to seek an extension of the restraining order. The struggle to move the gym was over.

CONCLUSIONS

The controversy needs to be viewed both in terms of a specific issue of the location of a proposed facility and a much broader issue of the general relationships which had developed on Kent State's campus between activist students and university officials. The specific issue of the site of the HPER facility was clearly defined at the outset of the controversy. The position of the coalition was that the entire area of the May 4th confrontation should be preserved. This was land of great historical significance, and they were determined to prevent construction of the facility on that site. The majority of the trustees, on the other hand, did not hold these same values. While they agreed that no facility should cover the area where most of the students were killed or wounded, they did not see the necessity for preserving the entire area. Many other considerations also affected the trustees. They believe that they had followed proper procedures for choosing the site, student input had occurred, the site selected was the best one available in terms of cost effectiveness and convenience, and too much money had already been spent to change the decision. Coalition members in turn rejected each of these arguments.

While the conflict over the specific site of the facility was the central issue in the controversy, developments in the struggle must be understood in terms of the more general attitudes of student activists toward the university leadership, attitudes which involved hostility and distrust. It was the feeling of many activists that university officials—trustees and administrators alike—were guilty of many sins: insensitivity toward the events of May 4th; disregard for student ideas and opinions on a wide range of matters; intransigence toward faculty complaints; and improper administration of the university, as seen most clearly in the scandals that had broken open. University leaders were thus in a situation in which they had little credibility with student activists, and little constructively was done to address this situation in the months prior to May 4, 1977 as critical issues continued to rise on almost a monthly basis in 1976-77 for a university caught in a leadership vacuum.

This general background is important to an understanding of the failure of the trustees and coalition to reach a settlement of their conflict before the contracts became final in late June. While a resolution of the controversy would not have been easy even at the early stages given the sharply contrasting positions of the two sides, not one meeting was held between the trustees and coalition during this period. Effective leadership to resolve the differences did not arise from the trustees or top level administrators. The efforts which were made by university officials only served to reinforce previous attitudes held by coalition members, and the vulnerability of the university to adverse publicity was exploited by the coalition to achieve its goal.

By mid-summer there were no longer any realistic chances for resolving the controversy with any degree of mutual satisfaction. Positions hardened and conflict escalated. The majority of the trustees adhered to their earlier views, but now additional factors further solidified their positions. They were by this time faced with the potential of major suits, including personal liability suits, if they changed the location, and the increasingly militant tactics and rhetoric of the coalition confirmed the earlier suspicions of some of the trustees that they were dealing with a radical, communist-oriented movement that could not be allowed to win. For many member of the coalition who had committed so much energy and time to a cause in which they believed deeply, they perceived that no alternative existed to increasingly militant tactics. The publicity which had been given to their movement had attracted many others to their cause, and these new recruits tended to be more militant than many of the

original coalition members. As coalition leaders saw themselves being subjected to increasing police arrests and harassment, even deeper resentment and opposition began to build. Under these conditions, a radical group, the Revolutionary Student Brigade, was able gradually to gain dominance within the coalition.

Responsibility is difficult to assess in such a complicated controversy, but reflections can be offered on the actions of the conflicting sides in the controversy. Concerning the university leadership, I found no evidence that there was a "cover-up" of any type throughout the long history of this controversy. I believe university officials were insensitive to the depth of feelings of some people concerning the events of May 4th, but it also seems to me that the trustees' decisions on November 11, 1976 and May 12, 1977 were reasonable given the circumstances which they faced at the time. Administrative officials and many trustees did fail, however, to exercise the leadership which could reasonably have been expected during the weeks of Tent City when a resolution of the conflict might have been achieved. After the contracts became final, compromise on the part of the trustees became more difficult for they were in a complex legal situation. Nevertheless, the hardline position taken by a majority of the trustees throughout the controversy probably created a self-fulfilling prophecy, for their actions served to stimulate the development of the militant student movement about which they were worried from the beginning.

The coalition is difficult to assess because it was composed of so many diverse individuals and groups and because it had undergone so many changes. I was impressed by the dedication and resourcefulness of the original coalition members. Tent City was a classic example of effective peaceful protest, and the civil disobedience act which culminated the Tent City period was both rational and responsible. It must also be pointed out, however, that the coalition did contribute substantially to the impasse during the early period before contracts became final by setting forth the position that none of the demands were negotiable, thus reducing the possibility of a compromise. It is difficult to condone some of the later actions of the coalition, even if one sympathizes with their cause. Especially after the legal avenues were exhausted and construction began, continued protest could only serve to punish university officials for their decision and actions.[137] Unfortunately, the punishment was felt also by the thousands of students, faculty, staff, and graduates of Kent State University who had no involvement in the selection of the site.

ENDNOTES

1. *Kent*, Volume 3, No. 6 (June 1970), p.1.
2. Especially useful studies have been undertaken by Glen Griffin, Ann Hutchinson, Cheryl Daly, Wendy Hellinger, and Andy Oeftering.
3. The only person to refuse an interview was George Janik, chairman of the Board of Trustees, who felt that it was too early to analyze the controversy because of the lack of complete documentation and historical perspective on the events. These are good methodological arguments, as I acknowledge below. Mr. Janik did talk informally with me for several hours, however, and many of his comments have been useful for my analysis.
4. Interview with Dr. Michael Schwartz on November 3, 1977.
5. Based upon my interviews and analysis of trustee minutes and other materials, four trustees appear to have played especially important decision making roles: trustee chairman George Janik, Robert Baumgardner, Michael Johnston, and Dr. James Fleming. Other members of the Board of Trustees were: Robert Blakemore, David Dix, Norman Jackson, Joyce Quirk, and William Williams.
6. *Akron Beacon Journal*, July 15, 1977, p. A10.
7. This analysis is based upon a variety of sources. The two most important pubic documents are (1) "Fact and Issue File" released on June 2, 1977 by Anthony J. May, Kent State University Director of Communications and updated on August 3, 1977 and (2) "Chronology of HPER Facility Planning and May 4th Coalition," issued in August 3, 1977, by the May 4th Coalition. In addition, I have been able to draw upon a large number of interdepartmental memos related to the planning and development of the HPER facility.
8. It is important to note that much disagreement arose over the purpose of the facility during the years of planning. An especially important point of controversy centered around the use of the facility for intercollegiate athletics, a position which was ultimately rejected.
9. Minutes of the Long Range Planning Committee, October 20, 1969.
10. Minutes of the Space Planning Committee, April 16, 1970.
11. Many important meetings were of course held in the years prior to 1974 when the site north of Memorial Gymnasium was specified in the plans forwarded to the regents. For the purposes of this study, however, the critical point is that the site of the facility was recommended *before* May 4, 1970.
12. Memo from President Glenn Olds to Dean Carl Erickson dated March 4, 1974.
13. Memo from Dean Carl Erickson to President Glenn Olds dated April 30, 1974.
14. Memo from President Glenn Olds to Dean Carl Erickson dated May 8, 1974.

15. Memo from Gae Russo to Vice President * Walter Bruska dated June 13, 1975.
16. Memo from Vice President Walter Bruska to University Architect Gae Russo dated June 27, 1975.
17. Memo from Gae Russo to Walter dated July 3, 1975
18. Attachment 3, Site Map, to memo from Gae Russo to Dr. Carl Erickson dated July 18, 1975.
19. The new facility had been discussed briefly by the trustees at a meeting in 1975, but the matter was not brought before the trustees for any official action at this time.
20. It needs to be pointed out that several students— particularly Scott Marburger, executive secretary of Student Caucus, Nancy Grim, and John Henrikson—had become concerned about the location of the HPER facility during the summer of 1976. They were unsuccessful in learning the exact location of the facility, however. A detailed analysis of student activities and attitudes during the planning stages of the HPER facility can be found in Matijasic and Bills, "The People United: A Tentative Commentary on the Kent State Struggle 1977." Matijasic wrote this portion of the article.
21. *Daily Kent Stater*, November 4, 1976, p.3
22. The Student Caucus was the elected student government body of Kent State University.
23. The May 4th Task Force is a group which coordinates the annual May 4th commemorative activities on the campus and also sponsors throughout the year various informational programs concerning May 4th.
24. "Fact and Issue File."
25. This analysis of the trustees' reasons draws heavily from my interview with trustee Joyce Quirk conducted on October 22, 1977 and from a memo from Quirk to Kent State president-elect Brage Golding dated August 24, 1977
26. Minutes of the Kent State University Board of Trustees, November 11, 1976, p. 18.
27. For example, see the following *Daily Kent Stater* papers: April 8, 1977, p. 4; April 15, 1977, p. 4; April 29, 1977, pp. 4 and 5; May 3, 1977, p. 4; and May 4, 1977, p. 4. Olds responded to these criticisms in a letter on April 28, 1977, p. 4, and Bob Hart, a leader in the May 4th Task Force, responded to Olds in a letter on May 3, 1977, p. 4.
28. Hyde Park was an area by the Commons where the ROTC building had stood before it was burned down in May of 1970.
29. The quotation is taken from Olds' letter of April 28, 1977 in the *Daily Kent Stater*, p. 4.
30. This was an ad hoc group formed around the issue of the refusal of the administration to cancel classes on May 4th.
31. *Daily Kent Stater*, April 19, 1977, p. 3.
32. *Ibid.*
33. *Ibid.*, p. 3.
34. *Ibid.*, p. 1.
35. *Daily Kent Stater*, May 4, 1977, p. 3.
36. The decision of the trustees to hold a meeting on May 4th has been a subject of much debate and criticism. Some people have suggested that the entire controversy would never have occurred if the trustees had not met that afternoon. Janik has indicated that members of the board were concerned about meeting on that day, but that the presidential search committee—composed of students and

faculty as well as trustees—was anxious to meet because of concern about losing candidates if any delays occurred.

37. *Daily Kent Stater*, May 4, 1977, p. 1
38. *Akron Beacon Journal*, May 4, 1977, p. A1.
39. *Akron Beacon Journal*, May 5, 1977, p.A9.
40. *Daily Kent Stater*, May 5, 1977, p. 3.
41. *Ibid.*
42. This list of demands is taken from a leaflet printed by the May 4th Coalition later in May following the Rockwell sit-in.
43. *Record-Courier*, May 5, 1977, p. 31.
44. *Akron Beacon Journal*, May 5, 1977, p. A1
45. *Record-Courier*, May 6, 1977, p. 1, 13.
46. Janik said the demand about discussions with UFPA would not be permitted nor would the other three demands, which contained new information and had not been evaluated by trustee subcommittees. See *Daily Kent Stater,* May 10, 1977, p. 1.
47. *Akron Beacon Journal*, May 13, 1977, p. A10.
48. The evidence suggests that several trustees took this latter view, i.e., that the coalition was a radical movement using the gym issue to promote radical political ideologies.
49. It is important to point out that several trustees—Quirk, Dix, Blakemore, and Janik—did visit Tent City and talk with coalition members. Coalition members believe that only Quirk and Dix really came to understand the Tent City movement.
50. The date on the contracts was June 24, 1977. The letter from the state informing primary contractor Bucky Arnes of the contracts was dated June 28, 1977.
51. This is a judgment which is offered retrospectively. The date was not perceived at that time as being so critical by most participants in the controversy.
52. *Akron Beacon Journal*, July 11, 1977, p. A8.
53. "Position Paper May 4th Coalition," June 23, 1977
54. Coalition members spent a great deal of time developing these arguments and trying to convince students, faculty, and others of the validity of the arguments. They hoped that by gaining large numbers of supporters, they could put pressure on the trustees.
55. Each of the area newspapers had several feature stories on Tent City, and all of the stories portrayed a positive image to the reader.
56. This information is based upon an interview with State Representative John Begala on November 4, 1977.
57. *Daily Kent Stater*, May 17, 1977, p. 3.
58. The distrust by the coalition of university officials is seen in the coalition's rejection of Biles' proposal: "It is obviously offered at this late time to divert attention from our proposals. A chapel would serve to preserve the memory of May 4, 1970 in the only way the administration would accept: a tragic incident frozen in the past, to be mourned in solitude behind stained glass windows. The administration refuses to acknowledge "May 4" as part of the living history of Kent State and the world." The quote is taken from the June 23, 1977 "Position Paper May 4th Coalition."
59. Minutes of the Kent State University Board of Trustees, June 9, 1977, p. 20.
60. *Ibid*, pp. 23-24.
61. *Ibid*. p, 20.
63. *Akron Beacon Journal*, July 8, 1977, p. B1.
62. *Akron Beacon Journal*, July 3, 1977, p. C1.
63. This tactic, as opposed to arrest for criminal trespass, relieved the trustees from direct responsibility for the removal of the protestors but it also gave the court and county sheriff authority over the site instead of maintaining control in the hands of the university.
64. Record-Courier, July 7, 1977, p.1.
65. *Ibid.*, p. 15.
66. The following analyses are based upon the respective interviews with trustee Joyce Quirk and State Representative John Begala.
67. A change order can only be issued if there is a small amount of money involved in the change.
68. Begala interpreted Riffe to be leaning toward supporting the request at this point.
69. Only $100 separated the two lowest bidders for the contract. A change order to rotate the facility would have involved much more than this, and hence the second lowest bidder would be able to bring a suit if a change order was issued.
70. Interview with State Representative John Begala on November 4, 1977.
71. According to newspaper accounts, 67 of those arrested were Kent State students, 9 were Kent State alums, and 117 were neither students nor alums. Subsequent analysis has shown that many of the 117 had various past connections to the university.
72. *Record-Courier*, July 12, 1977, p. 7. Considerable credit for the success for this operation should be given to members of the Kent State Center for Peaceful Change, especially Dr. Dennis Carey, and members of the American Friends Service Committee.
73. For example, in June, the Executive Committee of the Faculty Senate expressed to the Board of Trustees its opposition to the site chosen for the facility.
74. Interview with Dr. Michael Schwartz on November 3, 1977.
75. Interview with Dr. Michael Schwartz on November 3, 1977.
76. Coalition members were certainly aware of this, as evidenced by their continuous efforts to establish a "Tent City in exile."
77. This viewpoint was shared by many other individuals and groups associated with the coalition, including the Youth Socialist Alliance, a moderate group of Kent Sate students who favored peaceful, legal tactics; the Communist Youth Organization, composed of a few initially influential people who came to Kent after the arrests on Blanket Hill; the Youth International Party, a group of perhaps 15 to 30 persons who came to Kent later in the summer and who defy easy description because of their militant rhetoric and semi-comical behavior, including pie throwing at their opponents; and the Spartacus Youth League, a Trotskyite oriented group whose members attended some coalition meetings but never formally identified with the coalition, in part at least because of the SYL focus on issues such as ROTC on campus and its ideological clash with the more dominant RSB. It is important to recognize that all of these groups were small in size. Throughout most of the spring

and summer, all of the members of these groups together did not constitute a majority of the coalition membership.

78. The reasons for this development are analyzed later in this section.

79. *Akron Beacon Journal*, July 17, 1977, p. A4. Dr. James Laue of the University of Missouri at St. Louis was an important figure in promoting White House initiatives.

80. Coalition members included Alan and Chic Canfora, Dean Kahler, Jim Fry, Greg Rambo, John Rowe, Lynn Stoval, Reverend John Adams, and lawyer David Engdahl.

81. University officials included George Janik, Michael Johnston, Michael Schwartz, and Ted Curtis.

82. See *Record-Courier,* August 2, 1977, p. 1, 5.

83. In a letter dated July 22, 1977 to faculty members, UFPA president Dr. V. Edwin Bixenstine cited two primary reasons for the decision by the group's executive committee: fear of potential violent actions if construction begins and the economic costs to the university and faculty if continued protests adversely affected enrollment. Bixenstine also noted: "The Executive Committee, in arriving at its decision, did *not* render a judgment on the moral rightness or wrongness of the gym site or of the protestors' tactics. It is, however, our judgment that the numbers who believe that the gym site is wrong is both growing and serious."

84. Memo from President Michael Schwartz to all Academic Deans dated July 21, 1977.

85. *Record-Courier*, July 26, 1977, p.9.

86. *Record-Courier*, July 25, 1977, pp. 1, 13.

87. The number was subsequently expanded to fifteen to include the two students killed in1970 at Jackson State.

88. Temporary Restraining Order, Portage County Common Pleas Court, Judge Joseph Kainrad, July 25, 1977.

89. Coalition members had also been picketing the homes and offices of some trustees.

90. *Record-Courier*, July 27, 1977, p. 3.

91. On August 2, UFPA lawyer Staughton Lynd filed a motion with the appeals court asking the court to overrule Kainrad's decision. This appeal was rejected on August 26.

92. Verified Complaint for Injunctive Relief, filed 29 July 1977 in U. S. District Court, Northern District of Ohio, p. 4.

93. These possible reasons for Lambros' decision developed during the interview with Dr. David Luban on November 8, 1977.

94. The analysis of the negotiating sessions in federal district court draws heavily from the interviews with Dr. David Luban on November 8, 1977.

95. *Akron Beacon Journal*, August 9, 1977, p.A1

96. *Ibid.*

97. *Ibid.* This conflict was more apparent than real. Schwartz had instructed university attorney Parisi to inform Judge Lambros that the university was willing to consider the rotation plan, but apparently Judge Lambros received negative responses from the coalition lawyers for the reasons cited above. The three coalition representatives never did see the plans during the negotiations, but Schwartz was unaware of this.

98. Memorandum Opinion and Order, U. S. District Court, Northern District of Ohio Eastern Division, August 8, 1977, Judge Thomas D. Lambros, p. 3.

99. Akron Beacon Journal, August 2, 1977, p. A1.

100. Reverend John Adams had been involved since 1970 in court issues on behalf of the parents of the students killed on May 4th.

101. *Akron Beacon Journal*, August 5, 1977, p.A1.

102. *Akron Beacon Journal*, August 8, 1977, p. B1.

103. *Record-Courier*, August 6, 1977, p. 1.

104. *Record-Courier*, August 13, 1977, p. 1.

105. *Ibid.*

106. *Record-Courier*, August 18, 1977, p. A13.

107. *Akron Beacon Journal,* August 5, 1977, p. 1.

108. *Akron Beacon Journal*, August 8, 1977, p. A13

109. See *Record-Courier*, August 17, 1977, p. 3 and *Record-Courier*, August 18, 1977, p. 31.

110. *Christian Science Monitor*, August 4, 1977, p. 27.

111. See the earlier discussion in this section on the strains which confronted coalition unity.

112. Memorandum Opinion and Order, U. S. District Court, Northern District of Ohio Eastern Division, August 17, 1977, Judge Thomas D. Lambros, p. 6.

113. *Ibid.*

114. *Akron Beacon Journal*, August 18, 1977, p. 12.

115. Memorandum Opinion and Order, U. S. District Court, Northern District of Ohio Eastern Division, August 17, 1977, Judge Thomas D. Lambros, p. 6.

116. These announcements were apparently stimulated by contact initiated by coalition lawyer Tony Walsh in response to Lambros' position that "the method and procedure for declaring a particular location a national historic site is set forth by statute. Plaintiffs' grievance, seeking solely to achieve an administrative determination pursuant to congressional legislation, is necessarily bounded by the terms and conditions of that legislation. These terms and conditions include no provision for federal control over lands being investigated for but not having been declared as national historic sites." *Ibid.*, pp. 2, 3.

117. *Akron Beacon Journal*, August 19, 1977, p. 6.

118. The dissenting vote was cast by Robert Baumgardner. Trustees George Janik and William Williams were absent from the meeting.

119. The plan reportedly involved $2.5 million for renovation of the University School, $1.4 million for the renovation of Memorial Gymnasium, and $2 million for compensation to the contractors. See *Record-Courier*, August 23, 1977, p. 1.

120. *Akron Beacon Journal*, August 23, 1977, p. B1.

121. *Akron Beacon Journal,* August 23, 1977, p. A6 and *Record-Courier,* August 24, 1977, p. 4.

122. *Record-Courier*, August 23, 1977, p. 1.

123. *Record-Courier*, August 24, 1977, p. 2.

124. *Akron Beacon Journal*, August 23, 1977, p. B1

125. *Record-Courier*, September 9, 1977, p. 13.

126. The coalition saw these arrests as a clear example of police harassment, and these arrests served to anger and radicalize many coalition members. The arrested coalition members, including Chic Canfora and her brother Mark as well as a coalition lawyer, believe that they were set-up for these arrests by agent provocateurs working in close cooperation with the police.

127. A lot of attention focused on reestablishing Tent City.

128. Written comments from John Henrikson on an earlier version of this paper.

129. Interview with John Henrikson on November 11, 1977.

130. *Akron Beacon Journal*, September 6, 1977, p. A12.
131. *Daily Kent Stater*, September 14, 1977, p. 3.
132. *Ibid.*
133. *Daily Kent Stater*, September 14, 1977. p. 3.
134. Leaflet entitled "This Isn't a May 4th Coalition Leaflet, But. .. Move the Gym."
135. *Record-Courier*, September 19, 1977, p.1.

136. Temporary Restraining Order, Portage County Common Pleas Court, Judge J. Phillip Jones, October 21, 1977.
137. While continued protest could not succeed in altering the construction of the gym, protest over the gym issue could be used to promote the interests of a broader movement, and there is substantial evidence that this did occur.

The May 4th Coalition and Tent City: A Norm Oriented Movement[1]

Jerry M. Lewis
Kent State University

Introduction

This essay examines the events at Kent State University during the months of May to July 1977 related to the construction of a gym near the place where four students fell dead and nine were wounded as a result of gunfire from the Ohio National Guard on May 4th, 1970. There are two purposes for the essay. First, it is designed to provide the reader with an account of the facts of the events. Second, it is written to demonstrate the utility of Neil Smelser's (1962) model of collective behavior for looking at a variety of collective behavior events. In this regard, the essay should be seen as a companion to one written earlier by the author (Lewis, 1972) dealing with the hostile outburst that took place on the Kent campus on May 4, 1970.

Narrative[2]

On May 12, 1977 a group of protestors pitched tents on the campus of Kent State University, Kent, Ohio, on the site of the proposed gym. They hoped their efforts would result in the protection and preservation of what they considered to be an area of national historical significance. The protestors occupied the site for sixty-two days.

The genesis of "Tentropolis" (Tent City) began May 3 during an all-night candlelight vigil involving approximately 1000 participants who were commemorating the events of May 4, 1970. On the evening of May 4, about 200 persons, mostly students, occupied the administration building (Rockwell Hall) for eight hours. During the occupation the demonstrators created an organization known as the May 4 Coalition and a series of demands to be implemented by the Coalition. Early on the morning of May 5, the protestors left the building, had the demands read to the press by a student Dean Kahler, who was wounded on May 4th, 1970, and began efforts to mobilize students to support the demands.

On May 12, the University Board of Trustees, by a vote of 8-1, approved the completion of the bidding process, hence affirming their decision to build the gym on the proposed site. A crowd which had assembled outside the meeting began to talk of "stopping bulldozers with bodies." The crowd began a march around campus which culminated when about seventy protestors pitched eight tents within the proposed gym site area, and hence Tent City became a reality. By May 17 Tent City consisted of approximately fifty-five tents and one hundred inhabitants. University officials remained reticent while campus security officials were hoping rain would terminate the city.

On June 4th, a national rally was held by the May 4th Coalition. The city now included more than sixty tents and one hundred thirty people. The June 4 rally involved 550 participants including activist Dick Gregory. Lawyer William Kunstler was present and offered legal defense for those who might be arrested in the future.

In the weeks following the June 4 rally, both the University administration and the May 4th Coalition worked on their respective strategies. Developing appropriate methods for removing protestors from the hill was the administration's primary concern, while the Coalition was deciding whether to leave when confronted by the agents of social control.

On July 8th, the University president, Glenn A. Olds, made a midnight visit to Tent City to informally tell the Coalition of an imminent court order which would call for them to vacate the area. On Sunday morning Olds ordered the people of Tent City to disperse or face arrest; the protestors chose the latter. The following day the trustees voted 6-1 to seek an injunction which was subsequently obtained. The temporary restraining order, issued on July 11, ordered the protestors to vacate the site, but also ordering the University to delay construction for ten days.

On Tuesday, July 12th, the sixty-second day of Tent City's existence, one hundred ninety-three people chose to defy the court order which called for their dispersement. As a consequence they were arrested by police who were armed only with night sticks. With the arrests, Tent City ended as non-violently as it had begun. This time around neither blood nor bullets had painted the picture of the conflict.

METHODOLOGY

Data about the May 4th Coalition and Tent City were obtained in a variety of ways. First, I visited Tent City twice between May 12 and May 19th, 1977.[3] Then, from early in June to the arrests of July 12th, which ended Tent City, I visited the site regularly and attended Coalition meetings. In the course of these visits, I talked with Coalition leaders and members. Second, I used documents developed by the Coalition to present its views. Copies of these documents are available in the Kent State University Archival Services or can be obtained from the author.

Third, I drew on newspaper accounts for factual material not available to me. These accounts were primarily from the *Kent Record-Courier*, the *Akron Beacon Journal*, and the *Cleveland Plain Dealer*. Four, Professor Betty Kirschner and I conducted a survey of those arrested on July 12 (Lewis and Kirschner, 1977). Some of the data from this study are reported in this paper.

THEORETICAL CONSIDERATIONS

This study is organized around the general theoretical model of Neil Smelser (1962). He divides the analysis of collective behavior phenomena into five determinants, each having several subdeterminants. In this section, a brief review of the model is provided. In going beyond the earlier approach (Lewis, 1972), propositions about the May 4th Coalition and Tent City are provided as guides for the inquiry.

Smelser's approach to collective behavior is based on the work of Talcott Parsons as well as value-added approaches to economics. He feels that factors must combine in certain ways in order for various types of collective behavior to happen. To understand this process Smelser proposes an analytical model centered around five determinants, namely structural conduciveness, structural strain, growth of a generalized belief, mobilization for action, and social control.

Structural Conduciveness

Structural conduciveness refers to conditions that are necessary but not sufficient for an episode of collective behavior to occur. The activities of the May 4th Coalition to block the construction of a gym with the technique of Tent City are treated here as a norm-oriented movement. Smelser feels that a norm-oriented movement should be analyzed, in regard to structural conduciveness, by first looking at whether the movement attempts to protect or create norms without any efforts to make ". . . a more fundamental modification of values" (Smelser, 1962: 278). Second, the analysis should look at the movement in terms of its access to channels that influence the normative order. Third, one should ask if the norm-oriented movement develops social mechanisms for communication with members, as well as with other interested parties. These propositions are suggested:

1. The leaders and members of the May 4th Coalition proposed modifications of norms without calling for basic value changes.
2. The leaders and members of the May 4th Coalition had access to channels for expressing their grievances.

3. The leaders and members for the May 4th Coalition developed a social mechanism in the form of Tent City for communicating with each other as well as interested parties.

Structural Strain

What were the conditions of strain that were the basis of this norm-oriented movement? Strain for Smelser (1962: 47) is the assumption that ". . . people enter episodes of [collective behavior] because something is wrong in their social environment." For Smelser, in the tradition of Talcott Parsons, it is particularly important to look at strain at the level of values and norms. He (Smelser, 1962: 288) writes, "Any disharmony between normative standards and actual social conditions can provide the basis for a movement whose objective it is to modify the norms." Smelser (1962: 290), quoting V. O. Key, sees strain as generating norm-oriented movements which create "demands for readjustment in the social situation." Based on these ideas, the following proposition is suggested:

4. The leaders and members of the May 4th Coalition reported a perception of a disharmony between the ideal and real aspects of historical norms related to the building of the gym.

Growth of a Generalized Belief

Smelser believes that in all episodes of collective behavior beliefs develop which guide the actions of participants. Beliefs about norms serve to explain the condition of strain for movement participants. In addition, beliefs provide solutions for resolving the strain. These propositions are suggested:

5. The May 4th Coalition leaders and members stated their analysis of the gym dispute in beliefs about the sources of normative strain.
6. The May 4th Coalition leaders and members presented solutions to ameliorate strain in the form of normative beliefs.

Mobilization of Participants for Action

Smelser (1962: 355) argues that mobilization for action of the movement should be analyzed under four subdeterminants which he labels (1) leadership, (2) the real and derived aspects, (3) the effect of the success or failure of specific tactics, and (4) the direction and development after the success or failure for the movement.

Smelser sees two types of leadership roles: those which formulate beliefs and those that mobilize participants to action. This proposition is suggested:

7. The May 4th Coalition generated distinct belief and action leadership roles.

Smelser feels that a movement shifts from a real or initial stage to a derived stage. In addition, he states that a norm-oriented movement is likely to go through three temporal phases which he labels as incipient, enthusiastic mobilization, and institutionalization. This proposition is proposed:

8. The May 4th Coalition moved through three distinct temporal phases which can be characterized as incipient, enthusiastic mobilization, and institutionalization.

Smelser believes that movements are responsive to tactical successes or failures. He writes (Smelser, 1962: 302):

> The history of any given movement—its ebbs and flows, its switches, its bursts of enthusiasm—can be written in large part as a pattern of abandoning one method which appears to be losing effectiveness and adopting some new, more promising method.

Thus, this proposition is suggested:

9. The May 4th Coalition's tactic of civil disobedience was a response to the failure of other actions to stop the building of the gym.

Smelser notes that because of the generalized belief, most social movements will set goals that cannot be reached, and hence, there can never be complete success. Thus, this proposition is suggested:

10. The May 4th Coalition successfully achieved some but not all of its stated goals.

Social Control

In dealing with the determinant of social control, Smelser's ideas point to the issue of how authorities respond to the movement. The most important question is whether the social control authorities respond to a norm-oriented movement in such a manner that encourages the movement to retain its character, or whether the response turns the movement into an alternative form of collective behavior such as a hostile outburst or a panic. Smelser (1962: 307) writes:

> Beyond general encouragement of a movement, what kinds of behavior on the part of authorities encourage a norm-oriented movement to retain its norm-oriented character? The agencies of social control must (a) permit expression of grievances but insist that this expression remain within the confines of legitimacy, and (b) give a hearing—as defined by institutionalized standards of "fairness"—to the complaints at hand. This does not mean that authorities must accede to the demands of the movement; rather they must leave open the possibility that these demands, along with others, will be heard, and that some responsible decision will be taken with regard to them.

This proposition is suggested:

11. The response of the social control authorities to the May 4th Coalition facilitated the norm-oriented character of the movement.

ANALYSIS OF THE MAY 4TH COALITION AS A NORM ORIENTED MOVEMENT

Structural Conduciveness

What were the conditions of social structure that were conducive for a norm-oriented movement? These propositions were suggested:

1. The leaders and members in the May 4th Coalition proposed modification of norms without calling for basic value changes.
2. The leaders and members of the May 4th Coalition had access to channels for expressing their grievances.

3. The leaders and members of the May 4th Coalition developed a mechanism for communicating with each other as well as interested parties.

The May 4th Coalition formed during an eight hour sit-in in the central administration building (Rockwell Hall) on the evening of May 4th, 1977. At the end of the sit-in, KSU students and others emerged from the building and presented their demands to the waiting press and interested bystanders. The demands were later presented to the chairman of the Board of Trustees who agreed to present them at a Board of Trustees meeting on May 12th. The demands were:

1. The Kent State University administration must officially acknowledge the injustice of the Kent State Massacre of May 4, 1970.
2. The new p.e. building (gym) must not be built on the site of the shootings of May 4, 1970, and in the future, no construction or alteration of the site must be permitted.
3. The status of the Center for Peaceful Change shall be maintained as it is as an all university program.
4. Henceforth May 4 shall be set aside as a day of remembrance and education about the Kent State massacre; and the regular activities of this University will be canceled this May 4 and every May 4 hereafter.
5. The four buildings which have been named after the four slain students shall be officially recognized.
6. Amnesty must be given to all students, faculty and staff who commemorated May 4 and, as a result, are threatened with punishment of any kind.
7. The administration must reopen negotiations in good faith with the United Faculty Professional Association.
8. No punitive actions shall be taken against anyone who participated in the sit-in May 4, 1977 in Rockwell Hall.[4]

All of these demands presented to the Board of Trustees dealt with rules or norms of University procedures without calling for any major value change either in the University or the larger society. Demands 1, 2, 4, and 5 were central to the movement throughout the summer. In particular, demand number 2 served as the impetus for most of the activity. Demand 3 never was crucial because the University soon dropped its plan to change the personnel and programs of the Center for Peaceful Change. Demand 7, on the reopening of negotiations, was never a factor because the negotiations resumed shortly after the demands were issued. Both University and United Faculty Professional Association leaders indicated to me, in personal interviews, that demand 7 was not a major factor in reopening negotiations.

Yet, the Coalition believed the demand was an important factor. Consequently, many Coalition members were bitter towards the faculty for not providing more support in the efforts to move the gym.

Demands 6 and 8 never emerged again since the University administration took no action against people who had participated in May 4 activities or who had involved themselves in the Rockwell occupation. Thus, the first proposition is supported.

In regard to proposition 2, the May 4th Coalition identified the KSU Board of Trustees as the source of its grievances and attempted to open up channels of communication with the Board.[5] On May 6th, nine members of the Coalition met the chairman of the Board who indicated he would present the demands to the full Board. On May 12th, the Board held a regularly-scheduled public meeting, and members of the Coalition were present to speak about the demands. The University president spoke for the administration and defended the decision to build the new gym. He also explained the proper procedure for renaming buildings. One of the persons at the meeting pointed out that students had previously attempted to use the proper procedure for renaming the buildings but were not able to get any results.

At various times during the meeting, six people other than Board members addressed the Board of Trustees on the issue of moving the site of the new gymnasium. The result of the meeting was a vote by the Board of Trustees to approve the authorization of construction contracts. There was one dissenting vote.

The results of the meeting were clearly unsatisfactory to the Coalition. The Coalition decided to pitch tents on a part of the proposed construction area that had trees in order to protect the area from construction work. The tents varied from very small two-person tents to a large parachute canopy which served as "City Hall" for Tent City. Over the following weeks the president of the University and members of the Board of Trustees visited Tent City in order to talk with members of the Coalition. It can be concluded that proposition 2 is supported.

The third proposition instructs one to look for social mechanisms of communication. The May 4th Coalition developed three major techniques of communication. The first technique was Tent City itself. The physical presence of the City ensured that someone was always available to receive and distribute messages.

The press displayed considerable interest in Tent City by publishing many stories about it and about the goals of the Coalition. Because Tent City was visually interesting, television used it as a backdrop for communicating the goals of the Coalition. When Tent City was eliminated in the middle of the summer, the communication problem became very serious.

Second, the Coalition used the mechanism of the town meeting for discussing issues. On almost every evening during the summer, regular meetings of the Coalition were held. They began around 7:30 at Tent City, on a site overlooking the main construction area. The meetings were lengthy and attendance varied, from 50 to 200 people, depending on the importance of the issues being discussed. The chairperson was a rotating one early in the life of Tent City, but later one person served many meetings as chair. The chairpersons were quite effective in communicating a sense of fairness in the debate. Every person was allowed to speak, and considerable effort was made to avoid personal attacks on people because of their ideas. However, the personal attacks did occur and caused some tension among the Coalition. Voting rights were granted to all present, and decisions were made on the basis of a simple majority.

The third form of communication was the use of leaflets and handouts which are typical of a student movement. These materials were always available to the press and others who came to Tent City. New positions and developments were generally published in handouts and leaflets and were posted on a bulletin board near "City Hall." It can be concluded that the May 4th Coalition developed social mechanisms of communication, and thus proposition 3 is supported.

Summary

The analysis indicates that the May 4th Coalition called for changes in norms rather than values; identified channels for expressing their grievances; and developed social mechanisms of communication. It can be concluded that conditions were conducive for a norm-oriented social movement. However, it should be noted that some of the readers of this essay felt that the Coalition's activities should be characterized as a value-oriented movement. I have retained the norm-oriented position because the Coalition called for changes in University rules not for major value changes in regard to important educational policies and procedures.

Structural Strain

What were the conditions of strain that led to the creation of the May 4th Coalition and Tent City? This proposition guides the analysis of strain:

4. The leaders and members of the May 4th Coalition reported a perception of disharmony between the ideal and actual aspects for historical norms related to the building of the gym annex.

What type of strain was identified by the Coalition? That is, what was the nature of the disharmony between ideal and actual norms as perceived by the leaders and members of the Coalition?

It is possible to identify three factors of strain. They may be labeled as the denial of history; the destruction of legal evidence; and the insensitivity of the University to the death of four Kent State students and the wounding of nine others.

The three factors were generally intertwined in the arguments of the Coalition. For example, on May 19, 1977 the Coalition issued a lengthy press release explaining its actions. The release said in part:

> One Week ago today members of the May 4 Coalition claimed the sacred land where four of our brothers and sisters were massacred May 4, 1970.
>
> We chose this course of action as a last resort when it became painfully clear that the Board of Trustees and the administration of Kent State University were obstinately prepared to coverup

May 4, 1970 once and for all, by actually destroying the physical evidence with their plans to construct a massive gymnasium on this historic site. Their refusal to accede to other reasonable Coalition demands contributed to our decision to claim our land.

> When we moved on Taylor Hill we did so with every intention of staying to prevent the desecration of this historic and beautiful land. Make no mistake about it, we are here to stay. We have the support of the University community, the families and attorneys for the slain and wounded students and the good people of our nation. We shall not be moved.
>
> From our inception on May 4, 1977, our movement has been one of peaceful and nonviolent action. Any confrontation on this historic site, reminiscent of May 4, 1970, will once again not be provoked by students, but by the agents of the administration and the state of Ohio.[6]

The analysis now looks at the three factors in more detail.

The Denial of History

The Coalition believed that the student antiwar movement was a major part of American history of the late 1960s and early 1970s. Further, they felt that the events of May 4, 1970, represented a turning point in the antiwar movement because for the first time the "war had come home" and had raised the consciousness of the general public about the Vietnam War. The Coalition stated in a major policy paper that the administration of Kent State University "is obligated to preserve this site, as Boston must preserve the site of the Boston Massacre." The Coalition believed that while the actual sites from where the Guard fired and where the students fell dead would not be changed, many other important aspects of the site would be significantly altered. In particular, the gym and landscaping would result in ". . . covering the path of the Guard's march . . ." just prior to the shootings.[7] The Coalition's position on this issue is summarized in this concluding statement from its position paper:

> The administration refuses to acknowledge 'May 4' as part of the living history of Kent State and the world.[8]

Destruction of Legal Evidence

Much of the activity related to May 4 and afterward dealt with legal disputes. During most of the summer of 1977, the 1975 civil case was under appeal. The Coalition felt that should the case be reversed, as it subsequently was, the site would be partially destroyed for a jury view. The Coalition wrote,

> The civil suit brought by the nine wounded and the parents of the dead against Governor Rhodes, Guard officers and enlisted men and former KSU President White is presently under appeal in the Sixth District Court of Appeals. Because of numerous errors in the original trial, there is a strong chance that the plaintiffs will win a new trial. If so, a jury view of the site will almost certainly be necessary. There are so many photographs taken from various perspectives or distorted by telephoto lens, that interpretation is impossible without a view of the site. Judge Young ordered a jury view in the first trial, and any Judge is likely to do the same.[9]

University's Insensitive Attitude Toward the Death of Four Students

This dimension of strain is more difficult to describe than the other two, but it was a theme that could be clearly ascertained at Coalition meetings. The basic idea was that the University was perceived as having failed to recognize officially the killing of four students and the wounding of nine others. This strain dimension was stated in the demands of the Coalition to call off classes every year on May 4 and to name a building for each of the slain students.

Summary

There were at least three dimensions of strain perceived by the May 4th Coalition. They were the denial of history, the destruction of legal evidence, and the University's perceived insensitivity to the killings. Thus, it can be concluded that proposition 4 is supported.

Growth of Generalized Beliefs

What were the beliefs about strain and the sources of strain that shaped the action of the May 4th Coalition? Two propositions guide the analysis:

5. The May 4th Coalition leaders and members stated their analysis of the gym annex dispute in beliefs about the normative strain.
6. The May 4th Coalition leaders and members presented solutions to ameliorate strain in the form of normative beliefs.

The Coalition believed that the central reason for building the gym on the particular site was that the Board of Trustees and the University president wished to coverup Kent State's involvement in the shootings as well as its failure to show concern about the shootings. The Coalition noted in its major policy paper.

> For the past seven years the KSU administration has worked hard to distort the facts, confuse the issues and bury the history of May 4, 1970. The natural extension of this policy is to literally bury the site of the shootings under a sprawling building.[10]

The question often raised by interested observers to the dispute was why the KSU administration would wish to cover over the site. The two answers to the question provided by the Coalition throughout the summer may be interpreted as generalized beliefs. First, the Coalition felt that the University had been a party to the suppression of free expression on May 4th, 1970. The building of the gym on the particular site was seen as a coverup by the University's administration concerning its culpability. This coverup was reiterated throughout the summer. For example, a leaflet announcing a rally on July 22nd said in part, "Today, the May 4th Coalition is protesting the KSU administration's latest step in the coverup of the truth about May 4, 1970. They are attempting to bury the historic ground of the shootings under a massive gymnasium."[11]

The second answer to why a coverup was taking place had to do with the governor of the state, James Rhodes. The Coalition believed that the gym was being built to protect the governor who had been in office in 1970 and was still involved in the civil suit. They felt the governor was putting pressure on the Board to build the gym annex. Although the Coalition was never able to document this fact, the belief remained strong throughout the summer. It can be concluded that proposition number 5 is supported.

In regard to proposition number 6, the most important solution proposed by the Coalition was not to build the gym on the proposed site but rather move it to another location. In addition, the Coalition felt that the site should never be altered for any reason. This was to remain the central belief of the movement. The phrase "Move the gym" appeared on T-shirts, handouts and posters. The importance of the theme can be illustrated by the fact that a group organized against the Coalition late in the summer used the phrase "Move the Coalition." Thus, proposition 6 is supported.

Summary

In regard to generalized beliefs the analysis found that there were two sets of beliefs present. One set attributed the reason for building the gym to a desire of the University and the governor to coverup their violation of rules of justice. The other set of beliefs stressed rules for protection of the site, including the decision not to build the proposed gym.

Mobilization for Action

What patterns of action were carried out by the leaders and members of the May 4th Coalition as they tried to stop the building of the gym? In this section three propositions guide the analysis. The first is:

7. The May 4th Coalition generated distinct belief and action leadership roles.

The May 4th Coalition officially had no formal leaders and attempted to do things democratically through group consensus. But, outside demands, particularly from the press and from groups interested in working with the Coalition, exerted pressure on the Coalition to put some people into leadership responsibilities. There was one person who was placed in a belief oriented leadership role more than any other person associated with the Coalition. This person was Alan Canfora. Canfora was a charismatic leader who was perceived as being legitimate for a variety of reasons. First, he provided a tie directly to the events of May 4th, 1970 because he had been wounded by the National Guard. In October, 1970 he was indicted by a Portage County Grand Jury, as one of the "Kent-25,"

for second-degree rioting. The charge was subsequently dismissed.

Second, he had a very clear point of view about the wrong that was being done in the building of the gym. He was able to articulate this view effectively to the Coalition. Third, Canfora spent a good deal of time and effort working with the Coalition by staying on the hill and building group morale. Canfora's involvement eventually led to the involvement of his family. Among the 193 arrested on July 12 were Alan, his parents, two brothers, and his sister who became a spokesperson for the Coalition.[12]

In regard to action on tactics, the leadership of the May 4th Coalition was more diffuse. There were committees such as the press relations committee, the fund-raising committee, and the marshaling committee. Generally, the committees made recommendations to the Coalition which were then discussed in the general meetings. For example, the decision to be arrested was reached after a five-hour meeting the night before the arrests. Many spoke at the meeting on the issue of violating the court order to vacate the site by refusing to leave. The meeting was held at the Kent Student Center and the vote was taken by having who wished to be arrested moving to one side while those who chose not to be arrested moving to other side. It can be concluded that proposition seven is supported although the tactic roles were not as distinct as the proposition would suggest.[13]

The analysis now turns to phases in the mobilization for action. This proposition guides the inquiry:

8. The May 4th Coalition moved through three distinct temporal phases which can be characterized as incipient, enthusiastic mobilization, and institutionalization.

The real and derived phases of the development of the May 4th Coalition can be located in a temporal context. The real or incipient phase began with the Rockwell sit-in on May 4, 1977 and lasted until the Board of Trustees meeting on May 12th. The derived phase of enthusiastic mobilization began with the start of Tent City and lasted until June 4 when the first national rally to protest the building of the gym annex was held. The period of institutionalization began with the planning of the June rally and lasted until the end of Tent City on

July12. The recognition and institutionalization of Tent City are important points because they served as symbols of the legitimacy of the May 4th Coalition's concerns.

The University administration's position on Tent City was presented on June 2, 1977. In a question-and-answer format, the University News Service said:

> **Q** Why doesn't the University throw the students off the hill?
>
> **A** At this time, the campers are not in violation of any law or existing University rule. In addition, the campers are extremely well behaved and appear to be careful in their cleanliness and preservation of the site. Destruction of property, obstruction of bona fide University activities or actual construction would be grounds for removal.[14]

The University's position on Tent City changed as it became apparent that the construction of the gym would soon begin. However, the recognition of Tent City remained even after the decision to build had been reaffirmed by the Board of Trustees. This is illustrated by the notice to vacate which was issued by the University president on July 9th, 1977. It said in part, "all students and others having custody, ownership or control over any and all tents and other temporary structures on the University campus are hereby ordered to remove said tents...."[15] The next University recognition of Tent City came late in the conflict when the new University president[16] issued twelve proposals for recognition and protection of that part of the site not being changed by construction. One of the proposals recognized Tent City in stating:

> Build (I propose to do this myself) four benches to mark the places where the students died, perhaps tent- shaped shelters could be erected by other volunteers to shade these benches in symbolic recognition of the peaceful encampment on the site earlier this year.[17]

The press also recognized Tent City because the style of living and the location had considerable human interest. This recognition of Tent City can be illustrated by a story in the major paper in the area, the *Akron Beacon Journal*. It was a cover story in the June 26, 1977 Sunday magazine. The story entitled "Tent City: A Diary of Love and Anger" presented the story of the protestors through interviews with a number of its residents including two non-students.[18]

It can be concluded that proposition 8 is supported in that it was possible to identify the three temporal stages of incipient, enthusiastic mobilization, and institutionalization. However, this is the weakest proposition because the stages are not clearly defined.

9. The May 4th Coalition's tactic of civil disobedience was a response to the failure of other actions to stop the building of the gym.

The basic tactic of the Coalition was to activate public opinion against the building of the gym. Their primary effort was through the media and, as has been noted, through Tent City because it was an effective way for calling attention to the Coalition's concerns particularly in the densely populated northeast Ohio area. However, until the arrests July 12th, the national media paid little attention to the Coalition's cause.

As part of their public opinion campaign, the Coalition worked hard to persuade the Board of Trustees to change its position on the location of the gym. This was done primarily through meetings with the University president, and with trustee Joyce Quirk. Ms. Quirk had changed her mind and opposed construction of the gym on the proposed site.

The Coalition also attempted to mobilize Kent State faculty and students against the gym. This was done through the medium of Tent City which was a good place for informal conversations. In addition, there were talks in the dormitories, rallies, and leafleting. It is not completely clear how effective these tactics were because faculty support for the Coalition was not very strong in terms of actual behavior. However, a survey using a random sample of faculty and students (n = 345) showed that 51 percent were opposed to the gym site; 27 percent were for the site; 14 percent were undecided; and 8 percent refused to participate. The survey was conducted in late July after the 193 protestors had been arrested.[19]

The Coalition's tactics had been successful in calling attention to the debate over the gym but had not stopped the movement towards construction. Consequently, the Coalition began active consideration of the use of civil disobedience as construction day became imminent. The result of this consideration was a decision to resist peacefully police efforts to move Tent City.

On July 12 an order was read to vacate the site. Many of the Coalition's leaders and members sat down at the Tent City site, locked arms, and nonviolently refused to leave. The University police, who had removed their service pistols, arrested a total of 193 protestors. A questionnaire survey by my colleague, Betty F. Kirschner, and me (Lewis and Kirschner, 1977), showed that 67 percent of those who returned questionnaires were KSU students while another 19 percent had at some time been registered in Ohio universities. Sixty-three percent were males with the modal age being 22. In summary, the proto-typical person was a KSU male, Caucasian, under 24 years of age.[20] The tactic of civil disobedience received considerable media coverage in the northeast Ohio area as well as nationally in many major newspapers and the wire services. All three national television networks covered the arrests. The May 4th Coalition, with the death of Tent City, had succeeded in putting the gym issue before the general public in a rather dramatic way.

After the arrests had been completed, the tents were taken down and stored in University facilities for trial evidence. This action ended Tent City. The May 4th Coalition, to be sure, continued, but their tactics shifted dramatically away from the area of public opinion into the state and federal courts. Proposition 9 is supported.

10. The May 4th Coalition successfully achieved some but not all of its stated goals.

As is true of most social movement research, the evaluation of success or failure often only reflects the biases of the analyst. In the movement under consideration, there is an external standard by which the question of failure or success can be judged. This standard is the eight demands of the May 4th Coalition. As was noted earlier, four of the demands were never an issue. The recognition of the tragedy was clearly achieved in the twelve points proposed by the new president. The cancellation of classes on May 4th; the naming of the four buildings after students who were killed; and the moving of the gym were demands that were not achieved, although the cancellation of classes is still under consideration as this paper is being written

(November, 1977). Thus, two of the major demands of the Coalition were not achieved. Yet, in talking to Coalition members as well as attending meetings and listening to speakers, there was a "sense" of victory in that construction of the gym was stopped for four months. Furthermore, many believed that the activities of the University administration and Board of Trustees had been "exposed" to the nation. The Coalition may be correct in this feeling for on October 2, 1977 the *New York Times* editorially referred to the hard-line attitude and "obduracy" of some of the trustees.[21]

Summary

All propositions were supported. The analysis found all of the components suggested by Smelser that indicate the mobilization structure of a norm-oriented movement to be present.

Social Control

How did social control factors shape the action of the May 4th Coalition? This proposition guides the inquiry into the response of the social control forces.

11. The response of the social control authorities to the May 4th Coalition facilitated the norm-oriented character of the movement.

In looking at social control it is appropriate to divide the analysis into three component parts. They are internal social control, the police, and the courts.

Internal Social Control

In the analysis of the hostile outburst on May 4, 1970, I noted that internal social control should be considered as part of the social control process. This component was present primarily in the form of marshaling roles that developed as arrests became imminent. The May 4th Coalition rejected the use of faculty marshals in favor of using their own in this role. The marshals, about four to six members of the Coalition, encouraged the protestors in tactics of nonviolence. In addition, they developed opportunities to practice nonviolent procedures.

The faculty, including the author, served as observers representing the Faculty Senate and the United Faculty Professional Association (UFPA). The primary activity of the faculty observers was to serve as a conduit for information during the face-to-face conflicts.

One reader, Nancy Grim, suggested that the lifestyles of Tent City also contributed to internal social control. She wrote:

> An important factor in internal social control was the process of the Coalition. [There were] many hours spent discussing democratic process, responsibilities of people who took specific tasks, importance of nonviolence and of avoiding illegal substances.

The Police

For most of the life of Tent City the Kent State University police kept away from the political situation and allowed Tent City to stay where it had established. In fact, police often made sure that the residents were safe when they made their patrol rounds. The campus police moved from their low-profile service role to a high profile enforcement role when the University obtained an injunction against the May 4th Coalition and Tent City on July 11th. The reading of the order to vacate was done by the president of the University. However, most of the additional readings were done by the director of security, Robert Malone.

On July 12th, the Kent State police ordered the residents of Tent City to vacate the construction site. They refused to leave. The police, having removed their service weapons, began the arrests. They were supported by the county sheriff's police, also unarmed, who cordoned off the arrest area, but did not actually carry out the arrests.

The actions of the police were quite effective in not provoking a hostile outburst. There was no serious violence by either side. Consequently, the actions of the police facilitated the retention of the norm-oriented character of the movement.

The Courts

A more detailed analysis of the activities of the courts may be found elsewhere in this volume (see Hensley, *passim*). What is important here is the question of how the actions of the courts served to maintain the norm-oriented character of the May 4th Coalition's activities. This was achieved primarily by giving the May 4th Coalition a hearing through the mechanism of the temporary injunction. The first injunction to halt construction was issued on July 11 by Portage County Common Pleas Court. This was the pattern throughout the summer. The courts, state or federal, would halt construction while lawyers for the May 4th Coalition and the University would argue the issue of the gym annex site. The fact that the courts continued to hear the Coalition, combined with the resulting publicity, served to retain the character of the Coalition as a norm-oriented movement because it provided a channel for expressing grievances as well as a way to continue to get these grievances before the general public. Thus, the Coalition was not forced to go to other forms of collective behavior in an effort to achieve its goals until late in September, 1977.

Summary

The analysis shows that proposition 11 is supported in that all the mechanisms of social control including marshaling, Coalition lifestyles, the police, and the courts facilitated the retention of the May 4th Coalition's activities as a norm-oriented movement.

EVALUATION OF SMELSER'S MODEL

In my earlier work using Smelser, I commented that the usefulness of the approach was its ability to allow the researcher to organize, in a coherent pattern, a large amount of information about an event. I believe this to be true as a result of the present study because in this one I have worked with more diverse materials than in the earlier investigation.

In addition to this organizing factor, another advantage of Smelser's approach is its nomothetic dimension. That is, with the same model, the researcher has been able to propose generalizations about two distinctly different events, a hostile outburst and a norm-oriented movement.

A PERSONAL NOTE

I wish to close with a reflexive statement. I have tried to write fairly and objectively about the events of the May 4th Coalition and Tent City. To some extent, Smelser's model has facilitated this effort. However, readers should know that I supported the idea of building the gym on an alternative site because destruction of the original site would interfere with sociological research on social control violence. Further, I testified, for the Coalition's position, on these views at the hearings held in the Portage County Common Pleas Court.

REFERENCES

Lewis, Jerry M. 1972. "A Study of the Kent State Incident Using Smelser's Theory of Collective Behavior." *Sociological Inquiry* 42(2): 87-96.

Lewis, Jerry M. and Betty F. Kirschner. 1977. "Public Interpretation of Tent City Arrestees: Kent State, 1977." A paper presented at the Annual Meeting of the Southern Sociological Society in New Orleans, April, 1978.

Smelser, Neil J. 1962. *Theory of Collective Behavior.* New York: The Free Press.

ENDNOTES

1. I am indebted to Raymond Adamek, Richard Feinberg, Nancy Grim, Bob Hart, Thomas Hensley, Betty F. Kirschner and Diane L. Lewis for their helpful comments on an earlier version of this essay. It should be noted that all interpretations are mine and not necessarily agreed to by the various readers. I wish to also recognize and thank my research assistants Ed Ackerman, Karen Brown, and Terri Weaver for their contributions to this research.

2. This narrative was developed with the assistance of Ed Ackerman.

3. On the 19th I left for a research trip to England and I returned on June 4th.

4. They are quoted from a May 4th Coalition leaflet announcing a rally on May 12th. No date was on the leaflet.

5. This paragraph and the next two are based on the work of Karen Brown.

6. May 4th Coalition, "Quoting Official Sources," Press Release. May 19, 1977: pp. 5-6.

7. May 4th Coalition, "Position of the May 4th Coalition." Position Paper. June 23, 1977, p.2.

8. *Ibid.* p. 5.

9. *Ibid.* p. 3.

10. *Ibid.* p. 2.

11. May 4th Coalition, "National Rally," Leaflet, no date.

12. They are Albert and Ann Canfora and their children Alan, Roseann (Chic), Albert, Jr. and Mark.

13. One reader suggested, for example, that Alan Canfora had as much influence on tactics as he did on beliefs.

14. Kent State University News Service, "Fact and Issue File," June 2, 1977, p. 10.

15. Kent State University, "Notice to Vacate" Poster, July 9, 1977.

16. Dr. Brage Golding became president of the University in September, 1977.

17. Kent State University, "Update," October, 1977, p. 6.

18. William Bierman, "Tent City: A Diary of Love and Anger" *Akron Beacon Journal Sunday Magazine.* June 26, 1977.

19. Allen Bukoff, "The Gym Annex Survey." Typed Report. August 3, 1977: p. 2.

20. One hundred and twenty-nine out of 193 returned questionnaires. It is possible that Kent State students were more willing to return questionnaires.

21. *The New York Times*, "Remembering Kent State," Sunday, October 2, 1977, p. E-16.

Victims of Groupthink:
The Kent State University Board of Trustees and the 1977 Gymnasium Controversy

Thomas R. Hensley
Glen W. Griffin
Kent State University

ABSTRACT

An important theory in the study of small group decision making is groupthink, developed by Irving Janis. Groupthink refers to a process by which a small group of decision makers subjected to intense stress may become more concerned with achieving concurrence among their members than in arriving at carefully considered decisions. In this study, Janis's theory is applied to the 1977 gymnasium controversy at Kent State University where trustees decided to build an addition to the school's gymnasium on part of the area where students and Ohio National Guard members confronted each other just before the tragic shootings of May 4, 1970. Despite opposition from the student body and faculty, large-scale protest activities, massive arrests, and numerous third party efforts to resolve the conflict, the trustees not only refused to alter their decision but also refused even to reconsider their decision. A detailed analysis of Janis's theory reveals that each major condition of the theory was present in the conflict and that the trustees were indeed victims of groupthink.

Social scientists have long been fascinated by the decision-making processes of political elites. The analysis of decision making is a central concern of most fields of political science, and political scientists have borrowed extensively from psychology, sociology, and social psychology in trying to describe and explain the decisions of political authorities. An important contribution to this area of inquiry has been made by social psychologist Irving L. Janis in a book entitled

This is an expanded and revised version of a paper presented at the 1979 annual meeting of the Midwest Political Science Association, Chicago, Illinois.

Thomas R. Hensley and Glen W. Griffin, *The Journal of Conflict Resolution*, Vol. 30, Number 3 (September 1986), pp. 497-531, copyright 1986 by Sage Publications Inc. Reprinted by permission of Sage Publications, Inc.

So many individuals provided assistance to us in the preparation of this study that it is impossible to acknowledge them all. Two individuals—Dr. Jerry M. Lewis and Dr. Steven R. Brown—deserve special thanks, although they bear no responsibility for any shortcomings in this article.

Groupthink (1972, 1982). While trying to account for major American foreign policy fiascoes, such as Pearl Harbor, the invasion of North Korea, the Bay of Pigs invasion, and the Vietnam involvement, Janis found as a recurrent characteristic that foreign policy decision makers had "become more concerned with retaining the approval of the fellow members of their work group than with coming up with good solutions to the tasks at hand" (1982: vii). He labeled this phenomenon "groupthink." In the years since this work originally appeared in 1972, Janis and others have devoted considerable attention to the testing and refinement of the theory (Raven and Raven, 1974; Green and Conolley, 1974; Flowers, 1977; Janis and Mann, 1977; Raven and Raven, 1977; Courtright, 1978; Semmel and Minnix, 1978; Tetlock, 1979; Longley and Pruitt, 1980; Janis, 1982; Fodor and Smith, 1982; Stocker-Kreichgauer et al., 1982; Manz and Sims, 1982), but its nonlaboratory application to political contexts beyond the originally studied foreign policy decisions has been limited to the Watergate coverup (Green and Conolley, 1974; Raven and Raven, 1974; Janis, 1982). Janis argued in his original book that groupthink is probably operative across cultures and within both governmental and nongovernmental groups, and he called for research into a variety of decision-making situations.

Responding to these suggestions, we test the groupthink theory by analyzing the decision of the Kent State University Board of Trustees to build a physical education and recreation facility on part of the site where Kent State University students and Ohio National Guardsmen confronted each other on May 4, 1970, just prior to the fatal shooting of four students and the wounding of nine other students. This decision by the trustees led to continuous protests on the Kent State campus throughout the spring, summer, and fall of 1977; the arrests of over 300 protestors; involvement by the White House, members of Congress, members of the Ohio legislature, state courts, the lower federal courts, and eventually the U. S. Supreme Court; direct costs to the university of hundreds of thousands of dollars; and incalculable indirect costs to the university because of the adverse publicity associated with the protests. Despite these problems, however, the majority of the trustees not only held to their decision but also refused even to approve a motion for reconsidering the decision. These events suggest that groupthink may have been operative within the board.

This study presents data gathered from this controversy to test whether groupthink was operative. From a theoretical perspective, we seek to test the applicability of Janis's theory in a different context than it has ever been applied and also to assess if the theory can be made more parsimonious or if it needs expansion in order to account for additional factors. From a more applied perspective, the results of the analysis may provide insights into improving small group decision making as well as raise questions about the selection of members of boards of trustees for state universities. We will proceed by first discussing the basic elements of Janis's groupthink theory; next, we will discuss the methodological bases of the study; then we will describe the 1977 gymnasium controversy at Kent State to provide the necessary background for testing components of the theory; the next sections will be the heart of the article, testing the applicability of Janis's theory; and the final section will consist of our conclusions and policy recommendations.

THE THEORY OF GROUPTHINK

"Groupthink," writes Janis (1982: 9), "refers to a deterioration of mental efficiency, reality testing, and moral judgment that results from in-group pressures." These in-group pressures stem from a tendency in highly cohesive groups to seek concurrence, especially groups subjected to conditions of stress. The more cohesive the group becomes under conditions of stress, the more its members rely on each other for security and acceptance. The more members of a group rely on each other for approval, the more they will seek unanimity in their decisions so as to avoid conflict with one another. This concurrence-seeking tendency becomes an unannounced goal of the group and may take precedence over the group's other tasks, thus impairing the group's decision-making ability. Group cohesiveness can also lead to the group developing norms that can further impair its efficiency, and the tendency to seek concurrence can prevent the questioning or critical examination of these norms.

As identified in Figure 1, groupthink is a detailed conceptual framework positing that a variety of antecedent conditions can give rise to a

Figure 1: The Theory of Groupthink

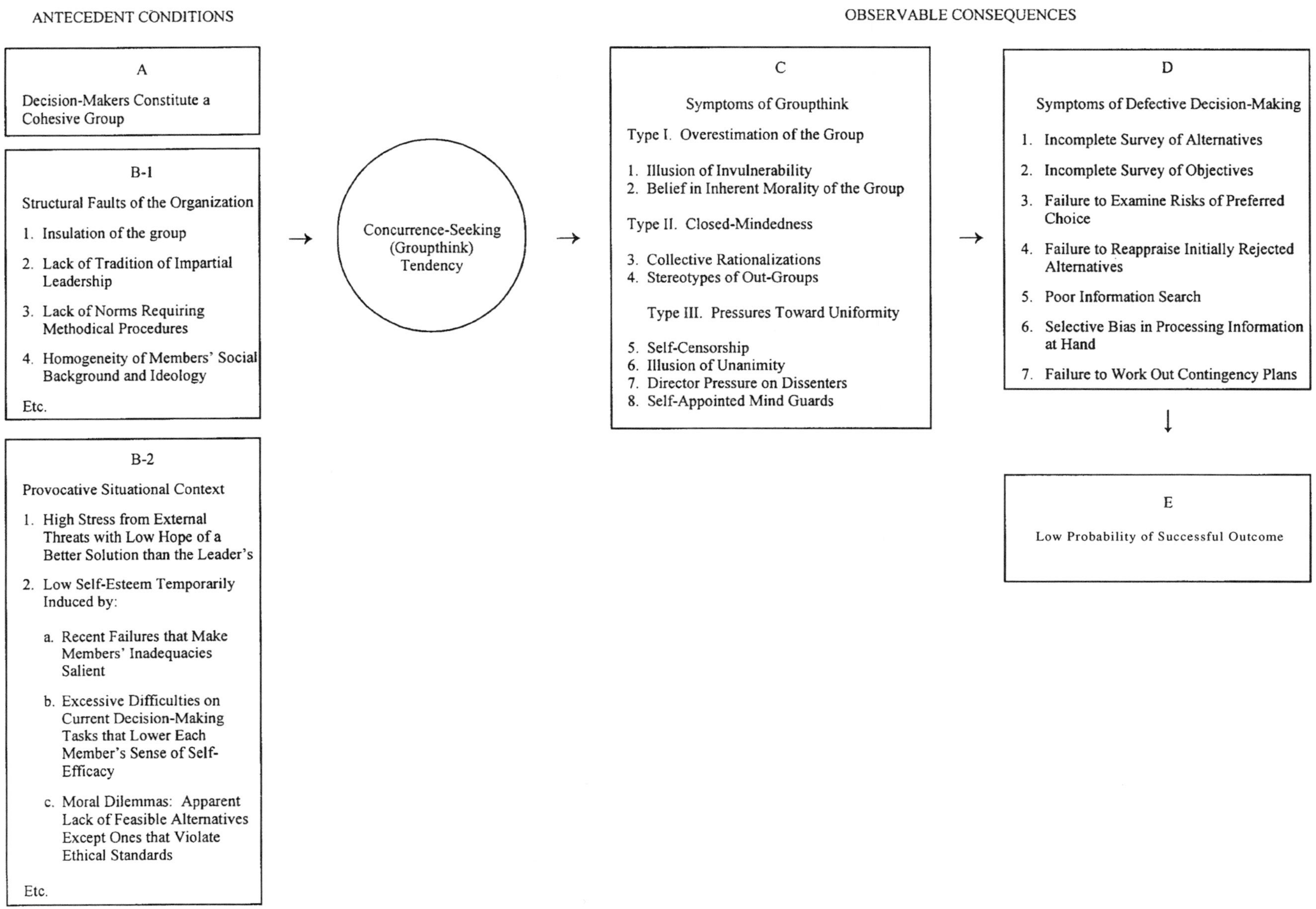

ANTECEDENT CONDITIONS

OBSERVABLE CONSEQUENCES

A

Decision-Makers Constitute a Cohesive Group

B-1

Structural Faults of the Organization

1. Insulation of the group
2. Lack of Tradition of Impartial Leadership
3. Lack of Norms Requiring Methodical Procedures
4. Homogeneity of Members' Social Background and Ideology

Etc.

B-2

Provocative Situational Context

1. High Stress from External Threats with Low Hope of a Better Solution than the Leader's
2. Low Self-Esteem Temporarily Induced by:

   a. Recent Failures that Make Members' Inadequacies Salient
   b. Excessive Difficulties on Current Decision-Making Tasks that Lower Each Member's Sense of Self-Efficacy
   c. Moral Dilemmas: Apparent Lack of Feasible Alternatives Except Ones that Violate Ethical Standards

Etc.

Concurrence-Seeking (Groupthink) Tendency

C

Symptoms of Groupthink

Type I. Overestimation of the Group

1. Illusion of Invulnerability
2. Belief in Inherent Morality of the Group

Type II. Closed-Mindedness

3. Collective Rationalizations
4. Stereotypes of Out-Groups

Type III. Pressures Toward Uniformity

5. Self-Censorship
6. Illusion of Unanimity
7. Director Pressure on Dissenters
8. Self-Appointed Mind Guards

D

Symptoms of Defective Decision-Making

1. Incomplete Survey of Alternatives
2. Incomplete Survey of Objectives
3. Failure to Examine Risks of Preferred Choice
4. Failure to Reappraise Initially Rejected Alternatives
5. Poor Information Search
6. Selective Bias in Processing Information at Hand
7. Failure to Work Out Contingency Plans

E

Low Probability of Successful Outcome

Source: Janis (1982:244)

concurrence-seeking tendency—groupthink—which in turn can result in the occurrence of the symptoms of groupthink, and these symptoms can in turn produce various symptoms of defective decision making and a resultant low probability of a successful outcome.

Before discussing the methodological foundations of the study, it is important to delineate the scope of explanatory power of the groupthink theory. Janis emphasizes that "the use of theory and research in group dynamics is intended to supplement, not to replace, the standard approaches to the study of political decision making" (1982: 6). *No claim is made that groupthink is capable of explaining completely the actions of a small group of decision makers.* The theory does, however, alert the researcher to the potential importance of small group dynamics, especially to the possibly detrimental effects of the consensus-seeking tendency in a cohesive group under considerable stress.

METHODOLOGY

Three subjects need to be discussed under the heading of methodology: the problem of objectivity, the requirements for accepting or rejecting various components of the theory, and the types of information available to test the theory. We have drawn heavily upon the guidelines provided by Janis (1982: chaps. 8 and 10) and Schwartz and Jacobs (1979).

The problem of objectivity is a tough one. We were emotionally involved in the controversy, believing that the trustees made serious mistakes in handling the conflict. We have no way to eliminate this problem. We have, however, delayed writing this study because we wanted time to pass to allow passions to cool and for a better historical perspective to emerge. Readers of the article will be the ultimate judges of our ability to approach the analysis of the events in an objective manner.

The second methodological concern can perhaps also be viewed as a problem of objectivity. Here our concern centers on the requirements used for the acceptance or rejection of various components of the theory. We will try to alleviate this danger in several ways. First, we will require more than one type of evidence before concluding that any specific condition or symptom has occurred; if only one example of a symptom or condition can be cited,

then we will not conclude that the factor was present. Second, in examining the sets of antecedent conditions, symptoms of groupthink, and symptoms of defective decision making, we will adopt the rule that a piece of evidence can only apply to one specific condition or symptom within each of these general categories. For example, the same piece of evidence cannot be used to establish the presence of two different symptoms of groupthink. Finally, we have attempted to accumulate the broadest possible data base in testing the components of the theory, and we will not use evidence from one source, the validity of which is challenged by another source.

This takes us into the third methodological concern we identified above, sources of information. In his original study, Janis was forced to rely primarily upon secondary data sources in testing the occurrence of groupthink, and he recognized the limitations imposed by such sources (1972: iv-v). We are in the fortunate position of having much better data; although the gymnasium controversy did receive statewide and nationwide attention, it did not involve matters of national security with the attendant secrecy and classified documents. We were able to conduct lengthy personal interviews with a wide variety of participants in the conflict, including many of the trustees, university administrators, protestors, and individuals who attempted third party intervention.* The verbatim minutes of the meetings of the trustees were another important source of information, and we also gathered voting data from the trustees meetings over a period of more than a decade. Area newspapers covered the conflict extensively, and we systematically collected every newspaper story on the controversy over a

---

*We have made the decision not to identify the specific individuals who were interviewed, with one exception. Most of the people interviewed specifically requested that we not use their names. Further, no useful purpose would be served by using their names, for these individuals are not widely known. Our position is consistent with Advisory Opinion No. 13, issued on August 16, 1973, by the Committee on Professional Ethics of the American Political Science Association, which recognizes the scholar's ethical obligation to protect confidential sources. The one individual whom we do identify is former Ohio State Representative John Begala, who expressed no reservations about our quoting him directly. One final point is that the senior author did conduct lengthy interviews with a majority of the Board of Trustees.

two-year period. Numerous interuniversity memos have also been made available to us.** Finally, we personally observed the conflict on a daily basis throughout its duration, and during this time we talked informally with dozens of involved people.

THE 1977 KENT STATE UNIVERSITY GYMNASIUM ADDITION CONTROVERSY

In this section of the study we will describe the controversy over the gymnasium addition site. This description is somewhat lengthy because it provides the foundation for analyzing the specific components of the theory and also because the details of the controversy are not widely known. Before we undertake this task, however, it is first necessary to discuss why the board of trustees had assumed a central decision-making role in Kent State University affairs.

During the 1976-1977 academic year, Kent State University was in a leadership crisis. President Glenn Olds had announced his resignation in November of 1976, but the resignation was not to become effective until the summer of 1977. Olds had lost his effectiveness long before the announcement of his resignation, and the trustees had found themselves becoming more closely involved in the management of the university than was normal. With Olds's announcement, a leadership vacuum was created, and members of the board became even more deeply involved in the daily administration of the university. Olds himself recognized this situation as he left Kent State in July of 1977: "It's been an absolutely atypical, almost absurd year, and that trend is catastrophic because no board can run a university. . . . The President has to" (*Akron Beacon Journal*, July 15, 1977: A10). The trustees were thus the key decision makers during most of the gymnasium addition controversy, for Olds's successor, Brage Golding, did not begin his presidency until September of 1977.

On May 12, 1977, a unique community was established on the campus of Kent State University. "Tent City" or "Tentropolis" was composed of

approximately 60 tents pitched on an area of campus called Blanket Hill. Tent City was established by a student-based group calling itself the May 4th Coalition, formed primarily to oppose construction of a large physical education and recreation facility to be attached to the existing Memorial Gymnasium and to be located on a site that included part of Blanket Hill and a practice football field just below Blanket Hill. These were areas where Kent State students and members of the Ohio National Guard had confronted each other just before the fatal shootings of May 4, 1970. At a board of trustee meeting on May 12, 1977, the coalition, a loosely organized group of a few hundred students and supporters, had presented to the trustees a set of eight demands concerning May 4th related issues, with the most central being that the new physical education and recreation facility must not be built on the site of the 1970 confrontation between students and guardsmen. When the trustees refused to agree to alter the site, the coalition established Tent City as a symbol of their determination to resist construction on the chosen site.

During the lengthy protest, three of the nine trustees—Joyce Quirk, the only woman on the board; David Dix, the local newspaper publisher; and Robert Blakemore, a prominent Akron, Ohio, attorney—each changed their minds in favor of locating the facility on a different site. The other members of the board did not change their decision, however. Further, they refused to approve any motions to reconsider their decision, and they never met with the May 4th Coalition following the meeting on May 12th.

Throughout the spring, summer, and fall of 1977, enormous pressures built up on the trustees to change their decision. The pressures came from a wide variety of local, state, and national sources. The initial pressure came from the May 4th Coalition. The coalition strategy was to attack the university administration at its weakest point, the concern over the badly tarnished public image of the university. By keeping constant media attention on the protest and posing the threat of increased conflict, the coalition believed it could create enormous public image problems for the leaders of the university, thereby forcing the trustees to change their decision. Continuous efforts by the coalition throughout May, June, and early July did create statewide and nationwide publicity, but the trustees did not reconsider their decision. By the first part of

---

**Again, we have chosen not to cite memos directly in order to provide confidentiality to persons writing the memos as well as to the persons who made the memos available to us.

July, construction was ready to begin, but the coalition still occupied Blanket Hill. This led to the decision by the trustees to seek a court order to remove the demonstrators, with the result that 193 persons were arrested on July 12 when they refused to leave Blanket Hill.

Having been evicted from the site and prohibited from reoccupying it, the coalition continued its struggle to prevent construction in a variety of other ways. During the months of July, August, and September, much of the coalition's attention was directed toward the courts, where a team of lawyers headed by William Kuntsler was successful in preventing construction until mid-September. On campus, this period was characterized by escalating rhetoric, increasing polarization of both campus and community, increasingly militant coalition tactics, and progressively harsher responses by law enforcement authorities, with dozens of additional arrests occurring as protestors tried on several occasions to reoccupy the construction site. By mid-September, however, all avenues of court delay had been exhausted by coalition lawyers, and construction finally began on September 19. The coalition was not finished, however, for two rallies were held at Kent State on September 24 and October 22. By this point the coalition had come largely under the control of a radical group, the Revolutionary Student Brigade, whose national leaders had focused upon Kent State as a cause to champion. About 3000 demonstrators rallied on the campus on September 22, and eventually about 1000 protestors broke down portions of the fence surrounding the site and briefly reoccupied it. Police kept a low profile at the September rally, but at the October rally, law enforcement personnel confronted approximately 500 demonstrators with horses and tear gas. Despite an afternoon of continuous confrontation, there were no serious injuries and few arrests. As May 4, 1978, approached, there was great tension on the Kent State campus over the possibilities of further protest and violence, but only a few individuals attempted unsuccessfully to break down the fence surrounding the construction site.

Whereas pressures on the trustees from the May 4th Coalition were continuous and intense, the members of the board also received substantial criticism and pressure from many other sources. One important group was the faculty. As the conflict escalated in July after the initial arrests, the faculty union—the United Faculty Professional Association—joined the coalition in its court effort to prevent the university from commencing construction. In addition, a survey of Kent State faculty members showed a majority of the faculty was opposed to building the facility on the chosen site. Opposition from the general student body also arose. A survey of the student body showed that the majority was against the decision of the trustees, and during the summer the student government filed suit against the trustees to prevent construction on the grounds that the board had not followed proper procedure in selecting the site.

The trustees not only faced opposition from the coalition, the faculty, and the general student body but also were confronted with efforts by state and national political figures who sought to find a compromise for the conflict. A leader in trying to resolve the controversy was State Representative John Begala, a Kent State University graduate and a lifelong resident of Kent. Concerned about the potential for violence and the damage to the university's reputation, Begala met with state legislative leaders and university officials in the state capital in early July before the arrests, but no compromise emerged from Begala's efforts. Following the arrests, the White House became involved when presidential aide Midge Constanza invited representatives of both sides to the White House in an attempt to resolve the conflict, but this attempt at third party intervention also failed. Yet another attempt at mediation occurred during the first week in August when federal district court judge Thomas Lambros ordered both sides to try to negotiate an out-of-court settlement of the dispute, but no agreement emerged. Representative Begala was again the main figure in a final third party effort to compromise the issue in mid-August. The proposal involved converting the university's laboratory school, which was on shaky financial footing, into a new physical education and recreation facility, for Begala argued that this could be done successfully within the existing monies allocated for the facility. The trustees had scheduled a meeting on August 26th to discuss this proposal, but the only trustees to attend the meeting were the three who had expressed their support of a change in location.

Many other individuals and groups expressed their opposition to the trustees' decision. For example, noted columnist Joseph Harsch, writing in the *Christian Science Monitor* on August 4, 1977 (p. 27), reacted as follows:

> It seems to me that it is as insensitive for the authorities of Kent State and of Ohio to try to obscure with a gymnasium the place where the four fell on the fourth of May, 1970, as it would be for Pennsylvania to put an office building where Picket launched his charge at Gettysburg.

Further examples are unnecessary to the central point of this lengthy discussion: Despite enormous pressures from a wide variety of sources, despite enormous direct financial costs to the university from the protests, despite the daily occurrence of damaging publicity to the university, and despite extensive third party efforts to reach a compromise solution to the controversy, *the majority of the trustees refused to vote to reconsider their decision on the location of the facility or to meet with the May 4th Coalition.* As these events unfolded, we pondered the reasons for this small group behavior, which seemed to defy the most basic tenets of good decision making. None of the more traditional theories of small group decision making seemed helpful. The theory of groupthink did seem to have significant explanatory potential, however, and discussions with colleagues encouraged us to explore the theory in depth. We did not undertake to test the theory in the belief that it would be capable of explaining fully the decision making of the trustees. It did seem to us, however, that important insights into their decisional processes might be gained through application of this theory.

ANTECEDENT CONDITIONS

We now turn to an analysis of the specific variables constituting the theory of groupthink. We begin by examining the antecedent conditions: A cohesive group of decision makers, structural faults of the organization, and a provocative situational context. The presence of these conditions, Janis argues, can lead to a concurrence-seeking tendency within the group that can cause groupthink to occur and lead to defective decision making.

Before analyzing each of these antecedent conditions, it is important to recognize the time dimension that is explicit in the theoretical framework, for all the antecedent conditions must precede the occurrence of the concurrence-seeking tendency of groupthink that leads to the symptoms of groupthink and the symptoms of defective decision making. In the Kent State gymnasium controversy, the concurrence-seeking tendency of groupthink seems to have emerged about one month after the establishment of Tent City, which occurred on May 12, 1977. An especially critical day was June 9, 1977, when a board of trustees meeting was held at which Quirk and Dix announced their opposition to the site. We will therefore use June 9 as the date before which the antecedent conditions must have occurred and after which groupthink may have become an important factor in the decision making of the trustee majority.

Group Cohesiveness

Janis (1982: 245) defines group cohesiveness as "a high degree of 'amiability and *esprit de corps*'" among a group's members. Janis cites Kurt Lewin, who defines group cohesiveness as the members' positive valuation of the group and their motivation to continue to belong to it. Cohesiveness is thus determined by the attractiveness of the group to its members, resulting from such factors as friendship, prestige, and mutual support. This is a centrally important antecedent condition; "the more amiability and *esprit de corps* among the members of an in-group of policy makers, the greater is the danger that independent critical thinking will be replaced by groupthink" (Janis, 1982: 245).

The evidence that we have suggests that the Kent State University trustees were a highly cohesive group prior to the development of the gymnasium controversy, although Ms. Quirk seems to have been an outsider. Interviews with a majority of the members of the board revealed that they all seemed to derive considerable satisfaction and prestige from serving as trustees. Several of them were personal friends, and the meetings before the gymnasium controversy were described as being warm and cordial. Voting records of the board provide empirical support concerning group cohesiveness, for the dominant voting pattern of the trustees was one of unanimity. In the year prior to the controversy, there were only nine nonunanimous votes, and seven of these votes were cast by Ms. Quirk.

Structural Faults of the Organization

High group cohesiveness is a necessary but not sufficient condition for groupthink to occur. Thus, Janis argues that an additional set of antecedent conditions involves four structural faults of the organization. These structural faults enhance the likelihood of groupthink occurring because they represent "the absence of a potential source of organizational *constraint* that could help to prevent the members of a cohesive policy-making group from developing a norm of indulging in uncritical conformity" (Janis, 1982: 249, emphasis in original). We will examine each of these four structural faults in turn.

Group Insulation

The insulation of the group from outside sources of information and opinions can result from both structural characteristics and informal group activities. Structurally, the group may be organized in such a way that no procedures exist for easy communication with nongroup members of the organization, e.g., the lack of representation at meetings for various constituencies. While this structural characteristic can lead to group insulation, it need not because less formalized means of input to the group can occur.

The Kent State Board of Trustees was insulated both structurally and informally. The board had neither student nor faculty representation; and in the critical month following the establishment of Tent City, the trustees as a group did not meet with the May 4th Coalition, student government representatives, or representatives of the faculty senate or the faculty union. Furthermore, the trustees who were to continue to oppose reconsideration of the site did not visit Blanket Hill to talk informally with the protestors who occupied Tent City. Thus, it can be concluded that the trustees were indeed insulated.

Lack of Tradition of Impartial Leadership

Another structural variable which can contribute to a concurrence-seeking tendency and groupthink is a lack of a tradition of impartial leadership. This involves the presence of directive leadership in which "the leader does not feel constrained by any organizational tradition to avoid pushing for his own preferred policies, and, instead, to encourage open,

unbiased inquiry into the available alternatives" (Janis, 1982: 249). It seems clear that the Kent State Board of Trustees was characterized by a lack of tradition of impartial leadership. University boards of trustees tend to be especially receptive to directive leadership because most university presidents are given substantial authority to conduct university affairs, with the board acting largely as a "rubber stamp" for the president's policies. The Kent State Board of Trustees was no exception. Evidence of this can be seen not only in the lack of serious debate over most issues in the minutes of the trustees' meetings but also in the unanimous and unchallenged support for the gymnasium addition proposal when it was presented to the Board in November of 1976.

Lack of Norms Requiring Methodical Procedures

A third antecedent condition under the category of structural faults of the organization is a lack of methodical procedures for search and appraisal. This condition differs from the previously discussed condition of group insulation, which focuses upon the barriers to a group getting adequate information from *outside* the group; the lack of norms requiring methodical procedures concerns the ability of the group *itself* to get reliable and complete information.

Of particular interest in discussing this antecedent condition of groupthink is the process by which the trustees originally approved the gymnasium addition site, for this evidence shows clearly the lack of procedures for search and appraisal. Initial trustee approval of the site came at a meeting on November 11, 1976; the trustees then confirmed their decision about this site at the meeting on May 12, 1977, when they voted to accept the lowest bids on the project. Planning of the facility, which began in the early sixties, was undertaken by members of the School of Health, Physical Education, and Recreation along with the university architect and other administrators. While a subcommittee of the trustees was kept informed about developments, by the time the proposed facility was first presented to the trustees for action on November 11, 1976, the trustees were in a poor position to challenge the plans for the proposed facility. Well over a decade of work had gone into the development of the facility, substantial costs had already been committed in architectural fees, and the presentation to the trustees about the convenience and economics of the proposed location seemed convincing. A number of members of the student government and other concerned students attended the meeting to protest the location of the facility, but to no avail. The trustees had no procedures for search and appraisal of alternative sites, and indeed none of the trustees were certain precisely where the facility would be located. A similar situation prevailed at the May 12, 1977, meeting of the trustees. Events had seemingly locked the trustees into their decision to approve the facility on the chosen site, for substantial additional developments had occurred between the November 1976 and May 1977 meetings. Added architectural and engineering funds had been committed, and formal bids on the project had now been submitted.

At a more general level, the trustees were never intended to be a group possessing methodical procedures for search and appraisal of information. The trustees are a general policy-making group, dependent upon administrators within the university to do their search and appraisal work. Unfortunately, in the administrative vacuum and leadership crisis at Kent State in 1976-1977, such work rarely got done.

Homogeneity of Members' Social Background and Ideology

The fourth structural fault of the organization which can contribute to the concurrence-seeking tendency so central to groupthink is the presence of homogeneity among the groups' members in terms of social background and ideology, and the Kent State Board of Trustees was indeed a rather homogeneous group. They were prominent, financially secure, middle-aged professional and executive people from the Northeast Ohio area. The process of selecting university trustees in Ohio virtually assures this homogeneity, for these appointments are made by the governor; the appointments have frequently gone to friends and financial supporters of the governor, and hence trustees come from a small pool of Ohio's upper social-economic class, who have a strong commitment to the established political and social systems. Differences did, of course, exist among the trustees in terms of their background; for example, five trustees were Republicans and four were Democrats. The differences in social background which did exist, however, were far less important than the similarities.

Provocative Situational Context

Having established that the Kent State Board of Trustees was a cohesive group which possessed each of the four structural faults of an organization susceptible to groupthink, we now turn to an analysis of the third and final antecedent condition, the presence of a provocative situational context. In Janis's theory, two factors comprise the provocative situational context. One is the presence of high stress from external threats coupled with low hope of finding a better solution than the leader's. The second factor involves temporary low self-esteem by the group's members, which can stem from three sources.

High Stress from External Sources

While Janis (1982: 250) emphasizes that high stress from external sources is neither a necessary nor sufficient condition for groupthink, an abundance of social psychology research informs us that group cohesiveness and concurrence-seeking tendencies can be enhanced by such forms of stress. The description of the controversy in the previous section makes it clear that the trustees were subjected to extreme external stress throughout the controversy. In the period before June 9, the May 4th Coalition's basic strategy was to build enormous pressure on the trustees to force them to change their decision. The coalition sponsored numerous rallies, marches, and demonstrations; the existence of Tent City was a constant reminder of the controversy; and trustees were accused not only of being insensitive to the tragedy of May 4 but also of trying to engage in a conspiracy to cover up the tragedy. The massive media coverage in the Northeast Ohio area assured that the trustees would feel the pressure and stress.

Janis couples the presence of high stress with a second variable, a low degree of hope for finding a better solution than the one favored by the leader or other influential persons. This was clearly the position in which the trustees found themselves when the controversy initially developed in May of 1977. When Tent City was established, the majority of the trustees saw themselves as locked into their decision to build on the site. Years of planning and thousands of dollars had already been committed to the project. Furthermore, contract bids had already been accepted for the project. Perhaps most important, the trustees believed this was the best place for the facility because of its central location on campus and its economical and convenient attachment to the already existing Memorial Gymnasium.

Temporary Low Self-Esteem

In his original formulation of the groupthink theory in his 1972 book, Janis did not identify the factor of the group's temporary low self-esteem. Subsequent thought and research convinced Janis, however, that a provocative situational context could be created by either external sources of stress or sources of stress internal to the group which produce a temporary lowering of self-esteem. Janis emphasizes that both sources of stress do not need to be present, and we have already established that high external stress was present. Evidence also exists, however, that the Kent State trustees were subject to sources of internal stress that could have temporarily lowered their self-esteem. Janis identifies three sources of such stress; while any one of them is sufficient to establish the presence of this factor, two can be identified in this unique controversy. The two sources of low self-esteem were recent failures and excessive difficulties in decision making. The moral dilemma variable does not seem to have been present.

It is possible to identify several recent failures that could have made the trustees question their adequacy. Interviews with the trustees made it clear that they had lost confidence in the president of the university, Glenn Olds. Given Olds's inability to run the university, the trustees had become closely involved in the daily operations of the university, and 1976-1977 was filled with continuous, serious problems which the trustees were unable to resolve. Enrollment was declining rapidly, two scandals embroiled the Business College in controversy, and an angry faculty had taken a strike vote over an impasse with the trustees on collective bargaining.

In addition to these recent failures, the trustees were also confronted with excessive difficulties in their decision-making tasks in regard to the gymnasium controversy. One problem was time. The trustees were busy people with demanding occupations, which left relatively little time to give to university affairs. The site controversy was one which grew and changed virtually every day, however, and it was extraordinarily difficult for the trustees to stay informed about these changing circumstances. A second major problem was the generational gap between the trustees and the

student protestors. Interviews with the trustees made it clear that they did not trust or understand the protestors, who represented a post-Vietnam generation with values and lifestyles that were threatening to many of the trustees. Thus, both the excessive time demands of the situation and the generational gap made the decision-making tasks of the trustees in this controversy exceptionally difficult.

CONCURRENCE-SEEKING (GROUPTHINK) TENDENCY

We have now examined each of the three classes of antecedent conditions of groupthink, and our analysis reveals that each of the conditions seems to have been present within the trustees. They were a cohesive group of decision makers, there were structural faults within the organization, and there was a provocative situational context with stress arising from both external and internal sources.

Janis postulates that these interacting antecedent conditions can lead to a concurrence-seeking tendency among members of a small group, with stress being a primary element. Janis writes: "The central explanatory concept I have in mind involves viewing concurrence-seeking as a form for striving for mutual support based on a powerful motivation in all group members to cope with the external or internal stresses of decision-making" (1982: 255). External sources of stress create the strong need for members to relieve the anxieties created by such stress, and internal sources of stress create the need for group members to bolster their self-esteem. To alleviate this stress, group members turn toward each other for social reassurance and affiliation, thus creating greater dependency on the group and a tendency to adhere to group norms. This in turn leads to concurrence-seeking because of the danger that if the group is not united then the stress will overwhelm the individual. All of this is much more likely to occur if the group is cohesive and lacks structural means of avoiding the concurrence-seeking tendency.

The presence of this concurrence-seeking tendency among the trustee majority is clear. At the May 12th meeting, the vote was 8-1 to approve the low bids on the project, which meant the facility would be built on the disputed site. Dix was the lone dissenter at this point, but even he argued that he approved the site in principle; he voted against accepting the bids at that point because he felt the trustees could spend a few more weeks going over the plans with the students in hope of creating greater understanding and harmony. While Dix, Quirk, and Blakemore were eventually to oppose the decision, the other members of the group remained committed to the chosen site. When Dix and Quirk moved to reconsider the decision about the site at the trustee meeting on June 9, the motion was tabled and was never removed from the table despite exhaustive efforts by many individuals. The concurrence of the majority was so solid that they resisted all efforts by third party mediators, and by August they refused even to attend a meeting at which an alternative site was to be discussed.

SYMPTOMS OF GROUPTHINK

If the antecedent conditions for groupthink are present within a small group and if a concurrence-seeking tendency exists, then the symptoms of groupthink may occur. These eight symptoms are divided into three types: overestimation of the group, closed-mindedness, and pressures toward uniformity. These symptoms reflect the group's defensive avoidance of anything that might threaten its consensus, with the result that perceptions of reality are distorted. These conditions in turn can lead to defective decision making. We turn now to an analysis of the presence or absence of the eight symptoms of groupthink. Not all eight symptoms need to be present to say that groupthink has occurred. Janis states: "Even when some symptoms are absent, the others may be so pronounced that we can predict all the unfortunate consequences of groupthink" (1982: 175).

Overestimation of the Group: Illusion of Invulnerability

Within the category of overestimation of the group, one important symptom of groupthink is "an illusion of invulnerability, shared by most or all of the members, which creates excessive optimism and encourages taking extreme risks" (Janis, 1982: 174). Based upon the actions of the majority of the trustees and personal interviews with a majority of them, it seems clear that this illusion of invulnerability was present among the trustee majority and that it did encourage extreme risk taking.

Throughout the controversy, the trustees acted as if they were so powerful that they had nothing to fear from the coalition. They failed to take the initiative to defuse resentment and opposition from the coalition, the general student body, and the faculty. In an interview, one trustee expressed the view that the trustees felt they could handle any trouble that came along. Another trustee indicated in an interview that the board saw no serious threat as the Tent City period began; the general perspective seemed to be "Let the kids play; they're not causing any problems." And as the conflict escalated, the trustees seemed to increase their view of their invulnerability. Interviews reveal that during the lengthy legal battles in July, August, and September, the trustees were not worried about losing in court. They believed that they would eventually triumph.

It seems reasonably certain that the majority of the trustees saw themselves as invulnerable, but was this an illusion or a reality? After all, they did win the court battles and the gymnasium addition was constructed on the site they chose. Clearly they won the conflict and the May 4th Coalition lost. This argument is valid, however, only if one views the controversy in the narrowest of perspectives. The trustees are responsible for the overall welfare of the university, and it is from this perspective that the illusion of invulnerability must be analyzed. The trustees were extremely vulnerable in regard to their broad responsibilities for the smooth operation and the long-term well-being of the university, and the damage to the university's reputation because of the lengthy controversy was enormous. Thus, the trustees assumed an invulnerability in regard to the specific conflict that was accurate, but they appear to have misperceived or neglected their vulnerability in regard to their most fundamental responsibility, the overall welfare of the university.

Overestimation of the Group: Belief in the Inherent Morality of the Group

A second symptom of groupthink is a belief in the inherent morality of the group. The members of the group view their motives and actions as being principled and just, and this can incline the group to ignore the ethical consequences of their decision.

It is difficult to determine whether this symptom of groupthink was present for the trustee majority. The statements and actions of the board members suggest, however, that this condition may have been present. The trustees continually defended themselves in terms of following correct procedures and being sensitive to the moral issues regarding the May 4th shootings. Further evidence of this symptom can be seen in the tendency of the trustees to view the conflict not so much in terms of substantive issues but rather in terms of a moral struggle between themselves as the proper and orderly governing authority of the university and the protestors as radicals bent upon creating disorder. At the trustee meeting on June 9, 1977, board member James Fleming stated: "The *Akron Beacon Journal*, the *Kent Stater*, the May 4th Coalition cannot run this board" (Minutes of the Kent State University Board of Trustees, June 9, 1977). In a personal interview, one trustee supporting the site said the issue confronting the board was one of strong leadership in the face of a small group of protestors trying to run the university. It therefore appears that the symptom of groupthink of a belief in the inherent morality of the group was present.

Closed Mindedness: Collective Rationalizations

In addition to symptoms of groupthink involving overestimation of the group, Janis also identifies two symptoms associated with closed-mindedness of the group. We now turn to an examination of these symptoms.

One aspect of closed-mindedness is "collective efforts to rationalize in order to discount warnings or other information that might lead the members to reconsider their assumptions before they commit themselves to their past policy decisions" (Janis, 1982: 174). These rationalizations reflect the group's desire not to question and possibly destroy the consensus they have established around their decision.

An analysis of the various arguments advanced by the trustees throughout the conflict suggests that four major rationalizations were advanced that served to defend the trustees' decision on the site and to protect them from seriously reconsidering the decision and possibly shattering their consensus. These rationalizations were: (1) Student representation had been present in the selection of the site, (2) the opponents of the site were not the proper constituency of the trustees, (3) there were no real options open to the trustees, and (4) the facility site was not the real issue in the struggle. The first two will be discussed in detail.

One position that the majority took throughout the controversy was that student representation occurred in the decision-making process to select the site of the facility. The trustees argued that students were present on committees within the School of Health, Physical Education, and Recreation and that students had been allowed to present their views at the meetings on November 11, 1976, and May 12, 1977. The position of the trustee majority was not convincing to student government leaders, however, for they argued that they had no representation on the board and they were not invited by the trustees to present their concerns; further, when they sought to present their views, the trustees paid only lip service to their concerns. The position of the trustees so infuriated members of student government that they brought suit against the trustees. It seems accurate to characterize the trustees' position as a collective rationalization. This is not to say that the trustees had any legal obligation to involve students directly in their decision-making process. No such obligation existed and no meaningful involvement occurred. The effort by members of the board to claim there was meaningful student representation was an attempt to rationalize their decision.

A second rationalization was that opponents of the chosen site were not the proper constituency of the trustees. As opposition to the trustees' decision became increasingly widespread, the members of the board found it necessary to redefine continually the constituency to whom they were responsible. Initially the trustee majority took the position that the May 4th Coalition was a small group composed of (1) nonstudents to whom the board had no responsibility and (2) students who were only a small portion of the student body. One trustee said in an interview that he did not care about protestors who were not faculty or students, for the board votes only in the interests of the majority of the students. Another trustee said that the coalition was obviously a small minority, and he did not know what the majority of the students wanted. It became apparent that the opposition to the site was widespread throughout the university community when both the faculty union and the student government went to court against the trustees and when an opinion poll by members of the university's Psychology Department showed both a majority of students and faculty opposed to the site (Bukoff and Watkins, 1978). In the face of these challenges, the position of the trustee majority began to shift, for now the trustees were defending their position as representing the people of the state of Ohio. Clearly, an element of rationalization was present in this line of argumentation.

Closed Mindedness: Stereotyped Views of Rivals and Enemies

This symptom involves "stereotyped views of enemy leaders as too evil to warrant genuine attempts to negotiate, or as too weak and stupid to counter whatever risky attempts are made to defeat their purposes" (Janis, 1982: 174). The trustees did not seem to view the protestors as weak or stupid. Substantial evidence exists, however, that the trustee majority saw the May 4th Coalition members as being threatening and morally bad, and this may have created an insurmountable barrier to genuine negotiations. From the beginning of the controversy, the trustee majority was distrustful of the members of the May 4th Coalition, labeling them as radicals and outsiders. Evidence from our personal interviews indicates that some trustees in private described the protestors as communists and anarchists. The public pronouncements of the trustee majority tended to label the protestors as outsiders, that is, non-Kent State University students.

The question must be raised as to whether the trustees were engaged in stereotyping their opponents or was the trustee majority accurate in its perceptions? It is true that by the late summer and into the fall the coalition had been taken over by radical elements, primarily the National Revolutionary Student Brigade, which sought to use the protest movement to further its own goals. These developments, however, led many original members of the coalition to drop out of the group and to criticize the actions of the coalition during the fall. The original members of the coalition were overwhelmingly Kent State students who were not members of radical political organizations (see Lewis, 1978). What appears to have happened is that the trustee majority misperceived the nature of the protest group, advanced false stereotypes about the group, refused to initiate effective negotiations with them, and thereby created a self-fulfilling prophecy through which the coalition became the type of group the trustees claimed they were.

Pressures Toward Uniformity: Self-Censorship of Personal Doubts

The third category of symptoms of groupthink identified by Janis involves pressures toward uniformity. He identifies four specific symptoms within this category.

One of the specific symptoms within the category is "self-censorship of deviations from the apparent group consensus, reflecting each member's inclination to minimize to himself the importance of his doubts and counterarguments" (Janis, 1982: 175). This is an especially difficult symptom to analyze; individuals are not likely to admit to this even if it occurred, and public statements and actions are indirect indicators at best of this symptom.

Although we are not in a position to offer a conclusive judgment, some evidence does exist that at least two members of the board's majority may have experienced substantial personal doubts about the decision to build on the controversial site and suppressed those doubts in their public positions. These two individuals were George Janik, chairman of the board, and Dr. James Fleming. Both men voted consistently with the majority throughout the controversy, and publicly defended the chosen site. Despite these public expressions of support for the trustees' decision, however, evidence exists that both men were uncertain about the decision. Fleming is said to have favored holding talks with the coalition during the Tent City period, and Representative Begala believed that in the early period of the conflict Fleming was willing to consider rotating the gym away from the site (Begala interview, November 4, 1977). Janik probably felt the cross-pressures of the conflict more severely than anyone. As chairman of the board, Janik was thrust into the public limelight, and he had long been among the most dedicated supporters of the university. Although he was committed to the site, he was acutely aware of the damage the controversy was doing to the reputation of the university. Further, Janik's wife was an outspoken critic of the gym site selection. One trustee reported that Janik was undergoing great indecision concerning the proper location of the facility throughout the controversy. Begala felt that Janik simply "agreed with whomever he talked to last" (Begala interview, November 4, 1977).

It appears, then, that both Fleming and Janik may have been involved in self-censorship of personal doubts. Other members of the board who were opposed to reconsidering the site may have also censored their personal doubts, but we have no evidence of this. Nonetheless, sufficient evidence of self-censorship exists to conclude that this symptom of groupthink was present.

Pressures Toward Uniformity: Illusion of Unanimity

Another symptom of groupthink is a "shared illusion of unanimity concerning judgments conforming to the majority view" (Janis, 1982: 175). Janis argues that this illusion of unanimity results partly from self-censorship of deviations as well as from the incorrect assumption that silence means consent. This symptom was not present among the trustees, for three of them were in open dissent against the policy of the majority. No illusion of unanimity could exist under these circumstances.

Pressures Toward Uniformity: Direct Pressure on Dissenting Group Members

A third symptom of groupthink within the category of pressures toward uniformity is "direct pressure on any member who expresses strong arguments against any of the group's stereotypes, illusions or commitments, making clear that this type of dissent is contrary to what is expected of all loyal members" (Janis, 1982: 175). Evidence to test the presence of this symptom is also difficult to ascertain, for such pressure tends to come in private conversations or in closed sessions of the group. Interviews with members of the board and newspaper accounts of meetings do suggest, however, that dissenting members of the board did experience substantial direct pressure from the majority. The pressure appears to have been directed primarily at the two early defectors, Quirk and Dix.

One example occurred at the trustee meeting of July 15. At this meeting Quirk tried to renew a tabled motion she made on June 9th that the trustees reconsider the site. This was resisted, and the trustees went into executive session. Emerging from the closed-door meeting two hours later, Quirk announced that she was withdrawing her motion "to avoid further polarization" (Minutes of the Kent State University Board of Trustees, July 15,1977: 8). It was reported that the meeting was highly emotional, with, according to one trustee, "terrible arguments and heated discussion" (*Akron Beacon Journal*, July 16, 1977: A1). It is clear that Quirk had been subjected to intense personal pressures because of her dissenting viewpoint.

Quirk and Dix were apparently subjected to similar pressures at a board meeting two weeks later, when they proposed a ten-day delay in construction to investigate sources of financial help for moving the facility. The majority of trustees refused to agree to the delay, and the meeting was described as emotionally charged (*Kent-Ravenna Record-Courier*, July 27, 1977: 1), again indicating that substantial pressure had been placed upon dissenting members of the group. We can thus conclude that this symptom was present.

Pressures Toward Uniformity: Emergence of Self-Appointed "Mind Guards"

The final symptom of pressures toward uniformity is the "emergence of self-appointed mind guards—members who protect the group from adverse information that might shatter their shared complacency about the effectiveness and morality of their decision" (Janis, 1982: 175). Considerable evidence exists that points to the presence of this symptom among the trustees. It appears to have occurred both within the trustees' meetings and in meetings between the trustees and third party negotiators. Janik, Baumgardner, and Johnston seem to have been the trustees who emerged as self-appointed mind guards.

On several occasions, Janik and Baumgardner undertook actions that sought to prevent the group from receiving potentially adverse information. Before the beginning of the June 9th meeting, Quirk told the other trustees she had changed her mind about the site and would propose a motion that the trustees reconsider the decision. Janik is reported to have made an unsuccessful effort to talk her out of proposing the motion. Another example of mind guarding seems to have occurred at the July 10th meeting of the trustees just prior to the arrest of the 193 persons at Blanket Hill. Quirk read a statement objecting to the seeking of a court injunction and expressing a desire that all other possibilities be examined first (*Kent-Ravenna Record-Courier*, July 11, 1977: 1, 3). After Quirk read her statement, Baumgardner called for an immediate vote on seeking the injunction, with no further discussion of the matter (*Akron Beacon Journal*, July 11, 1977: A1, A8). The trustees then voted to seek the injunction. Further examples of mind guarding could be presented, but these are sufficient to establish the presence of this symptom of groupthink.

Summary

Our examination of the eight symptoms of groupthink suggests strongly that groupthink did indeed occur within the Kent State University Board of Trustees during the 1977 gymnasium controversy, for substantial evidence exists that seven of the eight symptoms appear to have been operative among the majority of the trustees. Janis points out that not all symptoms have to be present for groupthink to occur, and we therefore conclude that the trustees were victims of groupthink.

SYMPTOMS OF DEFECTIVE DECISION MAKING

What does it mean to say that the trustees were victims of groupthink? The theory postulates that the antecedent conditions, the concurrence-seeking tendency, and the symptoms of groupthink can lead to defective decision making. Janis has suggested seven different ways a group's decision making can be impaired. It is important to recognize that the theory does not require all or even a majority of these defective procedures to occur. The occurrence of any one of them is enough to harm the effectiveness of the group; however, the greater the number of manifestations of defective decision making, the greater the likelihood of serious problems arising from the decisions of the group. It should also be mentioned that these seven deficiencies are not tied exclusively to groupthink. These defects can occur from other sources as well, for instance, an authoritarian leader. But having shown that groupthink did occur for the trustee majority, a strong case can be made that the occurrence of any of these symptoms was related to the presence of groupthink.

Incomplete Survey of Alternatives

The first type of defective decision making to be examined is an incomplete survey of alternatives; "the discussions are limited to a few alternative courses of action without a survey of the full range of alternatives" (Janis,1982: 10). Our previous discussions provide ample evidence that this symptom of defective decision making was present among the trustee majority. In terms of formal reconsideration of their decision, the trustee majority refused even to discuss any possible alternatives, let alone undertake a full survey of alternatives. The lack of formal reconsideration could have been the result of the failure of the trustees to arrive at viable alternatives through more informal channels, however. This informal survey of alternatives by the trustees thus deserves close analysis.

Although the trustees did search informally for alternatives to their original decision, the evidence is strong that there was not a complete survey of alternatives. Early in the controversy, after the establishment of Tent City, efforts were made to explore alternative courses of action. The most important of these involved (1) a study by the university architect to determine the feasibility and costs of rotating the facility away from Blanket Hill and (2) efforts by the university's vice-president for financial affairs, who explored the possibility of the university receiving state funds to cover any additional costs if a change in site occurred. It was determined, however, that substantial costs would be involved in rotating the facility and that state funds would not likely be available. Did these efforts, and perhaps other efforts not publicized, constitute a complete survey of alternatives? The answer seems to be no. The efforts early in the controversy to determine the feasibility of rotation and the availability of funds appear to have been less than adequate. In regard to rotation, the alternative explored in early May was a rotation of approximately 40 feet, whereas in court-ordered negotiations in August the trustees were discussing up to a 300 foot rotation. And whereas the trustees maintained in May that there were no funds to alter the site, Representative Begala did get a firm commitment from Senate majority leader Oliver Ocasek in early July to support an additional appropriation to alter the site (Begala interview, November 4, 1977). These circumstances do not prove conclusively that the trustee majority had an incomplete survey of alternatives, however. The strongest evidence is their resistance to cooperate with third party mediators seeking alternatives to the proposal location. Our interview data reveal that the majority was generally not receptive to and cooperative with Representative Begala, White House aide Midge Costanza, and federal mediator Richard Salem, who was involved in court ordered negotiations in August. The trustees were committed early in the controversy to their decision and closed themselves off to a full survey of available alternatives.

Incomplete Survey of Objectives

Another aspect of defective decision making stemming from the symptoms of groupthink is the incomplete survey of objectives. An analysis of the available data suggests that the trustees had two primary objectives throughout the controversy: (1) to build the facility on the chosen site and (2) to maintain their control over the university in the face of the perceived challenge to their authority, a challenge that they believed could lead to major problems in the future if the protestors won this battle. It can be argued that the trustee majority lost sight of their primary objective as trustees, the effective operation of a university. The trustee majority seems to have been convinced, however, that this ultimate goal was directly linked to defeating this perceived radical movement. Thus although it is possible to argue that the objectives of the trustee majority were based upon badly distorted images of reality, it is not possible to conclude that the trustees had an incomplete survey of objectives.

Failure to Examine Risks

The third type of defective decision making is the failure of a group to examine the risks associated with its decision. Although some indications exist that this condition may have been present among the board majority, the evidence does not seem strong enough to conclude that this symptom did occur. Certainly, after the arrests of the 193, no trustee was unaware of the variety of risks involved in building on the chosen site. Did the trustee majority examine the risks associated with their decision during the early months of the controversy in the Tent City period? Although there is no evidence of such an examination in the trustee minutes, our interviews lead us to believe that the trustees had given thought to the potential risks, for warnings of the risks were coming from many sources. The trustee majority thus seemed aware of, and seemed willing to take, these risks.

Failure to Reappraise Initially Rejected Alternatives

The fourth type of defective decision making involves the refusal of the group to reexamine courses of action that had been initially rejected. This is a likely result of groupthink, for such an appraisal could strike at the heart of the concurrence established by the group. Once again the trustee majority appears to have exhibited this aspect of defective decision making. An excellent illustration of this point involves the unwillingness of the majority of the trustees to consider the university school alternative in late August. One trustee stated flatly in an interview with a newspaperman who questioned him about the alternative:

> I think the majority [of the trustees] still feels it should be built where it's proposed. I'm still behind the building 100 percent as it's proposed.
> The idea to use the University School came up a long time ago when the financial affairs committee was considering the project. It's just not practical [*Akron Beacon Journal*, August 23, 1977: B1].

Consideration does have to be given to the fact that the trustee majority rejected the ideas of rotating the facility in May, but then in court-ordered negotiations in August they introduced a plan for rotating the structure. This can be viewed as a willingness of the trustees to appraise a course of action initially rejected. A more accurate interpretation seems to be, however, that this was simply public posturing, for it was rather obvious that the terms demanded of the coalition under the plan would make the proposal unacceptable to the coalition.

Poor Information Search

Another symptom of defective decision making is a poor search for information. Although the trustee majority did seek out some information related to the controversy in which they found themselves embroiled, they did so in an incomplete and inadequate manner. Our previous discussions in this section of the study dealing with the incomplete survey of alternatives and the failure to reappraise initially rejected alternatives contain evidence that relates directly to this symptom, but our validity standards do not allow us to use the same evidence for different symptoms of defective decision making. Ample independent evidence does exist, however, to establish the presence of this symptom of a poor information search. One glaring example of this symptom was that little information was sought concerning the University School proposal. A meeting of the trustees was scheduled for August 26 to discuss the proposal with members of the state legislature. All six members of the board opposed to changing the site boycotted the meeting, thus refusing to receive any new ideas and information about this alternative. Further evidence of an inadequate information search involves contacts with state officials concerning funding. Although information was sought, Representative Begala's comments suggest an inadequate information search; this position is supported by a quote from another state representative, Michael Stinziano, who asked the trustees to "seriously consider the offers that the Democratic [legislative] leadership has made to seek an answer to this conflict" (*Akron Beacon Journal,* August 8, 1977: A13). Perhaps the most critical inadequacy in searching out information involved the unwillingness of the trustee majority to learn about the composition and goals of the May 4th Coalition as the conflict escalated in July and August.

Selective Bias in Processing Information

The sixth symptom of defective decision making is a selective bias in processing information. The tendency here is to screen out information that does not support the group's decision and that might threaten group cohesion. Several specific examples of this symptom occurred during the lengthy controversy. The discussions throughout the efforts to secure state funding for any site change seem to have involved a selective bias in information processing. The trustees were repeatedly told that consideration would be given to a trustee request for funds and that chances of an appropriation would be good, but the trustee majority argued that they could not make such a request because they had not been promised funds. This is assuredly not an open and unbiased manner of interpreting information. The trustees' continually shifting position in regard to their proper constituency also shows how information was selectively processed, for as opposition from more and more groups became more publicized, the trustees reinterpreted their

position to eliminate as part of their proper constituency those groups that opposed them.

Failure to Work Out Contingency Plans

The last symptom of defective decision making involves the failure to work out contingency plans because little time is spent considering how the chosen plan might be hindered. This condition did not characterize the decision making of the trustee majority. During the Tent City period, the trustee majority developed a variety of plans to counteract the activities of the May 4th Coalition. The basic strategy was to maintain a low profile, hoping the protest would fade away as the factors of unpleasant weather, the ending of the regular academic year, and sheer exhaustion would take their toll. But if this did not work, they recognized they might have to use law enforcement personnel to remove the protestors from Blanket Hill. And following the arrests on July 12, if the trustees found themselves confronted with continued protest, they would allow the courts to settle the conflict, for they were confident they would win.

Summary

This analysis of the seven symptoms of defective decision making has led us to conclude that a majority of these symptoms did characterize the board's decision making during the gymnasium controversy. The trustees' decision making process was characterized by the incomplete survey of alternatives, the poor search for information, the failure to reappraise initially rejected alternatives, and a selective bias in processing information.

GROUPTHINK

Were the members of the trustee majority victims of groupthink? Our analysis leads us to answer "yes" to this question. We have argued that all of the antecedent conditions appear to have been present, a definite concurrence-seeking tendency could be observed in the actions of the trustees, most of the symptoms of groupthink seem to have been present, and a majority of the symptoms of defective decision making appear to have occurred. The evidence is thus rather strong that the trustee majority did become victims of groupthink, "a deterioration of mental efficiency, reality testing, and moral judgment that results from in-group pressures" (Janis, 1982: 9).

This conclusion does not mean that we have explained completely the decision-making process of the trustees. Small group decision making is too complex to be explained fully by any single theory. Nor can we offer a precise judgment as to how important groupthink may have been in the decision making of the trustee majority. We simply propose that the evidence strongly suggests that groupthink occurred, and the presence of groupthink seems to have contributed in important ways to defective decision making.

It needs to be recognized, however, that alternative explanations to groupthink can be offered. For example, a far less elaborate explanation of the decision of the trustee majority is that they were ideologically opposed to the protest movement and sought to exercise their authority over the protestors. Under this interpretation, even if all of the elements of rational decision making had been present in board considerations and even if an alternative site had been readily available, the trustees probably would have remained committed to the controversial site.

Although an explanation like this does have some appeal, it is deficient for two reasons. First, the theory of groupthink does include elements that incorporate these considerations into an explanation of the trustees' actions; the stereotyping of out-groups, one of the symptoms of groupthink, is especially relevant. Second, the ideological explanation is too simplistic; it does not help us to describe and explain the many facets of the decision-making process of the board. For example, why did self-appointed mind guards emerge, and why were there so many symptoms of defective decision making? The ideological answer by itself does not reach these concerns, but the rich detail of the groupthink theory not only alerts us to these phenomena but also allows us to place them in a meaningful integrated context.

A FIASCO?

Although the occurrence of a fiasco is not a necessary part of the theory of groupthink, Janis states that fiascoes may occur because of groupthink. We therefore cannot avoid the question. Did the trustee decision to build on the disputed site result in a fiasco? The standard meaning of fiasco is "a complete failure; action that comes to a ridiculous end" (*Webster's New World Dictionary*, 1982: 518). Using this definition, we must conclude that a fiasco did not occur. The facility has been completed and has been a valuable addition to the Kent State University campus. Fortunately, no one was seriously injured in the many confrontations, and the educational process of the university continued functioning in a nearly normal manner throughout the controversy. The direct and indirect costs to the university, however, were extraordinary, and, sadly, they were costs that probably could have been avoided.

THEORETICAL CONSIDERATIONS

When we began our analysis, we entertained the hope that we might find ways to make the theory more parsimonious by eliminating or combining various conditions or symptoms within the theory. After having worked through each element of the theory, we find ourselves in a rather different position. Each specific variable in the theory seems to us important and distinct; further, it appears to us that some additional symptoms of defective decision making need to be incorporated into the theory. One symptom is the *failure to initiate or maintain contact with an opposition group*. Certainly this was true in regard to the lack of trustee interaction with the May 4th Coalition, and it is probably characteristic of several foreign policy fiascoes, given the inherent difficulties of diplomatic negotiations. A second form of defective decision making that may stem directly from groupthink is *a lack of cooperation with third party mediators*. This was a distinctive pattern in the Kent State case, and there is evidence of this in some of the foreign policy cases Janis discusses, for instance, the disregard given by U. S. decision makers to Indian efforts to mediate prior to the North Korean invasion. Yet a third symptom missing from Janis's formulation is *the failure to extend the time period for reaching a decision*. On several occasions the trustee majority refused to postpone decisions in order to gain time to discuss matters with various groups or to explore alternative courses of action. The ability of Kennedy and his advisors to do this in the Cuban Missile Crisis is often cited as an important factor in the successful outcome of that situation, and the failure to do so was associated with several foreign policy fiascoes, for example, the Bay of Pigs.

POLICY IMPLICATIONS

Janis gives considerable attention to the question of how groupthink can be prevented, and he quite logically focuses upon the antecedent conditions that can give rise to the concurrence-seeking tendency so central to groupthink. We now wish to discuss briefly the direct policy implications of our study, focusing upon the antecedent conditions that gave rise to groupthink within the Kent State University Board of Trustees. Stated succinctly, is it possible to reduce the likelihood of groupthink occurring in a group like this?

Our answer is straightforward: change the selection process for the board. The current procedure for selecting members to a university's board of trustees in Ohio and many other states virtually assures that the members will be somewhat cohesive and well-insulated from outside sources of opinion and information, two important antecedent conditions of groupthink. Current procedures give a governor virtually unchecked authority to select trustees, and this has meant that trustees overwhelmingly have been upper-socioeconomic-class white males. A more diverse representation of groups on a trustee board is clearly needed in order that the divergent perspectives of students, faculty, and other groups in society can more faithfully be reflected in discussions and decisions.

REFERENCES

Akron Beacon Journal (1977) May 5 to August 25.

Begala, J. (1977) Personal Interview, November 4.

Bukoff, A. and P. Watkins (1978) "The false consensus effect in a real life conflict situation: the Kent State gym controversy." Presented at the 1978 Meeting of the Midwestern Psychological Association.

Courtright, J. A. (1978) "A laboratory investigation of groupthink." *Communications Monographs* 45 (August): 229-246.

Flowers, M. L. (1977) "A laboratory test of some implications of Janis's groupthink hypothesis." *Journal of Personality and Social Psychology* 35, 12: 888-896.

Fodor, E. M. and T. Smith (1982) "The power motive as an influence on group decision making." *Journal of Personality and Social Psychology* 42, 1: 178-185.

Green, D. and E. Conolley (1974) "'Groupthink' and Watergate." Presented at the 1974 Meeting of the American Psychological Association.

Janis, I. L. (1972) *Victims of Groupthink: A Psychological Study of Foreign Policy Decisions and Fiascoes.* Boston: Houghton Mifflin.

_____ (1982) *Groupthink: Psychological Studies of Policy Decisions and Fiascoes.* Boston: Houghton Mifflin.

_____ and L. Mann (1977) *Decision Making: A Psychological Analysis of Conflict, Choice, and Commitment.* New York: Free Press.

Kent-Ravenna Record-Courier (1977) May 5 to September 2.

Lewis, J. M. (1978) "The May 4th coalition and Tent City: a norm oriented movement," pp.149-158 in T. R. Hensley and J. M. Lewis (eds.) *Kent State and May 4th: A Social Science Perspective.* Dubuque, IA: Kendall/Hunt.

Longley, J. and D. G. Pruitt (1980) "Groupthink: A Critique of Janis's Theory." *Rev. of Personality and Social Psychology* 1: 74-93.

Manz, C. C. and H. P. Sims, Jr. (1982) "Potential for Groupthink in Autonomous Work Groups." *Human Relations.*

Minutes of the Kent State University Board of Trustees, 1963-1977.

Ohio Legislative Service Commission (1977) "Procedures for Site Change of a State Construction Project." Columbus, Ohio.

Raven, B. H. and J. Z. Raven (1974) "The Nixon group." *Journal of Social Issues* 30: 297-320.

_____ (1977) *Social Psychology: People in Groups.* New York: Wiley.

Schwartz, H. and J. Jacobs (1979) *Qualitative Sociology: A Method to the Madness.* New York: The Free Press.

Semmel, A. K. and D. Minnix (1978) "Group Dynamics and Risk-Taking: An Experimental Examination." *Experimental Study of Politics*, 6, 3 (March): 1-33.

Stocker-Kreichgauer, G., I. L. Janis, I. D. Steiner, and H. Brandstatter (1982) "Groupthink," in H. Brandstatter, J. H. Davis, and G. Stocker-Kreichgauer (eds.) *Group Decision Making.* New York: Academic.

Tetlock, P. E. (1979) "Identifying victims of groupthink from public statements of decision makers." *Journal of Personality and Social Psychology* 37: 1314-1324.

NAME INDEX

SUBJECT INDEX